Spanish
Phrasebook

LAROUSSE

Editors
José A Gálvez, Andrew Hastings

with
Christy Johnson, Donald Watt

Supplement on Spanish language and Hispanic culture
Josephine Grundy, Valerie Grundy

Publishing manager
Janice McNeillie

Design and typesetting
Sharon McTeir

© Larousse 2006
21, rue du Montparnasse
75283 Paris Cedex 06

ISBN: 2-03-542152-7

Sales: Houghton Mifflin Company, Boston

Introduction

This phrasebook is the ideal companion for your trip. It gets straight to the point, helping you to understand and make yourself understood so that you don't miss a thing. Use it like a dictionary to find the exact word you're looking for right away. And at each word we've provided a selection of key phrases that will help you in any situation, no matter how tricky things may have gotten.

The English–Spanish section contains all those essential expressions that you'll need to get by in Spain. And because you need to be able to pronounce the words properly, we've provided a simple and straightforward phonetic transcription that will enable you to make yourself understood with ease.

The Spanish–English section provides all the most important words and expressions that you might read or hear while on vacation.

And that's not all: we've added practical and cultural tips for getting by, a supplement on Spanish language, life and culture – everything, in fact, to make your trip go as smoothly as possible.

¡Buen viaje!

Pronunciation

So that you can say what you want to say in Spanish without running any risk of being misunderstood, we have devised a simple and straightforward phonetic transcription to show how every Spanish word or phrase used in this phrasebook is pronounced. This phonetic transcription, which is shown in brackets after each Spanish word or phrase, uses as many standard English sounds as possible, so that it is virtually self-explanatory. The following list provides further clarification:

[ah]	as in **fa**ther
[air]	as in f**air**
[aw]	as in p**aw**
[ay]	as in d**ay**
[ch]	as in **ch**eese
[CH]	as in lo**ch**
[e]	as in m**e**n
[ee]	as in tr**ee**
[eye]	as in m**y**
[o]	as in n**o**t
[oh]	as in g**o**
[oo]	as in s**oo**n
[ow]	as in n**ow**
[oy]	as in b**oy**
[RR]	a strongly rolled **r**
[th]	as in **th**in

Abbreviations

abbr	abbreviation
adj	adjective
adv	adverb
art	article
conj	conjunction
excl	exclamation
f	feminine
m	masculine
n	noun
num	numeral
pl	plural
prep	preposition
pron	pronoun
v	verb

English–Spanish phrasebook

a

able
▸ to be able to ... poder ... [pod-air]
▸ I'm not able to come tonight esta noche no puedo ir [es-ta no-chay noh pway-doh eer]

about más o menos [mas oh may-nos]
▸ I think I'll stay for about an hour creo que me quedaré más o menos una hora [kray-oh kay may kay-da-ray mas oh may-nos oo-na aw-ra]

abroad (live) en el extranjero [en el ek-stran-CHair-oh]; (travel) al extranjero [al ek-stran-CHair-oh]
▸ I've never been abroad before esta es la primera vez que viajo al extranjero [es-ta es la pri-mair-a-beth kay bya-CHoh al ek-stran-CHair-oh]

absolutely absolutamente [ab-so-loo-ta-men-tay]
▸ you're absolutely right tienes toda la razón [tyen-es toh-da la RRa-thohn]

accept aceptar [a-thep-tahr]
▸ do you accept traveler's checks? ¿aceptan cheques de viaje? [a-thep-tan chek-ays day bya-CHay]

access el acceso [ak-thay-soh]
▸ is there disabled access? ¿hay acceso para discapacitados? [eye ak-thay-soh pa-ra dis-ka-pa-thi-tah-dohs]

accident el accidente [ak-thi-den-tay]
▸ there's been an accident ha habido un accidente [a a-bee-doh oon ak-thi-den-tay]

according to según [se-goon]
▸ it's well worth seeing, according to the guidebook según la guía, vale la pena verlo [se-goon la gee-a bah-lay la pay-na bair-loh]

address (details of place) la dirección [di-rekth-yohn] ◆ (speak to) dirigirse a [di-ri-CHeer-say a]

---

addressing people

You say Señora(s), Señor(es), Señorita(s) for 'Mrs./Ms.' or 'm'am,' 'Mr.' or 'sir,' and 'Miss' (and their plurals). Don or Doña followed by the person's name or last name are really only used in Zorro. Or you could try on the style of Old Spain with Damas and Caballeros (Ladies and Gentlemen), much favored by TV-show hosts, just for fun!

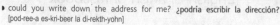

- could you write down the address for me? **¿podría escribir la dirección?** [pod-ree-a es-kri-beer la di-rekth-yohn]
- here is my address and phone number, if you're ever in the US **esta es mi dirección y mi número de teléfono, por si alguna vez viene a los Estados Unidos** [es-ta es mee di-rekth-yohn ee mee noo-mair-oh day te-lay-fon-oh por see al-goo-na beth byen-ay a es-tah-dos oo-nee-dohs]

adult el adulto [a-dool-toh], la adulta [a-dool-ta]
- two adults and one student, please **dos adultos y un estudiante, por favor** [dos a-dool-tohs ee oon es-tood-yan-tay por fa-bor]

advance *(money)* el adelanto [a-de-lan-toh] • **in advance** *(pay, reserve)* **por adelantado** [por a-de-lan-tah-doh]
- do you have to book in advance? **¿hay que reservar por adelantado?** [eye kay RRes-air-bahr por a-de-lan-tah-doh]

after *(in time, space)* después de [des-pwes day]
- the stadium is just after the traffic lights **el estadio está justo después del semáforo** [el es-tad-yoh es-ta CHoos-toh des-pwes del se-ma-fo-roh]
- it's twenty after eight **son las ocho y veinte** [son las o-choh ee bayn-tay]

afternoon tarde [tahr-day]
- is the museum open in the afternoons? **¿abre el museo por las tardes?** [ab-ray el moo-say-oh por las tahr-days]

aftershave la colonia [ko-lohn-ya]
- a bottle of aftershave **una botella de colonia** [oo-na bo-tel-ya day ko-lohn-ya]

afterwards después [des-pwes]
- join us afterwards **véngase con nosotros después** [ben-ga-say kon no-soh-trohs des-pwes]

again otra vez [oh-tra beth]
- the train is late again **el tren llega tarde otra vez** [el tren yay-ga tahr-day oh-tra beth]

age la edad [ay-dad]
- what ages are your children? **¿de qué edades son sus hijos?** [day kay ay-dad-ays son soos ee-CHohs]

---

agreement/disagreement

- absolutely! **¡por supuesto!** [por soo-pwes-toh]
- that's fine by me **por mí, bien** [por mee byen]
- you're right **tienes razón** [tyen-es RRa-thohn]
- go on, then **venga, vamos** [ben-ga bah-mos]
- I'm not at all convinced **no estoy nada convencido** [noh es-toy nah-da kom-ben-thee-doh]
- I disagree **no estoy de acuerdo** [noh es-toy day a-kwair-doh]

▸ we've been waiting for ages! ¡estamos esperando hace horas! [es-tah-mos es-pair-an-doh a-thay aw-ras]

agency la agencia [a-CHenth-ya]

▸ what is the contact number for the agency? ¿cuál es el número de contacto de la agencia? [kwal es el noo-mair-oh day kon-tak-toh day la a-CHenth-ya]

ago

▸ I've been before, several years ago ya había estado, hace varios años [ya a-bee-a es-tah-doh a-thay bahr-yohs an-yohs]

▸ a long time ago hace mucho tiempo [a-thay moo-choh tyem-poh]

ahead adelante [a-de-lan-tay]

▸ is the road ahead clear? ¿se puede pasar por la carretera más adelante? [say pway-day pa-sahr por la ka-RRe-tair-a mas a-de-lan-tay]

air *(wind)* el aire [eye-ray]

▸ the air is much fresher in the mountains el aire es mucho más fresco en la montaña [el eye-ray es moo-choh mas fres-koh en la mon-tan-ya]

air-conditioning el aire acondicionado [eye-ray a-kon-dith-yo-nah-doh]

▸ do you have air-conditioning? ¿tienen aire acondicionado? [tyen-en eye-ray a-kon-dith-yo-nah-doh]

airline la compañía aérea [kom-pan-yee-a a-air-ay-a]

▸ no, we're traveling with a different airline no, volamos con otra compañía aérea [noh bo-lah-mos kon oh-tra kom-pan-yee-a a-air-ay-a]

airmail el correo aéreo [ko-RRay-oh a-air-ay-oh]

▸ I'd like to send it airmail quería enviarlo por correo aéreo [kair–ee-a em-byahr-loh por ko-RRay-oh a-air-ay-oh]

airport el aeropuerto [eye-roh-pwair-toh]

▸ how long does it take to get to the airport? ¿cuánto se tarda en llegar hasta el aeropuerto? [kwan-toh say tahr-da en yay-gahr as-ta el eye-roh-pwair-toh]

at the airport

▸ where is gate number 2? ¿dónde está la puerta dos? [don-day es-ta la pwair-ta dos]

▸ where is the check-in desk? ¿dónde está el mostrador de facturación? [don-day es-ta el mos-tra-dawr day fak-too-rath-yohn]

▸ I'd like an aisle seat quiero un asiento de pasillo [kyair-oh oon as-yen-toh day pa-seel-yoh]

▸ where is the baggage claim? ¿dónde está la recogida de equipajes? [don-day es-ta la RRe-ko-CHee-da day e-ki-pa-CHays]

airport shuttle el servicio de autobús al aeropuerto [sair-beeth-yoh day ow-toh-boos al eye-roh-pwair-toh]
 ▶ is there an airport shuttle? ¿hay algún servicio de autobús al aeropuerto? [eye al-goon sair-beeth-yoh day ow-toh-boos al eye-roh-pwair-toh]

air pressure la presión (del aire) [pres-yohn (del eye-ray)]
 ▶ could you check the air pressure in the tires? ¿podría comprobar la presión de los neumáticos? [pod-ree-a kom-pro-bahr la pres-yohn day los new-ma-ti-kohs]

airsick mareado(da) [ma-ray-ah-doh]
 ▶ can I have an airsick bag? ¿me podría dar una bolsa para el mareo? [may pod-ree-a dahr oo-na bol-sa pa-ra el ma-ray-oh]

aisle *(between plane seats)* el pasillo [pa-seel-yoh]; *(plane seat)* el asiento de pasillo [as-yen-toh day pa-seel-yoh]
 ▶ two seats, please: one window and one aisle dos asientos, por favor: uno de ventana y otro de pasillo [dos as-yen-tohs por fa-bor oo-noh day ben-tah-na ee oh-troh day pa-seel-yoh]

aisle seat el asiento de pasillo [as-yen-toh day pa-seel-yoh]
 ▶ I'd like an aisle seat quería un asiento de pasillo [kair-ee-a oon as-yen-toh day pa-seel-yoh]

alarm (clock) el despertador [des-pair-ta-dawr]
 ▶ I set the alarm for nine o'clock he puesto el despertador para las nueve [ay pwes-toh el des-pair-ta-dawr pa-ra las nway-bay]

alcohol el alcohol [al-koh-ol]
 ▶ I don't drink alcohol no bebo alcohol [noh bay-boh al-koh-ol]

alcohol-free sin alcohol [seen al-koh-ol]
 ▶ what kind of alcohol-free drinks do you have? ¿qué bebidas sin alcohol tiene? [kay beb-ee-das seen al-koh-ol tyen-ay]

all todo(da) [toh-doh] ♦ *(everybody)* todos(das) [toh-dohs]
 ▶ all the time todo el rato [toh-doh el RRa-toh]
 ▶ all English people todos los ingleses [toh-dohs los in-glay-says]
 ▶ will that be all? ¿eso es todo? [e-soh es toh-doh]

allergic alérgico(ca) [a-lair-CHi-koh]
 ▶ I'm allergic to aspirin/nuts/wheat/dairy products soy alérgico a las aspirinas/los frutos secos/el trigo/los productos lácteos [soy a-lair-CHi-koh a las as-pi-ree-nas/los froo-tohs sek-ohs/el tree-goh/los pro-dook-tohs lak-tay-ohs]

allow permitir [pair-mi-teer]
 ▶ how much luggage are you allowed? ¿cuánto equipaje permiten? [kwan-toh e-ki-pa-CHay pair-mee-ten]
 ▶ are you allowed to smoke here? ¿se puede fumar aquí? [say pway-day foo-mahr a-kee]

almost casi [ka-si]
> it's almost one o'clock es casi la una [es ka-si la oo-na]

alone solo(la) [soh-loh]
> leave us alone! ¡déjanos en paz! [day-CHa-nos en path]

along a lo largo de [a loh lahr-goh day]
> along the river a lo largo del río [a loh lar-goh del RRee-oh]

altogether *(in total)* en total [en toh-tal]
> how much does it cost altogether? ¿cuánto cuesta en total? [kwan-toh kwes-ta en toh-tal]

always siempre [syem-pray]
> it's always the same thing es siempre lo mismo [es syem-pray loh mees-moh]

ambulance la ambulancia [am-boo-lanth-ya]
> could you send an ambulance right away to...? ¿podrían mandar una ambulancia ahora mismo a...? [pod-ree-an man-dahr oo-na am-boo-lanth-ya a-aw-ra mees-moh a]

ambulance service el servicio de ambulancias [sair-beeth-yoh day am-boo-lanth-yas]
> what's the number for the ambulance service? ¿cuál es el número del servicio de ambulancias? [kwal es el noo-mair-oh del sair-beeth-yoh del am-boo-lanth-yas]

America los Estados Unidos [es-tah-dohs oo-nee-dohs]
> I'm from America soy de los Estados Unidos [soy day los es-tah-dohs oo-nee-dohs]
> I live in America vivo en los Estados Unidos [bee-boh en los es-tah-dohs oo-nee-dohs]
> have you ever been to America? ¿ha estado en los Estados Unidos? [a es-tah-doh en los es-tah-dohs oo-nee-dohs]

American estadounidense [es-tah-doh-oo-ni-den-say] ♦ el estadounidense [es-tah-doh-oo-ni-den-say], la estadounidense [es-tah-doh-oo-ni-den-say]
> I'm American soy estadounidense [soy es-tah-doh-oo-ni-den-say]
> we're Americans somos estadounidenses [so-mos es-tah-doh-oo-ni-den-says]

ankle el tobillo [to-beel-yoh]
> I've sprained my ankle me he torcido el tobillo [may ay tor-thee-doh el to-beel-yoh]

announcement el anuncio [a-noonth-yoh]
> what was that announcement about the Barcelona train? ¿qué decía ese anuncio sobre el tren de Barcelona? [kay de-thee-a e-say a-noonth-yoh soh-bray el tren day bahr-thel-oh-na]

another otro(tra) [oh-troh]
> another coffee, please otro café, por favor [oh-troh ka-fay por fa-bor]
> would you like another drink? ¿quiere otra bebida? [kyair-ay oh-tra beb-ee-da]

answer la respuesta [RRes-pwes-ta] ♦ contestar [kon-tes-tar]
> there's no answer no contestan [noh kon-tes-tan]

▶ I phoned earlier but nobody answered llamé antes pero no contestaban [ya-may an-tes pay-roh noh kon-tes-tah-ban]

answering machine el contestador (automático) [kon-tes-ta-dawr (ow-toh-ma-ti-koh)]

▶ I left a message on your answering machine te dejé un mensaje en el contestador (automático) [tay de-CHay oon men-sa-CHay en el kon-tes-ta-dawr (ow-toh-ma-ti-koh)]

anti-dandruff shampoo el champú anticaspa [cham-poo an-ti-kas-pa]

▶ do you have anti-dandruff shampoo? ¿tiene champú anticaspa? [tyen-ay cham-poo an-ti-kas-pa]

anybody, anyone alguien [alg-yen]

▶ is there anybody there? ¿hay alguien ahí? [eye alg-yen eye-ee]

anything *(indeterminate)* algo [al-goh]; *(in negatives)* nada [nah-da]

▶ is there anything I can do? ¿hay algo que pueda hacer? [ay al-goh kay pway-da a-thair]

anywhere

▶ I can't find it anywhere no lo encuentro por ningún sitio [noh loh en-kwen-troh por ning-goon seet-yoh]

▶ do you live anywhere near here? ¿vive cerca de aquí? [bee-bay thair-ka day a-kee]

apartment el apartamento [a-par-ta-men-toh]

▶ we'd like to rent an apartment for one week queríamos alquilar un apartamento una semana [kair-ee-a-mos al-ki-lahr oon a-par-ta-men-toh oo-na se-mah-na]

apologize pedir perdón [ped-eer pair-dohn]

▶ there's no need to apologize no hace falta que pida perdón [noh a-thay fal-ta kay pee-da pair-dohn]

appetizer el aperitivo [a-pe-ri-tee-boh]

▶ which of the appetizers would you recommend? ¿cuál de los aperitivos recomendaría? [kwal day los a-pe-ri-tee-bohs RRe-ko-men-da-ree-a]

apple la manzana [man-thah-na]

▶ could I have a kilo of apples, please? ¿me pone un kilo de manzanas, por favor? [may poh-nay oon kee-loh day man-thah-nas por fa-bor]

apologizing

▶ excuse me! ¡perdón! [pair-dohn]

▶ I'm sorry, I can't come on Saturday lo siento, el sábado no puedo venir [loh syen-toh el sa-ba-doh noh pway-doh ben-eer]

▶ that's OK de acuerdo [day a-kwair-doh]

▶ it doesn't matter no importa [noh im-por-ta]

▶ don't mention it no hay de qué [noh eye day kay]

apple juice el zumo de manzana [thoo-moh day man-thah-na]

> I'd like some apple juice quería zumo de manzana [kair-ee-a thoo-moh day man-thah-na]

appointment la cita [thee-ta]

> could I get an appointment for tomorrow morning? ¿me podría dar hora para mañana por la mañana? [may pod-ree-a dahr aw-ra pa-ra man-yah-na por la man-yah-na]

> I have an appointment with Doctor ... tengo hora con el Doctor... [ten-goh aw-ra kon el dok-tawr]

April abril [ab-reel]

> April 6th seis de abril [seys day ab-reel]

area *(region, sector)* el área [ah-ray-a]; *(locality, of town)* la zona [thoh-na]

> I'm visiting the area estoy visitando la zona [es-toy bi-si-tan-doh la thoh-na]

> what walks can you recommend in the area? ¿qué paseos me recomienda en la zona? [kay pa-say-ohs may RRe-kom-yen-da en la thoh-na]

area code *(for telephoning)* el prefijo [pre-fee-CHoh]

> what's the area code for Andorra? ¿cuál es el prefijo de Andorra? [kwal es el pre-fee-CHoh day an-do-RRa]

arm el brazo [bra-thoh]

> I can't move my arm no puedo mover el brazo [noh pway-doh mob-air el bra-thoh]

around *(in all directions)* por todas partes [por toh-das pahr-tays]; *(nearby)* alrededor [al-RRe-de-dawr]; *(here and there)* por ahí [por a-ee] ♦ *(encircling, approximately)* alrededor de [al-RRe-de-dawr day]

> we've been traveling around Europe hemos estado viajando por Europa [ay-mos es-tah-doh bya-CHan-doh por ew-roh-pa]

> I don't know my way around yet todavía no me oriento [toh-da-bee-a noh may awr-yen-toh]

> I arrived around two o'clock llegué alrededor de las dos [yay-gay al-RRe-de-dawr day las dos]

> I'd like something for around 15 euros quería algo en torno a los 15 euros [kair-ee-a al-goh en tawr-noh a los keen-thay ew-rohs]

arrive llegar [yay-gahr]

> my luggage hasn't arrived todavía no ha llegado mi equipaje [toh-da-bee-a noh a yay-gah-doh mee e-ki-pa-CHay]

> we arrived late llegamos tarde [yay-gah-mos tahr-day]

> we just arrived acabamos de llegar [a-ka-bah-mos day yay-gahr]

art el arte [ahr-tay]

> I'm not really interested in art no me interesa mucho el arte [noh may in-tair-ay-sa moo-choh el ahr-tay]

as *(while)* mientras [myen-tras]; *(like, since)* como [kom-oh] ♦ *(in comparisons)* como [kom-oh]

- the lights went out just as we were about to eat se apagaron las luces justo cuando nos disponíamos a comer [say a-pa-gahr-on las loo-thays CHoos-toh kwan-doh nos dis-pon-ee-a-mos a-kom-air]
- as I said before como ya dije antes [kom-oh ya dee-CHay an-tes]
- leave it as it is déjalo tal y como está [day-CHA-loh tal ee kom-oh es-ta]
- as... as tan... como [tan ... kom-oh]
- as much as tanto como [tan-toh kom-oh]
- as many as tantos como [tan-tohs kom-oh], tantas como [tan-tas kom-oh]

ashtray el cenicero [then-ee-thair-oh]

- could you bring us an ashtray? ¿nos podría traer un cenicero? [nos pod-ree-a tra-air oon then-ee-thair-oh]

ask *(question)* preguntar [pre-goon-tahr]; *(time)* pedir [ped-eer]

- can I ask you a question? ¿le puedo hacer una pregunta? [lay pway-doh a-thair oo-na pre-goon-ta]

aspirin la aspirina [as-pi-ree-na]

- I'd like some aspirin quería unas aspirinas [kair-ee-a oo-nas as-pi-ree-nas]

asthma el asma [as-ma]

- I have asthma tengo asma [ten-goh as-ma]

at a [a]

- our bags are still at the airport nuestras bolsas todavía están en el aeropuerto [nwes-tras bol-sas toh-da-bee-a es-tan en el eye-roh-pwair-toh]
- we arrive at midnight llegamos a medianoche [yay-gah-mos a med-ya-no-chay]

ATM el cajero (automático) [ka-CHair-oh (ow-toh-ma-ti-koh)]

- I'm looking for an ATM estoy buscando un cajero (automático) [es-toy boos-kan-doh oon ka-CHair-oh (ow-toh-ma-ti-koh)]
- the ATM has eaten my card el cajero se ha tragado mi tarjeta [el ka-CHair-oh say a tra–gah–doh mee tar-Chay-ta]

attack *(of illness)* el ataque [a-ta-kay] ◆ *(person)* atacar [a-ta-kahr]

asking questions

- is this seat free? ¿está libre este asiento? [es-ta lee-bray es-tay as-yen-toh]
- where is the station? ¿dónde está la estación? [don-day es-ta la es-tath-yohn]
- could you help me get my suitcase down, please? ¿podría ayudarme a bajar la maleta, por favor? [pod-ree-a a-yoo-dahr-may a ba-CHahr la ma-lay-ta por fa-bor]
- could you give me a hand? ¿me podría echar una mano? [may pod-ree-a e-chahr oo-na mah-noh]
- could you lend me ten euros? ¿me podría prestar diez euros? [may pod-ree-a pres-tahr dyeth ew-rohs]

ATMs

There are ATMs (*cajeros automáticos*) pretty much everywhere. You can pay by credit card in most shops, hotels and restaurants as long as you show some ID.

- ▶ he had a heart attack sufrió un ataque al corazón [soo-free-oh oon a-ta-kay al ko-ra-thohn]
- ▶ I've been attacked me han atacado [may an a-ta-kah-doh]

attention la atención [a-tenth-yohn]
- ▶ may I have your attention for a moment? ¿podrían prestar atención un momento? [pod-ree-an pres-tahr a-tenth-yohn oon mo-men-toh]

attractive atractivo(va) [a-trak-tee-boh]
- ▶ I find you very attractive me pareces muy atractivo [may pa-reth-ays mwee a-trak-tee-boh]

August el agosto [a-gos-toh]
- ▶ we're arriving on August 29th llegamos el veintinueve de agosto [yay-gah-mos el bayn-ti-nway-bay day a-gos-toh]

automatic automático(ca) [ow-toh-ma-ti-koh] ◆ *(car)* el coche automático [ko-chay ow-toh-ma-ti-koh]
- ▶ I want a car with automatic transmission quiero un coche con transmisión automática [kyair-oh oon ko-chay kon trans-mees-yohn ow-toh-ma-ti-ka]
- ▶ is it a manual or an automatic? ¿es manual o automático? [es man-wal oh ow-toh-ma-ti-koh]

available disponible [dis-pon-eeb-lay]
- ▶ you don't have a table available before then? ¿no tiene una mesa disponible antes? [noh tyen-ay oo-na may-sa dis-pon-eeb-lay an-tes]

average medio(dia) [med-yoh]
- ▶ what's the average price of a meal there? ¿cuál es el precio medio de una comida ahí? [kwal es el preth-yoh med-yoh de oo-na kom-ee-da a-ee]

avoid evitar [e-bi-tahr]
- ▶ is there a route that would help us avoid the traffic? ¿hay algún itinerario que nos ayude a evitar el tráfico? [eye al-goon ee-tin-air-ahr-yoh kay nos a-yoo-day a e-bi-tahr el tra-fi-koh]

away
- ▶ the village is ten miles away el pueblo está a diez millas de distancia [el pweb-loh es-ta a dyeth meel-yas day dis-tanth-ya]
- ▶ how far away is Madrid? ¿a cuántos kilómetros está Madrid? [a kwan-tohs ki-lo-met-rohs es-ta mad-reed]
- ▶ we're looking for a cottage far away from the town buscamos una casa de

campo lejos de la ciudad [boos-kah-mos oo-na ka-sa day kam-poh lay-CHos day la thyoo-dad]

▶ do you have any rooms away from the main road? ¿tienen habitaciones lejos de la carretera principal? [tyen-en a-bi-tath-yoh-nes lay-CHos day la ka-RRe-tair-a preen-thi-pal]

baby bottle el biberón [bee-bair-ohn]

▶ I need to sterilize a baby bottle tengo que esterilizar el biberón [ten-goh kay es-tair-il-i-thahr el bee-bair-ohn]

back atrás [a-tras] ♦ *(part of body)* la espalda [es-pal-da]; *(of room)* el fondo [fon-doh]

▶ I'll be back in 5 minutes vuelvo en 5 minutos [bwel-boh en theen-koh mi-noo-tohs]

▶ I've got a bad back estoy mal de la espalda [es-toy mal day la es-pal-da]

▶ I prefer to sit at the back prefiero sentarme atrás [pref-yair-oh sen-tahr-may a-tras]

backache el dolor de espalda [dol-awr day es-pal-da]

▶ I've got a backache me duele la espalda [may dway-lay la es-pal-da]

backpack la mochila [mo-chee-la]

▶ my passport's in my backpack mi pasaporte está en la mochila [mee pa-sa-por-tay es-ta en la mo-chee-la]

back up retroceder [RRe-troh-thed-air]

▶ I think we have to back up and turn right me parece que tenemos que retroceder y girar a la derecha [may pa-reth-ay kay ten-ay-mos kay RRe-troh-thed-air ee CHi-rahr a la de-re-cha]

bad malo(la) [ma-loh]

▶ the weather's bad today hoy hace mal tiempo [oy a-thay mal tyem-poh]

bag la bolsa [bol-sa]; *(suitcase)* la maleta [ma-lay-ta]; *(purse)* el bolso [bol-soh]

▶ are these the bags from flight 502? ¿son éstas las bolsas del vuelo quinientos dos? [son es-tas las bol-sas del bway-loh kin-yen-tos dos]

▶ can someone take our bags up to the room, please? ¿alguien podría subir las maletas a nuestra habitación, por favor? [alg-yen pod-ree-a soo-beer las ma-lay-tas a nwes-tra a-bi-tath-yohn por fa-bor]

baggage el equipaje [e-ki-pa-CHay]

▶ my baggage hasn't arrived no ha llegado mi equipaje [noh a yay-gah-doh mee e-ki-pa-CHay]

▶ I'd like to report the loss of my baggage quería denunciar la pérdida de mi equipaje [kair-ee-a de-noonth-yahr la pair-di-da day mee e-ki-pa-CHay]

baggage cart el carrito (para equipaje) [ka-RRee-toh (pa-ra e-ki-pa-CHay)]
▶ I'm looking for a baggage cart estoy buscando un carrito (para equipaje) [es-toy boos-kan-doh oon ka-RRee-toh (pa-ra e-ki-pa-CHay)]

bakery la panadería [pan-ad-air-ee-a]
▶ is there a bakery nearby? ¿hay una panadería cerca? [eye oo-na pan-ad-air-ee-a thair-ka]

balcony el balcón [bal-kohn]
▶ do you have any rooms with a balcony? ¿tienen habitaciones con balcón? [tyen-en a-bi-tath-yohn-ays kon bal-kohn]

banana el plátano [pla-ta-noh]
▶ a kilo of bananas, please un kilo de plátanos, por favor [oon kee-loh day pla-ta-nohs por fa-bor]

bandage la venda [ben-da]
▶ I need a bandage for my ankle necesito una venda para el tobillo [ne-thes-ee-toh oo-na ben-da pa-ra el to-beel-yoh]

Band-Aid® la tirita [ti-ree-ta]
▶ can I have a Band-Aid® for my cut? ¿me podría dar una tirita para el corte? [may pod-ree-a dahr oo-na ti-ree-ta pa-ra el kawr-tay]

bank *(finance)* el banco [ban-koh]
▶ is there a bank nearby? ¿hay algún banco cerca? [eye al-goon ban-koh thair-ka]
▶ are banks open on Saturdays? ¿los bancos abren los sábados? [los ban-kohs ab-ren los sa-ba-dohs]

bank card la tarjeta bancaria [tahr-CHay-ta ban-kahr-ya]
▶ I've lost my bank card he perdido mi tarjeta bancaria [ay pair-dee-doh mee tahr-CHay-ta ban-kahr-ya]

---

at the bank

▶ I'd like to change 200 dollars into euros quería cambiar doscientos dólares en euros [kair-ee-a kamb-yahr dos-thyen-tos do-la-rays en ew-rohs]

▶ in small bills, please en billetes pequeños, por favor [en bil-yay-tays pe-kayn-yohs por fa-bor]

▶ what is the exchange rate for the euro? ¿cuál es el tipo de cambio del euro? [kwal es el tee-poh day kam-byoh del ew-roh]

▶ how much is that in euros? ¿cuánto es eso en euros? [kwan-toh es e-soh en ew-rohs]

▶ do you take traveler's checks? ¿aceptan cheques de viaje? [a-thep-tan chek-ays day bya-CHay]

▶ do you charge a commission? ¿cobran comisión? [koh-bran kom-ees-yohn]

bars

Spanish bars are great places to meet people. The Spanish love going from one bar to another (*ir de tapas*) to have a drink and try different *tapas*. There's even a famous Spanish song that says there are more bars in one single district of Madrid than there are in all of Norway!

bar *(establishment serving alcohol)* el bar [bahr]; *(counter)* la barra [ba-RRa]; *(of chocolate)* la tableta [tab-lay-ta]; *(of soap)* la pastilla [pas-teel-ya]

‣ are there any good bars around here? ¿hay buenos bares por aquí? [eye bway-nohs bahr-ays por a-kee]

base la base [ba-say]

‣ we're going to use the village as our base to explore the area vamos a usar el pueblo como base para explorar la zona [bah-mos a oo-sar el pweb-loh kom-oh ba-say pa-ra eks-plo-rahr la thoh-na]

‣ the base of the lamp got broken el pie de la lámpara está roto [el pyay day la lam-pa-ra es-ta RRoh-toh]

basic básico(ca) [ba-si-koh]

‣ do the staff all have a basic knowledge of English? ¿el personal tiene los conocimientos básicos de inglés? [el pair-son-al tyen-ay los ko-no-theem-yen-tohs ba-si-kohs day in-glays]

‣ the basics lo esencial [loh es-enth-yal]

‣ I know the basics, but no more than that conozco lo esencial, pero nada más [ko-noth-koh loh es-enth-yal pay-roh nah-da mas]

basis

‣ the price per night is on a double-occupancy basis el precio es por noche basado en dos personas [el preth-yoh es por no-chay ba-sah-doh en dos pair-soh-nas]

bat *(for table tennis)* la pala [pa-la]

‣ can you rent bats? ¿alquilan palas? [al-kee-lan pa-las]

bath el baño [ban-yoh]

‣ to take a bath darse un baño [dahr-say oon ban-yoh]

bathroom *(with toilet and bathtub or shower)* el cuarto de baño [kwahr-toh day ban-yoh]; *(with toilet)* el baño [ban-yoh]

‣ where's the bathroom? ¿dónde está el baño? [don-day es-ta el ban-yoh]

bathtub la bañera [ban-yair-a]

‣ there's no plug for the bathtub la bañera no tiene tapón [la ban-yair-a noh tyen-ay ta-pohn]

battery *(for radio, flashlight)* la pila [pee-la]; *(in car)* la batería [bat-air-ee-a]

‣ I need new batteries necesito pilas nuevas [ne-thes-ee-toh pee-las nway-bas]

- the battery needs to be recharged hay que recargar la batería [eye kay RRe-kahr-gahr la bat-air-ee-a]
- the battery's dead la batería está descargada [la bat-air-ee-a es-ta des-kahr-gah-da]

be *(with adj, n)* ser [sair]; *(referring to health)* estar [es-tahr]; *(referring to age)* tener [ten-air]; *(referring to weather)* estar [es-tahr]; *(referring to prices)* ser [sair]
- where are you from? ¿de dónde eres? [day don-day air-es]
- I'm a teacher soy profesor/profesora [soy pro-fe-sawr/pro-fe-saw-ra]
- I'm happy estoy contento [es-toy kon-ten-toh]
- what day is it? ¿qué día es? [kay dee-a es]
- it's eight o'clock son las ocho [son las o-choh]
- how are you? ¿cómo estás? [kom-oh es-tas]
- I'm fine estoy bien [es-toy byen]
- where is terminal 1? ¿dónde está la terminal uno? [don-day es-ta la tair-mi-nal oo-noh]
- could you show me where I am on the map? ¿me podría mostrar en el mapa dónde estoy? [may pod-ree-a en-sen-yahr en el ma-pa don-day es-toy]
- have you ever been to the United States? ¿has estado en los Estados Unidos? [as es-tah-doh en los es-tah-dos oo-nee-dohs]
- it's the first time I've been here es la primera vez que vengo aquí [es la pri-mair-a beth kay ben-goh a-kee]
- how old are you? ¿cuántos años tienes? [kwan-tohs an-yohs tyen-ays]
- I'm 18 (years old) tengo dieciocho años [ten-goh dyeth-ee-o-choh an-yohs]
- it was over thirty-five degrees hacía más de treinta y cinco grados [a-thee-a mas day trayn-ta ee- theen-koh grah-dohs]
- it's cold in the evenings por las noches hace frío [por las no-chays a-thay free-oh]
- how much is it? ¿cuánto es? [kwan-toh es]
- I'm 1.67 meters tall mido un metro sesenta y siete de altura [mee-doh oon met-roh se-sen-ta ee syet-ay day al-too-ra]

beach la playa [pleye-a]
- it's a sandy beach es una playa de arena [es oo-na pleye-a day a-ray-na]
- is it a quiet beach? ¿es una playa tranquila? [es oo-na pleye-a tran-kee-la]

beach umbrella la sombrilla [som-breel-ya]
- can you rent beach umbrellas? ¿se pueden alquilar sombrillas? [say pway-den al-ki-lahr som-breel-yas]

beautiful hermoso(sa) [air-moh-soh]
- isn't the weather beautiful today? ¿no hace un día hermoso hoy? [noh a-thay oon dee-a air-moh-soh oy]

bed la cama [ka-ma]
- is it possible to add an extra bed? ¿podrían añadir una cama adicional? [pod-ree-an an-ya-deer oo-na ka-ma a-deeth-yon-al]

bed and breakfasts

Pensiones, casas de huéspedes, hostales or *residencias* are all names for the same thing, small, family-run bed and breakfasts. You should ask to view the room before you take it, as standards of comfort can vary considerably. Watch out, as prices can double, or even triple, in the high season. In the country, opt for the charming *casas rurales*.

- do you have a children's bed? **¿tienen una cama para niños?** [tyen-en oo-na ka-ma pa-ra neen-yohs]
- to go to bed **irse a la cama** [eer-say a la ka-ma]
- I went to bed late **me acosté tarde** [may a-kos-tay tahr-day]
- I need to put my children to bed now **ahora tengo que acostar a los niños** [a-aw-ra ten-goh kay a-kos-tahr a los neen-yohs]

bedroom el dormitorio [dor-mi-tawr-yoh]
- how many bedrooms does the apartment have? **¿cuántos dormitorios tiene el apartamento?** [kwan-tohs dor-mi-tawr-yohs tyen-ay el a-pahr-ta-men-toh]

bedside lamp la lámpara de noche [lam-pa-ra day no-chay]
- the bedside lamp doesn't work **la lámpara de noche no funciona** [la lam-pa-ra day no-chay noh foonth-yoh-na]

beef la carne de vaca [kahr-nay day ba-ka]
- I don't eat beef **no como carne de vaca** [noh kom-oh kahr-nay day ba-ka]

beer la cerveza [thair-bay-tha]
- two beers, please **dos cervezas, por favor** [dos thair-bay-thas por fa-bor]

begin *(start)* **empezar** [em-pe-thahr]
- when does the performance begin? **¿a qué hora empieza la representación?** [a kay aw-ra em-pyay-tha la RRe-pre-sen-tath-yohn]

beginner principiante [prin-theep-yan-tay]
- I'm a complete beginner **soy principiante total** [soy prin-theep-yan-tay toh-tal]

behind detrás [day-tras]
- from behind **por la espalda** [por la es-pal-da]
- the rest of our party is in the car behind **el resto del grupo está en el coche de atrás** [el RRes-toh del groo-poh es-ta en el ko-chay day a-tras]

berth *(on ship)* **la litera** [lit-air-a]
- I'd prefer the upper berth **prefiero la litera de arriba** [pref-yair-oh la lit-air-a day a-RRee-ba]

beside al lado de [al lah-doh day]
- is there anyone sitting beside you? **¿hay alguien sentado a tu lado?** [eye alg-yen sen-tah-doh a too lah-doh]

best mejor [me-CHor]
  ▸ what's the best restaurant in town? ¿cuál es el mejor restaurante de la ciudad?
    [kwal es el me-CHor RRes-tow-ran-tay day la thyoo-dad]

better mejor [me-CHor]
  ▸ I've been on antibiotics for a week and I'm not any better **estoy tomando**
    antibióticos hace una semana y no me encuentro mejor [es-toy to-man-doh an-
    tee-byo-tee-kohs a-thay oo-na se-mah-na ee noh may en-kwen-troh me-CHor]
  ▸ the better situated of the two hotels **el mejor localizado de los dos hoteles** [el
    me-CHor loh-ka-li-thah-doh day los dos oh-tel-ays]

between entre [en-tray]
  ▸ the bus runs between the airport and the hotel **hay un autobús entre el**
    aeropuerto y el hotel [eye oon ow-toh-boos ba en-tray el ray-roh-pwair-toh ee el oh-tel]

bicycle la bicicleta [bi-thi-klay-ta]
  ▸ is there a place to leave bicycles? ¿hay algún lugar donde dejar las bicicletas?
    [eye al-goon loo-gahr don-day de-CHahr las bi-thi-klay-tas]

bicycle lane el carril-bici [ka-RReel-bee-thi]
  ▸ are there any bicycle lanes? ¿hay algún carril-bici? [eye al-goon ka-RReel-bee-thi]

bicycle pump la bomba (de bicicleta) [bom-ba day bi-thi-klay-ta]
  ▸ do you have a bicycle pump? ¿tienes una bomba para la bicicleta? [tyen-ays oo-
    na bom-ba day pa-ra la bi-thi-klay-ta]

big grande [gran-day]
  ▸ do you have it in a bigger size? ¿tiene una talla mayor? [tyen-ay oo-na tal-ya meye-awr]
  ▸ it's too big es demasiado grande [es de-mas-yah-doh gran-day]

bike la bici [bee-thi]
  ▸ I'd like to rent a bike for an hour quería alquilar una bici una hora [kair-ee-a al-ki-
    lahr oo-na bee-thi oo-na aw-ra]
  ▸ I'd like to do a bike tour me gustaría hacer un recorrido en bici [may goos-ta-ree-a
    a-thair oon RRe-ko-RRee-doh en bee-thi]

bill (in hotel) la cuenta [kwen-ta]; (for goods) la factura [fak-too-ra]; (paper
money) el billete [bil-yay-tay]
  ▸ I think there's a mistake with the bill creo que hay un error en la cuenta [kray-oh
    kay eye oon e-RRor en la kwen-ta]
  ▸ put it on my bill póngalo en mi cuenta [pon-ga-loh en mee kwen-ta]
  ▸ can you write up my bill, please? ¿me podría preparar la cuenta, por favor?
    [may pod-ree-a pre-pa-rahr la kwen-ta por fa-bor]

birthday el cumpleaños [koom-play-an-yohs]
  ▸ happy birthday! ¡feliz cumpleaños! [fe-leeth koom-play-an-yohs]

bite (of animal) la mordedura [mor-de-doo-ra]; (of insect) la picadura [pi-ka-doo-ra]
  ◆ (animal) morder [mor-dair]; (insect) picar [pi-kahr]
  ▸ do you have a cream for mosquito bites? ¿tiene alguna crema para picaduras de
    mosquito? [tyen-ay al-goo-na kray-ma pa-ra pi-ka-doo-ras day mos-kee-toh]

▶ I've been bitten by a mosquito me ha picado un mosquito [may a pi-kah-doh oon mos-kee-toh]

black negro(gra) [neg-roh]; *(coffee, tea)* solo(la) [soh-loh]
▶ I'm looking for a little black dress busco un vestido negro y pequeño [boos-koh oon bes-tee-doh neg-roh ee pe-kayn-yoh]

black-and-white en blanco y negro [en blan-koh ee neg-roh]
▶ I'd like to see a black-and-white movie me gustaría ver una película en blanco y negro [may goos-ta-ree-a bair oo-na pe-lee-koo-la en blan-koh ee neg-roh]

black ice las placas de hielo [pla-kas day yay-loh]
▶ there's black ice hay placas de hielo [eye pla-kas day yay-loh]

blanket la manta [man-ta]
▶ I'd like an extra blanket quería otra manta [kair-ee-a oh-tra man-ta]

bleed sangrar [san-grahr]
▶ it won't stop bleeding no para de sangrar [noh pa-ra day san-grahr]

blind *(on window)* la persiana [pair-see-ah-na]
▶ can we pull down the blinds? ¿podemos bajar las persianas? [pod-ay-mos ba-CHahr las pair-see-ah-nas]

blister la ampolla [am-pol-ya]
▶ I got a blister tengo una ampolla [ten-goh oo-na am-pol-ya]

block bloquear [blo-kay-ahr]
▶ the toilet's blocked el retrete está atascado [el RRe-tray-tay es-ta a-tas-kah-doh]
▶ my ears are completely blocked tengo los oídos completamente tapados [ten-goh los o-ee-dohs kom-ple-ta-men-tay ta-pah-dohs]

blond rubio(bia) [RRoob-yoh]
▶ I have blond hair tengo el pelo rubio [ten-goh el pay-loh RRoob-yoh]

blood la sangre [san-gray]
▶ traces of blood restos de sangre [RRes-tohs day san-gray]

blood pressure la tensión [tens-yohn], la presión sanguínea [pres-yohn san-gee-nay-a]
▶ I have high blood pressure tengo la tensión alta [ten-goh la tens-yohn al-ta]

blood type el grupo sanguíneo [groo-poh san-gee-nay-oh]
▶ my blood type is A positive mi grupo sanguíneo es A positivo [mee groo-poh san-gee-nay-oh es a po-si-tee-boh]

blue azul [a-thool]
▶ the blue one el azul [el a-thool]

board *(plane)* embarcar en [em-bahr-kahr en] ♦ embarcar [em-bahr-kahr]
▶ what time will the plane be boarding? ¿a qué hora será el embarque? [a kay aw-ra sair-a el em-bahr-kay]
▶ where is the flight to Dublin boarding? ¿desde dónde se embarca para el vuelo de Dublín? [des-day don-day say em-bahr-ka pa-ra el bway-loh day doob-leen]

boarding pass la tarjeta de embarque [tahr-CHay-ta day em-bahr-kay]
 ▶ I can't find my boarding pass no encuentro la tarjeta de embarque [noh en-kwen-troh mee tahr-CHay-ta day em-bahr-kay]

boat el barco [bahr-koh]
 ▶ can we get there by boat? ¿se puede ir en barco? [say pway-day eer en bahr-koh]

boat trip el paseo en barco [pa-say-oh en bahr-koh]
 ▶ are there boat trips on the river? ¿hay paseos en barco por el río? [eye pa-say-ohs en bahr-koh por el RRee-oh]

book *(for reading)* el libro [lee-broh]; *(of tickets)* el taco [ta-koh]; *(of stamps)* el librillo [li-breel-yoh]; *(of matches)* la caja [ka-CHa] ◆ *(ticket, room)* reservar [RRes-air-bahr]
 ▶ do you sell English–language books? ¿venden libros en inglés? [ben-den lee-brohs en in-glays]
 ▶ is it more economical to buy a book of tickets? ¿sale más barato comprar un taco de entradas? [sa-lay mas ba-ra-toh kom-prahr oon ta-koh day en-trah-das]
 ▶ I'd like to book a ticket quería reservar un billete [kair-ee-a RRes-air-bahr oon bil-yay-tay]
 ▶ do you need to book in advance? ¿hace falta reservar por anticipado? [a-thay fal-ta RRes-air-bahr por an-ti-thi-pah-doh]

born
 ▶ to be born nacer [na-thair]
 ▶ I was born on March 3rd, 1985 nací el tres de marzo de mil novecientos ochenta y cinco [na-thee el trays day mahr-thoh day meel no-bayth-yen-tohs o-chen-ta ee theen-koh]

bottle la botella [bo-tel-ya]
 ▶ a bottle of red wine, please una botella de vino tinto, por favor [oo-na bo-tel-ya day bee-noh teen-toh por fa-bor]

bottle opener el abrebotellas [ab-ray-bo-tel-yas]
 ▶ can you pass me the bottle opener? ¿me podrías pasar el abrebotellas? [may pod-ree-as pa-sahr el ab-ray-bo-tel-yas]

bottom *(of a well, of a box)* el fondo [fon-doh]
 ▶ my passport's at the bottom of my suitcase mi pasaporte está en el fondo de la maleta [mee pa-sa-por-tay es-ta en el fon-doh day mee ma-lay-ta]

box la caja [ka-CHa]
 ▶ could I have a box of matches, please? quería una caja de cerillas, por favor [kair-ee-a oo-na ka-CHa day thair-eel-yas por fa-bor]

boy *(young male)* el chico [chee-koh]; *(son)* el hijo [ee-CHoh]
 ▶ he seems like a nice boy parece un chico majo [pa-reth-ay oon chee-koh ma-CHoh]
 ▶ she has two boys tiene dos hijos [tyen-ay dos ee-CHohs]

boyfriend novio(via) [nohb-yoh]
 ▶ my boyfriend is a biologist mi novio es biólogo [mee nohb-yoh es bi-ol-oh-goh]

breakfast

Breakfast (*el desayuno*) is usually light: fruit juice, a pastry or a croissant and coffee. Serving times in hotels will vary slightly, but it will usually be between 7 and 10 o'clock. Many city dwellers just have a quick coffee before going in to work and then have their proper breakfast mid-morning. Then they eat lunch at about 2 or 3 o'clock. When in Rome...!

brake el freno [fray-noh]
- the brakes aren't working properly los frenos no funcionan correctamente [los fray-nohs noh foonth-yoh-nan ko-RRek-ta-men-tay]

brake fluid el líquido de frenos [lee-ki-doh day fray-nohs]
- could you check the brake fluid? ¿podría comprobar el líquido de frenos? [pod-ree-a kom-pro-bahr el lee-ki-doh day fray-nohs]

branch *(of bank)* la agencia [a-CHenth-ya]
- which branch should I visit to get the replacement traveler's checks? ¿a qué agencia tengo que ir para conseguir los cheques de viajero de sustitución? [a kay a-CHenth-ya ten-goh kay eer pa-ra kon-se-geer los chek-ays day bya-CHair-oh day soos-ti-tooth-yohn]

bread el pan [pan]
- do you have any bread? ¿tiene pan? [tyen-ay pan]
- could I have some more bread? ¿me podría dar más pan? [may pod-ree-a dahr mas pan]

break *(pause)* el descanso [des-kan-soh] • romper [RRom-pair]
- should we take a break? ¿hacemos un descanso? [a-thay-mos oon des-kan-soh]
- be careful you don't break it ten cuidado, no vayas a romperlo [ten kwi-dah-doh noh beye-as a RRom-pair-loh]
- I think I've broken my ankle creo que me he fracturado el tobillo [kray-oh kay may ay frak-too-rah-doh el to-beel-yoh]

break down averiarse [a-bair-yahr-say], estropearse [es-trop-ay-ahr-say]
- my car has broken down se ha averiado el coche [say a-bair-yah-doh el ko-chay]

breakdown la avería [a-bair-ee-a]
- we had a breakdown on the freeway tuvimos una avería en la autopista [too-bee-mos oo-na a-bair-ee-a en la ow-toh-pees-ta]

breakfast el desayuno [des-eye-oo-noh]
- to have breakfast desayunar [des-eye-oo-nahr]
- what time is breakfast served? ¿a qué hora sirven el desayuno? [a kay aw-ra seer-ben el des-eye-oo-noh]

bridge el puente [pwen-tay]

▸ do you have to pay a toll to use the bridge? ¿hay que pagar peaje para usar el puente? [eye kay pa-gahr pay-a-CHay pa-ra oo-sar el pwen-tay]

bring traer [tra-air]

▸ what should we bring to drink? ¿qué tenemos que traer de beber? [kay te-nay-mos kay tra-air day beb-air]

bring down *(bags, luggage)* bajar [ba-CHahr]

▸ could you get someone to bring down our luggage, please? ¿podría llamar a alguien para que bajara nuestro equipaje, por favor? [pod-ree-a yam-ahr a alg-yen pa-ra kay ba-Chah-ra nwes-troh e-ki-pa-CHay pa-ra fa-bor]

bring in *(bags, luggage)* entrar [en-trahr]

▸ can you bring in my bags, please? ¿podría entrar mis bolsas, por favor? [pod-ree-a en-trahr mees bol-sas por fa-bor]

broken roto(ta) [RRoh-toh]

▸ the lock is broken la cerradura está rota [la the-RRa-doo-ra es-ta RRoh-ta]

▸ I think I've got a broken leg creo que me he roto la pierna [kray-oh kay may ay RRoh-toh oo-na pyair-na]

bronchitis la bronquitis [bron-kee-tees]

▸ do you have anything for bronchitis? ¿tiene algo para la bronquitis? [tyen-ay al-goh pa-ra la bron-kee-tis]

brother el hermano [air-mah-noh]

▸ I don't have any brothers or sisters no tengo hermanos [noh ten-goh air-mah-nohs]

brown marrón [ma-RRohn]

▸ he has brown hair tiene el pelo castaño [tyen-ay el pay-loh kas-tan-yoh]

▸ I'm looking for a brown leather belt busco un cinturón de piel marrón [boos-koh oon thin-too-rohn day pyel ma-RRohn]

brush el cepillo [thep-eel-yoh] ◆ *(hair)* cepillar [thep-eel-yahr]

▸ where are the brush and dustpan? ¿dónde están la escoba y el recogedor? [don-day es-tan la es-koh-ba ee el RRe-ko-CHe-dawr]

▸ to brush one's teeth lavarse los dientes [la-bahr-say los dyen-tays]

bulb *(light)* la bombilla [bom-beel-ya]

▸ the bulb's out in the bathroom la bombilla del baño está fundida [la bom-beel-ya del ban-yoh es-ta foon-dee-da]

bunk beds la litera [lit-air-a]

▸ are there bunk beds for the children? ¿hay literas para los niños? [eye lit-air-as pa-ra los neen-yohs]

burn quemar [kay-mahr]

▸ the food's completely burnt la comida está completamente quemada [la ko-mee-da es-ta kom-ple-ta-men-tay kay-mah-da]

▸ I've burned my hand me he quemado la mano [may ay kay-mah-doh la mah-noh]

burst *(tire)* reventar [RRe-ben-tahr]
 ▸ one of my tires has burst se me ha reventado un neumático [say may a RRe-ben-tah-doh oon new-ma-ti-koh]

bus el autobús [ow-toh-boos]
 ▸ does this bus go downtown? ¿este autobús va al centro? [este ow-toh-boos ba al then-troh]
 ▸ which bus do I have to take to go to…? ¿qué autobús tengo que coger para ir a…? [kay ow-toh-boos ten-goh kay koCH-air pa-ra eer a]

bus driver el conductor de autobús [kon-dook-tawr day ow-toh-boos], la conductora de autobús [kon-dook-taw-ra day ow-toh-boos]
 ▸ can you buy tickets from the bus driver? ¿puedes comprarle los billetes al conductor del autobús? [pway-days kom-prahr-lay bil-yay-tays al kon-dook-tawr del ow-toh-boos]

business *(commerce)* los negocios [ne-gohth-yohs]; *(company)* la empresa [em-pray-sa]; *(concern, affair, matter)* el asunto [a-soon-toh]
 ▸ it's none of your business no es asunto tuyo [noh es a-soon-toh too-yoh]

business card la tarjeta de visita [tahr-CHay-ta day bi-see-ta]
 ▸ here's my business card aquí tiene mi tarjeta de visita [a-kee tyen-ay mee tahr-CHay-ta day bi-see-ta]

business class la clase ejecutiva [kla-say e-CHe-koo-tee-ba], la clase preferente [kla-say pre-fair-en-tay] ◆ en clase preferente [en kla-say pre-fair-en-tay]
 ▸ are there any seats in business class? ¿hay asientos en la clase ejecutiva? [eye as-yen-tohs en kla-say e-CHe-koo-tee-ba]
 ▸ I prefer to travel business class prefiero viajar en clase ejecutiva [pref-yair-oh bya-CHahr en kla-say e-CHe-koo-tee-ba]

bus station la estación de autobuses [es-tath-yohn day ow-toh-boos-ays]
 ▸ I'm looking for the bus station estoy buscando la estación de autobuses [es-toy boos-kan-doh la es-tath-yohn day ow-toh-boos-ays]

bus stop la parada de autobús [pa-rah-da day ow-toh-boos]
 ▸ where's the nearest bus stop? ¿dónde está la parada de autobús más cercana? [don-day es-ta la pa-rah-da day ow-toh-boos mas thair-kah-na]

busy *(person)* ocupado(da) [o-koo-pah-doh]; *(town, beach, street)* concurrido(da) [kon-koo-RRee-doh]; *(period)* ajetreado(da) [a-CHet-ray-ah-doh]; *(phone line)* ocupado [o-koo-pah-doh], comunicando [ko-moo-ni-kan-doh]
 ▸ I'm afraid I'm busy tomorrow me temo que mañana estoy ocupado [may tay-moh kay es-ta man-yah-na es-toy o-koo-pah-doh]
 ▸ the line's busy está comunicando [es-ta ko-moo-ni-kan-doh], comunica [ko-moo-nee-ka]

butter la mantequilla [man-te-keel-ya]
 ▸ could you pass the butter please? ¿me podrías pasar la mantequilla, por favor? [may pod-ree-as pa-sahr la man-te-keel-ya por fa-bor]

buy comprar [kom-prahr]

▶ where can I buy tickets? ¿dónde puedo comprar entradas? [don-day pway-doh kom-prahr en-trah-das]

▶ can I buy you a drink? ¿puedo invitarte a tomar algo? [pway-doh in-bi-tahr-tay a toh-mahr al-goh]

bye adiós [ad-yohs]

▶ bye, see you tomorrow! ¡adiós, hasta mañana! [ad-yohs as-ta man-yah-na]

C

cab el taxi [tak-si]

▶ can you order me a cab to the airport? ¿podría pedirme un taxi para llevarme al aeropuerto? [pod-ree-a ped-eer-may oon tak-si pa-ra yay-bahr-may al eye-roh-pwair-toh]

cab driver el taxista, la taxista [tak-sees-ta]

▶ does the cab driver speak English? ¿el taxista habla inglés? [el tak-sees-ta ab-la in-glays]

cabin *(on boat)* el camarote [ka-ma-roh-tay]; *(on plane)* la cabina [ka-bee-na]

▶ can I have breakfast in my cabin? ¿puedo desayunar en mi camarote? [pway-doh des-eye-oo-nahr en mee ka-ma-roh-tay]

cable la televisión por cable [te-le-bis-yohn por kah-blay]

▶ does the hotel have cable? ¿el hotel tiene televisión por cable? [el oh-tel tyen-ay te-le-bis-yohn por kah-blay]

café el café [ka-fay]

▶ is there a café near here? ¿hay algún café cerca? [eye al-goon ka-fay thair-ka]

cake el pastel [pas-tel]

▶ a piece of that cake, please un trozo de ese pastel, por favor [oon tro-thoh day es-ay pas-tel por fa-bor]

call *(on phone)* la llamada [ya-mah-da] ◆ llamar [ya-mahr]

▶ I have to make a call tengo que hacer una llamada [ten-goh kay a-thair oo-na ya-mah-da]

in a café

▶ is this table/seat free? ¿está libre esta mesa/este asiento? [es-ta lee-bray es-ta may-sa/es-tay as-yen-toh]

▶ excuse me! ¡perdón! [pair-dohn]

▶ two black coffees/coffees with cream, please dos cafés solos/cafés con leche, por favor [dos ka-fays soh-lohs/ka-fays kon le-chay por fa-bor]

camping

Camping rough can be a bit tricky. In theory it is permitted on some beaches and in designated areas. You need to take advice from the local tourist office. But if you ask for permission to camp on private land, or you camp somewhere off the beaten track that is at least 1 kilometer (0.62 miles) from a campsite, that's fine.

▶ what is this called? **¿cómo se llama esto?** [kom-oh say yah-ma es-toh]

▶ who's calling? **¿de parte de quién?** [day pahr-tay day kyen]

call back volver a llamar a [bol-bair a ya-mahr a] ◆ volver a llamar [bol-bair a ya-mahr]

▶ could you ask her to call me back? **¿podría pedirle que me volviera a llamar?** [pod-ree-a ped-eer-lay kay may bol-byair–a a ya-mahr]

▶ I'll call back (later) **llamaré (más tarde)** [ya-ma-ray (mas tahr-day)]

calm tranquilo(la) [tran-kee-loh]

▶ keep calm! **¡tranquilo!** [tran-kee-loh]

camera la cámara [ka-ma-ra]

▶ can I use my camera here? **¿puedo usar la cámara aquí?** [pway-doh oo-sar la ka-ma-ra a-kee]

camper la autocaravana [ow-toh-ka-ra-bah-na]

▶ do you have a space left for a camper? **¿les queda espacio para una autocaravana?** [les kay-da es-path-yoh pa-ra oo-na ow-toh-ka-ra-bah-na]

▶ I'd like to book space for a camper for the night of August 15th **quería reservar espacio para una autocaravana para la noche del quince de agosto** [kair-ee-a RRe-sair-bahr es-path-yoh pa-ra oo-na ow-toh-ka-ra-bah-na pa-ra la no-chay del keen-thay day a-gos-toh]

campground el camping [kam-peen]

▶ I'm looking for a campground **estoy buscando un camping** [es-toy boos-kan-doh oon kam-peen]

camping la acampada [a-kam-pah-da]

▶ I love going camping **me encanta ir de acampada** [may en-kan-ta eer day a-kam-pah-da]

can la lata [la-ta]

▶ a can of oil, please **una lata de aceite, por favor** [oo-na la-ta day a-thay-tay por fa-bor]

can *(be able to)* poder [pod-air]

▶ can I help you? **¿puedo ayudarle?** [pway-doh a-yoo-dahr-lay]

▶ can you speak English? **¿habla inglés?** [ab-la in-glays]

Canada Canadá [ka-na-da]

▶ I'm from Canada **soy de Canadá** [soy day ka-na-da]

- I live in Canada **vivo en Canadá** [bee-boh en ka-na-da]
- have you ever been to Canada? **¿has estado en Canadá?** [as es-tah-doh en ka-na-da]

Canadian canadiense [ka-nad-yen-say] ◆ el canadiense, la canadiense [ka-nad-yen-say]

- I'm Canadian **soy canadiense** [soy ka-nad-yen-say]
- we're Canadians **somos canadienses** [so-mos ka-nad-yen-says]

cancel anular [a-noo-lahr], cancelar [kan-thel-ahr]

- is it possible to cancel a reservation? **¿se puede anular una reserva?** [say pway-day a-noo-lahr oo-na RRe-sair-ba]

canoeing el piragüismo [pi-rag-wees-mo]

- I was told we could go canoeing **me dijeron que podríamos hacer piragüismo** [may di-CHair-on kay pod-ree-a-mos a-thair pi-rag-wees-mo]

car *(automobile)* el coche [ko-chay]; *(on train)* el vagón [ba-gohn]

- I'd like to rent a car for a week **quería alquilar un coche una semana** [kair-ee-a al-ki-lahr oon ko-chay oo-na se-mah-na]
- I've just crashed my car **acabo de chocar con el coche** [a-kah-boh day cho-kahr kon el ko-chay]
- can you help us push the car? **¿nos podría ayudar a empujar el coche?** [nos pod-ree-a a-yoo-dahr a em-poo-CHahr el ko-chay]
- my car's been towed away **la grúa se me ha llevado el coche** [la groo-a say may a yay-bah-doh el ko-chay]
- my car's broken down **se me ha averiado el coche** [say may a a-bair-yah-doh el ko-chay]

carafe la jarra [CHa-RRa]

- a large carafe of water, please **una jarra de agua grande, por favor** [oo-na CHa-RRa day ag-wa gran-day por fa-bor]
- a carafe of house wine **una jarra de vino de la casa** [oo-na CHa-RRa day bee-noh day la ka-sa]

renting a car

- with comprehensive insurance **con seguro a todo riesgo** [kon se-goo-roh a toh-doh RRee-es-goh]
- can I leave the car at the airport? **¿puedo dejar el coche en el aeropuerto?** [pway-doh de-CHar el ko-chay en el eye-roh-pwair-toh]
- can I see your driver's license, please? **¿me podría enseñar su carnet de conducir, por favor?** [may pod-ree-a en-sen-yahr soo kahr-nay day kon-doo-theer por fa-bor]

car crash el accidente de coche [ak-thi-den-tay day ko-chay]
- he's been killed in a car crash ha muerto en un accidente de coche [a mwair-toh en oon ak-thi-den-tay day ko-chay]

card la tarjeta [tahr-CHay-ta]
- the waiter hasn't brought my card back el camarero no me ha devuelto mi tarjeta [el ka-ma-rair-oh noh me a day-bwel-toh mee tahr-CHay-ta]
- I need to get a card for my parents for their anniversary necesito comprar una tarjeta para el aniversario de mis padres [ne-the-see-toh kom-prahr oo-na tahr-CHay-ta pa-ra el a-ni-bair-sahr-yoh day mees pad-rays]
- can I give you my card? ¿le puedo dar mi tarjeta? [lay pway-doh dahr mee tahr-CHay-ta]

cardigan la chaqueta de punto [cha-kay-ta day poon-toh]
- should I take a cardigan in case it gets cool in the evening? ¿llevo una chaqueta de punto por si refresca por la noche? [yay–boh oo-na cha-kay-ta day poon-toh por si RRe-fres-ka por la no-chay]

carpet la alfombra [al-fom-bra]
- the carpet hasn't been vacuumed no han aspirado la alfombra [noh an as-pi-rah-doh la al-fom-bra]

car rental el alquiler de coches [al-ki-lair day ko-chays]
- is car rental expensive? ¿el alquiler de coches es caro? [el al-ki-lair day ko-chays es kah-roh]

car rental agency la compañía de alquiler de coches [kom-pan-yee-a day al-ki-lair day ko-chays]
- do you know of any car rental agencies? ¿conoce alguna compañía de alquiler de coches? [ko-noth-ay al-goo-na kom-pan-yee-a day al-ki-lair day ko-chays]

carry *(baggage)* llevar [yay-bahr], transportar [trans-por-tahr] ◆ *(sound)* oírse [o-eer-say]
- could you help me carry something? ¿me podría ayudar a llevar algo? [may pod-ree-a a-yoo-dahr a yay-bahr al-goh]

carry-on bag la bolsa de mano [bol-sa day mah-noh]
- am I only allowed one carry-on bag? ¿sólo puedo llevar una bolsa de mano? [soh-loh pway-doh yay-bahr oo-na bol-sa day mah-noh]

cart el carrito [ka-RRee-toh]
- where can I get a cart? ¿dónde puedo conseguir un carrito? [don-day pway-doh kon-se-geer oon ka-RRee-toh]

carton *(of cigarettes)* el cartón [kahr-tohn]
- I'd like a carton of cigarettes quería un cartón de cigarrillos [kair-ee-a oon kahr-tohn day thi-ga-RReel-yohs]

in case por si [por see]
- just in case por si acaso [por see a-ka-soh]

cash *(notes and coins)* el efectivo [e-fek-tee-boh] ◆ *(check)* hacer efectivo [a-thair e-fek-tee-boh]
  ▶ I'll pay cash voy a pagar en efectivo [boy a pa-gahr en e-fek-tee-boh]
  ▶ I want to cash this traveler's check quiero hacer efectivo este cheque de viajero [kyair-oh a-thair e-fek-tee-boh es-tay che-kay day bya-CHair-oh]

castle el castillo [kas-teel-yoh]
  ▶ is the castle open to the public? ¿está abierto al público el castillo? [es-ta ab-yair-toh al poob-li-koh el kas-teel-yoh]

catalog el catálogo [ka-ta-loh-goh]
  ▶ do you have a catalog? ¿tiene un catálogo? [tyen-ay oon ka-ta-loh-goh]

catch *(with hands)* coger [koCH-air]; *(cold)* coger [koCH-air]; *(hear clearly)* oír [o-eer]
  ▶ I've caught a cold he cogido un resfriado [ay koCH-ee-doh oon RRes-free-ah-doh]
  ▶ I'm sorry, I didn't quite catch your name perdón, no oí bien su nombre [pair-dohn noh o-ee byen soo nom-bray]

Catholic católico(ca) [ka-to-li-koh] ◆ el católico [ka-to-li-koh], la católica [ka-to-li-ka]
  ▶ where is there a Catholic church? ¿dónde hay una iglesia católica? [don-day eye oo-na ee-glays-ya ka-to-li-ka]

CD el CD [thay-day]
  ▶ how much does this CD cost? ¿cuánto cuesta este CD? [kwan-toh kwes-ta es-tay thay-day]

cellphone el teléfono móvil [te-lay-fon-oh mob-eel], el móvil [mob-eel]
  ▶ what's your cellphone number? ¿cuál es el tu número de móvil? [kwal es el too noo-mair-oh day mob-eel]

center el centro [then-troh]
  ▶ we want to be based near the center of the region queremos establecernos cerca del centro de la región [kair-ay-mos es-tab-le-thair-nos thair-ka del then-troh day la RReCH-yohn]

chair la silla [seel-ya]
  ▶ could we have another chair in our room? ¿nos podrían poner otra silla en la habitación? [nos pod-ree-an pon-air oh-tra seel-ya en la a-bi-tath-yohn]

change el cambio [kam-byoh] ◆ cambiar [kam-byahr]
  ▶ do you have any change? ¿tiene cambio? [tyen-ay kam-byoh]
  ▶ keep the change quédese con el cambio [kay-day-say kon el kam-byoh]
  ▶ I don't have exact change no tengo el cambio exacto [noh ten-goh el kam-byoh ek-sak-toh]
  ▶ give me change for ten dollars cámbieme diez dólares [kam-byay-may dyeth doh-la-res]
  ▶ is it possible to change a reservation? ¿se puede cambiar una reserva? [say pway-day kam-byahr oo-na RRe-sair-ba]

- I'd like to change these traveler's checks quería cambiar estos cheques de viajero [kair-ee-a kam-byahr es-tohs chek-ays day bya-CHair-oh]
- can you help me change the tire? ¿me podría ayudar a cambiar la rueda? [may pod-ree-a a-yoo-dahr a kam-byahr la RRoo-ay-da]
- the oil needs to be changed hay que cambiar el aceite [eye kay kam-byahr el a-thay-tay]

changing table la mesa para cambiar los pañales [may-sa pa-ra kam-byahr los pan-yah-lays]

- is there a changing table? ¿hay una mesa para cambiar los pañales? [eye oo-na may-sa pa-ra kam-byahr los pan-yah-lays]

charge *(cost)* el precio [preth-yoh]

- is there a charge for the parking lot? ¿hay que pagar para usar el aparcamiento? [eye kay pa-gahr pa-ra oo-sahr el a-pahr-kam-yen-toh]
- is there a charge for using the facilities? ¿hay que pagar para usar las instalaciones? [eye kay pa-gahr pa-ra oo-sahr las in-sta-lath-yoh-nays]
- is there a charge for cancellations? ¿hay una comisión por cancelación? [eye oo-na ko-mis-yohn por kan-thel-ath-yohn]
- I'd like to speak to the person in charge quería hablar con el encargado [kair-ee-a ab-lahr kon el en-kahr-gah-doh]

charter flight el vuelo chárter [bway-loh chahr-tair]

- where do we board the charter flight to Málaga? ¿dónde embarcamos en el vuelo chárter a Málaga? [don-day em-bahr-kah-mos en el bway-loh chahr-tair a ma-la-ga]

cheap barato(ta) [ba-ra-toh]

- I'm trying to find a cheap flight home estoy intentando encontrar un vuelo

---

checking

- is it right and then left? ¿es a la derecha y luego a la izquierda? [es a la de-re-cha ee loo-ay-goh a la ith-kyair-da]
- is this the train for Seville? ¿éste es el tren de Sevilla? [es-tay es el tren day se-beel-ya]
- could you tell me where to get off, please? ¿me podría decir dónde me tengo que bajar, por favor? [may pod-ree-a de-theer don-day may ten-goh kay ba-CHahr por fa-bor]
- is this the right stop for ...? ¿esta es la parada de...? [es-ta es la pa-rah-da day]
- are you sure that he'll be able to come? ¿estás seguro de que va a poder venir? [es-tas se-goo-roh day kay ba a po-dair ben-eer]

barato de vuelta a casa [es-toy in-ten-tan-doh en-kon-trahr oon bway-loh ba-ra-toh day bwel-ta a ka-sa]

check *(for paying)* el cheque [chek-ay]; *(in restaurant)* la cuenta [kwen-ta] ♦ *(test, verify)* comprobar [kom-proh-bahr]

▶ the check, please! ¡la cuenta, por favor! [la kwen-ta por fa-bor]
▶ can I pay by check? ¿puedo pagar con cheque? [pway-doh pa-gahr kon chek-ay]
▶ can you check the oil? ¿podría comprobar el aceite? [pod-ree-a kom-proh-bahr el a-thay-tay]

checkbook el talonario de cheques [ta-loh-nahr-yoh day chek-ays]

▶ my checkbook's been stolen me han robado el talonario de cheques [may an RRob-ah-doh el ta-loh-nahr-yoh day chek-ays]

check in *(at airport)* facturar [fak-too-rahr]; *(at hotel)* registrarse [RRe-gis-trahr-say]

▶ I'd like to check in both these bags, please quería facturar estas dos bolsas, por favor [kair-ee-a fak-too-rahr es-tas dos bol-sas por fa-bor]
▶ what time do you have to be at the airport to check in? ¿a qué hora hay que estar en el aeropuerto para facturar? [a kay aw-ra eye kay es-tahr en el eye-roh-pwair-toh pa-ra fak-too-rahr]

check-in desk *(at airport)* el mostrador de facturación [mos-tra-dawr day fak-too-rath-yohn]

▶ where is the United Airlines check-in desk? ¿dónde está el mostrador de facturación de United Airlines? [don-day es-ta el mos-tra-dawr day fak-too-rath-yohn day oo-neye-ted eyer-leyens]

check out

▶ what time do you have to check out by? ¿a qué hora hay que dejar libre la habitación? [a kay aw-ra eye kay day-CHahr lee-bray la a-bi-tath-yohn]

cheers salud [sa-lood]

▶ cheers and all the best! ¡salud y todo lo mejor! [sa-lood ee toh-doh loh me-CHor]

cheese el queso [kay-soh]

▶ what are the best local cheeses? ¿cuáles son los mejores quesos del lugar? [kwa-lays son los me-CHor-ays kay-sohs del loo-gahr]

chicken el pollo [pol-yoh]

▶ half a roast chicken, please medio pollo asado, por favor [med-yoh pol-yoh a-sah-doh por fa-bor]
▶ a chicken sandwich and fries un bocadillo de pollo con patatas fritas [oon bo-ka-deel-yoh day pol-yoh kon pa-ta-tas free-tas]

child el niño [neen-yoh], la niña [neen-ya]

▶ do you have children? ¿tenéis niños? [ten-eys neen-yohs]
▶ two adults and two children, please dos adultos y dos niños, por favor [dos a-dool-tohs ee dos neen-yohs por fa-bor]

▶ do you have discounts for children? ¿hay descuentos para niños? [eye des-kwen-tohs pa-ra neen-yohs]

children's menu el menú infantil [men-oo in-fan-teel]
▶ do you have a children's menu? ¿tienen un menú infantil? [tyen-en oon men-oo in-fan-teel]

chilled *(wine)* frío(fría) [free-oh]
▶ this wine isn't chilled enough este vino no está bien frío [el bee-noh noh es-ta byen free-oh]

chocolate el chocolate [cho-koh-la-tay]
▶ I'd like a bar of chocolate quería una tableta de chocolate [kair-ee-a oo-na tab-lay-ta day cho-koh-la-tay]

choose elegir [el-eCH-eer]
▶ I don't know which one to choose no sé cuál elegir [noh say kwal el-eCH-eer]

Christmas la Navidad [na-bee-dad]
▶ Merry Christmas! ¡feliz Navidad! [fe-leeth na-bee-dad]
▶ I wish you a very merry Christmas ¡feliz Navidad! [fe-leeth na-bee-dad]

Christmas Day el día de Navidad [dee-a day na-bee-dad]
▶ we're closed on Christmas Day cerramos el día de Navidad [theRR-ah-mos el dee-a day na-bee-dad]

church la iglesia [i-glays-ya]
▶ how old is the church? ¿de cuándo es la iglesia? [day kwan-doh es la i-glays-ya]
▶ where can we find a Protestant church? ¿dónde podemos encontrar una iglesia protestante? [don-day pod-ay-mos en-kon-trahr oo-na i-glays-ya pro-tes-tan-tay]
▶ where is there a Catholic church? ¿dónde hay una iglesia católica? [don-day eye oo-na i-glays-ya ka-to-li-ka]

cigarette el cigarrillo [thi-ga-RReel-yo]
▶ can I ask you for a cigarette? ¿me podrías dar un cigarrillo? [may pod-ree-as dah oon thi-ga-RReel-yo]
▶ where can I buy cigarettes? ¿dónde puedo comprar cigarrillos? [don-day pway-doh kom-prahr thi-ga-RReel-yos]

cigarette lighter el encendedor [en-then-de-dawr], el mechero [me-chair-oh]
▶ do you have a cigarette lighter? ¿tienes un encendedor? [tyen-ays oon en-then-de-dawr]

city la ciudad [thyoo-dad]
▶ what's the nearest big city? ¿cuál es la ciudad grande más cercana? [kwal es la thyoo-dad gran-day mas thair-kah-na]

class *(on train, plane)* la clase [kla-say]
▶ which class are your seats in? ¿de qué clase son sus asientos? [day kay kla-sa son soos as-yen-tohs]

clean limpio(pia) [leem-pyoh] ◆ limpiar [leem-pyahr]

- the sheets aren't clean las sábanas no están limpias [las sa-ba-nas noh es-tan leem-pyas]
- do we have to clean the apartment before leaving? ¿tenemos que limpiar el apartamento antes de salir? [ten-ay-mos kay leem-pyahr el a-par-ta-men-toh an-tes day sal-eer]
- could you clean the windshield? ¿podría limpiar el parabrisas? [pod-ree-a leem-pyahr el pa-ra-bree-sas]

cleaning la limpieza [leem-pyay-tha]
- who does the cleaning? ¿quién hace la limpieza? [kyen a-thay la leem-pyay-tha]

clear (easily understood) claro(ra) [klah-roh]; (way) despejado(da) [des-pe-CHah-doh] ◆ (road, path) despejar [des-pe-CHahr]
- is that clear? ¿está claro? [es-ta klah-roh]
- is the road ahead clear? ¿está despejada la carretera más adelante? [es-ta des-pe-CHah-da la ka-RRe-tair-a mas a-de-lan-tay]
- when will the road be cleared? ¿cuándo van a despejar la carretera? [kwan-doh ban a des-pe-CHahr la ka-RRe-tair-a]

climb (mountaineer) escalar [es-ka-lahr]; (plane, road) subir [soo-beer]
- the road climbs steadily after you leave the village la carretera sube sin parar después de salir del pueblo [la ka-RRe-tair-a soo-bay seen pa-rahr des-pwes day sal-eer del pweb-loh]

climbing la escalada [es-ka-lah-da]
- can you go climbing here? ¿se puede hacer escalada aquí? [say pway-day a-thair es-ka-lah-da a-kee]

cloakroom (in a museum, a theater) el guardarropa [gwahr-da-RRoh-pa]
- is there a charge for the cloakroom? ¿hay que pagar para usar el guardarropa? [eye kay pa-gahr pa-ra oo-sar la gwahr-da-RRoh-pa]
- I'd like to leave my things in the cloakroom quería dejar mis cosas en el guardarropa [kair-ee-a de-CHahr mees koh-sas en la gwahr-da-RRoh-pa]

close cerrar(se) [theRR-ahr-(say)]
- what time do the stores close? ¿a qué hora cierran las tiendas? [a kay aw-ra thee-e-RRan las tyen-das]
- what time do you close? ¿a qué hora cierra? [a kay aw-ra thee-e-RRa]
- the door won't close no consigo cerrar esta puerta [noh kon-see-goh theRR-ahr es-ta pwair-ta]

closed cerrado(da) [theRR-ah-doh]
- are the stores closed on Sundays? ¿las tiendas están cerradas los domingos? [las tyen-das es-tan theRR-ah-das los do-meen-gohs]

clothes la ropa [RRoh-pa]
- where can we wash our clothes? ¿dónde podemos lavar la ropa? [don-day pod-ay-mos la-bahr la RRoh-pa]

ordering coffee

How do you like it? Black and very strong, like a lot of Spaniards? If so, ask for a *solo*. Or you can have an *americano*, which has some hot water added. Or a *cortado* with a splash of milk added. At breakfast time or with a cake as an afternoon snack it's usually drunk *con leche*. And finally, if you're out on the town, a *carajillo* is a coffee with brandy or rum.

club *(nightclub)* la discoteca [dis-ko-tay-ka]
  ▶ we could go to a club afterwards podríamos ir después a una discoteca [pod-ree-a-mos eer des-pwes a oo-na dis-ko-tay-ka]

coach el autocar [ow-toh-kahr]
  ▶ what time does the coach leave? ¿a qué hora sale el autocar? [a kay aw-ra sa-lay el ow-toh-kahr]

coast la costa [kos-ta]
  ▶ an island off the coast of France una isla cerca de la costa de Francia [oo-na ees-la thair-ka day la kos-ta day franth-ya]

coffee el café [ka-fay]
  ▶ coffee with milk or cream café con leche [ka-fay kon le-chay]
  ▶ black coffee café solo [ka-fay soh-loh]
  ▶ I'd like a coffee quería un café [kair-ee-a oon ka-fay]
  ▶ would you like some coffee? ¿quiere café? [kyair-ay ka-fay]

coin la moneda [mo-nay-da]
  ▶ the machine only takes coins la máquina solo acepta monedas [la ma-ki-na soh-loh a-thep-ta mo-nay-das]

cold frío(fría) [free-oh] ◆ *(illness)* el resfriado [RRes-free-ah-doh]; *(low temperature)* el frío [free-oh]
  ▶ it's cold today hoy hace frío [oy a-thay free-oh]
  ▶ I'm very cold tengo mucho frío [ten-goh moo-choh free-oh]
  ▶ to have a cold tener un resfriado [ten-air oon RRes-free-ah-doh]
  ▶ I've caught a cold he cogido un resfriado [ay koCH-ee-doh oon RRes-free-ah-doh]

collect a cobro revertido [a kob-roh RRe-bair-tee-doh]
  ▶ I have to call my parents collect tengo que llamar a mis padres a cobro revertido [ten-goh kay yam-ahr a mees pad-rays a kob-roh RRe-bair-tee-doh]

collect call la llamada a cobro revertido [ya-mah-da a kob-roh RRe-bair-tee-doh]
  ▶ to make a collect call hacer una llamada a cobro revertido [a-thair oo-na ya-mah-da a a kob-roh RRe-bair-tee-doh]

color el color [ko-lor]
- do you have it in another color? ¿lo tiene en otro color? [loh tyen-ay en oh-troh ko-lor]

color film el carrete en color [ka-RRay-tay en ko-lor]
- I'd like a roll of color film quería un carrete en color [kair-ee-a oon ka-RRay-tay en ko-lor]

come *(move here)* venir [ben-eer]; *(arrive)* llegar [yay-gahr]; *(pass by)* pasar [pa-sahr]
- come here! ¡ven aquí! [ben a-kee]
- coming! ¡ya voy! [ya boy]
- when does the bus come? ¿a qué hora pasa el autobús? [a kay aw-ra pa-sa el ow-toh-boos]

come from ser de [sair day]
- where do you come from? ¿de dónde eres? [day don-day air-ays]

come in *(enter)* entrar [en-trahr]; *(train)* llegar [yay-gahr]; *(tide)* subir [soo-beer]
- may I come in? ¿puedo entrar? [pway-doh en-trahr]
- come in! ¡entre! [en-tray]
- the tide's coming in está subiendo la marea [es-ta soob-yen-doh la ma-ray-a]

come on *(light, heating)* encenderse [en-then-dair-say]
- the heating hasn't come on no se ha encendido la calefacción [noh say a en-then-dee-doh la ka-lay-fakth-yohn]
- come on! ¡vamos! [bah-mos]

come with venir con [ben-eer kon]
- could you come with me to...? ¿podrías venir conmigo a...? [pod-ree-as ben-eer kon-mee-goh a]
- what does it come with? ¿con qué viene? [kon kay byen-ay]

comfortable *(person)* cómodo(da) [kom-oh-doh]
- we're very comfortable here aquí estamos muy cómodos [a-kee es-tah-mos mwee kom-oh-dohs]

commission la comisión [ko-mees-yohn]
- what commission do you charge? ¿qué comisión cobran? [kay ko-mees-yohn kohb-ran]

company *(firm)* la empresa [em-pray-sa], la compañía [kom-pan-yee-a]
- is it a big company? ¿es una empresa grande? [es oo-na em-pray-sa -gran-day]

compartment el compartimento [kom-par-ti-men-toh]
- which compartment are our seats in? ¿en qué compartimento están nuestros asientos? [en kay kom-par-ti-mon-toh es-tan nwes-tros as-yen-tohs]

complain quejarse [kay-CHahr-say]
- I will be writing to your headquarters to complain voy a escribir a su sede para quejarme [boy a es-kri-beer a soo say-day pa-ra kay-CHar-may]

complaint *(protest)* la queja [kay-CHa]; *(in store)* la reclamación [rek-la-math-yohn]

▸ I'd like to make a complaint *(protest)* quería presentar una queja [kair-ee-a pre-sen-tahr oo-na kay-CHa]; *(in store)* quería hacer una reclamación [kair-ee-a a-thair oo-na RRek-la-math-yohn]

complete *(form)* completar [kom-ple-tahr]

▸ here's the completed form aquí está el formulario completado [a-kee es-ta el for-moo-lahr-yoh kom-ple-tah-doh]

comprehensive insurance el seguro a todo riesgo [se-goo-roh a toh-doh RRee-es-goh]

▸ how much extra is the comprehensive insurance coverage? ¿cuánto cuesta añadir el seguro a todo riesgo? [kwan-toh kwes-ta el se-goo-roh a toh-doh RRee-es-goh]

computer el ordenador [or-den-a-dawr]

▸ is there a computer I could use? ¿podría usar un ordenador? [pod-ree-a oo-sar oon or-den-a-dawr]

concert el concierto [konth-yair-toh]

▸ did you like the concert? ¿te gustó el concierto? [tay goos-toh el konth-yair-toh]

condom el condón [kon-dohn]

▸ do you have any condoms? ¿tiene condones? [tyen-ay kon-doh-nays]

confirm confirmar [kon-feer-mahr]

▸ I confirmed my reservation by phone confirmé la reserva por teléfono [kon-feer-may la RRe-sair-ba por te-lay-fon-oh]

▸ I'd like to confirm my return flight quería confirmar mi vuelo de vuelta [kair-ee-a kon-feer-mahr mee bway-loh day bwel-ta]

---

complaints

▸ I'd like to see the manager, please quería ver al director, por favor [kair-ee-a bair al dee-rek-tawr por fa-bor]

▸ I have a complaint tengo una queja [ten-goh oo-na kay-cha]

▸ there's a problem with the heating hay un problema con la calefacción [eye oon prob-lay-ma kon la ka-le-fakth-yohn]

▸ I am relying on you to sort this problem out confío en usted para que resuelva este problema [kon-fee-oh en oos-ted pa-ra kay RRes-wel-ba es-tay prob-lay-ma]

▸ I expect the cost of the camera to be fully reimbursed espero que me reembolsen el coste total de la cámara [es-pair-oh kay may RRay-em-bol-sen el kos-tay toh-tal day la ka-ma-ra]

congratulations la enhorabuena [en-aw-ra-bway-na]
- congratulations! ¡enhorabuena! [en-aw-ra-bway-na]

connecting flight el vuelo de conexión [bway-loh day kon-eks-yohn]
- does the connecting flight leave from the same terminal? ¿el vuelo de conexión sale de la misma terminal? [el bway-loh day kon-eks-yohn sa-lay day la mees-ma tair-mee-nal]

connection la conexión [kon-eks-yohn]
- the connection is very bad: I can't hear very well hay una mala conexión, no oigo bien [eye oo-na ma-la kon-eks-yohn noh oy-goh byen]
- I've missed my connection he perdido mi conexión [ay pair-dee-doh mee kon-eks-yohn]

consulate el consulado [kon-soo-lah-doh]
- where is the American consulate? ¿dónde está el consulado de los Estados Unidos? [don-day es-ta el kon-soo-lah-doh day los es-tah-dohs oo-nee-dohs]

contact *(communication)* el contacto [kon-tak-toh] ◆ ponerse en contacto con [pon-air-say en kon-tak-toh kon]
- I need to contact my family in the States tengo que ponerme en contacto con mi familia en los Estados Unidos [ten-goh kay pon-air-may en kon-tak-toh kon mee fa-meel-ya en es-tah-dohs oo-nee-dohs]
- do you know how to get in contact with him? ¿sabe cómo puedo ponerme en contacto con él? [sa-bay kom-oh pway-doh pon-air-may en kon-tak-toh kon el]

contact lens la lente de contacto [len-tay day kon-tak-toh], la lentilla [len-teel-ya]
- I've lost a contact (lens) he perdido una lentilla [ay pair-dee-doh oo-na len-teel-ya]

cookie *(food)* la galleta [gal-yay-ta]
- a box of cookies, please una caja de galletas, por favor [oo-na ka-CHa day gal-yay-tas por fa-bor]

cooking la cocina [ko-thee-na]
- we prefer to do our own cooking preferimos prepararnos nuestra propia comida [pre-fair-ee-mos pre-pa-rahr-nos nwes-tra prop-ya ko-mee-da]
- do you like French cooking? ¿te gusta la comida francesa? [tay goos-ta la ko-mee-da fran-thay-sa]

cork *(for a bottle)* el corcho [kor-choh]
- where's the cork for the bottle? ¿dónde está el corcho de la botella? [don-day es-ta el kor-choh day la bo-tel-ya]

corked agrio(gria) [ag-ree-oh]
- this wine is corked el vino está agrio [el bee-noh es-ta ag-ree-oh]

corner *(outside)* la esquina [es-kee-na]; *(inside)* el rincón [RRin-kohn]
- stop at the corner pare en la esquina [pah-ray en la es-kee-na]
- the table in the corner la mesa del rincón [la may-sa del RRin-kohn]

coronary el infarto [in-fahr-toh]
▸ he's had a coronary ha sufrido un infarto [a soo-free-doh oon in-fahr-toh]

correct *(check)* correcto(to) [ko-RRek-toh]
▸ that's correct correcto [ko-RRek-toh]

cost costar [kos-tahr]
▸ how much will it cost to go to the airport? ¿cuánto costará ir hasta el aeropuerto? [kwan-toh kos-ta-ra eer as-ta el eye-roh-pwair-toh]
▸ it cost us 150 dollars nos costó ciento cincuenta dólares [nos kos-toh they-toh theen-kwen-ta doh-la-rays]

cot la cuna [koo-na]
▸ we can put a cot in the room for you podemos poner una cuna en el cuarto [pod-ay-mos pon-air oo-na koo-na en el kwahr-toh]

cough la tos [tos] ◆ toser [tos-air]
▸ I've got a cough tengo tos [ten-goh tos]
▸ I need something for a cough necesito algo para la tos [ne-thes-ee-toh al-goh pa-ra la tos]

could
▸ could you help me? ¿podría ayudarme? [pod-ree-a a-yoo-dahr-may]

count contar [kon-tahr]
▸ that doesn't count eso no cuenta [e-soh noh kwen-ta]

counter *(in store)* el mostrador [mos-tra-dawr]; *(in bank)* la ventanilla [ben-ta-neel-ya]
▸ which counter do I have to go to? ¿a qué ventanilla tengo que ir? [a kay ben-ta-neel-ya eye kay eer]
▸ do you sell this medication over the counter? ¿venden esta medicina sin receta? [ben-den es-ta me-di-thee-na seen RRe-thay-ta]

country el país [pa-ees]
▸ what country do you come from? ¿de qué país eres? [day kay pa-ees air-es]

couple la pareja [pa-ray-CHa]
▸ it's for a couple and two children es para una pareja y dos hijos [es pa-ra oo-na pa-ray-CHa ee dos ee-CHohs]

course *(of a meal)* el plato [pla-toh]; *(of a ship, a plane)* el rumbo [room-boh]; *(for a race)* el circuito [theer-kwee-toh]; *(in yoga, sailing)* el curso [koor-soh] ◆ **of course** *(inevitably)* por supuesto [por soo-pwes-toh]; *(for emphasis)* claro [klah-roh]
▸ is the set meal three courses? ¿el menú del día incluye tres platos? [el men-oo del dee-a in-kloo-yay tres pla-tohs]
▸ how much does the diving course cost? ¿cuánto cuesta el curso de buceo? [kwan-toh kwes-ta el koor-soh day boo-thay-oh]
▸ of course he'll come claro que vendrá [klah-roh kay ben-dra]

cream *(for the skin)* la crema [kray-ma]
▶ I need some cream for my sunburn necesito una crema para las quemaduras del sol [ne-thes-ee-toh oo-na kray-ma pa-ra las kay-ma-doo-ras del sol]

credit card la tarjeta de crédito [tahr-CHay-ta day kre-di-toh]
▶ do you take credit cards? ¿aceptan tarjetas de crédito? [a-thep-tan tahr-CHay-tas day kre-di-toh]

cross cruzar [kroo-thahr]
▶ how do we cross this street? ¿cómo cruzamos esta calle? [kom-oh kroo-thah-mos es-ta kal-yay]

cross-country skiing el esquí de fondo [es-kee day fon-doh]
▶ where can I go cross-country skiing around here? ¿dónde puedo hacer esquí de fondo aquí? [don-day pway-doh a-thair es-kee day fon-doh a-kee]

crosswalk el paso de peatones [pa-soh day pay-a-toh-nays]
▶ always cross at the crosswalk cruza siempre por el paso de peatones [kroo-tha syem-pray por el pa-soh day pay-a-toh-nays]

cruise el crucero [kroo-thair-oh]
▶ how much does a cruise on the Rhine cost? ¿cuánto cuesta un crucero por el Rhin? [kwan-toh kwes-ta kwes-ta oon kroo-thair-oh por el RReen]

cry llorar [yoh-rahr]
▶ don't cry no llores [noh yoh-rays]

cup la taza [ta-tha]
▶ I'd like a cup of tea quería una taza de té [kair-ee-a oo-na ta-tha day tay]
▶ a coffee cup una taza de café [oo-na ta-tha day ka-fay]
▶ could we have an extra cup? ¿nos podría traer otra taza? [nos pod-ree-a tra-air oh-tra ta-tha]

currency *(money)* la moneda [mo-nay-da]
▶ how much local currency do you have? ¿cuánta moneda local tienes? [kwan-ta mo-nay-da loh-kal tyen-es]

cut cortar [kor-tahr]
▶ I cut my finger me he cortado el dedo [may ay kor-tah-doh el day-doh]

daily diario(ria) [dee-ahr-yoh] ◆ *(newspaper)* el periódico [pe-ri-oh-di-koh]
▶ what's the name of the local daily newspaper? ¿cuál es el nombre del periódico local? [kwal es el nom-bray del pe-ri-oh-di-koh loh-kal]

damage dañar [dan-yahr]
▶ my suitcase was damaged in transit dañaron mi maleta durante el transporte [dan-yahr-on mee ma-lay-ya doo-ran-tay el trans-por-tay]

damp húmedo(da) [oo-me-doh]
- it's damp today hoy hay mucha humedad [oy eye moo-cha oo-me-dad]

dance bailar [beye-lahr]
- shall we dance? ¿bailamos? [beye-lah-mos]
- I can't dance no sé bailar [noh say beye-lahr]

dancing el baile [beye-lay]
- will there be dancing? ¿habrá baile? [ab-ra beye-lay]
- where can we go dancing? ¿dónde podemos ir a bailar? [don-day pod-ay-mos eer a beye-lahr]

dandruff la caspa [kas-pa]
- I have bad dandruff tengo mucha caspa [ten-goh moo-cha kas-pa]

danger el peligro [pe-lee-groh]
- hurry! someone's in danger! ¡rápido!, ¡hay alguien en peligro! [RRa-pi-doh eye alg-yen en pel-ee-groh]

dangerous peligroso(sa) [pe-li-groh-soh]
- the river is quite dangerous el río es bastante peligroso [el RRee-oh es bas-tan-tay pe-lee-groh-soh]

dark oscuro(ra) [os-koo-roh]
- it's dark es de noche [es day no-chay]
- she has dark hair tiene el pelo oscuro [tyen-ay el pay-loh os-koo-roh]

dark chocolate el chocolate negro [cho-ko-la-tay neg-roh]
- I prefer dark chocolate prefiero el chocolate negro [pref-yair-oh el cho-ko-la-tay neg-roh]

date *(in time)* la fecha [fe-cha]; *(appointment)* la cita [thee-ta]
- I've got a date tonight esta noche tengo una cita [es-ta no-chay ten-goh oo-na thee-ta]

date-stamp validar [ba-li-dahr]
- do I have to date-stamp this ticket? ¿tengo que validar este billete? [ten-goh kay ba-li-dahr es-tay bil-yay-tay]

daughter la hija [ee-CHa]
- this is my daughter esta es mi hija [es-ta es mee ee-CHa]

day el día [dee-a]
- what day is it? ¿qué día es? [kay dee-a es]
- I arrived three days ago llegué hace tres días [yay-gay a-thay tres dee-as]
- I'd like to do a round trip in a day me gustaría hacer un viaje de ida y vuelta en un día [may goos-ta-ree-a a-thair oon bya-CHay day ee-da ee bwel-ta en oon dee-a]
- how much is it per day? ¿cuánto cuesta por día? [kwan-toh kwes-ta por dee-a]

dead muerto(ta) [mwair-toh]
- he was pronounced dead at the scene fue declarado muerto en el lugar [fway dek-la-rah-doh mwair-toh en el loo-gahr]
- the battery's dead la batería está agotada [la bat-air-ee-a es-ta a-goh-tah-dah]

dead end el callejón sin salida [kal-ye-CHohn seen sal-ee-da]
> it's a dead end es un callejón sin salida [es oon kal-ye-CHohn seen sal-ee-da]

deal *(business agreement)* el acuerdo [ak-wair-doh]
> I got a good deal on the room la habitación me salió bien de precio [la a-bi-tath-yohn may sal-yoh byen day preth-yoh]

death la muerte [mwair-tay]
> there were two deaths hubo dos muertes [oo-boh dos mwair-tays]

decaf, decaffeinated el descafeinado [des-kaf-ay-nah-doh] ◆ descafeinado(da) [des-kaf-ay-nah-doh]
> a decaf/decaffeinated coffee, please un descafeinado, por favor [oon des-kaf-ay-nah-doh por fa-bor]

December diciembre [deeth-yem-bray]
> December 10th diez de diciembre [dyeth day deeth-yem-bray]

decide decidir [de-thi-deer]
> we haven't decided yet no nos hemos decidido todavía [noh nos ay-mos de-thi-dee-doh toh-da-bee-a]

deck *(of ship)* la cubierta [koob-yair-ta]; *(of cards)* la baraja [ba-ra-CHa]
> how do I get to the upper deck? ¿cómo se sube a la cubierta superior? [kom-oh say soo-bay a la koob-yair-ta soo-pair-yawr]

deckchair la tumbona [toom-boh-na]
> I'd like to rent a deckchair quería alquilar una tumbona [kair-ee-a al-ki-lahr oo-na toom-boh-na]

declare declarar [dek-la-rahr]
> I have nothing to declare no tengo nada que declarar [noh ten-goh nah-da kay dek-la-rahr]
> I have a bottle of brandy to declare tengo que declarar una botella de coñac [ten-goh kay dek-la-rahr oo-na bo-tel-ya day kon-yak]

definitely claramente [klah-ra-men-tay]
> we'll definitely come back here claramente volveremos aquí [klah-ra-men-tay bol-bair-ay-mos a-kee]

degree el grado [grah-doh]
> it's 5 degrees below freezing estamos a cinco grados bajo cero [es-tah-mos a theen-koh grah-dos ba-CHoh thair-oh]

delay el retraso [RRe-tra-soh]
> is there a delay for this flight? ¿tiene algún retraso este vuelo? [tyen-ay al-goon RRe-tra-soh es-tay bway-loh]

delayed retrasado(da) [RRe-tra-sah-doh]
> how long will the flight be delayed? ¿cuánto tiempo se va a retrasar el vuelo? [kwan-toh tyem-poh say ba a RRe-tra-sahr el bway-loh]

delighted encantado(da) [en-kan-tah-doh]
> we're delighted you could make it estamos encantados de que hayas podido venir [es-tah-mohs en-kan-tah-dohs day kay eye-as po-dee-doh ben-eer]

dentist el dentista, la dentista [den-tees-ta]
> I need to see a dentist urgently necesito un dentista urgentemente [ne-thes-ee-toh oon den-tees-ta oor-CHen-te-men-tay]

department *(in store)* la sección [sekth-yohn], el departamento [de-par-ta-men-toh]
> I'm looking for the menswear department busco la sección de caballeros [boos-koh-la sekth-yohn day ka-bal-yair-ohs]

department store los grandes almacenes [gran-days al-ma-then-ays]
> where are the department stores? ¿dónde están los grandes almacenes? [don-day es-tan los gran-days al-ma-then-ays]

departure la salida [sa-lee-da]
> 'departures' *(in airport)* 'salidas' [sa-lee-das]

departure lounge la sala de embarque [sa-la day em-bahr-kay]
> where's the departure lounge? ¿dónde está la sala de embarque? [don-day es-ta la sa-la day em-bahr-kay]

deposit *(against loss or damage)* la fianza [fee-an-tha]; *(down payment)* la entrada [en-trah-da]
> is there a deposit to pay on the equipment? ¿hay que pagar una fianza por el equipo? [eye kay pa-gahr oo-na fee-an-tha por el e-kee-poh]
> how much is the deposit? ¿de cuánto es la fianza? [day kwan-toh es la fee-an-tha]

desk *(in office, home)* la mesa [may-sa]; *(at hotel)* la recepción [RRe-thepth-yohn]; *(for cashier)* la caja [ka-CHa]; *(at airport)* el mostrador [mos-tra-dawr]
> where can I find the American Airlines desk? ¿dónde está el mostrador de American Airlines? [don-day es-ta el mos-tra-dawr day a-mair-i-kan eyer-leyens]

dessert el postre [pos-tray]
> what desserts do you have? ¿qué postres tienen? [kay pos-trays tyen-en]

dessert wine el vino dulce [bee-noh dool-thay]
> can you recommend a good dessert wine? ¿me podría recomendar un buen vino dulce? [may pod-ree-a RRe-ko-men-dahr oon bwen bee-noh dool-thay]

detour el desvío [des-bee-oh]
> is there a detour ahead? ¿hay un desvío más adelante? [eye oon des-bee-oh mas a-de-lan-tay]

develop revelar [RRe-be-lahr]
> how much does it cost to develop a roll of 36 photos? ¿cuánto cuesta revelar un carrete de treinta y seis fotos? [kwan-toh kwes-ta RRe-be-lahr oon ka-RRay-tay day treyn-ta ee seys foh-tohs]

diabetic diabético(ca) [dee-a-bet-í-koh] ◆ el diabético, la diabética [dee-a-bet-i-koh]

dinner

Because the Spanish eat lunch (*la comida*) so late (and linger over it so long!), they often don't have dinner (*la cena*) before 9 o'clock in the evening – sometimes even later. It all depends on how many *tapas* you eat with your aperitif at 7 o'clock. If you have overdone it, you can put off your dinner until between 10 o'clock and midnight. That's how they do things in the South!

▶ I'm diabetic and I need a prescription for insulin soy diabético y necesito una receta para comprar insulina [soy dee-a-bet-i-koh ee ne-thes-ee-toh oo-na RRe-thay-ta pa-ra kom-prahr in-soo-lee-na]

diarrhea la diarrea [dee-a-RRay-a]
▶ I'd like something for diarrhea quiero algo para la diarrea [kyair-oh-a al-goh pa-ra la dee-a-RRay-a]

difference *(in price, cost)* la diferencia [di-fair-enth-ya]
▶ will you pay the difference? ¿pagarás la diferencia? [pa-ga-ras la di-fair-enth-ya]

difficult difícil [di-fee-theel]
▶ I find some sounds difficult to pronounce algunos sonidos son difíciles de pronunciar [al-goo-nohs so-nee-dohs son di-fee-thee-les day pro-noonth-yahr]

difficulty *(trouble)* la dificultad [di-fi-kool-tad]
▶ I'm having difficulty finding the place estoy teniendo dificultades para encontrar el lugar [es-toy ten-yen-doh di-fi-kool-tad-ays pa-ra en-kon-trahr el loo-gahr]

digital camera la cámara digital [ka-ma-ra di-CHi-tal]
▶ my digital camera's been stolen me han robado la cámara digital [may an RRo-bah-doh la ka-ma-ra di-CHi-tal]

dining room el comedor [kom-e-dawr]
▶ do you have to have breakfast in the dining room? ¿hay que desayunar en el comedor? [eye kay des-eye-oo-nahr en el kom-e-dawr]

dinner la cena [thay-na]
▶ up to what time do they serve dinner? ¿hasta qué hora sirven la cena? [as-ta kay aw-ra seer-ben la thay-na]

direct directo(ta) [di-rek-toh]
▶ is that train direct? ¿ese tren es directo? [e-say tren es di-rek-toh]

direction *(heading)* la dirección [di-rekth-yohn]
▶ am I going in the right direction for the train station? ¿voy en la dirección correcta para ir a la estación de tren? [boy en la di-rekth-yohn ko-RRek-ta pa-ra eer a la es-tath-yohn day tren]

directory assistance la información telefónica [in-for-math-yohn te-le-fo-ni-ka]
▶ what's the number for directory assistance? ¿cuál es el número de la información telefónica? [kwal es el noo-mair-oh day la in-for-math-yohn te-le-fo-ni-ka]

dirty sucio(cia) [sooth-yoh]
  ▸ the sheets are dirty las sábanas están sucias [las sa-ba-nas es-tan sooth-yas]

disability la discapacidad [dis-ka-path-i-dad]
  ▸ do you have facilities for people with disabilities? ¿tienen instalaciones para discapacitados? [tyen-en in-sta-lath-yoh-nays pa-ra dis-ka-path-i-tah-dohs]

disabled discapacitado(da) [dis-ka-path-i-tah-doh]
  ▸ where's the nearest disabled parking spot? ¿dónde está el estacionamiento para discapacitados más cercano? [don-day es-ta el es-tath-yon-am-yen-toh pa-ra dis-ka-path-i-tah-dos mas thair-kah-noh]

disco (club) la discoteca [dees-koh-tay-ka]
  ▸ are there any discos around here? ¿hay discotecas por aquí? [eye dees-koh-tay-kas por a-kee]

discount el descuento [des-kwen-toh]
  ▸ is there any chance of a discount? ¿me podría dar algún descuento? [may pod-ree-a dahr al-goon des-kwen-toh]

dish el plato [pla-toh]
  ▸ what's the dish of the day? ¿cuál es el plato del día? [kwal es el pla-toh del dee-a]
  ▸ can I help you with the dishes? ¿te puedo ayudar a lavar los platos? [tay pway-doh a-yoo-dahr a la-bahr los pla-tohs]

disposable desechable [de-se-chah-blay]
  ▸ I need some disposable razors necesito cuchillas de afeitar desechables [ne-thes-ee-toh koo-cheel-yas day a-fay-tahr de-se-chab-lays]
  ▸ do you sell disposable cameras? ¿venden cámaras de usar y tirar? [ben-den ka-ma-ras day oo-sahr ee ti-rahr]

distance la distancia [dis-tanth-ya]
  ▸ the hotel is only a short distance from here el hotel está a poca distancia de aquí [el oh-tel es-ta a poh-ka dis-tanth-ya day a-kee]

district (of town) el barrio [baRR-yoh]
  ▸ which district do you live in? ¿en qué barrio vives? [en kay baRR-yoh bee-bays]

dive (from poolside) tirarse de cabeza [ti-rahr-say day ka-bay-tha]; (as sport) bucear [boo-thay-ahr] ♦ el buceo [boo-thay-oh]
  ▸ can we do a night dive? ¿podemos hacer un buceo nocturno? [po-day-mos a-thair oon boo-thay-oh nok-toor-noh]

diving (scuba diving) el buceo [boo-thay-oh]
  ▸ what's the diving like around here? ¿cómo es el buceo por aquí? [kom-oh es el boo-thay-oh por a-kee]
  ▸ I'd like to take diving lessons me gustaría hacer un curso de buceo [may goos-ta-ree-a a-thair oon koor-soh day boo-thay-oh]
  ▸ do you rent out diving equipment? ¿alquilan equipo de buceo? [al-kee-lan e-kee-poh day boo-thay-oh]

diving board el trampolín [tram-po-leen]
- ▶ is there a diving board? ¿hay un trampolín? [eye oon tram-po-leen]

dizzy spell el mareo [ma-ray-oh]
- ▶ I've been having dizzy spells me dan mareos [may dan ma-ray-ohs]

do hacer [a-thair]
- ▶ what do you do for a living? ¿en qué trabajas? [en kay tra-ba-CHas]
- ▶ is there anything I can do (to help)? ¿puedo hacer alguna cosa (para ayudar)? [pway-doh a-thair al-goo-na koh-sa (pa-ra a-yoo-dahr)]
- ▶ what are you doing tonight? ¿qué vas a hacer esta noche? [kay bas a a-thair es-ta no-chay]
- ▶ what is there to do here on Sundays? ¿qué se puede hacer aquí los domingos? [kay say pway-day a-thair a-kee los do-meen-gohs]

doctor el médico [may-di-koh], el doctor [dok-tawr]
- ▶ I have to see a doctor tengo que ver a un médico [ten-goh kay bair a oon may-di-koh]

dollar el dólar [doh-lar]
- ▶ I'd like to change some dollars into euros quería cambiar dólares por euros [kair-ee-a kamb-yahr doh-lar-ays por ew-rohs]

door la puerta [pwair-ta]
- ▶ do you want me to answer the door? ¿quieres que abra la puerta? [kyair-ays kay ab-ra la pwair-ta]

dormitory (in youth hostel) el dormitorio (colectivo) [dor-mi-tawr-yoh (ko-lek-tee-boh)]; (for students) el colegio mayor [ko-leCH-yoh meye-awr]
- ▶ are you staying in the dormitory? ¿estás alojado en el colegio mayor? [es-tas a-lo-CHah-doh en el ko-leCH-yoh meye-awr]

double doble [doh-blay] ◆ el doble [el doh-blay] ◆ duplicarse [doo-pli-kahr-say]
- ▶ it's spelled with a double 'm' se escribe con dos 'emes' [say es-kree-bay kon dos em-ays]
- ▶ prices have doubled since last year los precios se han duplicado desde el año pasado [los preth-yohs say an doo-pli-kah-doh des-day el an-yoh pa-sah-doh]

double bed la cama de matrimonio [ka-ma day mat-ri-mohn-yoh]
- ▶ does the room have a double bed? ¿la habitación tiene una cama de matrimonio? [la a-bi-tath-yohn tyen-ay oo-na ka-ma day mat-ri-mohn-yoh]

double room la habitación doble [a-bi-tath-yohn doh-blay]
- ▶ I'd like a double room for 5 nights, please quería una habitación doble para cinco noches, por favor [kair-ee-a oon a-bi-tath-yohn doh-blay pa-ra theen-koh no-chays por fa-bor]

downtown del centro [del then-troh] ◆ al centro [al then-troh] ◆ el centro [then-troh]
- ▶ we're looking for a good downtown hotel buscamos un buen hotel en el centro [boos-kah-mos oon bwen oh-tel en el then-troh]
- ▶ does this bus go downtown? ¿este autobús va al centro? [es-tay ow-toh-boos ba al then-troh]

ordering drinks

Your guide to being the perfect barfly: if you ask for *una cerveza* (a beer) you'll be given a beer in a bottle. For a small glass of draft beer, ask for *una caña*. For something a little bigger, ask for *un tubo*, and if you're really thirsty, *una jarra*. A mixture of beer and lemonade is called *una clara*, and a glass of wine *una copa de vino*.

draft beer la cerveza de barril [thair-bay-ha day ba-RReel]
- a draft beer, please una cerveza de barril, por favor [oo-na thair-bay-ha day ba-RReel por fa-bor]

dream el sueño [swayn-yoh] ♦ soñar [son-yahr]
- to have a dream tener un sueño [ten-air oon swayn-yoh]
- I dreamt (that)... soñé que... [son-yay kay]

drink la bebida [beb-ee-da] ♦ beber [beb-air]
- I'll have a cold drink quería una bebida fría [kair-ee-a oo-na beb-ee-da free-a]
- I could do with a drink no me vendría mal una bebida [noh may ben-dree-a mal oo-na beb-ee-da]
- what kind of hot drinks do you have? ¿qué bebidas calientes tienen? [kay beb-ee-das kal-yen-tays tyen-en]
- shall we go for a drink? ¿vamos a tomar una copa? [bah-mos a tom-ahr oo-na koh-pa]
- can I buy you a drink? ¿puedo invitarte a tomar algo? [pway-doh im-bi-tahr-tay a tom-ahr al-goh]

drinking water el agua potable [ag-wa po-tah-blay]
- I'm looking for bottled drinking water busco una botella de agua mineral [boos-koh oo-na bo-tel-ya day ag-wa min-air-al]

drive *(in vehicle)* el viaje [bya-CHay] ♦ *(vehicle)* conducir [kon-doo-theer]
- is it a long drive? ¿es un viaje largo? [es oon bya-CHay lahr-goh]
- could you drive me home? ¿me podría llevar a casa? [may pod-ree-a yay-bahr a ka-sa]
- she was driving too close conducía demasiado cerca [kon-doo-thee-a de-mas-yah-doh thair-ka]

driver el conductor [kon-dook-tawr], la conductora [kon-dook-taw-ra]; *(of taxi)* el taxista, la taxista [tak-sees-ta]
- the other driver wasn't looking where he was going el otro conductor no miraba por dónde iba [el oh-troh kon-dook-tawr noh mi-rah-ba por don-day ee-ba]

driver's license el carnet de conducir [kahr-nay day koon-doo-theer]
- can I see your driver's license? su carnet de conducir, por favor [soo kahr-nay day koon-doo-theer, por fa-bor]

drop la gota [goh-ta] ◆ *(let fall)* dejar caer [de-CHahr ka-air]; *(let out of vehicle)* dejar [de-CHahr]

▸ could I just have a drop of milk? ¿me podía poner una gota de leche? [may pod-ree-a pon-air oo-na goh-ta day le-chay]

▸ I dropped my scarf se me cayó la bufanda [say may ka-yoh la boo-fan-da]

▸ could you drop me off at the corner? ¿me podría dejar en la esquina? [may pod-ree-a de-CHahr en la es-kee-na]

drop off *(let out of vehicle)* dejar [de-CHahr]

▸ could you drop me off here? ¿me podría dejar aquí? [may pod-ree-a de-CHahr a-kee]

drown ahogarse [a-o-gahr-say]

▸ he's drowning: somebody call for help se está ahogando, que alguien pida ayuda [say es-ta a-o-gan-doh kay alg-yen pee-da a-yoo-da]

drugstore la farmacia [far-math-ya]

▸ where is the nearest drugstore? ¿dónde está la farmacia más cercana? [don-day es-ta la far-math-ya mas thair-kah-na]

drunk borracho(cha) [bo-RRa-choh]

▸ he's very drunk está completamente borracho [es-ta kom-play-ta-men-tay bo-RRa-choh]

dry seco(ca) [say-koh] ◆ secar [se-kahr] ◆ secarse [se-kahr-say]

▸ a small glass of dry white wine un vaso pequeño de vino blanco seco [oon ba-soh pe-kayn-yoh day bee-noh blan-koh say-koh]

▸ where can I put my towel to dry? ¿dónde puedo poner la toalla para que se seque? [don-day pway-doh pon-air la twal-ya pa-ra kay say say-kay]

dry cleaner's la tintorería [tin-to-rair-ee-a]

▸ is there a dry cleaner's nearby? ¿hay una tintorería por aquí cerca? [eye oo-na tin-to-rair-ee-a por a-kee]

dryer *(for laundry)* la secadora [se-ka-daw-ra]

▸ is there a dryer? ¿hay secadora? [eye se-ka-daw-ra]

---

at the drugstore

▸ I'd like something for a headache/a sore throat/diarrhea quería algo para el dolor de cabeza/el dolor de garganta/la diarrea [kair-ee-a el-algoh pa-ra el do-lawr day ka-bay-tha/el do-lawr day gar-gan-ta/la dee-a-RRay-a]

▸ I'd like some aspirin/some Band-Aids® quiero aspirinas/tiritas [kair-ee-a as-pi-ree-nas/ti-ree-tas]

▸ could you recommend a doctor? ¿podría recomendarme un médico? [pod-ree-a RRe-ko-men-dahr-may oon may-di-koh]

dub *(movie)* doblar [dob-lahr]
- do they always dub English-language movies? ¿siempre doblan las películas en inglés? [syem-pray dob-lan las pe-lee-koo-las en in-glays]

during durante [doo-ran-tay]
- is there restricted parking during the festival? ¿se puede aparcar normalmente durante el festival? [say pway-day a-par-kahr nor-mal-men-tay doo-ran-tay el fes-ti-bal]

duty *(tax)* el impuesto [im-pwes-toh]
- do I have to pay duty on this? ¿tengo que pagar impuestos por esto? [ten-goh kay pa-gahr im-pwes-tohs por es-toh]
- I want to see the doctor on duty quiero ver al médico de guardia [kair-ee-a bair al may-di-koh day gwahrd-ya]

duty-free shop la tienda libre de impuestos [tyen-da lee-bray day im-pwes-tohs]
- where are the duty-free shops? ¿dónde están las tiendas libres de impuestos? [don-day es-tan las tyen-das lee-brays day im-pwes-tohs]

DVD el DVD [day oo-bay day]
- which region is this DVD coded for? ¿cuál es el código regional de este DVD? [kwal es el koh-di-goh RReCH-yoh-nal day es-tay day oo-bay day]

ear el oído [o-ee-doh]
- I have a ringing in my ears me zumban los oídos [may thoom-ban los o-ee-dohs]

earache el dolor de oídos [do-lawr day o-ee-dohs]
- he has an earache le duelen los oídos [lay dway-len los o-ee-dohs]

ear infection la infección en el oído [in-fekth-yohn en el o-ee-doh]
- I think I have an ear infection creo que tengo una infección en el oído [kray-oh kay ten-goh oo-na in-fekth-yohn en el o-ee-doh]

early temprano(na) [tem-prah-noh] ♦ *(before the expected time, in the day)* temprano [tem-prah-noh], pronto [pron-toh]; *(at the beginning)* a principios [a prin-theep-yohs]
- is there an earlier flight? ¿hay algún vuelo antes? [eye al-goon bway-loh an-tes]
- we arrived early llegamos temprano [yay-gah-mos tem-prah-noh]
- I'll be leaving early in the morning me voy por la mañana temprano [may boy por la man-yah-na tem-prah-noh]

Easter la Pascua [pas-kwa], la Semana Santa [se-mah-na san-ta]
- Happy Easter! ¡felices pascuas! [fe-leeth-es pas-kwas]

easy fácil [fa-theel]
- is it easy to use? ¿es fácil de usar? [es fa-theel day oo-sahr]

▶ I'd like something easy to carry quiero algo que sea fácil de transportar [kyair-oh kay say-a fa-theel day trans-por-tahr]

eat comer [kom-air]
▶ I'm afraid I don't eat meat me temo que no como carne [may tay-moh kay noh kom-oh kahr-nay]
▶ where can we get something to eat? ¿dónde podemos comer algo? [don-day pod-ay-mos kom-air al-goh]

economy (class) la clase turista [kla-say too-rees-ta] ◆ en clase turista [en kla-say too-rees-ta]
▶ are there any seats in economy class? ¿hay asientos en la clase turista? [eye as-yen-tohs en kla-say too-rees-ta]
▶ I'd prefer to go economy prefiero viajar en clase turista [pref-yair-oh bya-CHahr en kla-say too-rees-ta]

egg el huevo [way-boh]
▶ I'd like a fried egg with fries quería un huevo frito con patatas fritas [kair-ee-a oon way-boh kon pa-ta-tas free-tas]

eight ocho [o-choh]
▶ there are eight of us somos ocho [so-mos o-choh]

electric heater el radiador eléctrico [RRad-ya-dawr e-lek-tri-koh]
▶ do you have an electric heater? ¿tiene un radiador eléctrico? [tyen-ay oon RRad-ya-dawr e-lek-tri-koh]

electricity la electricidad [e-lek-tri-thi-dad]
▶ there's no electricity in the room no hay electricidad en la habitación [noh eye e-lek-tri-thi-dad en la a-bi-tath-yohn]

electric razor, electric shaver la máquina de afeitar [ma-ki-na day a-fay-tahr]
▶ where can I plug in my electric razor? ¿dónde puedo enchufar la máquina de afeitar? [don-day pway-doh en-choo-fahr la ma-ki-na day a-fay-tahr]

elevator el ascensor [as-then-sawr]
▶ is there an elevator? ¿hay ascensor? [eye as-then-sawr]
▶ the elevator is out of order el ascensor no funciona [el as-then-sawr noh foonth-yoh-na]

eleven el once [on-thay]
▶ there are eleven of us somos once [so-mos on-thay]

e-mail el correo electrónico [ko-RRay-oh e-lek-tro-ni-koh]
▶ I'd like to send an e-mail quería enviar un correo electrónico [kair-ee-a emb-yahr oon ko-RRay-oh e-lek-tro-ni-koh]
▶ where can I check my e-mail? ¿dónde puedo ver mi correo electrónico? [don-day pway-doh bair mee ko-RRay-oh e-lek-tro-ni-koh]

emergencies

If you need medical attention, go to an *ambulatorio* (medical center) or to a hospital emergency room (*urgencias*). You can dial 061 for medical emergencies, but the new unified emergency number (112) will get you through to whatever emergency service you require anywhere in Spain.

e-mail address la dirección de correo electrónico [di-rekth-yohn day ko-RRay-oh e-lek-tro-ni-koh]

▶ do you have an e-mail address? ¿tiene una dirección de correo electrónico? [tyen-ay oo-na di-rekth-yohn day ko-RRay-oh e-lek-tro-ni-koh]

emergency la emergencia [em-air-CHenth-ya]

▶ it's an emergency! ¡es una emergencia! [es oo-na em-air-CHenth-ya]

▶ what number do you call in an emergency? ¿a qué número hay que llamar en caso de emergencia? [a kay noo-mair-oh eye kay ya-mahr en ka-soh day em-air-CHenth-ya]

emergency brake el freno de mano [fray-noh day mah-noh]

▶ I'm sure I put the emergency brake on estoy seguro de que puse el freno de mano [es-toy se-goo-roh day kay poo-say el fray-noh day mah-noh]

emergency cord la palanca de emergencia [pa-lan-ka day em-air-CHenth-ya]

▶ someone's pulled the emergency cord alguien accionó la palanca de emergencia [alg-yen akth-yon-oh la pa-lan-ka day em-air-CHenth-ya]

emergency exit la salida de emergencia [sa-lee-da day em-air-CHenth-ya]

▶ remember that the nearest emergency exit may be behind you *(on plane)* recuerde que la salida de emergencia más próxima puede estar detrás suyo [RRe-kwair-day kay la sa-lee-da day em-air-CHenth-ya mas prok-si-ma pway-day es-tahr de-tras soo-yoh]

emergency room las urgencias [oor-CHenth-yas]

▶ I need to go to the emergency room right away tengo que ir a urgencias inmediatamente [ten-goh kay eer a oor-CHenth-yas in-med-ya-ta-men-tay]

emergency services los servicios de urgencia [sair-beeth-yohs day oor-CHenth-ya]

▶ do you a have a listing of emergency services numbers? ¿tiene una lista de números de los servicios de urgencia? [tyen-en oo-na lees-ta day los noo-mair-ohs day sair-beeth-yohs day oor-CHenth-ya]

end *(conclusion, finish)* el final [fee-nal]

▶ at the end of July a finales de julio [a fee-nahl-es day CHool-yoh]

engine el motor [moh-tawr]

▶ the engine is making a funny noise el motor está haciendo un ruido raro [el moh-tawr es-ta ath-yen-doh oon RRoo-ee-doh RRah-roh]

English inglés(esa) [in-glays] ◆ *(language)* el inglés [in-glays]
- I'm English soy inglés/inglesa [soy in-glays/in-glay-sa]
- that's not how you say it in English no se dice así en inglés [noh say dee-thay a-see en in-glays]
- do you understand English? ¿entiendes inglés? [en-tyen-days in-glays]

enjoy pasarlo bien [pa-sahr-loh byen]
- to enjoy oneself pasárselo bien [pa-sahr-tay-loh byen]
- enjoy your meal! ¡que aproveche! [kay a-proh-bech-ay]
- did you enjoy your meal? ¿le gustó la comida? [lay goos-toh la ko-mee-da]

enough suficiente [soo-fith-yen-tay], bastante [bas-tan-tay] ◆ bastante [bas-tan-tay]
- I don't have enough money no tengo suficiente dinero [noh ten-goh soo-fith-yen-tay di-nair-oh]
- that's enough! ¡basta ya! [bas-ta ya]
- no thanks, I've had quite enough no gracias, ya he comido bastante [noh grath-yas ya ay ko-mee-doh bas-tan-tay]

enter *(type in)* introducir [in-tro-doo-theer]
- do I enter my PIN number now? ¿introduzco ahora mi PIN? [in-tro-dooth-koh a-aw-ra mee peen]

entrance la entrada [en-trah-da]
- where's the entrance to the subway? ¿dónde está la entrada del metro? [don-day es-ta la en-trah-da del met-roh]

entry *(to place)* la entrada [en-trah-da]
- entry to the exhibit is free la entrada a la exposición es gratuita [la en-trah-da a la eks-po-seeth-yohn es grat-wee-ta]

envelope el sobre [soh-bray]
- I'd like a pack of envelopes quería un paquete de sobres [kair-ee-a oon pa-kay-tay day soh-brays]

equipment el equipo [e-kee-poh]
- do you provide the equipment? ¿ustedes proporcionan el equipo? [oos-ted-ays pro-porth-yoh-nan el e-kee-poh]

escalator la escalera mecánica [es-ka-lair-a me-ka-ni-ka]
- is there an escalator? ¿hay una escalera mecánica? [eye oo-na es-ka-lair-a me-ka-ni-ka]

euro el euro [ew-roh]
- I'd like to change some dollars into euros quería cambiar dólares por euros [kair-ee-a kamb-yahr doh-lar-ays por ew-rohs]

evening *(earlier)* la tarde [tahr-day]; *(later)* la noche [no-chay]
- why don't we meet up this evening? ¿por qué no nos vemos por la tarde/noche? [por kay noh nos bay-mos por la tahr-day/no-chay]
- in the evening *(of every day)* por la tarde/noche [por la tahr-day/no-chay]

event *(cultural)* la actividad [ak-ti-bi-dad]
- what's the program of events? ¿cuál es el programa de actividades? [kwal es el pro-gra-ma day ak-ti-bi-da-days]

ever *(before now)* alguna vez [al-goo-na beth]
- have you ever been to Boston? ¿has estado alguna vez en Boston? [as es-tah-doh al-goo-na beth en bos-ton]
- if you're ever in New York, let me know si alguna vez vas a Nueva York, avísame [see al-goo-na beth bas a nway-ba york a-bee-sa-may]

everything todo [toh-doh]
- that's everything, thanks eso es todo, gracias [e-soh es toh-doh grath-yas]
- we didn't have time to see everything no tuvimos tiempo de ver todo [noh too-bee-mos tyem-poh day bair toh-doh]

excess baggage el exceso de equipaje [eks-thay-soh day e-ki-pa-CHay]
- what's your policy on excess baggage? ¿cuáles son sus normas respecto del exceso de equipaje? [kwah-lays son soos nor-mas RRes-pek-toh del eks-thay-soh day e-ki-pa-CHay]

exchange cambiar [kamb-yahr]
- I'd like to exchange this T-shirt quería cambiar esta camiseta [kair-ee-a kamb-yahr es-ta ka-mi-say-ta]

exchange rate el tipo de cambio [tee-poh day kamb-yoh]
- what is today's exchange rate? ¿cuál es el tipo de cambio de hoy? [kwal es el tee-poh day kamb-yoh day oy]

excursion la excursión [eks-koors-yohn]
- I'd like to sign up for the excursion on Saturday quería apuntarme a la excursión del sábado [kair-ee-a a-poon-tahr-may a la eks-koors-yohn del sa-ba-doh]

excuse *(behavior, person)* disculpar [dis-kool-pahr]
- excuse me? *(asking for repetition)* ¿cómo? [kom-oh]
- excuse me! *(to get attention, when interrupting, to apologize)* ¡perdón! [pair-dohn]; *(to get by, when leaving)* ¡con permiso! [kon pair-mee-soh]; *(expressing disagreement)* ¡un momento! [oon mo-men-toh]
- you'll have to excuse my (poor) Spanish tiene que disculpar lo mal que hablo español [tyen-ay kay dis-kool-pahr loh mal kay ab-loh es-pan-yol]

exhaust el tubo de escape [too-boh day es-ka-pay]
- the exhaust is making a strange noise el tubo de escape está haciendo un ruido extraño [el too-boh day es-ka-pay es-ta ath-yen-doh oon RRoo-ee-doh eks-tran-yoh]

exhausted *(tired)* agotado(da) [a-goh-tah-doh]
- I'm exhausted estoy agotado [es-toy a-goh-tah-doh]

exhibit la exposición [eks-po-seeth-yohn]
- I'd like a ticket for the temporary exhibit quería una entrada para la exposición temporal [kair-ee-a oo-na en-trah-da pa-ra la eks-po-seeth-yohn tem-po-ral]

▸ is this ticket valid for the exhibit too? ¿la entrada también vale para la exposición? [la en-trah-da tamb-yen ba-lay pa-ra la eks-po-seeth-yohn]

exit la salida [sa-lee-da]

▸ where's the exit? ¿dónde está la salida? [don-day es-ta la sa-lee-da]

expect *(baby, letter)* esperar [es-pair-ahr]

▸ I'll be expecting you at eight o'clock at... te esperaré a las ocho en... [tay es-pair-a-ray a las o-choh en]

▸ when do you expect it to be ready? ¿cuándo esperas que esté listo? [kwan-doh es-pair-as kay es-tay lees-toh]

expensive caro(ra) [kah-roh]

▸ do you have anything less expensive? ¿tiene alguna cosa menos cara? [tyen-ay al-goo-na koh-sa may-mos kah-ra]

expire *(visa)* caducar [ka-doo-kahr]

▸ my passport has expired me ha caducado el pasaporte [may a ka-doo-kah-doh el pa-sa-por-tay]

explain explicar [eks-pli-kahr]

▸ please explain how to get to the airport por favor, me explique cómo se llega al aeropuerto [por fa-bor may eks-plee-kay kom-oh say yay-ga al eye-roh-pwair-toh]

▸ can you explain what this means? ¿puede explicarme qué significa esto? [pway-day eks-pli-kahr-may kay sig-ni-fee-ka es-toh]

express (train) el tren rápido [tren RRa-pi-doh]

▸ how long does it take by express train? ¿cuánto se tarda en el tren rápido? [kwan-toh say tahr-da en el tren RRa-pi-doh]

extension *(phone line)* la extensión [eks-tens-yohn]; *(cord)* el alargador [a-lahr-ga-dawr]

▸ could I have extension 358, please? con la extensión tres cinco ocho, por favor [kon la eks-tens-yohn tres theen-koh o-choh por fa-bor]

extra adicional [a-dith-yoh-nal]

▸ is it possible to add an extra bed? ¿podrían colocar una cama adicional? [pod-ree-an ko-lo-kahr oo-na ka-ma a-dith-yoh-nal]

▸ would it be possible to stay an extra night? ¿podríamos quedarnos una noche más? [pod-ree-a-mos kay-dahr-nos oo-na no-chay mas]

extra charge el recargo [RRe-kahr-goh]

▸ what would the extra charge be for this service? ¿cuál sería el recargo por este servicio? [kwal sair-ee-a el RRe-kahr-goh por es-tay sair-beeth-yoh]

▸ at no extra charge sin cargo adicional [seen kahr-goh a-dith-yoh-nal]

eye el ojo [o-CHoh]

▸ she has blue eyes tiene los ojos azules [tyen-ay los o-CHohs a-thoo-lays]

▸ can you keep an eye on my bag for a few minutes? ¿podría vigilar mi bolsa unos minutos? [pod-ree-a bi-CHi-lahr mee bol-sa oo-nohs mi-noo-tohs]

eye drops el colirio [ko-leer-yoh]
- do you have any eye drops? ¿tiene colirio? [tyen-ay ko-leer-yoh]

eye shadow la sombra de ojos [som-bra day o-CHohs]
- is this the only eye shadow you've got? ¿esta es la única sombra de ojos que tiene? [es-ta es la oo-ni-ka som-bra day o-CHohs kay tyen-ay]

eyesight la vista [bees-ta]
- I don't have very good eyesight no tengo muy bien la vista [noh ten-goh mwee byen la bees-ta]

face *(of person)* la cara [kah-ra]
- the attacker had a broad face el atacante tenía la cara ancha [al a-ta-kan-tay ten-ee-a la kah-ra an-cha]

facilities las instalaciones [in-sta-lath-yoh-nays]
- what kind of exercise facilities do you have here? ¿qué clase de instalaciones para hacer ejercicio tienen? [kay kla-say day in-sta-lath-yoh-nays pa-ra a-thair eCH-air-theeth-yoh tyen-en]
- do you have facilities for people with disabilities? ¿tienen instalaciones para discapacitados? [tyen-en in-sta-lath-yoh-nays pa-ra dis-ka-pa-thi-tah-dohs]
- are there facilities for children? ¿hay instalaciones para niños? [eye in-sta-lath-yoh-nays pa-ra neen-yohs]

faint desmayarse [des-meye-ahr-say]
- I fainted twice last week me desmayé dos veces la semana pasada [may des-meye-ay dos beth-ays la se-mah-na pa-sah-da]

fair *(person, situation, price)* justo(ta) [CHoos-toh]; *(hair)* rubio(bia) [RRoob-yoh]; *(skin, complexion)* claro(ra) [klah-roh]
- this isn't a fair price este precio no es justo [es-tay preth-yoh noh es Choos-toh]
- it's not fair! ¡no es justo! [noh es CHoos-toh]

fall caerse [ka-air-say]
- I fell on my back me caí de espaldas [may ka-ee day es-pal-das]

family la familia [fa-meel-ya]
- do you have any family in the area? ¿tienes familia en la zona? [tyen-es fa-meel-ya en la thoh-na]

fan el ventilador [ben-ti-la-dawr]
- how does the fan work? ¿cómo funciona el ventilador? [kom-oh foonth-yoh-na el ben-ti-la-dawr]

far lejos [lay-CHohs]
- am I far from the village? ¿estoy lejos del pueblo? [es-toy lay-CHohs del pweb-loh]
- is it far to walk? ¿andando está lejos? [an-dan-doh es-ta lay-CHohs]
- is it far by car? ¿en coche está lejos? [el ko-chay es-ta lay-CHohs]
- how far is the market from here? ¿a qué distancia de aquí está el mercado? [a kay dis-tanth-ya day a-kee es-ta el mair-kah-doh]
- far away/off lejos [lay-CHohs]
- so far hasta el momento

fast rápido(da) [RRa-pi-doh] ◆ rápido [RRa-pi-doh]
- please don't drive so fast por favor, no conduzca tan rápido [por fa-bor noh kon-dooth-ka tan RRa-pi-doh]
- to be fast *(watch, clock)* estar adelantado [es-tahr a-de-lan-tah-doh]
- my watch is five minutes fast mi reloj está cinco minutos adelantado [mee RRe-loCH es-ta theen-koh mi-noo-tohs a-de-lan-tah-doh]

fat *(in diet)* la grasa [gra-sa]
- it's low in fat tiene bajo contenido de grasa [tyen-ay ba-CHoh kon-te-nee-doh day gra-sa]

father el padre [pah-dray]
- this is my father este es mi padre [es-tay es mee pah-dray]

fault *(responsibility)* la culpa [kool-pa]
- it was my fault fue culpa mía [fway kool-pa mee-a]

favor *(kind act)* el favor [fa-bor]
- can I ask you a favor? ¿le podría pedir un favor? [lay pod-ree-a ped-eer oon fa-bor]

favorite favorito(ta) [fa-bo-ree-toh] ◆ el favorito [fa-bo-ree-toh], la favorita [fa-bo-ree-ta]
- it's my favorite book es mi libro favorito [es mee lee-broh fa-bo-ree-toh]

feather la pluma [ploo-ma]
- are these feather pillows? ¿éstas almohadas son de plumas? [es-tas al-moh-ah-das son day ploo-mas]

February febrero [feb-rair-oh]
- February 8th ocho de febrero [o-choh day feb-rair-oh]

feed dar de comer a [dahr day kom-air a]
- where can I feed the baby? ¿dónde puedo darle de comer al bebé? [don-day pway-doh dahr-lay day kom-air al beb-ay]

feel *(touch)* tocar [tok-ahr]; *(sense)* sentir [sen-teer] ◆ *(physically)* sentirse [sen-teer-say]
- I can't feel my feet no siento los pies [noh syen-toh los pyays]
- I don't feel well no me siento bien [noh may syen-toh byen]

ferry el ferry [fe-RRi], el transbordador [trans-bor-da-dawr]
- when does the next ferry leave? ¿a qué hora sale el próximo ferry? [a kay aw-ra sa-kay el prok-si-moh fe-RRi]

ferry terminal la terminal de ferries [tair-mi-nal day fe-RRis]
> which way is the ferry terminal? ¿por dónde se va a la terminal de ferries? [por don-day say ba a la tair-mi-nal day fe-RRis]

fever la fiebre [fyeb-ray]
> the baby's got a fever el bebé tiene fiebre [el beb-ay tyen-ay fyeb-ray]

few pocos(cas) [poh-kohs] ◆ **a few** algunos(nas) [al-goo-nohs]
> there are few sights worth seeing around here hay pocas cosas que valga la pena ver por aquí [eye poh-kas koh-sas kay bal-ga la pay-na bair por a-kee]
> we're thinking of staying a few more days pensábamos quedarnos algunos días más [pen-sah-ba-mos kay-dahr-nos al-goo-nos dee-as mas]
> I spent a month in Spain a few years ago pasé un mes en España hace algunos años [pa-say oon mes en es-pan-ya a-thay al-goo-nohs an-yohs]

fifth quinto(ta) [keen-toh] ◆ *(gear)* la quinta [keen-ta]
> I can't get it into fifth no me entra la quinta [noh may en-tra la keen-ta]

filling *(in a tooth)* el empaste [em-pas-tay]
> one of my fillings has come out se me ha soltado un empaste [say may a sal-tah-doh oon em-pas-tay]

fill up llenar [yay-nahr] ◆ llenarse [yay-nahr-say]
> fill it up, please lleno, por favor [yay-noh por fa-bor]

film *(for camera)* el carrete [ka-RRay-tay] ◆ filmar [feel-mahr]
> I'd like to have this film developed quería revelar este carrete [kair-ee-a RRe-be-lahr es-tay ka-RRay-tay]
> do you have black-and-white film? ¿tiene un carrete en blanco y negro? [tyen-ay oon ka-RRay-tay en blan-koh ee neg-roh]
> is filming allowed in the museum? ¿se puede filmar en el museo? [say pway-day feel-mahr en el moo-say-oh]

find encontrar [en-kon-trahr]
> has anyone found a watch? ¿alguien ha encontrado un reloj? [a en-kon-trah-doh alg-yen oon RRe-loCH]
> where can I find a doctor on a Sunday? ¿dónde puedo encontrar un médico en domingo? [don-day pway-doh en-kon-trahr oon may-di-koh en do-meen-goh]

find out enterarse de [en-tair-ahr-say day]
> I need to find out the times of trains to Lisbon me tengo que enterar de los horarios de los trenes a Lisboa [may ten-goh kay en-tair-ahr day los o-rahr-yohs day los tren-ays a lees-boh-aa]

fine *(in health etc.)* bien [byen] ◆ la multa [mool-ta]
> fine thanks, and you? bien gracias, ¿y tú? [byen grath-yas ee too]
> how much is the fine? ¿de cuánto es la multa? [day kwan-toh es la mool-ta]

finger el dedo [day-doh]
> I've cut my finger me he cortado el dedo [may ay kor-tah-doh el day-doh]

finish terminar [tair-mi-nahr]
  ▸ can we leave as soon as we've finished our meal? ¿podemos salir en cuanto terminemos la comida? [po-day-mos sa-leer en kwan-toh tair-mi-nay-mos la ko-mee-da]

fire el fuego [fway-goh]; *(out of control)* el incendio [in-thend-yoh]
  ▸ to make a fire encender un fuego [en-then-dair oon fway-goh]
  ▸ on fire *(forest, house)* ardiendo [ard-yen-doh]

fire department los bomberos [bom-bair-ohs]
  ▸ call the fire department! ¡llamen a los bomberos! [ya-men a los bom-bair-ohs]

fireworks los fuegos artificiales [fway-gohs ar-ti-fith-yah-lays]
  ▸ what time do the fireworks start? ¿a qué hora comienzan los fuegos artificiales? [a kay aw-ra kom-yen-than los fway-gohs ar-ti-fith-yah-lays]

first primero(ra) [pri-mair-oh] ◆ *(before all others)* el primero [pri-mair-oh], la primera [pri-mair-a]; *(gear, class)* la primera [pri-mair-a]
  ▸ it's the first time I've been here es la primera vez que vengo aquí [es la pri-mair-a beth kay ben-goh a-kee]
  ▸ you have to take the first left after the lights tienes que girar en la primera a la izquierda después del semáforo [tyen-es kay CHi-rahr en la pri-mair-a a la ith-kyair-da des-pwes del se-ma-fo-roh]
  ▸ put it into first mete la primera [may-tay la pri-mair-a]

first-aid kit el botiquín [bo-ti-keen]
  ▸ do you have a first-aid kit? ¿tiene un botiquín? [tyen-ay oon bo-ti-keen]

first class la primera clase [pri-mair-a kla-say] ◆ en primera clase [en pri-mair-a kla-say]
  ▸ are there any seats in first class? ¿hay algún asiento en primera clase? [eye al-goon as-yeh-toh en pri-mair-a kla-say]
  ▸ I'd like to send this first class quería enviar esto en el correo más rápido [kair-ee-a emb-yahr es-toh en el ko-RRay-oh mas RRa-pi-doh]
  ▸ I prefer to travel first class prefiero viajer en primera clase [pref-yair-oh bya-CHahr en pri-mair-a kla-say]

fish *(animal)* el pez [peth]; *(food)* el pescado [pes-kah-doh]
  ▸ I don't eat fish no como pescado [noh kom-oh pes-kah-doh]

fishing permit la licencia de pesca [li-thenth-ya day pes-ka]
  ▸ do you need a fishing permit to fish here? ¿hace falta licencia de pesca para pescar aquí? [a-thay fal-ta li-thenth-ya day pes-ka pa-ra pes-kahr a-kee]

fit *(of laughter, tears)* el ataque [a-ta-kay] ◆ *(be correct size for)* quedar bien [kay-dahr byen] ◆ *(be correct)* encajar [en-ka-CHahr]
  ▸ I think she's having some kind of fit creo que está teniendo un ataque [kray-oh kay es-ta ten-yen-doh oon a-ta-kay]
  ▸ those pants fit you better esos pantalones te quedan mejor [es-tohs pan-ta-loh-nays tay kay-dan me-CHor]
  ▸ the key doesn't fit in the lock la llave no encaja en la cerradura [la yah-bay noh en-ka-CHa en la theRR-a-doo-ra]

» we won't all fit around one table no vamos a caber todos en una mesa [noh bah-mos a ka-bair toh-dohs en oo-na may-sa]

fit in *(go in)* encajar [en-ka-CHahr] • *(put in)* meter [met-air]

» I can't get everything to fit in my suitcase no consigo meter todo en la maleta [noh kon-see-goh met-air toh-doh en la ma-lay-ta]

» how many people can you fit in this car? ¿cuánta gente puede meter en este coche? [kwan-ta CHen-tay pway-day met-air en es-tay ko-chay]

fitting room el probador [pro-ba-dawr]

» where are the fitting rooms? ¿dónde están los probadores? [don-day es-tan los pro-ba-daw-rays]

five cinco [theen-koh]

» there are five of us somos cinco [so-mos theen-koh]

fix arreglar [a-RReg-lahr]

» where can I find someone to fix my bike? ¿dónde puedo encontrar a alguien que me arregle la bici? [don-day pway-doh en-kon-trahr a alg-yen kay may a-RReg-lay la bee-thi]

fixed price el precio fijo [preth-yoh fee-CHoh]

» do taxis to the airport charge a fixed price? ¿los taxis al aeropuerto cobran un precio fijo? [los tak-sis al eye-roh-pwair-toh koh-bran oon preth-yoh fee-CHoh]

flash el flash [flas]

» I'd like some batteries for my flash necesito pilas para el flash [ne-thes-ee-toh pee-las pa-ra el flas]

flash photography la fotografía con flash [foh-toh-gra-fee-a kon flas]

» is flash photography allowed here? ¿se pueden hacer fotografías con flash aquí? [say pway-den a-thair foh-toh-gra-fee-as kon flas a-kee]

flat *(tire)* desinflado(da) [des-in-flah-doh]

» the tire's flat la rueda está desinflada [la RRoo-ay-da es-ta des-in-flah-da]

flavor el sabor [sa-bawr]

» I'd like to try a different flavor of ice cream me gustaría probar un helado de un sabor diferente [may goos-ta-ree-a pro-bahr oon e-lah-doh day oon sa-bawr di-fair-en-tay]

flight el vuelo [bway-loh]

» how many flights a day are there? ¿cuántos vuelos hay por día? [kwan-tohs bway-los eye por dee-a]

» what time is the flight? ¿a qué hora es el vuelo? [a kay aw-ra es el bway-loh]

flight of stairs la escalera [es-ka-lair-a]

» your room's up that flight of stairs su habitación está subiendo esa escalera [soo a-bi-tath-yohn es-ta soob-yen-doh e-sa es-ka-lair-a]

floor *(story)* el piso [pee-soh]

» which floor is it on? ¿en qué piso está? [en kay pee-soh es-ta]

» it's on the top floor está en el último piso [es-ta en el ool-ti-moh pee-soh]

flower la flor [flawr]
> do you sell flowers? ¿vende flores? [ben-day flaw-rays]

flu la gripe [gree-pay]
> I'd like something for the flu quería algo para la gripe [kair-ee-a al-goh pa-ra la gree-pay]

flush la cisterna [thees-tair-na] ♦ *(person)* ruborizarse [RRoo-bo-ri-thahr-say]
> to flush the toilet tirar de la cadena [ti-rahr day la ka-day-na]
> the toilet won't flush la cisterna del váter no funciona [la thees-tair-na del ba-tair noh foonth-yoh-na]

fog la niebla [nyeb-la]
> is there a lot of fog today? ¿hay mucha niebla hoy? [eye moo-cha nyeb-la oy]

food la comida [ko-mee-da]
> is there someplace to buy food nearby? ¿hay algún lugar cerca donde poder comprar comida? [eye al-goon loo-gahr don-day pod-air pre-pa-rahr ko-mee-da]
> the food here is excellent la comida de aquí es excelente [la ko-mee-da day a-kee es eks-thel-en-tay]

food cart *(on train, plane)* el carrito de la comida [ka-RRee-toh day la ko-mee-da]
> is there food cart service on this train? ¿este tren tiene carrito de comida? [es-tay tren tyen-ay ka-RRee-toh day ko-mee-da]

food section *(in store)* la sección de comida [sekth-yohn day ko-mee-da]
> where's the food section? ¿dónde está la sección de comida? [don-day es-ta la sekth-yohn day ko-mee-da]

foot el pie [pyay]
> on foot a pie [a pyay]

for *(expressing purpose, function)* para [pa-ra]; *(indicating direction, destination)* de [day]; *(indicating duration)* durante [doo-ran-tay]; *(showing preference)* a favor [a fa-bor]
> what's that for? ¿para qué es? [pa-ra kay es]
> the flight for London el vuelo de Londres [el bway-loh day lon-drays]
> is this the right train for Madrid? ¿es éste el tren de Madrid? [es es-tay el tren day mad-reed]
> I'm staying for two months me voy a quedar dos meses [may boy a kay-dahr dos mes-ays]
> I've been here for a week llevo aquí una semana [yay-boh a-kee oo-na se-mah-na]
> I need something for a cough necesito algo para la tos [ne-thes-ee-toh al-goh pa-ra la tos]

foreign *(country, language)* extranjero(ra) [eks-tran-CHair-oh]
> I don't speak any foreign languages no hablo ninguna lengua extranjera [noh ab-loh nin-goo-na len-gwa eks-tran-CHair-a]

foreign currency la moneda extranjera [mo-nay-da eks-tran-CHair-a]

> do you change foreign currency? ¿cambian moneda extranjera? [kamb-yan mo-nay-da eks-tran-CHair-a]

foreigner el extranjero [eks-tran-CHair-oh], la extranjera [eks-tran-CHair-a]

> as a foreigner, this custom seems a bit strange to me como extranjero, esa costumbre me parece extraña [kom-oh eks-tran-CHair-oh e-sa kos-toom-bray may pa-re-thay eks-tran-ya]

forever para siempre [pa-ra syem-pray]

> our money won't last forever el dinero no nos va a durar para siempre [el di-nair-oh noh nos ba a doo-rahr pa-ra syem-pray]

fork el tenedor [te-ne-dawr]

> could I have a fork? ¿me podría traer un tenedor? [may pod-ree-a tra-air oon te-ne-dawr]

forward remitir [RRe-mit-eer]

> can you forward my mail? ¿me podrían remitir el correo? [may pod-ree-an RRe-mit-eer el ko-RRay-oh]

four cuatro [kwat-roh]

> there are four of us somos cuatro [so-mos kwat-roh]

fourth cuarto(ta) [kwahr-toh] ◆ *(gear)* la cuarta [kwahr-ta]

> it's hard to get it into fourth no entra bien la cuarta [noh en-tra byen la kwahr-ta]

four-wheel drive el cuatro por cuatro [kwat-roh por kwat-roh]

> I'd like a four-wheel drive quería un cuatro por cuatro [kair-ee-a oon kwat-roh por kwat-roh]

fracture la fractura [frak-too-ra]

> she has a wrist fracture tiene la muñeca fracturada [tyen-ay la moon-yay-ka frak-too-rah-da]

free *(offered at no charge)* gratis [gra-tees]; *(not occupied, available)* libre [lee-bray]

> is it free? ¿es gratis? [es gra-tees]
> is this seat free? ¿está libre este asiento? [es-ta lee-bray es-tay as-yen-toh]
> are you free on Thursday evening? ¿estás libre el jueves por la noche? [es-tas lee-bray el CHway-bays por la no-chay]

freeway la autopista [ow-to-pees-ta]

> what is the speed limit on freeways? ¿cuál es el límite de velocidad en las autopistas? [kwal es el lee-mi-tay day be-loth-ee-dad en las ow-to-pees-tas]
> how do I get onto the freeway? ¿cómo entro en la autopista? [kom-oh en-troh en la ow-to-pees-ta]

freezing (cold) *(room, day)* helado(da) [e-lah-doh]

> I'm freezing (cold) estoy helado [es-toy e-lah-doh]

frequent frecuente [fre-kwen-tay]
- how frequent are the trains to the city? ¿cuál es la frecuencia de los trenes a la ciudad? [kwal es la frek-wenth-ya day los tren-ays a la thyoo-dad]

fresh *(fruit, vegetables)* fresco(ca) [fres-koh]; *(bread, cakes)* recién hecho(cha) [RReth-yen e-choh]
- is the bread fresh? ¿el pan está recién hecho? [el pan es-ta RReth-yen e-choh]

freshly recién [reth-yen]
- freshly squeezed orange juice zumo de naranja recién exprimido [thoo-moh day na-ran-CHa RReth-yen eks-pri-mee-doh]

Friday el viernes [byair-nes]
- we're arriving/leaving on Friday llegaremos/nos iremos el viernes [yay-ga-ray-mos/nos ee-ray-mos el byair-nes]

fried egg el huevo frito [way-boh free-toh]
- I'd prefer a fried egg preferiría un huevo frito [pre-fair-ee-ree-a oon way-boh free-toh]

friend el amigo [a-mee-goh], la amiga [a-mee-ga]
- are you with friends? ¿estás con tus amigos? [es-tas kon toos a-mee-gohs]
- I've come with a friend he venido con un amigo [ay ben-ee-doh kon oon a-mee-goh]
- I'm meeting some friends me voy a encontrar con unos amigos [may boy a en-kon-trahr kon oo-nohs a-mee-gohs]

from de [day]
- I'm from the United States soy de los Estados Unidos [soy day los es-tah-dohs oo-nee-dohs]
- how many flights a day are there from Madrid to Atlanta? ¿cuántos vuelos por día hay de Madrid a Atlanta? [kwan-tohs bway-lohs por dee-a eye day mad-reed a at-lan-ta]

front *(of train)* la parte delantera [pahr-tay de-lan-tair-a] + **in front** de delante [day de-lan-tay] + **in front of** delante de [day de-lan-tay day]
- the car in front braked suddenly el coche de delante frenó de repente [el ko-chay day de-lan-tay fray-noh day RRe-pen-tay]
- I'd like a seat toward the front of the train quería un asiento en la parte delantera del tren [kair-ee-a oon as-yen-toh en la pahr-tay de-lan-tair-a del tren]
- I'll meet you in front of the museum nos encontraremos delante del museo [nos en-kon-tra-ray-mos de-lan-tay del moo-say-oh]

front door la puerta principal [pwair-ta prin-thi-pal]
- which is the key to the front door? ¿cuál es la llave de la puerta principal? [kwal es la yah-bay day la pwair-ta prin-thi-pal]
- the front door is closed la puerta principal está cerrada [la pwair-ta prin-thi-pal es-ta theRR-ah-da]

frozen congelado(da) [kon-CHe-lah-doh]
- I'm absolutely frozen estoy completamente congelado [es-toy kom-ple-ta-men-tay kon-CHe-lah-doh]

▶ the lock is frozen la cerradura está congelada [la theRR-a-doo-ra es-ta kon-CHe-lah-da]

frozen food la comida congelada [ko-mee-da kon-CHe-lah-da]

▶ is that all the frozen food you have? ¿esta es toda la comida congelada que tiene? [es-ta es toh-da la ko-mee-da kon-CHe-lah-da kay tyen-ay]

fruit juice el zumo de frutas [thoo-moh day froo-tas]

▶ what types of fruit juice do you have? ¿qué tipos de zumo de frutas tiene? [kay tee-pohs day thoo-moh day froo-tas tyen-ay]

full lleno(na) [yay-noh]

▶ is it full? ¿está lleno? [es-ta yay-noh]

▶ I'm quite full, thank you estoy bastante lleno, gracias [es-toy bas-tan-tay yay-noh grath-yas]

full up *(with food)* lleno(na) [yay-noh]

▶ I'm full up estoy lleno [es-toy yay-noh]

fun *(pleasure, amusement)* la diversión [di-bairs-yohn]

▶ to have fun divertirse [di-bair-teer-say]

g

gallery *(for art)* la galería [ga-lair-ee-a], el museo [moo-say-oh]

▶ what time does the gallery open? ¿a qué hora abre la galería? [a kay aw-ra ab-ray la ga-lair-ee-a]

game *(fun activity)* el juego [CHway-goh]; *(of sport)* el partido [par-tee-doh]

▶ do you want to play a game of tennis tomorrow? ¿quieres echar un partido de tenis mañana? [kyair-es e-chahr oon par-tee-doh day te-nees man-yah-na]

garage *(for car repair)* el taller [tal-yair]

▶ is there a garage near here? ¿hay un taller cerca? [eye oon tal-yair thair-ka]

▶ could you tow me to a garage? ¿me podría remolcar hasta un taller? [may pod-ree-a RRe-mol-kahr as-ta oon tal-yair]

garbage can el cubo de la basura [koo-boh day la ba-soo-ra]

▶ where is the garbage can? ¿dónde está el cubo de la basura? [don-day es-ta el koo-boh day la ba-soo-ra]

gas *(for vehicle)* la gasolina [ga-so-lee-na]; *(for domestic and medical use)* el gas [gas]

▶ where can I get gas? ¿dónde puedo echar gasolina? [don-day pway-doh e-chahr ga-so-lee-na]

▶ I've run out of gas me he quedado sin gasolina [may ay kay-dah-doh seen ga-so-lee-na]

gas pump el surtidor [soor-ti-dawr]
▸ how do you use this gas pump? ¿cómo se usa este surtidor? [kom-oh say oo-sa es-tay soor-ti-dawr]

gas station la gasolinera [ga-so-li-nair-a]
▸ where can I find a gas station? ¿dónde puedo encontrar una gasolinera? [don-day pway-doh en-kon-trahr oo-na ga-so-li-nair-a]

gas stove la estufa de gas [es-too-fa day gas]
▸ do you have a gas stove we could borrow? ¿nos podría dejar una estufa de gas? [nos pod-ree-a de-CHahr oo-na es-too-fa day gas]

gas tank el depósito de gasolina [de-po-si-toh day ga-so-lee-na]
▸ the gas tank is leaking el depósito de gasolina tiene una fuga [el de-po-si-toh day ga-so-lee-na tyen-ay oo-na foo-ga]

gate la puerta [pwair-ta]
▸ where is Gate 2? ¿dónde está la Puerta dos? [don-day es-ta la pwair-ta dos]

gear *(of a car, a bike)* la marcha [mahr-cha]
▸ how many gears does the bike have? ¿cuántas marchas tiene la bicicleta? [kwan-tas mahr-chas tyen-ay la bi-thi-klay-ta]

get *(obtain)* conseguir [kon-se-geer]; *(understand)* entender [en-ten-dair] ◆ *(make one's way)* llegar [yay-gahr]
▸ where can we get something to eat this time of night? ¿dónde podemos conseguir algo de comer a estas horas de la noche? [don-day po-day-mos kon-se-geer al-goh day kom-air a es-tas aw-ras day la no-chay]
▸ I can't get it into reverse no consigo meter la marcha atrás [noh kon-see-goh met-air la mahr-cha a-tras]
▸ now I get it ahora lo entiendo [a-aw-ra loh ent-yen-doh]
▸ I got here a month ago llegué aquí hace un mes [yay-gay a-kee a-thay oon mes]
▸ can you get there by car? ¿se puede llegar ahí en coche? [say pway-day yay-gahr a-ee en ko-chay]
▸ how can I get to... ¿cómo puedo llegar a...? [kom-oh pway-doh yay-gahr a]
▸ could you tell me the best way to get to Bilbao? ¿me podría decir cuál es la mejor forma de llegar a Bilbao? [may pod-ree-a de-theer kwal es la me-CHor for-ma day yay-gahr a beel-bow]
▸ how do we get to Terminal 2? ¿cómo llegamos a la Terminal dos? [kom-oh yay-gah-mos a la tair-mi-nal dos]

get back *(money)* devolver [day-bol-bair]
▸ I just want to get my money back simplemente quiero que me devuelvan mi dinero [seem-ple-men-tay kyair-oh kay may day-bwel-ban mee di-nair-oh]

get back onto *(road)* volver [bol-bair]
▸ how can I get back onto the freeway? ¿cómo puedo volver a la autopista? [kom-oh pway-doh bol-bair a la ow-to-pees-ta]

get in *(arrive)* llegar [yay-gahr]; *(gain entry)* entrar [en-trahr]
> what time does the train get in to Santiago? ¿a qué hora llega el tren a Santiago? [a kay aw-ra yay-ga el tren a sant-yah-goh]
> what time does the flight get in? ¿a qué hora llega el vuelo? [a kay aw-ra yay-ga el bway-loh]
> do you have to pay to get in? ¿hay que pagar para entrar? [eye kay pa-gahr pa-ra en-trahr]

get off *(bus, train, bike)* bajarse de [ba-CHahr-say day]; *(road)* salir [sa-leer]
♦ bajarse [ba-CHahr-say]
> where do we get off the bus? ¿dónde nos bajamos del autobús? [don-day nos ba-CHah-mos del ow-toh-boos]
> where do I get off the freeway? ¿dónde salgo de la autopista? [don-day sal-goh day la ow-toh-pees-ta]

get on subirse [soo-beer-say]
> which bus should we get on to go downtown? ¿a qué autobús nos tenemos que subir para ir al centro? [a kay ow-toh-boos nos te-nay-mos kay soo-beer pa-ra eer al then-troh]

get past pasar [pa-sahr]
> sorry, can I get past, please? con permiso, ¿puedo pasar, por favor? [kon pair-mee-soh pway-doh pa-sahr por fa-bor]

get up *(in morning)* levantarse [le-ban-tahr-say]
> I get up very early me levanto muy temprano [may le-ban-toh mwee tem-prah-noh]

gift-wrap envolver para regalo [em-bol-bair pa-ra RRe-gah-loh]
> could you gift-wrap it for me? ¿me lo podría envolver para regalo? [may loh pod-ree-a em-bol-bair pa-ra RRe-gah-loh]

girl *(young female)* la chica [chee-ka]; *(daughter)* la hija [ee-CHa]
> who is that girl? ¿quién es esa chica? [kyen es e-sa chee-ka]
> I've got two girls tengo dos hijas [ten-goh dos ee-CHas]

girlfriend la novia [nohb-ya]
> is she your girlfriend? ¿es tu novia? [es too nohb-ya]

give dar [dahr]
> I can give you my e-mail address le puedo dar mi dirección de correo electrónico [lay pway-doh dahr mee di-rekth-yohn day ko-RRay-oh e-lek-tro-ni-koh]
> can you give me a hand? ¿me podría ayudar? [may pod-ree-a a-yoo-dahr]

glass *(material)* el cristal [kris-tal]; *(for drinking)* el vaso [ba-soh] *(with stem)* la copa [koh-pa] ♦ **glasses** las gafas [ga-fas]
> can I have a clean glass? ¿me podría dar un vaso limpio? [may pod-ree-a dahr oon ba-soh leemp-yoh]
> would you like a glass of champagne? ¿quiere una copa de champán? [kyair-a oo-na koh-pa day cham-pan]
> I've lost my glasses he perdido las gafas [ay pair-dee-doh las ga-fas]

glove el guante [gwan-tay]
▸ I've lost a brown glove he perdido un guante marrón [ay pair-dee-doh oon gwan-tay ma-RRohn]

go *(move, travel)* ir [eer]; *(depart)* irse [eer-say]; *(lead)* llevar [yay-bahr]
▸ let's go to the beach vamos a la playa [bah-mos a la pleye-a]
▸ where can we go for breakfast? ¿a dónde podemos ir para desayunar? [a don-day pod-ay-mos eer pa-ra des-eye-oo-nahr]
▸ where does this path go? ¿adónde lleva este camino? [a-don-day yay-ba es-tay ka-mee-noh]
▸ I must be going me tengo que ir [may ten-goh kay eer]
▸ we're going home tomorrow nos vamos a casa mañana [nos bah-mos a ka-sa man-yah-na]

go away *(person)* irse [eer-say]; *(pain)* desaparecer [de-sa-pa-re-thair]
▸ go away and leave me alone! ¡vete y déjame en paz! [bay-tay ee day-CHa-may en path]

go back *(return)* volver [bol-bair]
▸ we're going back home tomorrow volvemos a casa mañana [bol-bay-mos a ka-sa-man-yah-na]

go down bajar [ba-CHahr]
▸ go down that street and turn left at the bottom baje por esa calle y gire a la izquierda al final [ba-CHay por e-sa kal-yay ee CHee-ray a la ith-kyair-da al fee-nal]

gold *(metal)* el oro [aw-roh]
▸ is it made of gold? ¿es de oro? [es day aw-roh]

golf el golf [golf]
▸ I play golf juego al golf [CHway-goh al golf]

golf club el palo de golf [pah-loh day golf]
▸ where can I rent golf clubs? ¿dónde puedo alquilar palos de golf? [don-day pway-doh al-ki-lahr pah-lohs day golf]

golf course el campo de golf [kam-poh day golf]
▸ is there a golf course nearby? ¿hay algún campo de golf cerca? [eye al-goon kam-poh day golf thair-ka]

good bueno(na) [bway-noh]
▸ this isn't a very good restaurant este no es un restaurante muy bueno [es-tay noh es oon RRes-tow-ran-tay mwee bway-noh]
▸ you're really good at surfing! ¡eres muy bueno haciendo surf! [air-ays mwee bway-noh ath-yen-doh soorf]
▸ we had a good time nos lo pasamos muy bien [nos loh pa-sah-mos mwee byen]

good afternoon buenas tardes [bway-nas tahr-days]
▸ good afternoon! isn't it a beautiful day? buenas tardes, ¿no es un día maravilloso? [bway-nas tahr-days noh es oon dee-a ma-ra-beel-yoh-soh]

goodbye adiós [ad-yohs]
▶ I'd better say goodbye now será mejor que diga adiós ahora [sair-a me-CHor kay dee-ga ad-yohs a-aw-ra]

good evening *(earlier)* buenas tardes [bway-nas tahr-days]; *(later)* buenas noches [bway-nas no-chays]
▶ good evening! how are you tonight? buenas noches, ¿cómo estáis? [bway-nas no-chays kom-oh es-teyes]

good morning buenos días [bway-nohs dee-as]
▶ good morning! how are you today? buenos días, ¿cómo estáis? [bway-nohs dee-as kom-oh es-teyes]

good night buenas noches [bway-nas no-chays]
▶ I'll say good night, then entonces voy a dar las buenas noches [en-ton-thays boy a dahr las bway-nas no-chays]

go out *(leave house, socially, on date)* salir [sa-leer]; *(tide)* bajar [ba-CHahr]
▶ what's a good place to go out for a drink? ¿cuál es un buen sitio para tomar algo? [kwal es oon bwen seet-yoh pa-ra tom-ahr al-goh]
▶ the tide's going out baja la marea [ba-CHa la ma-ray-a]

grapefruit el pomelo [po-may-loh]
▶ I'll have the grapefruit tomaré el pomelo [tom-a-ray el po-may-loh]

great *(very good)* genial [CHen-yal]
▶ that's great! ¡genial! [CHen-yal]
▶ it was really great! ¡fue realmente genial! [fway RRay-al-men-tay CHen-yal]

green verde [bair-day]
▶ the green one el verde [el bair-day]

grocery store la tienda de comestibles [tyen-da day ko-mes-tee-blays]
▶ is there a grocery store around here? ¿hay alguna tienda de comestibles por aquí? [eye al-goo-na tyen-da day ko-mes-tee-blays por a-kee]

ground cloth el suelo [sway-loh]
▶ I brought a ground cloth traje un suelo [tra-CHay oon sway-loh]

group el grupo [groo-poh]
▶ there's a group of 12 of us somos un grupo de doce [so-mos oon groo-poh day doh-thay]
▶ are there reductions for groups? ¿hay descuentos para grupos? [eye des-kwen-tohs pa-ra groo-pohs]

group rate el precio para grupos [preth-yoh pa-ra groo-pohs]
▶ are there special group rates? ¿hay precios especiales para grupos? [eye preth-yohs es-peth-yah-lays pa-ra groo-pohs]

guarantee *(for purchased product)* la garantía [ga-ran-tee-a]
▶ it's still under guarantee todavía está en garantía [toh-da-bee-a es-ta en ga-ran-tee-a]

guesthouse la casa de huéspedes [ka-sa day wes-pe-days]
 ‣ we're looking for a guesthouse for the night estamos buscando una casa de huéspedes para pasar la noche [boos-kah-mos oo-na ka-sa day wes-pe-days pa-ra pa-sahr la no-chay]

guide *(person)* el guía, la guía [gee-a]; *(book)* la guía [gee-a]
 ‣ does the guide speak English? ¿el guía habla inglés? [el gee-a ab-la in-glays]

guidebook la guía [gee-a]
 ‣ do you have a guidebook in English? ¿tiene una guía en inglés? [tyen-ay oo-na gee-a en in-glays]

guided tour la visita guiada [bi-see-ta gee-ah-da]
 ‣ what time does the guided tour begin? ¿a qué hora empieza la visita guiada? [a kay aw-ra em-pyay-tha la bi-see-ta gee-ah-da]
 ‣ is there a guided tour in English? ¿hay una visita guiada en inglés? [eye oo-na bi-see-ta gee-ah-da en in-glays]
 ‣ are there guided tours of the museum? ¿hay visitas guiadas al museo? [eye bi-see-tas gee-ah-das al moo-say-oh]

hair el pelo [pay-loh]
 ‣ she has short hair tiene el pelo corto [tyen-ay el pay-loh kor-toh]
 ‣ he has red hair es pelirrojo [es pe-li-RRo-CHoh]

hairbrush el cepillo [thep-eel-yoh]
 ‣ do you sell hairbrushes? ¿vende cepillos? [ben-day thep-eel-yohs]

hairdryer el secador (de pelo) [se-ka-dawr (day pay-loh)]
 ‣ do the rooms have hairdryers? ¿hay secadores en las habitaciones? [eye se-ka-daw-rays en las a-bi-tath-yoh-nays]

hair salon la peluquería [pe-loo-kair-ee-a]
 ‣ does the hotel have a hair salon? ¿hay peluquería en el hotel? [eye pe-loo-kair-ee-a en el oh-tel]

half medio(dia) [med-yoh] ◆ a medias [a med-yas] ◆ la mitad [mee-tad]
 ‣ shall we meet in half an hour? ¿nos vemos dentro de media hora? [nos bay-mos den–troh day med-ya aw-ra]
 ‣ it's half past eight son las ocho y media [son las o-choh ee med-ya]

half-bottle la media botella [med-ya bo-tel-ya]
 ‣ a half-bottle of red wine, please media botella de vino tinto, por favor [med-ya bo-tel-ya day bee-noh teen-toh por fa-bor]

ham el jamón [CHa-mohn]

> I'd like five slices of ham quería cinco rodajas de jamón [kair-ee-a theen-koh RRoda-CHas day CHa-mohn]

hand la mano [mah-noh]

> where can I wash my hands? ¿dónde me puedo lavar las manos? [don-day may pway-doh la-bahr las mah-nohs]

handbag el bolso [bol-soh]

> someone's stolen my handbag me han robado el bolso [may ah RRo-bah-doh el bol-soh]

hand baggage el equipaje de mano [e-ki-pa-CHay day mah-noh]

> I have one suitcase and one piece of hand baggage tengo una maleta y un bulto de equipaje de mano [ten-goh oo-na ma-lay-ta ee oon bool-toh day e-ki-pa-CHay day mah-noh]

handkerchief el pañuelo [pan-yoo-ay-loh]

> do you have a spare handkerchief? ¿tienes un pañuelo de sobras? [tyen-es oon pan-yoo-ay-loh day soh-bras]

handle (of a door) la manilla [ma-neel-ya]; (of a suitcase) el asa [a-sa]

> the handle's broken el asa está rota [el a-sa es-ta RRoh-ta]

handmade hecho(cha) a mano [e-choh a mah-noh]

> is this handmade? ¿esto es hecho a mano? [es-toh es e-choh a mah-noh]

happen (occur) pasar [pa-sahr]

> what happened? ¿qué pasó? [kay pa-soh]
> these things happen estas cosas pasan [e-sas koh-sas pa-san]

happy (not sad) feliz [fe-leeth]; (satisfied) contento(ta) [kon-ten-toh]

> I'd be happy to help me encantaría ayudar [may en-kan-ta-RRee-a a-yoo-dahr]
> Happy Birthday! ¡feliz cumpleaños! [fe-leeth koom-play-an-yohs]
> Happy New Year! ¡feliz Año Nuevo! [fe-leeth an-yoh nway-boh]

hat el sombrero [som-brair-oh]

> I think I left my hat here creo que me he dejado el sombrero aquí [kray-oh kay ay may de-CHah-doh el som-brair-oh a-kee]

hate odiar [od-yahr]

> I hate golf odio el golf [od-yoh el golf]

have (possess, as characteristic) tener [ten-air]; (meal, drink) tomar [tom-ahr]
+ (be obliged) tener que [ten-air kay]

> do you have any bread? ¿tiene pan? [tyen-ay pan]
> do you have them in red? ¿los tiene en rojo? [los tyen-ay en RRo-CHoh]
> he has brown hair tiene el pelo castaño [tyen-ay el pay-loh kas-tan-yoh]
> where could we go to have a drink? ¿dónde podríamos ir para tomar algo? [don-day pod-ree-a-mos eer pa-ra tom-ahr al-goh]

▸ I have to be at the airport by six (o'clock) tengo que estar en el aeropuerto a las seis [ten-goh kay es-tahr en el eye-roh-pwair-toh a las seys]

▸ we have to go tenemos que irnos [ten-ay-mos kay eer-nos]

head *(of a person)* la cabeza [ka-bay-tha]; *(of a shower)* la alcachofa [al-ka-choh-fa]

▸ I hit my head when I fell me golpeé en la cabeza cuando me caí [may gol-pay-ay en la ka-bay-tha kwan-doh may ka-ee]

▸ the shower head is broken la alcachofa de la ducha está rota [la al-ka-choh-fa day la doo-cha es-ta RRoh-ta]

headache el dolor de cabeza [dol-awr day ka-bay-tha]

▸ I've got a headache me duele la cabeza [may dway-lay la ka-bay-tha]

▸ do you have anything for a headache? ¿tiene algo para el dolor de cabeza? [tyen-ay al-goh pa-ra el dol-awr day ka-bay-tha]

headlight el faro [fah-roh]

▸ one of my headlights got smashed uno de los faros quedó destrozado [oo-noh day los fah-rohs kay-doh des-tro-thah-doh]

headphones los auriculares [ow-ri-koo-lahr-ays]

▸ did you find my headphones? ¿encontraste mis auriculares? [en-kon-tras-tay mees ow-ri-koo-lahr-ays]

health la salud [sa-lood]

▸ in good/poor health bien/mal de salud [byen/mal day sa-lood]

hear oír [o-eer]

▸ I've heard a lot about you he oído muchas cosas de ti [ay o-ee-doh moo-chas koh-sas day tee]

heart el corazón [ko-ra-thohn]

▸ he's got a weak heart está mal del corazón [es-ta mal del ko-ra-thohn]

heart attack el infarto [in-fahr-toh], el ataque al corazón [a-ta-kay al ko-ra-thohn]

▸ he had a heart attack le dio un infarto [lay dyoh oon in-fahr-toh]

▸ I nearly had a heart attack! ¡casi me da un infarto! [ka-si may da oon in-fahr-toh]

heart condition la afección cardiaca [a-fekth-yohn kahr-dee-a-ka]

▸ to have a heart condition sufrir una afección cardiaca [soo-freer oo-na a-fekth-yohn kahr-dee-a-ka]

heat *(hot quality, weather)* el calor [ka-lawr]; *(for cooking)* el fuego [fway-goh]

▸ there's no heat from the radiator in my room no sale calor del radiador de mi habitación [noh sa-lay ka-lawr del RRad-ya-dawr en mee a-bi-tath-yohn]

heating la calefacción [ka-le-fakth-yohn]

▸ how does the heating work? ¿cómo funciona la calefacción? [kom-oh foonth-yoh-na la ka-le-fakth-yohn]

heavy pesado(do) [pe-sah-doh]

▸ my bags are very heavy mis bolsas son muy pesadas [mees bol-sas son mwee pe-sah-das]

saying hello

¡Hola! is the equivalent of 'Hi!' and is used by people from all walks of life as it has no pejorative overtones. *¡Buenas!* or *¡Muy buenas!*, on the other hand, are more familiar. If you want to be formal, say *¡Buenos días!* (in the morning, including lunchtime), *¡Buenas tardes!* (in the afternoon) or *¡Buenas noches!* (in the evening and at night).

heel *(of a foot)* el talón [ta-lohn]; *(of a shoe)* el tacón [ta-kohn]
▸ can you put new heels on these shoes? ¿podría poner tacones nuevos en estos zapatos? [pod-ree-a pon-air ta-koh-nays nway-bohs en es-tohs tha-pa-tohs]

hello *(as a greeting)* hola [oh-la]; *(answering the phone)* ¿diga? [dee-ga]
▸ hello, is this ...? hola, ¿es el...? [oh-la es el]

helmet el casco [kas-koh]
▸ do you have a helmet you could lend me? ¿me podrías prestar un casco? [may pod-ree-as pres-tahr oon kas-koh]

help la ayuda [a-yoo-da] ◆ ayudar [a-yoo-dahr]
▸ help! ¡socorro! [so-ko-RRoh]
▸ go and get help quickly! ¡rápido, ve a buscar ayuda! [RRa-pi-doh bay a boos-kahr a-yoo-da]
▸ thank you for your help gracias por tu ayuda [grath-yas por too a-yoo-da]
▸ could you help me? ¿podría ayudarme? [pod-ree-a a-yoo-dahr-may]
▸ could you help us push the car? ¿podría ayudarnos a empujar el coche? [pod-ree-a a-yoo-dahr-nos a em-poo-CHahr el ko-chay]
▸ let me help you with that déjeme que le ayude con eso [day-CHay-may kay lay a-yoo-day kon e-soh]
▸ could you help me with my bags? ¿podría ayudarme kon las maletas? [pod-ree-a a-yoo-dahr-may kon las ma-lay-tas]

herbal tea la infusión [in-foos-yohn]
▸ I'd like a herbal tea quería una infusión [kair-ee-a oo-na in-foos-yohn]

here aquí [a-kee]
▸ I've been here two days llevo aquí dos días [yay-boh a-kee dos dee-as]
▸ I came here three years ago llegué aquí hace tres años [yay-gay a-kee a-thay tres an-yohs]
▸ are you from around here? ¿eres de por aquí? [air-es day por a-kee]
▸ I'm afraid I'm a stranger here myself me temo que soy un forastero [may tay-moh kay soy oon fo-ras-tair-oh]
▸ it's five minutes from here está a cinco minutos de aquí [est-a a theen-koh mi-noo-tohs day a-kee]
▸ here is/are... aquí tiene... [a-kee tyen-ay]

▶ here are my passport and ticket aquí tiene mi pasaporte y mi billete [a-kee tyen-ay mee pa-sa-pawr-tay ee mee bil-yay-tay]

hi hola [oh-la]

▶ hi, I'm Julia hola, soy Julia [oh-la soy CHool-ya]

high beam las luces largas [loo-thays lahr-gas]

▶ put your lights on high beam pon las luces largas [pon las loo-thays lahr-gas]

high chair la trona [troh-na]

▶ could we have a high chair for the baby? ¿nos podría traer una trona para el bebé? [nos pod-ree-a tra-air oo-na troh-na pa-ra el beb-ay]

high season la temporada alta [tem-po-rah-da alta]

▶ is it very expensive in the high season? ¿es muy caro en la temporada alta? [es mwee kah-roh en la tem-po-rah-da alta]

high tide la marea alta [ma-ray-a al-ta]

▶ what time is high tide? ¿a qué hora es la marea alta? [a kay aw-ra es la ma-ray-a al-ta]

hike la caminata [ka-mi-nah-ta]

▶ are there any good hikes around here? ¿hay alguna caminata buena por aquí? [eye al-goo-na ka-mi-nah-ta bway-na por a-kee]

hiking el senderismo [sen-dair-ees-moh]

▶ to go hiking hacer senderismo [a-thair sen-dair-ees-moh]

▶ are there any hiking trails? ¿hay caminos para hacer senderismo? [eye ka-mee-nohs pa-ra a-thair sen-dair-ees-moh]

hiking boot la bota de senderismo [boh-ta day sen-dair-ees-moh]

▶ do you need to wear hiking boots? ¿tienes que llevar botas de senderismo? [tyen-es kay yay-bahr boh-tas day sen-dair-ees-moh]

hitchhike hacer autoestop [a-thair ow-toh-es-top]

▶ we hitchhiked here vinimos aquí haciendo autoestop [bi-nee-mos a-kee ath-yen-doh ow-toh-es-top]

holiday la fiesta [fyes-ta]

▶ is tomorrow a holiday? ¿mañana es fiesta? [man-yah-na es fyes-ta]

home *(house)* la casa [ka-sa] ◆ a casa [a ka-sa]

▶ to stay at home quedarse en casa [kay-dahr-say en ka-sa]

▶ we're going home tomorrow mañana nos vamos a casa [man-yah-na nos bah-mos a ka-sa]

homemade casero(ra) [ka-sair-oh]

▶ is it homemade? ¿es casero? [es ka-sair-oh]

hood *(of car)* el capó [ka-poh]

▶ I've dented the hood he abollado el capó [ay a-bol-yah-doh el ka-poh]

horrible horrible [o-RReeb-lay]

▶ what horrible weather! ¡qué tiempo tan horrible! [kay tyem-poh tan o-RReeb-lay]

hotel rooms

The Spanish have a nice word for a hotel room: *habitación*. If you're traveling with your partner, ask for *una habitación con una cama de matrimonio* (a double bed). Otherwise, it's better to specify *una habitación con dos camas* (with two beds).

horseback riding la equitación [e-ki-tath-yohn]
> can we go horseback riding? ¿podemos ir a montar a caballo? [po-day-mos eer a mon-tahr a ka-bal-yoh]

hospital el hospital [os-pi-tal]
> where is the nearest hospital? ¿dónde está el hospital más cercano? [don-day esta el os-pi-tal mas thair-kah-noh]

hot *(in temperature)* caliente [kal-yen-tay]; *(spicy)* picante [pi-kan-tay]
> I'm too hot tengo mucho calor [ten-goh moo-choh ka-lawr]
> this dish is really hot este plato es muy picante [es-tay pla-toh es mwee pi-kan-tay]
> there's no hot water no hay agua caliente [noh eye ag-wa kal-yen-tay]

hotel el hotel [oh-tel]
> do you have a list of hotels in this area? ¿tiene una lista de hoteles en la zona? [tyen-ay oo-na lees-ta day oh-tel-ays day la thoh-na]
> are there any reasonably priced hotels near here? ¿hay algún hotel con un precio razonable por aquí? [eye al-goon oh-tel kon oon preth-yoh RRa-tho-nah-blay por a-kee]
> is the hotel downtown? ¿el hotel está en el centro? [el oh-tel es-ta en el then-troh]
> could you recommend another hotel? ¿podría recomendarme otro hotel? [pod-ree-a RRe-ko-men-dahr-may oh-troh oh-tel]

at the hotel

> we'd like a double room/two single rooms queríamos una habitación doble/dos habitaciones individuales [kair-ee-a-mos oo-na a-bi-tath-yohn doh-blay/dos a-bi-tath-yoh-nays in-di-bid-wah-lays]
> I have a reservation in the name of Smith tengo una reserva a nombre de Smith [ten-goh oo-na RRe-sair-ba a nom-bray day es-meet]
> what time is breakfast/dinner served? ¿a qué hora se sirve el desayuno/la cena? [a kay aw-ra say seer-bay el des-eye-oo-noh/la thay-na]
> could I have a wake-up call at 7 a.m.? ¿me podrían llamar para despertarme a las siete de la mañana? [may pod-ree-an ya-mahr pa-ra des-pair-tahr-may a las syet-ay day la man-yah-na]

how are you?

If you want to say hello to your friend Pedro, you say *¿qué hay, Pedro?* (how are you, Pedro?). If you think you should be less familiar, say *¿qué tal?* or *¿qué tal está usted?* Or you could say *¿cómo estas?*, to people you know well, or *¿cómo está?*, which is more polite, to people you've just met or mere acquaintances.

hour la hora [aw-ra]
> I'll be back in an hour volveré dentro de una hora [bol-bair-ay den-troh day oo-na aw-ra]
> the flight takes three hours el vuelo dura tres horas [el bway-loh doo-ra tres aw-ras]

house la casa [ka-sa]
> is this your house? ¿esta es tu casa? [es-ta es too ka-sa]

house wine el vino de la casa [bee-noh day la ka-sa]
> a bottle of house wine, please una botella de vino de la casa, por favor [oo-na bo-tel-ya day bee-noh day la ka-sa por fa-bor]

how cómo [kom-oh]
> how are you? ¿cómo estás? [kom-oh es-tas]
> how do you spell it? ¿cómo se escribe? [kom-oh say es-kree-bay]
> how about a drink? ¿qué tal si tomamos algo? [kay tal see to-mah-mos al-goh]

humid húmedo(da) [oo-me-doh]
> it's very humid today hoy hay mucha humedad [oy eye moo-cha oo-me-dad]

hungry
> to be hungry tener hambre [ten-air am-bray]
> I'm starting to get hungry estaba comenzando a tener hambre [es-tah-ba ko-men-than-doh a ten-air am-bray]

hurry
> to be in a hurry tener prisa [ten-air pree-sa]

hurry up darse prisa [dahr-say pree-sa]
> hurry up! ¡date prisa! [da-tay pree-sa]

hurt *(to cause physical pain)* hacer daño a [a-thair dan-yoh a] ◆ doler [dol-air]
> you're hurting me! ¡me estás haciendo daño! [may es-tas ath-ten-doh dan-yoh]
> to hurt oneself hacerse daño [a-thair-say dan-yo]
> I hurt myself me he hecho daño [may ay e-choh dan-yoh]
> I hurt my hand me he hecho daño en la mano [may ay e-choh dan-yoh en la mah-noh]
> it hurts me duele [may dway-lay]

i

ice el hielo [yay-loh]
  ▸ the car skidded on the ice el coche patinó en el hielo [el ko-chay pa-ti-noh en el yay-loh]
  ▸ a Diet Coke® without ice, please una Coca-Cola Light® sin hielo, por favor [oo-na ko-ka koh-la lait seen yay-loh por fa-bor]

ice cream el helado [e-lah-doh]
  ▸ I'd like some ice cream quería un helado [kair-ee-a oon e-lah-doh]

ice cube el cubito de hielo [koo-bee-toh day yay-loh]
  ▸ could I have a carafe of water with no ice cubes in it? ¿me podría traer una jarra de agua sin cubitos de hielo? [may pod-ree-a tra-air oo-na CHa-RRa day ag-wa seen koo-bee-tohs day yay-loh]

iced coffee el café con hielo [ka-fay kon yay-loh]
  ▸ I'd like an iced coffee quería un café con hielo [kair-ee-a oon ka-fay kon yay-loh]

ice rink la pista de hielo [pees-ta day yay-loh]
  ▸ is there an ice rink nearby? ¿hay una pista de hielo por aquí? [eye oo-na pees-ta day yay-loh por a-kee]

ice skate el patín (para hielo) [pa-teen (pa-ra yay-loh)]
  ▸ I'd like to rent some ice skates quería alquilar unos patines (para hielo) [kair-ee-a al-ki-lahr oo-nohs pa-tee-nays (pa-ra yay-loh)]

ice-skate
  ▸ would you like to go ice-skating tomorrow? ¿te gustaría ir a patinar sobre hielo mañana? [tay goos-ta-ree-a eer a pa-ti-nahr soh-bray yay-loh man-yah-na]

ID card el carnet de identidad [kahr-nay day i-den-ti-dad]
  ▸ I don't have an ID card: will a passport work? no tengo un carnet de identidad, ¿sirve el pasaporte? [noh ten-goh oon kahr-nay day i-den-ti-dad seer-bay el pa-sa-pawr-tay]

if si [see]
  ▸ we'll go if you want iremos si quieres [i-ray-mos see kyair-ays]

ill enfermo(ma) [en-fair-moh]
  ▸ my son is ill mi hijo está enfermo [mee e-CHoh es-ta en-fair-moh]

immediately inmediatamente [in-mayd-ya-ta-men-tay]
  ▸ can you do it immediately? ¿puedes hacerlo inmediatamente? [pway-days a-thair-loh in-mayd-ya-ta-men-tay]

improve mejorar [me-CHo-rahr]
  ▸ I'm hoping to improve my Spanish while I'm here espero mejorar mi español mientras esté aquí [es-pair-oh me-CHo-rahr mee es-pan-yol myen-tras es-tay a-kee]

in en [en]
- our bags are still in the room nuestras bolsas todavía están en la habitación [nwes-tras bol-sas toh-da-bee-a es-tan en la a-bi-tath-yohn]
- do you live in Vigo? ¿vives en Vigo? [bee-bes en bee-goh]

included incluido(da) [in-kloo-ee-doh]
- is breakfast included? ¿el desayuno está incluido? [el des-eye-oo-noh es-ta in-kloo-ee-doh]
- is sales tax included? ¿está incluido el IVA? [es-ta in-kloo-ee-doh el ee-ba]
- is the tip included? ¿está incluida la propina? [es-ta in-kloo-ee-doh la pro-pee-na]

indoor cubierto(ta) [koob-yair-toh]
- is there an indoor pool? ¿hay una piscina cubierta? [eye oo-na pis-thee-na koob-yair-ta]

infection la infección [in-fekth-yohn]
- I have an eye infection tengo una infección en el ojo [ten-goh oo-na in-fekth-yohn en el o-CHoh]

information la información [in-for-math-yohn]
- a piece of information una información [oo-na in-for-math-yohn]
- may I ask you for some information? quería una información, por favor [kair-ee-a oo-na in-for-math-yohn por fabor]
- where can I find information on...? ¿dónde puedo encontrar información sobre...? [don-day pway-doh en-kon-trahr in-for-math-tohn soh-bray]

injection *(medicine)* la inyección [in-yekth-yohn]
- am I going to need an injection? ¿me van a tener que poner una inyección? [may ban a ten-air kay pon-er oo-na in-yekth-yohn]

injure lesionar [les-yoh-ahr]
- to injure oneself lesionarse [les-yon-ahr-say]
- I injured myself me he lesionado [may ay les-yon-ah-doh]

inside dentro de [den-troh day] ◆ dentro [den-troh]
- are you allowed inside the castle? ¿se puede entrar en el castillo? [say pway-day en-trahr en el kas-teel-yoh]
- we'd prefer a table inside ¿preferiríamos una mesa dentro [pre-fair-ee-ree-a-mos oo-na may-sa den-troh]

insurance el seguro [se-goo-roh]
- what does the insurance cover? ¿qué cubre el seguro? [kay koo-bray el se-goo-roh]

insure *(house, car)* asegurar [a-se-goo-rahr]
- yes, I'm insured sí, tengo seguro [see ten-goh se-goo-roh]

interesting interesante [in-tair-e-san-tay]
- it's not a very interesting place no es un lugar muy interesante [noh es oon loo-gahr mwee in-tair-e-san-tay]

international call la llamada internacional [ya-mah-da in-tair-nath-yoh-nal]
  ▶ I'd like to make an international call quería hacer una llamada internacional [kair-ee-a a-thair oo-na ya-mah-da in-tair-nath-yoh-nal]

Internet Internet [een-tair-net]
  ▶ where can I connect to the Internet? ¿dónde puedo conectarme a Internet? [don-day pway-doh ko-nek-tahr-may a een-tair-net]

introduce (present) presentar [pre-sen-tahr]
  ▶ to introduce oneself presentarse [pre-sen-tahr-say]
  ▶ allow me to introduce myself: I'm Michael permítame que me presente: soy Michael [pair-mee-ta-may kay may pre-sen-tay soy mai-kel]

invite invitar [im-bi-tahr]
  ▶ I'd like to invite you to dinner next weekend quería invitarle a cenar el próximo fin de semana [kair-ee-a im-bi-tahr-lay a then-ahr el prok-si-moh feen day se-mah-na]

iron (for ironing) la plancha [plan-cha] ◆ planchar [plan-chahr]
  ▶ I need an iron necesito una plancha [ne-thes-ee-toh oo-na plan-cha]

itch el picor [pi-kawr]
  ▶ I've got an itch on my left leg tengo un picor en la pierna izquierda [ten-goh oon pi-kawr en la pyair-na ith-kyair-da]

itinerary el itinerario [ee-ti-nair-ahr-yoh]
  ▶ is it possible to modify the planned itinerary? ¿sería posible modificar el itinerario previsto? [sair-ee-a po-see-blay mo-di-fi-kahr el ee-ti-nair-ahr-yoh pre-bees-toh]

j

January enero [en-air-oh]
  ▶ January 4th cuatro de enero [kwat-roh day en-air-oh]

Jet Ski® la moto acuática [moh-toh a-kwa-ti-ka]
  ▶ I'd like to rent a Jet Ski® quería alquilar una moto acuática [kair-ee-a al-ki-lahr oo-na moh-toh a-kwa-ti-ka]

job (employment) el trabajo [tra-ba-CHoh]
  ▶ I'm looking for a summer job in the area busco un trabajo de verano en la zona [boos-koh oon tra-ba-CHoh day bair-ah-noh en la thoh-na]

joke la broma [broh-ma] ◆ bromear [broh-may-ahr]
  ▶ it's beyond a joke! ¡esto pasa de castaño oscuro! [es-toh pa-sa day kas-tan-yoh os-koo-roh]
  ▶ I was just joking estaba de broma [es-tah-ba day broh-ma]

journey el viaje [bya-CHay]
  ▶ how long does the journey take? ¿cuánto dura el viaje? [kwan-toh doo-ra el bya-CHay]

juice *(from fruit)* el zumo [thoo-moh]
▸ what types of juice do you have? ¿qué tipos de zumo tienen? [kay too-pos day thoo-moh tyen-en]

July julio [CHool-yoh]
▸ July 4th cuatro de julio [kwat-roh day CHool-yoh]

June el junio [CHoon-yoh]
▸ June 2nd el dos de junio [el dos day CHoon-yoh]

just *(recently, at that moment)* justo [CHoos-toh]; *(only, simply)* sólo [soh-loh], solamente [soh-la-men-tay]
▸ he just left se acaba de ir [say a-kah-ba day eer]
▸ I'll just have one sólo quiero uno [soh-loh kair-ee-a oo-noh]

k

kayak el kayak [ka-yak]
▸ can we rent kayaks? ¿podemos alquilar kayaks? [pod-ay-mos al-ki-lahr ka-yaks]

keep *(retain)* quedarse con [kay-dahr-say kon]; *(promise)* cumplir [koom-pleer]; *(appointment)* acudir a [a-koo-deer a]
▸ I'm sorry, I won't be able to keep the appointment lo siento, no voy a poder acudir a la cita [loh syen-toh noh boy a po-dair a-koo-deer a la thee-ta]
▸ keep the change quédese con el cambio [kay-day-say kon el kamb-yoh]

key *(for a lock)* la llave [yah-bay]; *(on a keyboard, phone)* la tecla [tek-la]
▸ which is the key to the front door? ¿cuál es la llave de la puerta principal? [kwal es la yah-bay day la pwair-ta prin-thi-pal]

kilometer el kilómetro [ki-lo-met-roh]
▸ how much is it per kilometer? ¿cuánto cuesta por kilómetro? [kwan-toh kwes-ta por ki-lo-met-roh]

kind *(nice)* amable [a-mah-blay] ◆ *(sort, type)* el tipo [tee-poh]
▸ that's very kind of you es muy amable de tu parte [es mwee a-mah-blay day too pahr-tay]
▸ what's your favorite kind of music? ¿cuál es tu tipo favorito de música? [kwal es too tee-poh fa-bo-ree-toh day moo-si-ka]

kitchen la cocina [ko-thee-na]
▸ is the kitchen shared? ¿la cocina es compartida? [la ko-thee-na es kom-pahr-tee-da]

Kleenex® el kleenex® [klee-neks]
▸ do you have any Kleenex®? ¿tiene kleenex®? [tyen-ay klee-neks]

knife el cuchillo [koo-cheel-yoh]
  ▸ could I have a knife? ¿me podría traer un cuchillo? [may pod-ree-a tra-air oon koo-cheel-yoh]

know conocer [ko-no-thair]
  ▸ I don't know this town very well no conozco muy bien esta ciudad [noh ko-noth-koh mwee byen es-ta thyoo-dad mwee byen]
  ▸ I know the basics but no more than that conozco lo fundamental, pero nada más [ko-noth-koh loh foon-da-men-tal pair-oh nah-da mas]
  ▸ do you know each other? ¿se conocen? [say ko-no-then]

knowledge el conocimiento [ko-no-thim-yen-toh]
  ▸ she has a good knowledge of Spanish tiene buenos conocimientos de español [tyen-ay bway-nohs ko-no-thim-yen-tohs del es-pan-yol]
  ▸ without my knowledge sin que yo lo supiera [seen kay yoh loh soop-yair-a]

ladies' room el servicio de señoras [sair-beeth-yoh day sen-yaw-ras]
  ▸ where's the ladies' room? ¿dónde está el servicio de señoras? [don-day es-ta el sair-beeth-yoh day sen-yaw-ras]

lake el lago [lah-goh]
  ▸ can you go swimming in the lake? ¿se puede nadar en el lago? [say pway-day na-dahr en el lah-goh]

lamp la lámpara [lam-pa-ra]
  ▸ the lamp doesn't work la lámpara no funciona [la lam-pa-ra noh foonth-yoh-na]

land *(plane)* aterrizar [a-te-RRi-thahr]
  ▸ what time is the plane scheduled to land? ¿a qué hora está previsto que aterrice el avión? [a kay aw-ra es-ta pre-bees-toh kay a-te-RRee-thay el ab-yohn]

landmark el punto de referencia [poon-toh day RRe-fair-enth-ya]
  ▸ do you recognize any landmarks? ¿reconoces algún punto de referencia? [RRe-ko-no-thays al-goon poon-toh day RRe-fair-enth-ya]

lane el carril [ka-RReel]
  ▸ a four-lane highway una autopista de cuatro carriles [oo-na ow-to-pes-ta day kwat-roh ka-RRee-lays]

laptop el portátil [por-ta-teel]
  ▸ my laptop's been stolen me han robado el portátil [may an RRo-bah-doh el por-ta-teel]

last último(ma) [ool-ti-moh] ◆ durar [doo-rahr]
  ▸ when does the last bus go? ¿a qué hora sale el último autobús? [a kay aw-ra sa-lay el ool-ti-moh ow-toh-boos]

▸ when is the last subway train? ¿a qué hora es el último metro? [a kay aw-ra es el ool-ti-moh met-roh]

last name el apellido [a-pel-yee-doh]
▸ could I have your last name? ¿me podría decir su apellido? [may pod-ree-a de-theer soo a-pel-yee-doh]

late tarde [tahr-day]
▸ the plane was two hours late el avión llegó dos horas tarde [el ab-yohn yay-goh dos aw-ras tahr-day]
▸ could you tell me if the 1:17 to Cádiz is running late? ¿podría decirme si el de la una y diecisiete a Cádiz va con retraso? [pod-ree-a de-theer-may see el day la oo-na ee dyeth-ee-syet-ay a ka–deeth ba kon RRe-tra-soh]

later posterior [pos-tair-yawr] ◆ más tarde [mas tahr-day]
▸ is there a later train? ¿hay un tren más tarde? [eye oon tren mas tahr-day]
▸ see you later! ¡hasta luego! [as-ta loo-ay-goh]

latest último(ma) [ool-ti-moh]
▸ what's the latest time we can check out? ¿a qué hora tenemos que dejar el hotel? [a kay aw-ra ten-ay-mos kay de-CHahr el oh-tel]

laugh la risa [RRee-sa] ◆ reír [RRe-eer]
▸ I just did it for a laugh lo hice para divertirme [loh ee-thay pa-ra di-bair-teer-may]

Laundromat® la lavandería [la-ban-dair-ee-a]
▸ is there a Laundromat® nearby? ¿hay alguna lavandería cerca? [eye al-goo-na la-ban-dair-ee-a thair-ka]

laundry *(clothes)* la ropa [RRoh-pa]; *(business, room)* la lavandería [la-ban-dair-ee-a]
▸ where can we do our laundry? ¿dónde podemos lavar la ropa? [don-day pod-ay-mos la-bahr la RRoh-pa]
▸ where's the nearest laundry? ¿dónde está la lavandería más cercana? [don-day es-ta la la-ban-dair-ee-a mas thair-kah-na]

lawyer el abogado [a-bo-gah-doh], la abogada [a-bo-gah-da]
▸ I'm a lawyer soy abogado/abogada [soy a-bo-gah-doh/a-bo-gah-da]
▸ I need a lawyer necesito un abogado [ne-thes-ee-toh oon a-bo-gah-doh]

leaflet el folleto [fol-yay-toh]
▸ do you have any leaflets in English? ¿tiene algún folleto en inglés? [tyen-ay al-goon fol-yay-toh en in-glays]

learn aprender [ap-ren-dair]
▸ I've just learned a few words from a book he aprendido unas pocas palabras en un libro [ay ap-ren-dee-doh oo-nas poh-kas pa-lab-ras day oon lee-broh]

least menor [men-awr] ◆ menos [may-nos] ◆ **at least** por lo menos [por loh may-nos]
▸ it's the least I can do es lo menos que puedo hacer [es loh may-nos kay pway-doh a-thair]

▶ not in the least **en absoluto** [en ab-so-loo-toh]
▶ to say the least **por no decir otra cosa** [por noh de-theer oh-tra koh-sa]
▶ it's at least a three-hour drive **son por lo menos tres horas conduciendo** [son por loh may-nos tres aw-ras kon-dooth-yen-doh]

leave *(go away from)* **irse de** [eer-say day]; *(put)* **dejar** [de-CHahr]; *(forget to take)* **dejar** [de-CHahr] ♦ *(go away)* **irse** [eer-say]
▶ can I leave my backpack at the reception desk? **¿puedo dejar la mochila en recepción?** [pway-doh de-CHahr la mo-chee-la en RRe-thepth-yohn]
▶ can I leave the car at the airport? **¿puedo dejar el coche en el aeropuerto?** [pway-doh de-CHahr el ko-chay en el eye-roh-pwair-toh]
▶ leave us alone! **¡déjanos en paz!** [day-CHa-nos en path]
▶ I've left something on the plane **me he dejado algo en el avión** [may ay de-CHah-doh al-goh en el ab-yohn]
▶ I'll be leaving at nine o'clock tomorrow morning **me voy mañana a las nueve de la mañana** [may boy man-yah-na a las nway-bay day la man-yah-na]
▶ what platform does the train for Murcia leave from? **¿de qué andén sale el tren de Murcia?** [day kay an-dayn sa-lay el tren day moorth-ya]

left *(not right)* **izquierdo(da)** [ith-kyair-doh] ♦ **la izquierda** [ith-kyair-da]
▶ to be left **quedar** [kay-dahr]
▶ are there any tickets left for...? **¿quedan billetes para...?** [kay-dan bil-yay-tays pa-ra]
▶ to the left (of) **a la izquierda (de)** [a la ith-kyair-da]

left-hand de la izquierda [day la ith-kyair-da]
▶ on your left-hand side **a tu izquierda** [a too ith-kyair-da]

leg la pierna [pyair-na]
▶ I have a pain in my left leg **me duele la pierna izquierda** [may dway-lay la pyair-na ith-kyair-da]
▶ I can't move my leg **no puedo mover la pierna** [noh pway-doh mo-bair la pyair-na]

lemon el limón [li-mohn]
▶ can I have some lemons? **¿me puede poner unos limones?** [may pway-day pon-air oo-nohs li-moh-nays]

lend prestar [pres-tahr]
▶ could you lend us your car? **¿nos podrías prestar el coche?** [nos pod-ree-as pres-tahr el ko-chay]

lens *(of camera)* **el objetivo** [ob-CHe-tee-boh]; *(contact lens)* **la lentilla** [len-teel-ya], **la lente de contacto** [len-tay day kon-tak-toh]
▶ there's something on the lens **hay algo en el objetivo** [eye al-goh en el ob-CHe-tee-boh]
▶ I have hard/soft lenses **uso lentillas duras/blandas** [oo-soh len-teel-yas doo-ras/blandas]

less menos [may-nos]
▶ less and less **cada vez menos** [kah-da beth may-nos]
▶ a little less **un poco menos** [oon poh-koh may-nos]

lesson la clase [kla-say]
> how much do lessons cost? ¿cuánto cuestan las clases? [kwan-toh kwes-tan las kla-says]
> can we take lessons? ¿podemos recibir clases? [pod-ay-mos RRe-thi-beer klas-ays]

let off *(allow to disembark)* dejar [de-CHahr]
> could you let me off here, please? ¿me puede dejar aquí, por favor? [may pway-day de-CHahr a-kee, por fa-bor]

letter la carta [kahr-ta]
> I would like to send this letter to the States quería enviar esta carta a los Estados Unidos [kair-ee-a emb-yahr es-ta kahr-ta a es-tah-dohs oo-nee-dohs]
> I confirmed my reservation by letter confirmé la reserva por carta [kon-feer-may la RRe-sair-ba por kahr-ta]

level *(amount)* el nivel [nee-bel]; *(of a building, a ship)* el piso [pee-soh]
> do you know if cabin 27 is on this level? ¿sabe si el camarote veintisiete está en este piso? [sa-bay see el ka-ma-roh-tay beyn-ti-syet-ay es-ta en es-tay pee-soh]

license la licencia [lee-thenth-ya]; *(for driving)* el carnet de conducir [kahr-nay day kon-doo-theer]
> do you need a license to hunt here? ¿hace falta licencia para cazar aquí? [a-thay fal-ta lee-thenth-ya pa-ra ka-thahr a-kee]
> I left my driver's license in my hotel room me he dejado el carnet de conducir en el cuarto del hotel [may ay de-CHah-doh el kahr-nay day kon-doo-theer en el kwahr-toh del oh-tel]

license number el número de matrícula [noo-mair-oh day ma-tree-koo-la]
> I got the license number apunté el número de matrícula [a-poon-tay el noo-mair-oh day ma-tree-koo-la]

license plate la matrícula [ma-tree-koo-la]
> the license plate is broken la matrícula está rota [la ma-tree-koo-la es-ta RRoh-ta]

lifebelt el flotador [flo-ta-dawr]
> throw me a lifebelt! ¡tírenme un flotador! [tee-ren-may oon flo-ta-dawr]

lifeboat el bote salvavidas [boh-tay sal-ba-bee-das]
> how many lifeboats are there? ¿cuántos botes salvavidas hay? [kwan-tohs boh-tays sal-ba-bee-das eye]

lifejacket el chaleco salvavidas [cha-lay-koh sal-ba-bee-das]
> are there any lifejackets? ¿hay chalecos salvavidas? [eye cha-lay-kohs sal-ba-bee-das]

light *(brightness, on a car, in a lamp)* la luz [looth]; *(regulating traffic)* el semáforo [se-ma-fo-roh]; *(for a cigarette)* el fuego [fway-goh]
> the light doesn't work la luz no funciona [la looth noh foonth-yoh-na]
> could you check the lights? ¿podría comprobar las luces? [pod-ree-a kom-pro-bahr las loo-thays]
> stop at the next light para en el próximo semáforo [pa-ra en el prok-si-moh se-ma-fo-roh]
> do you have a light? ¿tiene fuego? [tyen-ay fway-goh]

likes

- I really love that painting realmente me encanta ese cuadro [RRay-al-men-tay may en-kan-ta e-say kwad-roh]
- I like your brother tu hermano me cae bien [too air-mah-noh may ka-ay byen]
- I've got a soft spot for her tengo debilidad por ella [ten-goh de-bi-li-dad por el-ya]
- I think she's very nice me parece que es encantadora [may pa-re-thay kay es en-kan-ta-daw-ra]

lighter el encendedor [en-then-de-dawr], el mechero [me-chair-oh]

- can I borrow your lighter? ¿me deja el encendedor? [may day-CHa el en-then-de-dawr]

lighthouse el faro [fah-roh]

- are there boat trips to the lighthouse? ¿hay paseos en barco hasta el faro? [eye pa-say-ohs en bahr-koh as-ta el fah-roh]

like como [kom-oh] • gustar [goos-tahr]

- it's quite like English se parece bastante al inglés [say pa-re-thay bas-tan-tay al in-glays]
- I like it me gusta [may goos-ta]
- I don't like it no me gusta [noh may goos-ta]
- do you like it here? ¿te gusta el lugar? [tay goos-ya el loo-gahr]
- I like Chinese food very much me gusta mucho la comida china [may goos-ta moo-choh la ko-mee-da chee-na]
- do you like the movies? ¿te gusta el cine? [tay goos-ta el thee-nay]
- would you like a drink? – yes, I'd love one ¿quieres una copa? – sí, gracias, me encantaría [kyair-ays oo-na koh-pa – see grath-yas may en-kan-ta-ree-a]
- I'd like to speak to the manager quería hablar con el encargado [kair-ee-a ab-lahr kon el en-kahr-gah-doh]

lime la lima [lee-ma]

- can I have some limes? ¿me podría poner unas limas? [may pod-ree-a ponair oo-nas lee-mas]

dislikes

- I hate football odio el fútbol [od-yoh el foot-bol]
- I can't stand him no lo aguanto [noh loh ag-wan-toh]
- I don't really like him/her no me cae muy bien [noh may ka-ay mwee byen]
- I'm not really into walking no me gusta mucho caminar [noh may goos-ta moo-choh ka-mi-nahr]

limit el límite [lee-mi-tay] ♦ limitar [li-mi-tahr]
▸ is that area off limits? ¿está prohibido entrar en esa zona? [es-ta pro-ee-bee-doh en-trahr en es-ta thoh-na]

line la línea [lee-nay-a]; *(of people waiting)* la cola [koh-la]
▸ the line was busy comunicaba [ko-moo-ni-kah-ba]
▸ we had to stand in line for 15 minutes tuvimos que hacer quince minutos de cola [too-bee-mos kay a-thair keen-thay mi-noo-tohs day koh-la]
▸ which line do I take to get to ...? ¿qué línea tengo que coger para ir a...? [kay lee-nay-a ten-goh kay koCH-air pa-ra eer a]

lipstick el pintalabios [peen-ta-lab-yohs]
▸ I need to buy some lipstick necesito comprar pintalabios [ne-thes-ee-toh kom-prahr peen-ta-lab-yohs]

listen escuchar [es-koo-chahr]
▸ listen, I really need to see a doctor escucha, realmente necesito un médico [es-koo-cha RRay-al-men-tay ne-thes-ee-toh oon may-di-koh]
▸ listen to me carefully escúchame con atención [es-koo-cha-may kon a-tenth-yohn]

liter el litro [lee-troh]
▸ a two-liter bottle of water una botella de agua de dos litros [oo-na bo-tel-ya day ag-wa day dos lee-trohs]

little pequeño(ña) [pe-kayn-yoh] ♦ poco [poh-koh] ♦ **a little** un poco [oon poh-koh]
▸ it's for a little girl es para una niña pequeña [es pa-ra oo-na neen-ya pe-kayn-ya]
▸ as little as possible lo mínimo [loh mee-ni-moh]
▸ I speak a little Spanish hablo un poco de español [ab-loh oon poh-koh day es-pan-yol]
▸ we've only got a little money left sólo nos queda un poco de dinero [soh-loh nos kay-da oon poh-koh day di-nair-oh]
▸ a little bit un poquito [oon po-kee-toh]
▸ a little less un poco menos [oon poh-koh may-nos]
▸ a little more un poco más [oon poh-koh mas]

live vivir [bib-eer]
▸ do you live around here? ¿vive por aquí? [bee-bay por a-kee]
▸ I live in Bilbao vivo en Bilbao [bee-boh en beel-bow]

live music la música en directo [moo-si-ka en di-rek-toh]
▸ I'd like to go to a bar with live music me gustaría ir a un bar con música en directo [may goos-ta-ree-a eer a oon bahr kon moo-si-ka en di-rek-toh]

living room el salón [sa-lohn]
▸ I can sleep in the living room puedo dormir en el salón [pway-doh dor-meer en el sa-lohn]

loaf (of bread) el pan [pan]
▸ I'd like one of those large loaves quería uno de esos panes grandes [kair-ee-a oo-na day e-sohs pan-ays gran-days]

local local [loh-kal]
> what's the local specialty? ¿cuál es el plato típico de la región? [kwal es el pla-toh tee-pi-koh day la RReCH-yohn]

lock la cerradura [theRR-a-doo-ra] • cerrar (con llave) [theRR-ahr(kon yah-bay)]
> the lock's broken la cerradura está rota [la theRR-a-doo-ra es-ta RRoh-ta]
> I locked the door cerré la puerta (con llave) [theRR-ay la pwair-ta(kon yah-bay)]

lock out
> to lock oneself out dejarse las llaves de casa dentro [de-CHahr-say las yah-bays day ka-sa den-troh]
> I've locked myself out me he dejado las llaves de casa dentro [may ay de-CHah-doh las yah-bays day ka-sa den-troh]

long largo(ga) [lahr-goh] • largo [lahr-goh]
> it's 10 feet long mide diez pies de largo [mee-day dyeth pyays day lahr-goh]
> I waited for a long time esperé mucho tiempo [es-pair-ay moo-choh tyem-poh]
> how long? ¿cuánto? [kwan-toh]
> how long will it take? ¿cuánto llevará? [kwan-toh yay-ba-ra]
> we're not sure how long we're going to stay no estamos seguros de cuánto tiempo nos vamos a quedar [noh es-tah-mos se-goo-rohs day kwan-toh tyem-poh nos bah-mos a kay-dahr]

look (with eyes) la mirada [mi-rah-da]; (appearance) el aspecto [as-pek-toh] • (with eyes) mirar [mi-rahr]; (seem) parecer [pa-reth-air]
> could you have a look at my car? ¿podría echar un vistazo al coche? [pod-ree-a e-chahr oon bis-ta-thoh al ko-chay]
> no, thanks, I'm just looking no, gracias, sólo estoy mirando [noh grath-yas so-loh es-toy mi-ran-doh]
> what does she look like? ¿cómo es? [kom-oh es]
> you look like your brother te pareces a tu hermano [tay pa-reth-ays a too air-mah-noh]
> it looks like it's going to rain parece que va a llover [pa-reth-ay kay ba a yoh-bair]

look after cuidar [kwee-dahr]
> can someone look after the children for us? ¿podría cuidar alguien de nuestros niños? [pod-ree-a kwee-dahr alg-yen day nwes-trohs neen-yohs]
> can you look after my things for a minute? ¿podría cuidar mis cosas un minuto? [pod-ree-a kwee-dahr mees koh-sas oon mi-noo-toh]

look for buscar [boos-kahr]
> I'm looking for a good restaurant that serves regional cuisine estoy buscando un restaurante bueno que sirva comida regional [es-toy boos-kan-doh oon RRes-tow-ran-tay bway-noh kay seer-ba ko-mee-da RReCH-yoh-nal]

lose (be unable to find) perder [pair-dair]
> I've lost the key to my room he perdido la llave de mi habitación [ay pair-dee-doh la yah-bay day mee a-bi-tath-yohn]
> I've lost my way me he perdido [may ay pair-dee-doh]

lost perdido(da) [pair-dee-doh]

▸ who do you have to see about lost luggage? ¿a dónde hay que ir para tratar de equipaje perdido? [a-don-day eye kay eer pa-ra tra-tahr day e-ki-pa-CHay pair-dee-doh]

▸ could you help me? I seem to be lost ¿me podría ayudar? creo que me he perdido [may pod-ree-a a-yoo-dahr. kray-oh kay may ay pair-dee-doh]

▸ to get lost perderse [pair-dair-say]

▸ get lost! ¡piérdete! [pyair-day-tay]

lost-and-found la oficina de objetos perdidos [o-fi-thee-na day ob-CHay-tohs pair-dee-dohs]

▸ where's the lost-and-found? ¿dónde está la oficina de objetos perdidos? [don-day es-ta la o-fi-thee-na day ob-CHay-tohs pair-dee-dohs]

lot ◆ **a lot** mucho [moo-choh]

▸ a lot of ... mucho ... [moo-choh]

▸ are there a lot of things to see around here? ¿hay muchas cosas para ver por aquí? [eye moo-chas koh-sas pa-ra bair por a-kee]

▸ will there be a lot of other people there? ¿habrá mucha gente ahí? [ab-ra moo-cha CHen-tay a-ee]

▸ thanks a lot muchas gracias [moo-chas grath-yas]

loud *(noise, voice)* fuerte [fwair-tay]; *(music)* alto(ta) [al-toh]

▸ the television is too loud la televisión está muy alta [la te-le-bis-yohn es-ta mwee al-ta]

loudly *(speak)* alto [al-toh]

▸ can you speak a little more loudly? ¿podría hablar un poco más alto? [pod-ree-a ab-lahr oon poh-koh mas al-toh]

love amar [a-mahr]

▸ I love you te amo [tay a-moh]

▸ I love the movies me encanta el cine [may en-kan-ta el thee-nay]

▸ I love cooking me encanta cocinar [may en-kan-ta ko-thi-nahr]

lovely encantador(ra) [en-kan-ta-dawr]

▸ what a lovely room! ¡qué cuarto tan encantador! [kay kwahr-toh tan en-kan-ta-dawr]

▸ it's lovely today hoy hace un tiempo estupendo [oy a-thay oon tyem-poh es-too-pen-doh]

low *(temperature)* bajo(ja) [ba-CHoh]; *(speed)* lento(ta) [len-toh]

▸ temperatures are in the low twenties las temperaturas pasan un poco de veinte grados [las tem-pair-a-too-ras pa-san oon po-koh day bayn-tay grah-dohs]

low beam las luces cortas [loo-thays kawr-tas]

▸ keep your lights on low beam deja las luces cortas [day-CHa las loo-thays kawr-tas]

lower bajar [ba-CHahr] ◆ inferior [in-fair-yawr]

▸ is it OK if I lower the blind a little? ¿le molesta si bajo un poco la persiana? [lay mo-les-ta see ba-CHoh oon poh-koh la pairs-yah-na]

▸ how do we get to the lower level? ¿cómo bajamos al nivel inferior? [kom-oh ba-CHah-mos al ni-bel in-fair-yawr]

low-fat *(yogurt)* bajo(ja) en grasas [ba-CHoh en gra-sas]
- do you have any low-fat yogurt? ¿tienen yogures bajos en grasas? [tyen-en yo-goo-rays ba-CHohs en gra-sa]

low season la temporada baja [tem-po-rah-da ba-CHa]
- what are prices like in the low season? ¿cómo son los precios durante la temporada baja? [kom-oh son los preth-yohs doo-ran-tay la tem-po-rah-da ba-CHa]

low tide la marea baja [ma-ray-a ba-CHa]
- what time is low tide today? ¿a qué hora es la marea baja hoy? [a kay aw-ra es la ma-ray-a ba-CHa oy]

luck la suerte [swair-tay]
- good luck! ¡buena suerte! [bway-na swair-tay]

luggage el equipaje [e-ki-pa-CHay]
- my luggage hasn't arrived mi equipaje no ha llegado [mee e-ki-pa-CHay noh a yay-gah-doh]
- I'd like to report the loss of my luggage quería denunciar la pérdida de mi equipaje [kair-ee-a de-noonth-yahr la par-di-da day mee e-ki-pa-CHay]

luggage cart el carrito para el equipaje [ka-RRee-toh pa-ra el a-ki-pa-CHay]
- I'm looking for a luggage cart estoy buscando un carrito para el equipaje [es-toy boos-kan-doh oon ka-RRee-toh pa-ra el a-ki-pa-CHay]

lunch la comida [ko-mee-da], el almuerzo [alm-wair-thoh]
- to have lunch comer [kom-air]
- what time is lunch served? ¿a qué hora se sirve la comida? [a kay aw-ra say seer-bay la kom-ee-da]

m

machine-washable lavable a máquina [la-bah-blay a ma-ki-na]
- is it machine-washable? ¿es lavable a máquina? [es la-bah-blay a ma-ki-na]

maid la camarera [ka-ma-rair-a]
- what time does the maid come? ¿a qué hora viene la camarera? [a kay aw-ra byen-ay la ka-ma-rair-a]

maid service el servicio de habitaciones [sair-beeth-yoh day a-bi-tath-yoh-nays]
- is there maid service? ¿hay servicio de habitaciones? [eye sair-beeth-yoh day a-bi-tath-yoh-nays]

mailbox el buzón [boo-thohn]
- where's the nearest mailbox? ¿dónde está el buzón más próximo? [don-day es-ta el boo-thohn mas prok-si-moh]

main course el plato principal [pla-toh prin-thi-pal]
- what are you having for your main course? ¿qué vas a tomar de plato principal? [kay bas a toh-mahr day pla-toh prin-thi-pal]

mainline de línea principal [day lee-nay-a prin-thi-pal]
- where are the mainline trains? ¿dónde están los trenes de largo recorrido? [don-day es-tan los tren-ays day lahr-goh RRe-ko-RRee-doh]

make hacer [a-thair]
- how is this dish made? ¿cómo se hace este plato? [kom-oh say a-thay es-tay pla-toh]
- I hope to make new friends here espero hacer nuevos amigos aquí [es-pair-oh a-thair nway-bohs a-mee-gohs a-kee]

make up (compensate for) recuperar [RRe-koo-pair-ahr]; (invent) inventar [im-ben-tahr]
- will we be able to make up the time we've lost? ¿conseguiremos recuperar el tiempo perdido? [kon-se-gi-ray-mos RRe-koo-pair-ahr el tyem-poh pair-dee-doh]

man el hombre [om-bray]
- that man is bothering me ese hombre me está molestando [e-say om-bray may es-ta mo-les-tan-doh]

man-made artificial [ahr-ti-fith-yal]
- it's man-made es artificial [es ahr-ti-fith-yal]

many mucho [moo-choh]
- there are many good restaurants here aquí hay muchos restaurantes buenos [a-kee eye moo-chohs RRes-tow-ran-tays bway-nohs]
- how many? ¿cuántos? [kwan-tohs]
- how many days will you be staying? ¿cuántos días se van a a quedar? [kwan-tohs dee-as say ban a kay-dahr]

map (of a country) el mapa [ma-pa]; (of a town, a network) el plano [plah-noh]
- where can I buy a map of the area? ¿dónde puedo comprar un mapa de la zona? [don-day pway-doh kom-prahr oon ma-pa day la thoh-na]
- can you show me where we are on the map? ¿me podría mostrar en el plano dónde nos encontramos? [may pod-ree-a mos-trahr en el pla-noh don-day nos en-kon-trah-mos]
- can I have a map of the subway? quería un plano del metro [kair-ee-a oon plah-noh del met-roh]

March el marzo [mahr-thoh]
- March 1st el primero de marzo [el pri-mair-oh day mahr-thoh]

market el mercado [mair-kah-doh]
- is there a market in the square every day? ¿hay mercado en la plaza todos los días? [eye mair-kah-doh en la pla-tha toh-dohs los dee-as]

married casado(da) [ka-sah-doh]
- are you married? ¿estás casado? [es-tas ka-sah-doh]

meals

In Spain, lunch is the main meal of the day and you start with a *primer plato/primero* (starter) which might be a dish of green vegetables (*verduras*) or legumes (*legumbres*), salad (*ensalada*), soup (*sopa*) or cooked meats (*embutidos*). Then there's the main course, *segundo plato/segundo*, of meat, fish or maybe an omelette, garnished with green vegetables or potatoes, perhaps. Finally, there's the dessert (*postre*). Then it's time for a chat over a liqueur or a coffee, which might go on for quite a while. It's called the *sobremesa*.

mass *(religious)* la misa [mee-sa]
▸ what time is mass? ¿a qué hora es la misa? [a kay aw-ra es la mee-sa]

match *(for lighting)* la cerilla [thair-eel-ya]
▸ do you have any matches? ¿tiene cerillas? [tyen-ay thair-eel-yas]

matter importar [im-por-tahr]
▸ it doesn't matter no importa [noh im-pawr-ta]

mattress el colchón [kol-chohn]
▸ the mattresses are saggy los colchones están hundidos [los kol-choh-nays es-tan oon-dee-dohs]

May mayo [meye-oh]
▸ May 9th nueve de mayo [nway-bay day meye-oh]

maybe tal vez [tal beth]
▸ maybe the weather will be better tomorrow tal vez el tiempo mejore mañana [tal beth el tyem-poh me-CHaw-ray man-yah-na]

meal la comida [ko-mee-da]
▸ are meals included? ¿están incluídas las comidas? [es-tan in-kloo-ee-das las ko-mee-das]

mean *(signify)* significar [sig-ni-fi-kahr]; *(intend)* querer [kair-air]
▸ what does that word mean? ¿qué significa esa palabra? [kay sig-ni-fee-ka e-sa pa-lab-ra]
▸ I mean it lo digo en serio [loh dee-goh en sair-yoh]
▸ I didn't mean it no lo dije en serio [noh loh dee-CHay en sair-yoh]

meat la carne [kahr-nay]
▸ I don't eat meat no como carne [noh kom-oh kahr-nay]

mechanic el mecánico [me-ka-ni-koh], la mecánica [me-ka-ni-ka]
▸ what did the mechanic say was wrong with the car? ¿qué dijo el mecánico que le pasaba al coche? [kay dee-CHoh el me-ka-ni-koh kay lay pa-sah-ba al ko-chay]

cooked meats

It's tough if you're a vegetarian. Spanish cooked meats, found particularly in *tapas* and in *bocadillos* (sandwiches), are absolutely delicious: *chorizo*, *jamón serrano* (similar to Parma ham), *salchichón* (salami), *salchicha* (sausage), *morcilla negra* or *blanca* (blood sausage or a sausage of ground pork suet, bread, and oatmeal), etc. In Madrid, there are *museos del jamón*, delis that are so big they are known as 'museums!'

medication la medicación [me-di-kath-yohn]
- ▶ I'm not taking any other medication at the moment en estos momentos no estoy tomando ninguna otra medicación [en es-tohs mo-men-tohs noh es-toy toman-doh nin-goo-na oh-trah me-di-kath-yohn]

medicine la medicina [me-di-thee-na]
- ▶ how many times a day do I have to take the medicine? ¿cuántas veces por día tengo que tomar la medicina? [kwan-tas beth-ays por dee-a ten-goh kay tom-ahr la me-di-thee-na]

medium *(size)* medio(dia) [med-yoh]; *(steak)* poco hecho(cha) [poh-koh e-CHoh]
- ◆ *(in size)* la talla mediana [tal-ya med-yah-na]
- ▶ I'd like my steak medium, please quiero mi filete poco hecho, por favor [kair-ee-a mee fi-lay-tay poh-koh e-choh por fa-bor]
- ▶ do you have this shirt in a medium? ¿tiene esta camisa en talla mediana? [tyen-ay es-ta ka-mee-sa en oo-na tal-ya med-yah-na]

meet *(by chance, arrangement)* encontrar(se) [en-kon-trahr-(say)]; *(become acquainted)* conocer(se) [ko-no-thair-(say)]
- ▶ meet you at 9 o'clock in front of the town hall te encontraré a las nueve delante del ayuntamiento [tay en-kon-trah-ray a las nway-bay de-lan-tay del a-yoon-tam-yen-toh]
- ▶ I have to meet my friend at nine o'clock tengo que encontrarme con un amigo a las nueve [ten-goh kay en-kon-trahr-may kon oon a-mee-goh a las nway-bay]
- ▶ pleased to meet you encantado de conocerle [en-kan-tah-doh day ko-no-thair-lay]
- ▶ goodbye! it was nice meeting you ¡adiós!, encantado de conocerle [ad-yohs en-kan-tah-doh day ko-no-thair-lay]
- ▶ Chris, I'd like you to meet Mr. López Chris, quiero que conozcas al señor López [krees, kair-ee-a kay ko-noth-kas al sen-yawr loh-peth]
- ▶ where shall we meet? ¿dónde nos encontraremos? [don-day nos en-kon-trah-ray-mos]
- ▶ what time are we meeting tomorrow? ¿a qué hora nos encontraremos mañana? [a kay aw-ra nos en-kon-trah-ray-mos man-yah-na]

member *(of a club)* el socio [sohth-yoh], la socia [sohth-ya]
- ▶ do you have to be a member? ¿hay que ser socio? [eye kay sair sohth-yoh]

men's room el servicio de caballeros [sair-beeth-yoh day ka-bal-yair-ohs]
- where's the men's room? ¿dónde está el servicio de caballeros? [don-day es-ta el sair-beeth-yoh day ka-bal-yair-ohs]

menu *(list of dishes)* la carta [kahr-ta] *(set menu)* el menú [men-oo]
- menu of the day menú del día [men-oo del dee-a]
- can we see the menu? ¿podría traernos la carta? [pod-ree-a tra-air-nos la kahr-ta]
- do you have a menu in English? ¿tiene una carta en inglés? [tyen-ay oo-na kahr-ta en in-glays]
- do you have a children's menu? ¿tiene menú infantil? [tyen-ay men-oo in-fan-teel]

message el mensaje [men-sa-CHay]
- can you take a message? ¿puedo dejar un recado? [pway-doh de-CHahr oon RRe-kah-doh]
- can I leave a message? ¿puedo dejar un recado? [pway-doh de-CHahr oon RRe-kah-doh]
- did you get my message? ¿recibiste mi mensaje? [re-thi-bees-tay mee men-sa-CHay]

meter *(measurement)* el metro [met-roh]; *(device)* el contador [kon-ta-dawr]
- it's about five meters long mide aproximadamente cinco metros de largo [mee-day a-prok-si-mah-da-men-tay theen-koh met-rohs day lahr-goh]

midday el mediodía [med-yoh-dee-a]
- we have to be there by midday tenemos que estar ahí antes del mediodía [te-nay-mos kay es-tahr a-ee an-tays del med-yoh-dee-a]

midnight la medianoche [med-ya-no-chay]
- it's midnight es medianoche [es med-ya-no-chay]

mileage *(distance)* el kilometraje [kee-loh-met-ra-CHay]
- is there unlimited mileage? ¿el kilometraje es ilimitado? [el kee-loh-met-ra-CHay es i-li-mi-tah-doh]

milk la leche [le-chay]
- a liter of milk un litro de leche [oon lee-troh day le-chay]
- tea with milk té con leche [tay kon le-chay]

milk chocolate el chocolate con leche [cho-koh-la-tay kon le-chay]
- I prefer milk chocolate prefiero el chocolate con leche [pref-yair-oh el cho-koh-la-tay kon le-chay]

mind *(object)* importar [im-por-tahr]
- I don't mind no me importa [noh may im-pawr-ta]
- do you mind if I smoke? ¿le importa si fumo? [lay im-pawr-ta see foo-moh]
- do you mind if I open the window? ¿le importa si abro la ventana? [lay im-pawr-ta see ab-roh la ben-tah-na]
- never mind no importa [noh im-pawr-ta]

mineral water el agua mineral [ag-wa min-air-al]
- could I have a bottle of mineral water, please? ¿me podría traer una botella de agua mineral, por favor? [may pod-ree-a tra-air oo-na bot-el-ya day ag-wa min-air-al por fa-bor]

minus menos [may-nos]
- it's minus two degrees outside! ¡fuera hace dos bajo cero! [fwair-a a-thay dos ba-CHoh thair-oh]

minute el minuto [mi-noo-toh]
- we'll go in a minute nos iremos en un minuto [nos i-ray-mos en oon mi-noo-toh]

mirror el espejo [es-pay-CHoh]
- the mirror's cracked el espejo está rajado [el es-pay-CHoh es-ta RRa-CHa-doh]

miss *(be too late for)* perder [pair-dair]; *(regret the absence of)* echar en falta a [e-chahr en fal-ta a]
- I've missed my connection he perdido mi conexión [ay pair-dee-doh mee kon-eks-yohn]
- we're going to miss the train vamos a perder el tren [bah-mos a pair-dair el tren]
- I missed you te eché en falta [tay e-chay en fal-ta]

missing perdido(da) [pair-dee-doh]
- one of my suitcases is missing no sé dónde está una de mis maletas [noh say don-day es-ta oo-na day mees ma-lay-tas]

mistake el error [e-RRor]
- I think there's a mistake with the bill creo que hay un error en la cuenta [kray-oh kay eye oon e-RRor en la kwen-ta]
- you've made a mistake with my change me ha dado el cambio equivocado [may a dah-doh el kamb-yoh e-ki-bo-kah-doh]

moment el momento [mo-men-toh]
- for the moment, we prefer staying in Madrid por el momento, preferimos quedarnos en Madrid [por el mo-men-toh pre-fair-ee-mos kay-dahr-nos en mad-reed]

Monday el lunes [loo-nes]
- we're arriving/leaving on Monday llegaremos/nos iremos el lunes [yay-ga-ray-mos/nos ee-ray-mos el loo-nes]

money el dinero [di-nair-oh]
- I don't have much money no tengo mucho dinero [noh ten-goh moo-choh di-nair-oh]
- where can I change money? ¿dónde puedo cambiar dinero? [don-day pway-doh kamb-yahr di-nair-oh]
- I want my money back quiero que me devuelvan mi dinero [kair-ee-a kay may de-bwel-ban mee di-nair-oh]

money order la transferencia [trans-fair-enth-ya]
- I'm waiting for a money order estoy esperando una transferencia [es-toy es-pair-an-doh oo-na trans-fair-enth-ya]

m mo

month el mes [mays]

▶ I'm leaving in a month me voy dentro de un mes [may boy den-troh day oon mays]

monument el monumento [mo-noo-men-toh]

▶ what does this monument commemorate? ¿qué conmemora este monumento? [kay kon-me-maw-ra es-tay mo-noo-men-toh]

more más [mas]

▶ can we have some more bread? ¿nos puede traer más pan? [nos pway-day tra-air mas pan]

▶ a little more un poco más [oon poh-koh mas]

▶ could I have a little more wine? ¿me podría poner un poco más de vino? [may pod-ree-a pon-air oon poh-koh mas day bee-noh]

▶ I don't want any more, thank you no quiero más, gracias [noh kyair-oh mas grath-yas]

▶ I don't want to spend any more no quiero gastar más [noh kyair-oh gas-tahr mas]

morning la mañana [man-yah-na]

▶ the museum is open in the morning el museo está abierto por la mañana [el moo-say-oh es-ta ab-yair-toh por la man-yah-na]

morning-after pill la píldora del día siguiente [peel-do-ra del dee-a sig-yen-tay]

▶ I need the morning-after pill necesito la píldora del día siguiente [ne-thes-ee-toh la peel-do-ra del dee-a sig-yen-tay]

mosque la mezquita [meth-kee-ta]

▶ where's the nearest mosque? ¿dónde está la mezquita más próxima? [don-day es-ta la meth-kee-ta mas prok-si-ma]

most la mayoría de [la meye-aw-ree-a day] ◆ la mayoría [la meye-aw-ree-a] ◆ *(to the greatest extent)* el más [el mas], la más [la mas]; *(very)* muy [mwee]

▶ are you here most days? ¿estás aquí la mayoría de los días? [es-tas a-kee la meye-aw-ree-a day los dee-as]

▶ that's the most I can offer es lo máximo que puedo ofrecer [es loh mak-si-moh kay pway-doh of-re-thair]

mother la madre [mah-dray]

▶ this is my mother esta es mi madre [es-ta es mee mah-dray]

motorboat la lancha motora [lan-cha mo-taw-ra]

▶ can we rent a motorboat? ¿podemos alquilar una lancha motora? [pod-ay-mos al-ki-lahr oo-na lan-cha mo-taw-ra]

motorcycle la motocicleta [moh-toh-thi-klay-ta]

▶ I'd like to rent a motorcycle me gustaría alquilar una motocicleta [may goos-ta-ree-a al-ki-lahr oo-na moh-toh-thi-klay-ta]

mountain la montaña [mon-tan-ya]

▶ in the mountains en la montaña [en la mon-tan-ya]

museums

You have to pay to visit museums and major sites, which tend to be more expensive than other tourist attractions. Some offer free admission one day a week (get there at opening time!). Monday is the usual closing day and on Sundays and national holidays they will normally be open only till lunchtime.

mountain hut la cabaña de montaña [ka-ban-ya day mon-tan-ya]
- we slept in a mountain hut dormimos en una cabaña de montaña [dor-mee-mos en oo-na ka-ban-ya day mon-tan-ya]

mouth la boca [boh-ka]
- I've got a strange taste in my mouth siento un sabor extraño en la boca [syen-toh oon sa-bawr eks-tran-yoh en la boh-ka]

move el movimiento [mob-eem-yen-toh] ◆ mover [mob-air] ◆ moverse [mob-air-say]
- I can't move my leg no puedo mover la pierna [noh pway-doh mob-air la pyair-na]
- don't move him no lo muevas [noh loh mway-bas]

movie la película [pe-lee-koo-la]
- have you seen ...'s latest movie? ¿has visto la última película de...? [as bees-toh la ool-ti-ma pe-lee-koo-la day]
- it's a subtitled movie es una película subtitulada [es oo-na pe-lee-koo-la soob-ti-too-lah-da]

movie theater el cine [thee-nay]
- where is there a movie theater? ¿dónde hay un cine? [don-day eye oon thee-nay]
- what's on at the movie theater? ¿qué ponen en el cine? [kay poh-nen en el thee-nay]

much mucho(cha) [moo-choh] ◆ mucho [moo-choh]
- I don't have much money no tengo mucho dinero [noh ten-goh moo-choh di-nair-oh]
- how much is it? ¿cuánto es? [kwan-toh es]
- how much is it for one night? ¿cuánto cuesta una noche? [kwan-toh kwes-ta oo-na no-chay]
- how much is it per day and per person? ¿cuánto es por día y por persona? [kwan-toh es por dee-a ee por pair-soh-na]
- how much does it cost per hour? ¿cuánto cuesta por hora? [kwan-toh kwes-ta por aw-ra]
- how much is a ticket to Pamplona? ¿cuánto cuesta un billete a Pamplona? [kwan-toh kwes-ta oon bil-yay-tay a pam-ploh-na]

museum el museo [moo-say-oh]
- what time does the museum open? ¿a qué hora abre el museo? [a kay aw-ra a-bray el moo-say-oh]

music la música [moo-si-ka]
▸ what kind of music do they play in that club? ¿qué tipo de música ponen en esa discoteca? [kay tee-poh day moo-si-ka poh-nen en esa dis-ko-tay-ka]

must deber [deb-air]
▸ that must cost a lot debe de costar mucho [deb-ay day kos-tahr moo-choh]

mustard la mostaza [mos-ta-tha]
▸ is it strong mustard? ¿es fuerte la mostaza? [es fwair-tay la mos-ta-tha]

n

nail *(on a finger, a toe)* la uña [oon-ya]
▸ I need to cut my nails necesito cortarme las uñas [ne-thes-ee-toh kor-tahr-may las oon-yas]

nail polish el esmalte de uñas [es-mal-tay day oon-yas]
▸ I'd like to find nail polish in a dark shade of red tengo que encontrar esmalte de uñas de una tonalidad rojo oscuro [ten-goh kay en-kon-trahr es-mal-tay day oon-yas day oo-na to-na-li-dad RRo-CHoh os-koo-roh]

name el nombre [nom-bray]
▸ what is your name? ¿cómo te llamas? [kom-oh tay yah-mas]
▸ my name is Patrick me llamo Patrick [may yah-moh pat-rik]
▸ hello, my name's David hola, mi nombre es David [oh-la mee nom-bray es dei-bid]
▸ I have a reservation in the name of Jackson tengo una reserva a nombre de Jackson [ten-goh oo-na RRes-air-ba a nom-bray day dyak-son]

napkin la servilleta [sair-beel yay-ta]
▸ could I have a clean napkin, please? ¿me podría traer una servilleta limpia, por favor? [may pod-ree-a pon-air oo-na sair-beel-yay-ta leem-pya por fa-bor]

national holiday la fiesta nacional [fyes-ta nath-yoh-nal]
▸ tomorrow is a national holiday mañana es fiesta nacional [man-yah-na es fyes-ta nath-yoh-nal]

nationality la nacionalidad [nath-yo-na-li-dad]
▸ what nationality are you? ¿de qué nacionalidad eres? [day kay nath-yo-na-li-dad air-ays]

nature la naturaleza [na-too-ra-lay-tha]
▸ I like to take long walks outdoors and enjoy nature me gusta hacer caminadas al aire libre y disfrutar de la naturaleza [may goos-ta a-thair ka-mi-nah-das al eye-ray lee-bray ee dis-froo-tahr day la na-too-ra-lay-tha]

nausea las náuseas [now-say-as]
▸ I've had nausea all day he tenido náuseas todo el día [ay te-nee-doh now-say-as toh-doh el dee-a]

near cercano(na) [thair-kah-noh], próximo(ma) [prok-si-moh] ◆ cerca [thair-ka] ◆ cerca de [thair-ka day]

▶ where's the nearest subway station? ¿dónde está la estación de metro más cercana? [don-day es-ta la es-tath-yohn day met-roh mas thair-kah-na]
▶ it's near the station está cerca de la estación [es-ta thair-ka day la es-tath-yohn]
▶ very near ... muy cerca de.... [mwee thair-ka day]

nearby cerca [thair-ka]

▶ is there a supermarket nearby? ¿hay un supermercado cerca? [eye oon soo-pair-mair-kah-doh thair-ka]

neck el cuello [kwel-yoh]

▶ I have a sore neck me duele el cuello [may dway-lay el kwel-yoh]

need la necesidad [ne-thes-i-dad] ◆ necesitar [ne-thes-i-tahr]

▶ I need something for a cough necesito algo para la tos [ne-thes-ee-toh al-goh pa-ra la tos]
▶ I need to be at the airport by six (o'clock) tengo que estar en el aeropuerto a las seis [ten-goh kay es-tahr en el eye-roh-pwair-toh a las seys]
▶ we need to go tenemos que ir [ten-ay-mos k eer]

neither ninguno(na) [nin-goo-noh] ◆ tampoco [tam-poh-koh] ◆ ni [nee]

▶ neither of us ninguno de nosotros [nin-goo-noh day no-soh-trohs]
▶ me neither yo tampoco [yoh tam-poh-koh]

neutral el punto muerto [poon-toh mwair-toh]

▶ make sure the car's in neutral asegúrate de que el coche esté en punto muerto [a-se-goo-ra-tay day kay el ko-chay es-tay en poon-toh mwair-toh]

never nunca [noon-ka]

▶ I've never been to Spain before nunca había estado en España [noon-ka a-bee-a es-tah-doh en es-pan-ya]

new nuevo(va) [nway-boh]

▶ could we have a new tablecloth, please? ¿nos podrían poner un mantel nuevo, por favor? [nos pod-ree-an po-nair oon man-tel nway-boh por fa-bor]

news las noticias [noh-teeth-yas]

▶ a piece of news una noticia [oo-na noh-teeth-ya]
▶ that's great news! ¡qué noticia tan buena! [kay noh-teeth-ya tan bway-na]
▶ I heard it on the news lo escuché en las noticias [loh es-koo-chay en las noh-teeth-yas]

newspaper el periódico [pair-yoh-di-koh]

▶ do you have any English-language newspapers? ¿tiene algún periódico en inglés? [tyen-ay al-goon pair-yoh-di-koh en in-glays]

New Year el año nuevo [an-yoh nway-boh]

▶ Happy New Year! ¡feliz Año Nuevo! [fe-leeth an-yoh nway-boh]

New Year's Day el día de año nuevo [dee-a day an-yoh nway-boh]

> are stores open on New Year's Day? ¿las tiendas abren el día de año nuevo?
> [las tyen-das ab-ren el dee-a day an-yoh nway-boh]

next próximo(ma) [prok-si-moh] ✦ **next to** al lado de [al lah-doh day]

> when is the next guided tour? ¿a qué hora es la próxima visita? [a kay aw-ra es la
> prok-si-ma bi-see-ta]
> when is the next train to Valencia? ¿cuándo es el próximo tren a Valencia?
> [kwan-doh es el prok-si-moh tren a bal-enth-ya]
> what time is the next flight to London? ¿a qué hora es el próximo vuelo a
> Londres? [a kay aw-ra es el prok-si-moh bway-koh a lon-dres]
> can we park next to the tent? ¿podemos aparcar al lado de la tienda? [pod-ay
> mos a-pahr-kahr al lah-doh day la tyen-da]

nice *(vacation, food)* bueno(na) [bway-noh]; *(kind)* agradable [ag-ra-dah-blay]
(likable) simpático(ca) [sim-pa-ti-koh]

> have a nice vacation! ¡que tengáis unas buenas vacaciones! [kay ten-geyes oo-nas
> bway-nas ba-kath-yoh-nays]
> we found a really nice little hotel encontramos un hotelito muy bueno [en-kon
> tram-mos oon oh-te-lee-toh mwee bway-noh]
> goodbye! it was nice meeting you ¡adiós!, fue un placer conocerte [ad-yohs fwa
> oon pla-thair ko-no-thair-tay]

night la noche [no-chay]

> how much is it per night? ¿cuánto es por noche? [kwan-toh es por no-chay]
> I'd like to stay an extra night me gustaría quedarme otra noche [may goos-ta-ree
> a kay-dahr-may oh-tra no-chay]

nightclub la discoteca [dis-koh-tay-ka]

> are there any good nightclubs in this town? ¿hay buenas discotecas en est
> ciudad? [eye bway-nas dis-koh-tay-kas en es-ta thyoo-dad]

nine nueve [nway-bay]

> there are nine of us somos nueve [so-mos nway-bay]
> we have a reservation for nine (o'clock) tenemos una reserva para las nuev
> [ten-ay-mos oo-na RRe-sair-ba pa-ra las nway-bay]

no no [noh]

> no thanks! ¡no, gracias! [noh grath-yas]
> a cup of tea with no milk or sugar, please una taza de té sin leche ni azúcar, po
> favor [oon ta-tha day tay seen le-chay nee a-thoo-kahr por fa-bor]

nobody nadie [nad-yay]

> there's nobody at the reception desk no hay nadie en recepción [noh eye nad-ya
> en RRe-thepth-yohn]

noise el ruido [RRoo-ee-doh]

> to make a noise hacer ruido [a-thair RRoo-ee-doh]
> I heard a funny noise oí un ruido extraño [o—ee oon RRoo-ee-doh eks-tran-yoh]

noisy ruidoso(sa) [RRoo-ee-doh-soh]
> I'd like another room: mine is too noisy quería otra habitación, la mía es demasiado ruidosa [kair-ee-a oh-tra a-bi-tath-yohn la mee-a es de-mas-yah-doh RRoo-ee-doh-sa]

nonsmoker el no fumador [noh foo-ma-dawr], la no fumadora [noh foo-ma-daw-ra]
> we're nonsmokers somos no fumadores [so-mos noh foo-ma-daw-rays]

nonsmoking de no fumadores [day noh foo-ma-daw-rays]
> is this restaurant nonsmoking? ¿es un restaurante de no fumadores? [es oon RRes-tow-ran-tay day noh foo-ma-daw-rays]

nonsmoking compartment el compartimento de no fumadores [kom-pahr-ti-men-toh day noh foo-ma-daw-rays]
> I'd like a seat in a nonsmoking compartment quería un asiento en un compartimento de no fumadores [kair-ee-a oon as-yen-toh en oon kom-pahr-ti-men-toh day noh foo-ma-daw-rays]

nonsmoking section la zona de no fumadores [thoh-na day noh foo-ma-daw-rays]
> do you have a nonsmoking section? ¿tiene una zona de no fumadores? [tyen-ay oo-na thoh-na day noh foo-ma-daw-rays]

nonstop directo(ta) [di-rek-toh] ◆ sin parar [seen pa-rahr]
> I'd like a nonstop flight from Madrid to Chicago quería un vuelo directo de Madrid a Chicago [kair-ee-a oon bway-loh di-rek-toh day mad-reed a chi-kah-goh]

noon el mediodía [med-yoh-dee-a]
> we leave at noon nos vamos al mediodía [nos bah-mos al med-yoh-dee-a]

no one nadie [nad-yay]
> there's no one there no hay nadie [noh eye nad-yay]

normal normal [nor-mal] ◆ lo normal [nor-mal]
> is it normal for it to rain as much as this? ¿es normal que llueva tanto? [es nor-mal kay yoo-ay-ba tan-toh]

not no [noh]
> I don't like spinach no me gustan las espinacas [noh may goos-tan las es-pi-na-kas]
> I don't think so creo que no [kray-oh kay noh]
> not at all en absoluto [en ab-so-loo-toh]

note la nota [noh-ta]
> could I leave a note for him? ¿podría dejarle una nota? [pod-ree-a de-CHahr-lay oo-na noh-ta]

nothing nada [nah-da]
> there's nothing to do here in the evening aquí no hay nada que hacer por las noches [a-kee noh eye nah-da kay a-thair por las no-chays]
> there's nothing I can do about it no puedo hacer nada al respecto [noh pway-doh a-thair nah-da al RRes-pek-toh]

November noviembre [nov-yem-bray]
- November 7th siete de noviembre [syet-ay day nov-yem-bray]

now ahora [a-aw-ra]
- what should we do now? ¿y ahora qué hacemos? [ee a-aw-ra kay a-thay-mos]

number el número [noo-mair-oh]
- my name is... and my number is... me llamo... y mi número es el... [may yah-moh ... ee mee noo-mair-oh es]

occupied *(bathroom)* ocupado(da) [o-koo-pah-doh]
- the restroom's occupied el aseo está ocupado [el a-say-oh es-ta o-koo-pah-doh]

ocean el océano [oh-thay-ah-noh]
- we'd like to see the ocean while we're here nos gustaría ver el mar durante nuestra estancia aquí [nos goos-ta-ree-a bair el mahr doo-ran-tay nwes-tra es-tanth-ya a-kee]

o'clock
- it's eight o'clock son las ocho [son las o-choh]

October octubre [ok-too-bray]
- October 12th doce de octubre [doh-thay day ok-too-bray]

of de [day]
- one of us uno de nosotros [oo-noh day no-soh-trohs]

off
- an island off the coast of France una isla cerca de la costa francesa [oo-na ees-la thair-ka day la kos-ta fran-thay-sa]
- this sweater is 50 percent off! ¡el jersey tiene una rebaja del cincuenta por ciento! [el CHair-say tyen-ay oo-na RRe-ba-CHa del thin-kwen-ta por thyen-toh]

offer ofrecer [of-reth-air]
- can I offer you a cigarette? ¿le puedo ofrecer un cigarrillo? [lay pway-doh of-reth-air oon thi-ga-RReel-yoh]

office la oficina [o-fi-thee-na]
- where is the hotel office? ¿dónde está la oficina del hotel? [don-day es-ta la o-fi-thee-na del oh-tel]

often a menudo [a me-noo-doh]
- how often does the ferry sail? ¿con qué frecuencia sale el ferry? [kon kay frek-wenth-ya sa-lay el fe-RRi]

oil el aceite [a-thay-tay]
- could you check the oil, please? ¿podría comprobar el aceite, por favor? [pod-ree-a kom-pro-bahr el a-thay-tay por fa-bor]

OK bien [byen] ◆ vale [bah-lay]
- that's OK está bien [es-ta byen]
- do you think it's still OK? ¿te parece que sigue estando bien? [tay pa-re-thay kay see-gay es-tan-doh byen]

old viejo(ja) [byay-CHoh]
- how old are you? ¿cuántos años tienes? [kwan-tohs an-yohs tyen-es]
- I'm 18 years old tengo dieciocho años [ten-goh dyeth-yoch-oh]
- have you visited the old town? ¿has visitado el casco antiguo? [as bi-si-tah-doh el kas-koh an-tee-gwoh]

on *(working)* encendido(da) [en-then-dee-doh]
- how long is the program on for? ¿cuánto dura el programa? [kwan-toh doo-ra el pro-gra-ma]

once una vez [oo-na beth]
- I've been here once before había estado aquí una vez [a-bee-a es-tah-doh a-kee oo-na beth]
- please do it at once por favor, hazlo ahora mismo [por fa-bor ath-loh a-aw-ra mees-moh]

one uno(na) [oo-noh]
- a table for one, please una mesa para uno, por favor [oo-na may-sa pa-ra oo-noh por fa-bor]

one-way (ticket) el billete de ida [bil-yay-tay day ee-da]
- how much is a one-way ticket downtown? ¿cuánto cuesta un billete de ida al centro? [kwan-toh kwes-ta oon bil-yay-tay day ee-da al then-troh]
- a second-class one-way ticket to Toledo un billete de ida en segunda a Toledo [oon bil-yay-tay day ee-da en-se-goon-da a to-lay-doh]

only solo [soh-loh], solamente [soh-la-men-tay]
- there's only one left solo queda uno [soh-loh kay-da oo-noh]

open abierto(ta) [ab-yair-toh] ◆ abrir [ab-reer] ◆ *(door, window)* abrirse [ab-reer-say]
- is the bank open on Saturday? ¿el banco abre los sábados? [el ban-koh ab-ray los sa-ba-dohs]
- is the museum open all day? ¿el museo abre todo el día? [el moo-say-oh ab-ray toh-doh el dee-a]
- at what time is ... open? ¿a qué hora abre...? [a kay aw-ra ab-ray]
- can I open the window? ¿puedo abrir la ventana? [pway-doh ab-reer la ben-tah-na]
- what time do you open? ¿a qué hora abre? [a kay aw-ra ab-ray]

open-air al aire libre [a- eye-ray lee-bray]
- is there an open-air swimming pool? ¿hay una piscina al aire libre? [eye oo-na pis-thee-na al eye-ray lee-bray]

operating room el quirófano [ki-ro-fa-noh]
- is she still in the operating room? ¿todavía está en el quirófano? [toh-da-bee-a es-ta en el ki-ro-fa-noh]

opinion la opinión [o-peen-yohn]

> in my opinion, ... en mi opinión, ... [en mee o-peen-yohn]

orange naranja [na-ran-CHa] ◆ *(fruit)* la naranja [na-ran-CHa]; *(color)* el naranja [na-ran-CHa]

> I'd like a kilo of oranges quería un kilo de naranjas [kair-ee-a oon kee-loh day na-ran-CHas]

orange juice el zumo de naranja [thoo-moh day na-ran-CHa]

> I'll have a glass of orange juice quería un vaso de zumo de naranja [kair-ee-a oon ba-soh day thoo-moh day na-ran-CHa]
> I'd like a freshly squeezed orange juice quería un zumo de naranja recién exprimido [kair-ee-a oon thoo-moh day na-ran-CHa RReth-yen eks-pri-mee-doh]

order el pedido [pe-dee-doh] ◆ pedir [ped-eer]

> this isn't what I ordered: I asked for... esto no es lo que había pedido. Pedí... [es-toh noh es loh kay ay ped-ee-doh ped-ee]
> I ordered a coffee pedí un café [ped-ee oon ka-fay]
> we'd like to order now queríamos pedir [kair-ee-a-mos ped-eer]

organize organizar [or-ga-ni-thahr]

> can you organize the whole trip for us? ¿podría organizarnos toda la excursión? [pod-ree-a or-ga-ni-thahr-nos toh-da la eks-koors-yohn]

other otro(tra) [oh-troh] ◆ el otro [oh-troh], la otra [oh-tra]

> I'll have the other one tomaré el otro [to-ma-tay el oh-troh]
> on the other side of the street en el otro lado de la calle [en el oh-troh lah-doh day la kal-yay]
> go ahead; I'm going to wait for the others adelántate, yo voy a esperar a los otros [a-de-lan-tay yoh boy a es-pair-ahr a los oh-trohs]

out-of-date caducado(da) [ka-doo-kah-doh]

> I think my passport is out-of-date creo que mi pasaporte está caducado [kray-oh kay mee pa-sa-pawr-tay es-ta ka-doo-kah-doh]

outside call la llamada (al exterior) [ya-mah-da (al eks-tair-yawr)]

> I'd like to make an outside call quería hacer una llamada (al exterior) [kair-ee-a a-thair oo-na ya-mah-da (al eks-tair-yawr)]

opinions

> personally, I don't think it's fair personalmente, no me parece justo [pair-soh-nal-men-tay noh may pa-re-thay CHoos-toh]
> I think he's right creo que tiene razón [kray-oh kay tyen-ay RRa-thohn]
> I don't want to say no te lo digo [noh tay loh dee-goh]
> I'm not sure no estoy seguro [noh es-toy se-goo-roh]
> no idea! ¡ni idea! [nee ee-day-a]
> it depends depende [de-pen-day]

outside line la línea exterior [lee-nay-a eks-tair-yawr]
- how do you get an outside line? ¿cómo consigo una línea exterior? [kom-oh kon-see-goh oo-na lee-nay-a eks-tair-yawr]

overheat recalentarse [RRe-ka-len-tahr-say]
- the engine is overheating el motor se está recalentando [el mo-tawr say es-ta RRe-ka-len-tan-doh]

owner el dueño [dwayn-yoh], la dueña [dwayn-ya]
- do you know who the owner is? ¿sabe quién es el dueño? [sa-bay kyen es el dwayn-yoh]

pack *(of cigarettes, chewing gum)* el paquete [pa-kay-tay] ♦ *(for a trip)* hacer el equipaje [a-thair el e-ki-pa-CHay]
- how much is a pack of cigarettes? ¿cuánto cuesta un paquete de cigarrillos? [kwan-toh kwes-ta oon pa-kay-tay day thi-ga-RReel-yohs]
- I need to pack tengo que hacer el equipaje [ten-goh kay a-thair el e-ki-pa-CHay]

package el paquete [pa-kay-tay]
- I'd like to send this package to Seattle by airmail quería enviar este paquete a Seattle por correo aéreo [kair-ee-a emb-yahr es-tay pa-kay-tay a say-at-el por ko-RRay-oh a-air-ay-oh]
- do you have weekend packages? ¿tienen paquetes de fin de semana? [tyen-en pa-kay-tays day feen day se-mah-na]

package tour el paquete turístico [pa-kay-tay too-rees-ti-koh]
- it's my first time on a package tour es la primera vez que voy en un paquete turístico [es la pri-mair-ra beth kay koy en oon pa-kay-tay too-rees-ti-koh]

padlock el candado [kan-dah-doh]
- I'd like to buy a padlock for my bike quería comprar un candado para la bici [kair-ee-a kom-prahr oon kan-dah-doh pa-ra la bee-thi]

pain *(physical)* el dolor [dol-awr]
- I'd like something for pain quería algo para el dolor [kair-ee-a al-goh pa-ra el dol-awr]
- I have a pain here me duele aquí [may dway-lay a-kee]

painkiller el analgésico [an-al-CHe-si-koh]
- I have a really bad toothache: can you give me a painkiller, please? tengo un dolor de muelas muy fuerte, ¿me podría dar un analgésico, por favor? [ten-goh oon dol-awr day mway-las mwee fwair-tay may pod-ree-a dahr oon an-al-CHe-si-koh por fa-bor]

pair *(of gloves, socks)* el par [pahr]
▶ a pair of shoes un par de zapatos [oon pahr day tha-pa-tohs]
▶ a pair of pants unos pantalones [oo-nohs pan-ta-loh-nays]
▶ do you have a pair of scissors? ¿tiene unas tijeras? [tyen-ay oo-nas tiCH-air-as]

pants los pantalones [pan-ta-loh-nays]
▶ a pair of pants unos pantalones [oo-nohs pan-ta-loh-nays]
▶ there is a hole in these pants hay un agujero en estos pantalones [eye oon a-gooCH-air-oh en es-tohs pan-ta-loh-nays]

pantyhose la media [med-ya]
▶ I got a run in my pantyhose tengo una carrera en la media [ten-goh oo-na ka-RRair-a en la med-ya]

paper *(for writing on)* el papel [pa-pel]; *(newspaper)* el periódico [pair-yoh-di-koh]
◆ **papers** *(official documents)* los papeles [pa-pel-ays]
▶ a piece of paper un papel [oon pa-pel]
▶ here are my papers aquí están mis papeles [a-kee es-tan mees pa-pel-ays]

parasol la sombrilla [som-breel-ya]
▶ can you rent parasols? ¿se pueden alquilar sombrillas? [say pway-den al-ki-lahr som-breel-yas]

pardon *(forgiveness)* el perdón [pair-dohn] ◆ *(forgive)* perdonar [pair-doh-nahr]
▶ I beg your pardon? *(asking for repetition)* ¿cómo dice? [kom-oh dee-thay]
▶ I beg your pardon! *(to apologize)* ¡discúlpeme! [dis-kool-pay-may]; *(showing disagreement)* ¿cómo dice? [kom-oh dee-thay]
▶ pardon me? *(asking for repetition)* ¿cómo dice? [kom-oh dee-thay]
▶ pardon me! *(to get past)* ¡con permiso! [kon pair-mee-soh]; *(to apologize)* ¡discúlpeme! [dis-kool-pay-may]; *(showing disagreement)* ¿cómo dice? [kom-oh dee-thay]

park el parque [pahr-kay] ◆ aparcar [a-pahr-kahr]
▶ where's the park? ¿dónde está el parque? [don-day es-ta el pahr-kay]
▶ can we park our trailer here? ¿podemos aparcar aquí nuestra caravana? [pod-ay-mos a-pahr-kahr a-kee nwes-tra ka-ra-ba-na]
▶ am I allowed to park here? ¿se puede aparcar aquí? [say pway-day a-pahr-kahr a-kee]

parking el aparcamiento [a-pahr-kam-yen-toh]
▶ is there any parking near the hostel? ¿hay algún aparcamiento cerca del hotel? [eye al-goon a-pahr-kam-yen-toh thair-ka del oh-tel]

parking lot el parking [pahr-king]
▶ is there a parking lot nearby? ¿hay un parking por aquí cerca? [eye oon pahr-king por a-kee thair-ka]

parking space el aparcamiento [a-pahr-kam-yen-toh]
▶ is it easy to find a parking space in town? ¿es fácil encontrar aparcamiento en el centro? [es fa-theel en-kon-trahr a-pahr-kam-yen-toh en el then-troh]

part la parte [pahr-tay]
- what part of Spain are you from? ¿de qué parte de España eres? [day kay pahr-tay day es-pan-ya air-es]
- I've never been to this part of Spain before nunca había estado en esta parte de España [noon-ka a-bee-a es-tah-doh en es-ta pahr-tay day es-pan-ya]

party la fiesta [fyes-ta] ♦ estar de fiesta [es-tahr day fyes-ta]
- I'm planning a little party tomorrow estoy planeando una pequeña fiesta para mañana [es-toy plan-ay-an-doh oo-na pe-kayn-ya fyes-ta pa-ra man-yah-na]

pass (hand) pasar [pa-sahr]; (in a car) adelantar [a-de-lan-tahr]
- can you pass me the salt? ¿me podrías pasar la sal? [may pod-ree-as pa-sahr la sal]
- can you pass on this road? ¿se puede adelantar en esta carretera? [say pway-day a-de-lan-tahr en es-ta ka-RRe-tair-a]

passage (corridor) el pasillo [pa-seel-yoh]
- I heard someone outside in the passage oí a alguien en el pasillo [o-ee a alg-yen en el pa-seel-yoh]

passenger el pasajero [pa-saCH-air-oh], la pasajera [pa-saCH-air-a]
- is this where the passengers from the Barcelona flight arrive? ¿es aquí donde llegan los pasajeros del vuelo de Barcelona? [es a-kee don-day yay-gan los pa-saCH-air-ohs del bway-loh day bar-thel-oh-na]

passport el pasaporte [pa-sa-pawr-tay]
- I've lost my passport he perdido el pasaporte [ay pair-dee-doh el pa-sa-pawr-tay]
- I forgot my passport me olvidé el pasaporte [may ol-bi-day el pa-sa-pawr-tay]
- my passport has been stolen me han robado el pasaporte [may an RRo-bah-doh el pa-sa-pawr-tay]

past y [ee]
- twenty past twelve las doce y veinte [las doh-thay ee bayn-tay]

path (track) el camino [ka-mee-noh]
- is the path well-marked? ¿el camino está bien señalizado? [el ka-mee-noh es-ta byen sen-ya-li-thah-doh]

pay pagar [pa-gahr]
- do I have to pay a deposit? ¿tengo que pagar un depósito? [ten-goh kay pa-gahr oon de-po-si-toh]
- do you have to pay to get in? ¿hay que pagar para entrar? [eye kay pa-gahr pa-ra en-trahr]
- can you pay by credit card? ¿se puede pagar con tarjeta de crédito? [say pway-day pa-gahr kon tahr-CHay-ta day kre-di-toh]
- we're going to pay separately vamos a pagar por separado [bah-mos a pa-gahr por se-pa-rah-doh]

pay-per-view TV la televisión de pago [te-le-bis-yohn day pah-goh]
- is there pay-per-view TV in the room? ¿hay televisión de pago en la habitación? [eye te-le-bis-yohn day pah-goh en la a-bi-tath-yohn]

pay-per-view channel el canal de pago por visión [ka-nal day pah-goh por bees-yohn]
- are there any pay-per-view channels? ¿hay canales de pago por visión? [eye ka-nah-lays day pah-goh por bees-yohn]

pedestrian el peatón [pay-a-tohn] ♦ peatonal [pay-a-toh-nal]
- is this just a pedestrian street? ¿esta calle es sólo peatonal? [es-ta kal-yay es soh-loh pay-a-toh-nal]

pedestrian mall la zona peatonal [thoh-na pay-a-toh-nal]
- can you direct me to the pedestrian mall? ¿me podría decir cómo llegar a la zona peatonal? [may pod-ree-a de-theer kom-oh yay-gahr a la thoh-na pay-a-toh-nal]

pen el bolígrafo [bo-lee-gra-foh]
- can you lend me a pen? ¿me podría dejar un bolígrafo? [may pod-ree-a de-CHahr oon bo-lee-gra-foh]

pencil el lápiz [la-peeth]
- can you lend me a pencil? ¿me podría dejar un lápiz? [may pod-ree-a de-CHahr oon la-peeth]

penicillin la penicilina [pe-ni-thi-lee-na]
- I'm allergic to penicillin soy alérgico a la penicilina [soy a-lair-CHi-koh a la pe-ni-thi-lee-na]

pepper la pimienta [pim-yen-tah]
- pass the pepper, please pásame la pimienta, por favor [pa-sa-may la pim-yen-ta por fa-bor]

percent el porcentaje [por-then-ta-CHay]
- could you knock 10 percent off the price? ¿podría descontarme diez por ciento del precio? [pod-ree-a des-kon-tahr-may dyeth por thyen-toh del preth-yoh]

performance *(show)* la representación [RRe-pre-sen-tath-yohn]; *(in a movie theater)* la sesión [ses-yohn]
- what time does the performance begin? ¿a qué hora empieza la representación? [a kay aw-ra em-pyay-tha la RRe-pre-sen-tath-yohn]

perfume el perfume [pair-foo-may]
- how much is this perfume? ¿cuánto cuesta este perfume? [kwan-toh kwes-ta es-tay pair-foo-may]

perhaps quizás [ki-thas]
- perhaps you can help me? a lo mejor puede ayudarme [a loh me-CHor pway-day a-yoo-dahr-may]

person la persona [pair-soh-na]
- how much is it per hour and per person? ¿cuánto cuesta por hora y por persona? [kwan-toh kwes-ta por aw-ra ee por pair-soh-na]

pet el animal doméstico [a-ni-mal do-mes-ti-koh]
- are pets allowed? ¿se pueden llevar animales domésticos? [say pway-den yay-bahr a-ni-mah-lays do-mes-ti-kohs]

phone el teléfono [te-lay-fo-noh] ✦ llamar por teléfono [yam-ahr por te-lay-fo-noh]
▸ can I use the phone? ¿puedo usar el teléfono? [pway-doh oo-sahr el te-lay-fo-noh]

phone booth la cabina telefónica [ka-bee-na te-le-fo-ni-ka]
▸ is there a phone booth near here? ¿hay alguna cabina telefónica cerca de aquí? [eye al-goo-na ka-bee-na te-le-fo-ni-ka thair-ka day a-kee]

phone call la llamada telefónica [ya-mah-da te-le-fo-ni-ka]
▸ I'd like to make a phone call quería hacer una llamada telefónica [kair-ee-a a-thair oo-na ya-mah-da te-le-fo-ni-ka]

phonecard la tarjeta telefónica [tahr-CHay-ta te-le-fo-ni-ka]
▸ where can I buy a phonecard? ¿dónde puedo comprar una tarjeta telefónica? [don-day pway-doh kom-prahr oo-na tahr-CHay-ta te-le-fo-ni-ka]

photo la foto [foh-toh]
▸ can I take photos in here? ¿se pueden hacer fotos aquí? [say pway-den a-thair foh-tos a-kee]
▸ could you take a photo of us? ¿podría hacernos una foto? [pod-ree-a a-thair-nos oo-na foh-toh]
▸ I'd like copies of some photos quería copias de algunas fotos [kair-ee-a kop-yas day al-goo-nas foh-tohs]

photography la fotografía [foh-toh-gra-fee-a]
▸ is photography allowed in the museum? ¿se pueden hacer fotos en el museo? [say pway-den a-thair foh-tohs en el moo-say-oh]

picnic el picnic [peek-neek]
▸ could we go for a picnic by the river? ¿podríamos hacer un picnic al lado del río? [pod-ree-a-mos a-thair oon peek-neek al lah-doh del RRee-oh]

---

on the phone

▸ hello? ¿diga? [dee-ga]
▸ Ted Stewart speaking soy Ted Stewart [soy ted es-tee-wahrt]
▸ I'd like to speak to Mr. Adams quería hablar con el Sr Adams [kair-ee-a ab-lahr kon el sen-yawr a-dams]
▸ hold the line espere un momento [es-pair-ay oon mo-men-toh]
▸ can you call back in ten minutes? ¿podría volver a llamar dentro de diez minutos? [pod-ree-a bol-bair a yam-ahr den-troh day dyeth mi-noo-tohs]
▸ would you like to leave a message? ¿quiere dejar un mensaje? [kyair-ay de-CHahr oon men-sa-CHay]
▸ you have the wrong number se ha equivocado de número [say a e-ki-bo-kah-doh day noo-mair-oh]

piece el trozo [tro-thoh]
- a piece of cake, please un trozo de pastel, por favor [oon tro-thoh day pas-tel por fa-bor]
- a piece of advice un consejo [oon kon-say-CHoh]
- a piece of news una noticia [oo-na no-teeth-ya]

pill la pastilla [pas-teel-ya]
- a bottle of pills un frasco de pastillas [oon fras-koh day pas-teel-yas]
- the Pill *(contraceptive)* la píldora [la peel-do-ra]

pillow la almohada [al-moh-ah-da]
- could I have another pillow? ¿me podrían dar otra almohada? [may pod-ree-an dahr oh-tra al-moh-ah-da]

pizza la pizza [peet-sa]
- I'd like a large mushroom pizza quería una pizza grande de setas [kair-ee-a oo-na peet-sa gran-day day say-tas]

place *(area)* el lugar [loo-gahr]; *(house)* la casa [ka-sa]; *(seat)* el sitio [seet-yoh]; *(place setting)* el cubierto [koob-yair-toh]
- can you recommend a nice place to eat? ¿me podría recomendar un lugar agradable para comer? [may pod-ree-a RRe-ko-men-dahr oon loo-gahr ag-ra-dah-blay pa-ra kom-air]
- do you want to change places with me? ¿quieres cambiar de sitio conmigo? [kyair-es kamb-yahr day seet-yoh kon-mee-goh]

plain natural [na-too-ral]
- do you have any plain yogurt? ¿tiene yogurt natural? [tyen-ay yo-goor na-too-ral]

plan el plan [plan] ◆ planear [pla-nay-ahr]
- do you have plans for tonight? ¿tienes planes para esta noche? [tyen-es pla-nays pa-ra es-ta no-chay]
- I'm planning to stay for just one night estoy planeando quedarme una sola noche [es-toy plan-ay-an-doh kay-dahr-may oo-na soh-la no-chay]

plane el avión [ab-yohn]
- which gate does the plane depart from? ¿de qué puerta sale el avión? [day kay pwair-ta sa-lay el ab-yohn]
- when's the next plane to Palma? ¿cuándo es el próximo avión a Palma? [kwan-doh es el pro-si-moh ab-yohn a pal-ma]

plate el plato [pla-toh]
- this plate's got a crack in it este plato tiene una raja [es-tay pla-toh tyen-ay oo-na RRa-CHa]

platform *(at a station)* el andén [an-dayn]
- which platform does the train leave from? ¿de qué andén sale el tren? [day kay an-dayn sa-lay el tren]

play *(at a theater)* la obra [oh-bra] ◆ *(sport, game)* jugar [CHoo-gahr]; *(instrument, music)* tocar [toh-kar]

police

Officers of the *policía nacional*, dressed in navy blue, will take care of any problems you may have in terms of losing something or having something stolen. Don't mix them up with the *policía local*, who also wear blue but who take care of traffic and neighborhood problems. In rural areas, go to the officers of the *Guardia Civil*, in their dark green uniforms.

▸ do you play tennis? ¿juegas al tenis? [CHway-gas al te-nees]
▸ I play the cello toco el violonchelo [to-koh el bee-o-lon-chay-loh]

playroom el cuarto de juegos [kwahr-toh day CHway-gohs]
▸ is there a children's playroom here? ¿aquí hay un cuarto de juegos infantil? [a-kee eye oon kwahr-toh day CHway-gohs in-fan-teel]

please por favor [por fa-bor]
▸ please sit down siéntate, por favor [syen-ta-tay por fa-bor]
▸ can I come in? – please do ¿puedo entrar? – por favor [pway-doh en-trahr – por fa-bor]

pleased contento(ta) [kon-ten-toh]
▸ pleased to meet you encantado de conocerle [en-kan-tah-doh day ko-noth-air-lay]

pleasure el placer [pla-thair]
▸ with pleasure! ¡con mucho gusto! [kon moo-choh goos-toh]
▸ it's a pleasure ¡no hay de qué! [noh eye day kay]

plug *(on electrical equipment)* el enchufe [en-choo-fay]
▸ where can I find an adaptor for the plug on my hairdryer? ¿dónde puedo encontrar un adaptador para el enchufe de mi secador? [don-day pway-doh en-kon-trahr oon a-dap-ta-dawr pa-ra el en-choo-fay day mee se-ka-dawr]

plug in enchufar [en-choo-fahr]
▸ can I plug my cellphone in here to recharge it? ¿puedo enchufar mi móvil aquí para cargarlo? [pway-doh en-choo-fahr mi mob-eel a-kee pa-ra kahr-gahr-loh]

point *(moment)* el momento [mo-men-toh]; *(spot, location)* el punto [poon-toh]
♦ *(direct)* dirigir [di-ri-CHeer]
▸ points of the compass puntos cardinales [poon-tohs kar-di-nah-lays]
▸ can you point me in the direction of the freeway? ¿podría indicarme la dirección de la autopista? [pod-ree-a in-di-kahr-may la di-rekth-yohn day la ow-to-pees-ta]

police la policía [po-li-thee-a]
▸ call the police! ¡llama a la policía! [yah-ma a la po-li-thee-a]
▸ what's the number for the police? ¿cuál es el número de la policía? [kwal es el noo-mair-oh day la po-li-thee-a]

police station la comisaría de policía [ko-mi-sa-ree-a day po-li-thee-a]
> where is the nearest police station? ¿dónde está la comisaría de policía más cercana? [don-day es-ta la ko-mi-sa-ree-a day po-li-thee-a mas thair-kah-na]

pool *(for swimming)* la piscina [pis-thee-na]
> main pool piscina principal [pis-thee-na prin-thi-pal]
> children's pool piscina infantil [pis-thee-na in-fan-teel]
> is the pool heated? ¿es una piscina climatizada? [es oo-na pis-thee-na clee-ma-ti-thah-da]
> is there an indoor pool? ¿hay una piscina cubierta? [eye oo-na pis-thee-na koob-yair-ta]

pork la carne de cerdo [kahr-nay day thair-doh]
> I don't eat pork no como carne de cerdo [noh kom-oh kahr-nay day thair-doh]

portable portátil [por-ta-teel]
> do you have a portable heater we could borrow? ¿tiene un calefactor portátil que nos pudiera dejar? [tyen-ay oon ka-le-fak-tawr por-ta-teel kay nos pood-yair-a de-CHahr]

portion la ración [RRath-yohn]
> the portions at that restaurant are just right las raciones en ese restaurante son perfectas [las RRath-yoh-nays day e-say RRes-tow-ran-tay son pair-fek-tas]

possible posible [po-see-blay]
> without sauce, if possible sin salsa, si es posible [seen sal-sa see es po-see-blay]

postcard la postal [pos-tal]
> where can I buy postcards? ¿dónde puedo comprar postales? [don-day pway-doh kom-prahr pos-tah-lays]
> how much are stamps for postcards to the States? ¿cuánto cuestan los sellos para los Estados Unidos? [kwan-toh kwes-tan los sel-yohs pa-ra los es-tah-dohs oo-nee-dohs]

post office la oficina de correos [o-fi-thee-na day ko-RRay-ohs]
> where is the nearest post office? ¿dónde está la oficina de correos más cercana? [don-day es-ta la o-fi-thee-na day ko-RRay-ohs mas thair-kah-na]

power *(electricity)* la electricidad [e-lek-tri-thi-dad]
> there's no power no hay electricidad [noh eye e-lek-tri-thi-dad]

power failure el corte de corriente [kor-tay day koRR-yen-tay]
> there's a power failure ha habido un corte de corriente [a a-bee-doh oon kor-tay day koRR-yen-tay]
> how long is the power failure expected to last? ¿cuánto se espera que dure el corte de corriente? [kwan-toh say es-pair-a kay doo-ray el kor-tay day koRR-yen-tay]

prawn la gamba [gam-ba]
> I'd like to try a dish with prawns quería un plato con gambas [kair-ee-a oon pla-toh kon gam-bas]

prefer preferir [pre-fair-eer]

▸ I'd prefer black tea **prefiero el té solo** [pref-yair-oh el tay soh-loh]

▸ I'd prefer you not smoke **preferiría que no fumaras** [pre-fair-i-ree-a kay noh foo-mah-ras]

prescription *(medicine)* **la receta** [RRe-thay-ta]

▸ is it only available by prescription? **¿sólo se puede comprar con receta?** [soh-loh say pway-day kom-prahr kon RRe-thay-ta]

present **el regalo** [RRe-gah-loh]

▸ where can we buy presents around here? **¿dónde podemos comprar regalos por aquí?** [don-day pod-ay-mos kom-prahr RRe-gah-lohs por a-kee]

pretty **bonito(ta)** [bo-nee-toh]

▸ she's a very pretty girl **es una chica muy bonita** [es oo-na chee-ka mwee bo-nee-ta]

price *(cost)* **el precio** [preth-yoh]

▸ what's the price of gas today? **¿cuál es el precio de la gasolina hoy?** [kwal es el preth-yoh day la ga-so-lee-na oy]

▸ if the price is right **si el precio fuera bueno** [see el preth-yoh fwair-a bway-noh]

price list **la lista de precios** [lees-ta day preth-yohs]

▸ do you have a price list? **¿tiene una lista de precios?** [tyen-ay oo-na lees-ta day preth-yohs]

print *(photograph)* **la copia** [kop-ya]

▸ could I have another set of prints? **quería otro juego de copias** [kair-ee-a oh-troh CHway-goh day kop-yas]

private *(not public)* **particular** [pahr-ti-koo-lahr]; *(personal)* **personal** [pair-so-nal]

▸ is it a private beach? **¿es una playa particular?** [es oo-na pleye-a pahr-ti-koo-lahr]

problem **el problema** [prob-lay-ma]

▸ there's a problem with the central heating **la calefacción central tiene algún problema** [la ka-lay-fakth-yohn tyen-ay al-goon prob-lay-ma]

▸ no problem **no hay problema** [noh eye prob-lay-ma]

program *(for an event)* **el programa** [proh-gra-ma]

▸ could I see a program? **¿podría ver un programa?** [pod-ree-a bair oon proh-gra-ma]

---

expressing a preference

▸ I prefer red wine to white wine **prefiero el vino tinto al blanco** [pref-yair-oh el bee-noh teen-toh al blan-koh]

▸ I'd rather fly than go by train **prefiero volar a ir en tren** [pref-yair-oh bo-lahr a eer en tren]

▸ Saturday would suit me better **el sábado me vendría mejor** [el sa-ba-doh may ben-dree-a me-CHor]

pronounce *(word)* pronunciar [pro-noonth-yahr]
> how is that pronounced? ¿cómo se pronuncia? [kom-oh say pro-noonth-ya]

public público(ca) [poob-li-koh] ◆ el público [poob-li-koh]
> let's go somewhere less public vamos a un lugar menos público [bah-mos a oon loo-gahr may-nos poob-li-koh]
> is the castle open to the public? ¿el castillo está abierto al público? [el kas-teel-yoh es-ta ab-yair-toh al poob-li-koh]

public holiday el día festivo [dee-a fes-tee-boh]
> is tomorrow a public holiday? ¿mañana es un día festivo? [man-yah-na es fes-tee-boh]

public transportation el transporte público [trans-por-tay poo-bli-koh]
> can you get there by public transportation? ¿se puede llegar usando el transporte público? [say pway-day yay-gahr oo-san-doh el trans-por-tay poo-bli-koh]

pull *(muscle)* desgarrar [des-ga-RRahr]; *(tooth)* arrancar [a-RRan-kahr]
> I've pulled a muscle me he desgarrado un músculo [may he des-ga-RRah-doh oon moos-koo-loh]

puncture pinchar [pin-chahr]
> the tire's been punctured hemos pinchado [ay-mos pin-chah-doh]

purpose el propósito [pro-po-si-toh] ◆ **on purpose** a propósito [a pro-po-si-toh]
> sorry, I didn't do it on purpose perdón, no lo hice a propósito [pair-dohn noh loh ee-thay a pro-po-si-toh]

purse *(handbag)* el bolso [bol-soh]; *(change purse)* el monedero [mo-ne-dair-oh]
> my purse was stolen me robaron el bolso [may RRo-bah-ron el bol-soh]

push empujar [em-poo-CHahr]
> can you help us push the car? ¿nos podría ayudar a empujar el coche? [nos pod-ree-a a-yoo-dahr a em-poo-CHahr el ko-chay]

put *(into place, position)* poner [pon-air]
> is there somewhere I can put my bags? ¿hay algún lugar dónde pueda poner las bolsas? [eye al-goon loo-gahr don-day pway-da pon-air las bol-sas]

put down *(set down)* dejar [de-CHahr]
> can we put our things down in the corner? ¿podemos dejar nuestras cosas en el rincón? [pod-ay-mos de-CHahr nwes-tras koh-sas en el RRin-kohn]

put on *(clothes)* ponerse [pon-air-say]; *(TV, radio, heating)* encender [en-then-dair]
> can you put the heat on? ¿puedes encender la calefacción? [pway-days en-then-dair la ka-le-fakth-yohn]
> can you put Mrs. Martin on, please? ¿me podría poner con la señora Martin, por favor? [may pod-ree-a pon-air kon la sen-yaw-ra mahr-tin por fa-bor]

put out *(cigarette, fire)* apagar [a-pa-gahr]
> can you please put your cigarette out? ¿podría apagar el cigarrillo, por favor? [pod-ree-a a-pa-gahr el thi-ga-RReel-yoh por fa-bor]

put up *(erect)* montar [mon-tahr]; *(provide accommodations for)* alojar [a-lo-CHahr]
▸ can we put up our tent here? ¿podemos montar la tienda aquí? [pod-ay-mos mon-tahr la tyen-da a-kee]

q

quarter *(fourth)* el cuarto [kwahr-toh]
▸ I'll be back in a quarter of an hour volveré dentro de un cuarto de hora [bol-bair-ay den-troh day oon kwahr-toh day aw-ra]
▸ a quarter past/after one la una y cuarto [la oo-na ee kwahr-toh]
▸ a quarter to/of one la una menos cuarto [la oo-na may-nos kwahr-toh]

quay el muelle [mwel-yay]
▸ is the boat at the quay? ¿el barco está en el muelle? [el bahr-koh es-ta en el mwel-yay]

question la pregunta [pre-goon-ta]
▸ can I ask you a question? ¿te puedo hacer una pregunta? [tay pway-doh a-thair oo-na pre-goon-ta]

quickly rápido [RRa-pi-doh]
▸ everyone speaks so quickly todo el mundo habla tan rápido [toh-doh el moon-doh ab-la tan RRa-pi-doh]

quiet tranquilo(la) [tran-kee-loh]
▸ is it a quiet beach? ¿es una playa tranquila? [es oo-na pleye-a tran-kee-la]
▸ do you have anything quieter? ¿tiene algo más tranquilo? [tyen-ay al-goh mas tran-kee-loh]

quite *(rather)* bastante [bas-tan-tay]
▸ it's quite expensive around here las cosas están bastante caras por aquí [las koh-sas es-tan bas-tan-tay kah-ras por a-kee]

racket *(for tennis)* la raqueta [RRa-kay-ta]
▸ can you rent rackets? ¿alquilan raquetas? [al-kee-lan RRa-kay-tas]

radiator el radiador [RRad-ya-dawr]
▸ the radiator's leaking el radiador tiene un escape [el RRad-ya-dawr tyen-ay oon es-ka-pay]

radio *(set)* la radio [RRad-yoh]
‣ the radio doesn't work la radio no funciona [la RRad-yoh noh foonth-yoh-na]

radio station la emisora de radio [e-mi-saw-ra day RRad-yoh]
‣ can you get any English-language radio stations here? ¿aquí se coge alguna emisora de radio en inglés? [a-kee say coCH-ay al-goo-na e-mi-saw-ra day RRad-yoh en in-glays]

railroad *(system, organization)* el ferrocarril [fe-RRo-ka-RReel]; *(track)* la vía férrea [bee-a fe-RRay-a]
‣ what region does this railroad cover? ¿qué región cubre este ferrocarril? [kay RReCH-yohn koo-bray es-tay fe-RRo-ka-RReel]

rain llover [yo-bair]
‣ it's raining está lloviendo [es-ta yob-yen-doh]

random
‣ at random al azar [al a-thahr]

rare *(meat)* muy poco hecho(cha) [mwee poh-koh e-choh]
‣ rare, please muy poco hecho, por favor [mwee poh-koh e-choh por fa-bor]

rate *(price)* la tarifa [ta-ree-fa]
‣ what's your daily rate? ¿cuál es su tarifa diaria? [kwal es soo ta-ree-fa dee-ahr-ya]

rate of exchange el tipo de cambio [tee-poh day kamb-yoh]
‣ they offer a good rate of exchange ofrecen un buen tipo de cambio [of-reth-en oon bwen tee-poh day kamb-yoh]

razor la maquinilla de afeitar [ma-ki-neel-ya day a-fay-tahr]
‣ where can I buy a new razor? ¿dónde puedo comprar una maquinilla de afeitar? [don-day pway-doh kom-prahr oo-na ma-ki-neel-ya day a-fay-tahr]

razor blade la cuchilla de afeitar [koo-cheel-ya day a-fay-tahr]
‣ I need to buy some razor blades necesito comprar cuchillas de afeitar [ne-thes-ee-toh comprahr koo-cheel-yas day a-fay-tahr]

ready *(prepared)* listo(ta) [lees-toh]; *(willing)* dispuesto(ta) [dis-pwes-toh]
‣ when will it be ready? ¿cuándo estará listo? [kwan-doh es-ta-ra lees-toh]

really *(actually)* de verdad [day bair-dad]; *(very)* realmente [RRay-al-men-tay]
‣ really? ¿de verdad? [day bair-dad]

rear *(of a train)* la parte trasera [pahr-tay tra-sair-a]
‣ your seats are in the rear of the train sus asientos están en la parte trasera del tren [soos as-yen-tohs es-tan en la pahr-tay tra-sair-a]

receipt el recibo [RRe-thee-boh]
‣ can I have a receipt, please? quería un recibo, por favor [kair-ee-a oon RRe-thee-boh por fa-bor]

receive *(package, letter)* recibir [RRe-thi-beer]
‣ I should have received the package this morning debería haber recibido el paquete esta mañana [de-bair-ee-a a-bair RRe-thi-beee-doh el pa-kay-tay es-ta man-yah-na]

reception *(welcome)* el recibimiento [RRe-thi-bim-yen-toh]; *(party)* la recepción [RRe-thepyh-yohn]; *(for TV or radio)* la recepción [RRe-thepyh-yohn]; *(for a cellphone)* la cobertura [ko-bair-too-ra]
  ▶ there's no reception no hay cobertura [noh eye ko-bair-too-ra]
  ▶ I'm looking for the Mackenzie wedding reception busco el banquete de boda de los Mackenzie [boos-koh el ban-kay-tay day boh-da day los ma-ken-si]

reception desk *(at hotel)* la recepción [RRe-thepyh-yohn]
  ▶ can I leave my backpack at the reception desk? ¿puedo dejar la mochila en recepción? [pway-doh de-CHAhr la mo-chee-la en RRe-thepyh-yohn]

recline reclinar [RRe-kli-nahr]
  ▶ do you mind if I recline my seat? ¿le importa si reclino el asiento? [lay im-por-ta see RRe-klee-noh mee a-yen-toh]

recommend recomendar [RRe-ko-men-dahr]
  ▶ could you recommend another hotel? ¿me podría recomendar otro hotel? [may pod-ree-a RRe-ko-men-dahr oh-troh oh-tel]
  ▶ could you recommend a restaurant? ¿me podría recomendar un restaurante? [may pod-ree-a RRe-ko-men-dahr oon RRes-tow-ran-tay]
  ▶ what do you recommend? ¿que recomendaría? [kay RRe-ko-men-da-ree-a]

record store la tienda de discos [tyen-da day dees-kohs]
  ▶ I'm looking for a record store estoy buscando una tienda de discos [es-toy boos-kan-doh oo-na tyen-da day dees-kohs]

rec center, recreation center el centro recreativo [then-troh RRek-ray-a-tee-boh]
  ▶ what kinds of activities does the recreation center offer? ¿qué tipo de actividades ofrece el centro recreativo? [kay tee-poh day ak-ti-bi-dah-days of-reth-ay el then-troh RRek-ray-a-tee-boh]

red *(dress)* rojo(ja) [RRo-CHOh]; *(hair)* pelirrojo(ja) [pe-li-RRO-CHOh] ◆ *(color)* el rojo [RRo-CHOh]; *(wine)* el tinto [teen-toh]
  ▶ dressed in red de rojo [day RRo-CHOh]
  ▶ what kinds of red wine do you have? ¿qué tipos de tinto tienen? [kay tee-pohs day teen-toh tyen-en]

redhead el pelirrojo [pe-li-RRo-CHOh], la pelirroja [pe-li-RRo-CHa]
  ▶ a tall redhead wearing glasses una pelirroja alta con gafas [oo-na pi-li-RRo-CHa al-ta kon ga-fas]

red light el semáforo en rojo [se-ma-fo-roh en RRo-CHOh]
  ▶ you failed to stop at a red light te saltaste un semáforo en rojo [tay sal-tas-tay oon se-ma-fo-roh en RRo-CHOh]

reduced *(price, rate)* reducido(da) [RRe-doo-thee-doh]
  ▶ is there a reduced rate for students? ¿hay una tarifa reducida para estudiantes? [eye oo-na ta-ree-fa RRe-doo-thee-da pa-ra es-tood-yan-tays]

reduced-price *(ticket)* a precio reducido [a preth-yoh RRe-doo-thee-doh]
  ▶ two reduced-price tickets and one full-price dos entradas a precio reducido y

una a precio normal [dos en-trah-das a preth-yoh RRe-doo-thee-doh ee oo-na a preth-yoh nor-mal]

reduction el descuento [des-kwen-toh]

▶ do you have reductions for groups? ¿tienen descuentos para grupos? [tyen-en des-kwen-tohs pa-ra groo-pohs]

red wine el vino tinto [bee-noh teen-toh]

▶ a bottle of red wine una botella de vinto tinto [oo-na bo-tel-ya day bee-noh teen-toh]

refresher course el cursillo de reciclaje [koor-seel-yoh day RRe-thi-kla-CHay]

▶ I need a refresher course necesito un cursillo de reciclaje [ne-thes-ee-toh oon koor-seel-yoh day RRe-thi-kla-CHay]

refuge *(for animals)* el refugio [RRe-fooCH-yoh]

▶ we'd like to visit the wildlife refuge nos gustaría visitar la reserva animal [nos goos-ta-ree-a bi-si-tahr la re-sair-ba a-ni-mal]

refundable reembolsable [RRay-em-bol-sah-blay]

▶ are the tickets refundable? ¿las entradas son reembolsables? [las en-trah-das son RRay-em-bol-sah-blays]

regards los saludos [sa-loo-dohs] ◆ **with regard to** con respecto a [kon RRes-pek-toh a]

▶ give my regards to your parents! ¡saluda a tus padres de mi parte! [sa-loo-da a toos pad-rays day mee paahr-tay]

▶ I'm calling you with regard to ... llamo con respecto a ... [yah-moh kon RRes-pek-toh a]

region la región [RReCH-yohn]

▶ in the northern region of the country en la región norte del país [en la RReCH-yohn nor-tay del pa-ees]

registered mail el correo certificado [ko-RRay-oh thair-ti-fi-kah-doh]

▶ I would like to send a letter by registered mail quería enviar una carta por correo certificado [kair-ee-a emb-yahr oo-na kahr-ta por ko-RRay-oh thair-ti-fi-kah-doh]

registration *(of vehicle)* el permiso de circulación [pair-mee-soh day theer-koo-lath-yohn]

▶ here's the car's registration aquí tiene el permiso de circulación [a-kee tyen-ay el pair-mee-soh day theer-koo-lath-yohn]

relative el pariente [pahr-yen-tay], la pariente [pahr-yen-tay]

▶ I have relatives in Galicia tengo parientes en Galicia [ten-goh pahr-yen-tays en ga-leeth-ya]

remember recordar [RRe-kor-dahr], acordarse de [a-kor-dahr-say day]

▶ do you remember me? ¿te acuerdas de mí? [tay a-kwair-das day mee]

▶ I can't remember his name no recuerdo su nombre [noh RRe-kwair-doh soo nom-bray]

remote (control) el mando a distancia [man-doh a dis-tanth-ya]
▶ I can't find the remote for the TV no encuentro el mando a distancia de la tele [noh en-kwen-troh el man-doh a dis-tanth-ya day la tay-lay]

rent el alquiler [al-ki-lair] ◆ alquilar [al-ki-lahr]
▶ how much is the rent per week? ¿cuánto cuesta el alquiler por semana? [kwan-toh kwes-ta el al-ki-lair por se-mah-na]
▶ I'd like to rent a car for a week me gustaría alquilar un coche una semana [may goos-ta-ree-a al-ki-lahr oon ko-chay oo-na se-mah-na]
▶ I'd like to rent a boat me gustaría alquilar un barco [may goos-ta-ree-a al-ki-lahr oon bahr-koh]
▶ does it work out cheaper to rent the equipment by the week? ¿sale más barato alquilar el equipo por semanas? [sa-lay mas ba-ra-toh al-ki-lahr el e-kee-poh por se-mah-nas]

rental (renting) el alquiler [al-ki-lair]; (apartment) el apartamento alquilado [a-pahr-ta-men-toh al-ki-lah-doh]; (house) la casa alquilada [ka-sa al-ki-lah-da]; (car) el coche alquilado [ko-chay al-ki-lah-doh]
▶ we have the rental for two weeks tenemos el coche alquilado dos semanas [ten-ay-mos el ko-chay al-ki-lah-doh dos se-mah-nas]

repair la reparación [RRe-pa-rath-yohn] ◆ reparar [RRe-pa-rahr]
▶ will you be able to make the repairs today? ¿podrá hacer las reparaciones hoy? [pod-ra a-thair las RRe-pa-rath-yoh-nays oy]
▶ how long will it take to repair? ¿cuánto tardará en repararlo? [kwan-toh tahr-da-ra en RRe-pa-rahr-loh]

repeat repetir [RRe-pe-teer]
▶ can you repeat that, please? ¿podría repetir eso, por favor? [pod-ree-a RRe-pe-teer e-soh por fa-bor]

report (theft) denunciar [de-noonth-yahr]
▶ I'd like to report something stolen quería denunciar un robo [kair-ee-a de-noonth-yahr oon RRoh-boh]
▶ I'd like to report the loss of my credit cards quería denunciar la pérdida de mis tarjetas de crédito [kair-ee-a de-noonth-yahr la pair-di-da day mees tahr-CHay-tas day kre-di-toh]

reservation la reserva [RRe-sair-ba]
▶ do you have to make a reservation? ¿hay que hacer reserva? [eye kay a-thair RRe-sair-ba]
▶ I have a reservation in the name of Gordon tengo una reserva a nombre de Gordon [ten-goh oo-na RRe-sair-ba a nom-bray day gor-don]

reserve (ticket, room) reservar [RRe-sair-bahr]
▶ hello, I'd like to reserve a table for two for tomorrow night at 8 hola, quería reservar una mesa para dos para mañana a las ocho de la noche [oh-la kair-ee-a RRe-sair-bahr oo-na may-sa pa-ra dos pa-ra man-yah-na a las o-choh day la no-chay]

reserved *(booked)* reservado(da) [RRe-sair-bah-doh]
- is this table reserved? ¿esta mesa está reservada? [es-ta may-sa es-ta RRe-sair-bah-da]

rest *(relaxation)* el descanso [des-kan-soh] ♦ *(relax)* descansar [des-kan-sahr]
- I've come here to get some rest he venido a aquí a descansar [ay be-nee-doh a-kee a des-kan-sahr]

restaurant el restaurante [RRes-tow-ran-tay]
- are there any good restaurants around here? ¿hay algún restaurante bueno por aquí cerca? [eye al-goon RRes-tow-ran-tay bway-noh por a-kee thair-ka]

restriction la restricción [RRes-treekth-yohn]
- are there restrictions on how much luggage you can take? ¿hay alguna restricción en cuanto a la cantidad de equipaje que se puede llevar? [eye al-goo-na RRes-treekth-yohn en kwan-toh a la kan-ti-dad day e-ki-pa-CHay kay say pway-day yay-bahr]

restroom el aseo [a-say-oh]
- is there a restroom on the bus? ¿hay un aseo en el autobús? [eye oon a-say-oh en el ow-toh-boos]

retired jubilado(da) [CHoo-bi-lah-doh]
- I'm retired now ahora estoy jubilado [a-aw-ra es-toy CHoo-bi-lah-doh]

return *(arrival back)* la vuelta [bwel-ta] ♦ devolver [day-bol-bair]
- when do we have to return the car? ¿cuándo tenemos que devolver el coche? [kwan-doh ten-ay-mos kay day-bol-bair el ko-chay]

return trip el viaje de vuelta [bya-CHay day bwel-ta]
- the return trip is scheduled for 6 o'clock el viaje de vuelta está programado a las seis [el bya-CHay day bwel-ta es-ta pro-gra-mah-doh a las seys]

rice el arroz [a-RRoth]
- I'd like some rice, please quería arroz, por favor [kair-ee-a a-RRoth por fa-bor]

ride el paseo [pa-say-oh]
- do you want a ride? ¿quieres que te lleve? [kyair-ays kay tay yay-bay]
- where can we go for a ride around here? ¿por dónde podemos dar un paseo en la zona? [por don-day pod-ay-mos dahr oon pa-say-oh en la thoh-na]

---

at a restaurant

- I'd like to reserve a table for tonight quería reservar una mesa para esta noche [kair-ee-a RRe-sair-bahr oo-na may-sa pa-ra es-ta no-chay]
- can we see the menu? ¿podemos ver el menú? [pod-ay-mos bair el men-oo]
- do you have a set menu? ¿tienen menú del día? [tyen-en men-oo del dee-a]
- rare/medium/well done, please muy poco hecho/poco hecho/pasado, por favor [mwee poh-koh e-choh/poh-koh e-choh/pa-sah-doh por fa-bor]
- can I have the check, please? la cuenta, por favor [la kwen-ta por fa-bor]

riding *(on horseback)* la equitación [e-ki-tath-yohn]
- to go riding ir a montar a caballo [eer a mon-tahr a ka-bal-yoh]

right *(correct)* correcto(ta) [ko-RRek-toh]; *(not left)* derecho(cha) [de-re-choh] ◆ la derecha [de-re-cha] ◆ directamente [di-rek-ta-men-tay]
- to the right (of) a la derecha (de) [a la de-re-cha]
- that's right eso es [e-soh es]
- I don't think the check's right me parece que la cuenta no está correcta [may pa-re-thay kay la kwen-ta noh es-ta ko-RRek-ta]
- is this the right train for Irún? ¿es este el tren de Irún? [es es-tay el tren day i-roon]
- is this the right number? ¿es este el número correcto? [es es-tay el noo-mair-oh ko-RRek-toh]
- take the next right gire a la derecha en la próxima [CHee-ray a la de-re-cha en la prok-si-ma]
- you have to turn right tiene que girar a la derecha [tyen-ay kay CHi-rahr a la de-re-cha]

right-hand a la derecha [a la de-re-cha]
- it's on the right-hand side of the steering column está a la derecha de la columna de dirección [es-ta a la de-re-cha day la ko-loom-na day di-rekth-yohn]

right of way la preferencia [pre-fair-enth-ya]
- who has the right of way here? ¿quién tiene preferencia aquí? [kyen tyen-ay pre-fair-enth-ya a-kee]

road la carretera [ka-RRe-tair-a]
- which road do I take for Madrid? ¿qué carretera cojo para ir a Madrid? [kay ka-RRe-tair-a koCH-oh pa-ra eer a mad-reed]
- what is the speed limit on this road? ¿cuál es el límite de velocidad en esta carretera? [kwal es el lee-mi-tay day be-lo-thi-dad en es-ta ka-RRe-tair-a]

rob *(person)* robar [RRo-bahr]
- I've been robbed me han robado [may an RRo-bah-doh]

rock climbing la escalada en roca [es-ka-lah-da en RRoh-ka]
- can you go rock climbing here? ¿se puede hacer escalada en roca aquí? [say pway-day a-thair es-ka-lah-da en RRoh-ka a-kee]

roller skate el patín (de ruedas) [pa-teen (day RRoo-ay-das)]
- where can we rent roller skates? ¿dónde podemos alquilar patines (de ruedas)? [don-day pod-ay-mos al-ki-lahr pa-tee-nays (day RRoo-ay-das)]

room *(bedroom)* el cuarto [kwahr-toh]; *(in a house, building)* la habitación [a-bi-tath-yohn]; *(space)* el espacio [es-path-yoh], el sitio [seet-yoh]
- do you have any rooms available? ¿tienen habitaciones? [tyen-en a-bi-tath-yoh-nays]
- how much is a room with a bathroom? ¿cuánto cuesta la habitación con baño? [kwan-toh kwes-ta la a-bi-tath-yohn kon ban-yoh]
- I've reserved a room for tonight under the name Pearson he reservado una habitación para esta noche a nombre de Pearson [ay RRe-sair-bah-doh oo-na a-bi-tath-yohn pa-ra es-ta no-chay a nom-bray day pay-ahr-son]

r ro

▶ can I see the room? ¿puedo ver la habitación? [pway-doh bair la a-bi-tath-yohn]

rosé *(wine)* rosado(da) [RRo-sah-doh] ♦ el rosado [RRo-sah-doh]

▶ could you recommend a good rosé? ¿podría recomendar un buen rosado? [pod-ree-a RRe-ko-men-dahr oon bwen RRo-sah-doh]

round trip el viaje de ida y vuelta [bya-CHay day ee-da ee bwel-ta]

▶ how long will the round trip take? ¿cuánto llevará el viaje de ida y vuelta? [kwan-toh yay-ba-ra el bya-CHay day ee-da ee bwel-ta]

round-trip ticket el billete de ida y vuelta [bil-yay-tay day ee-da ee bwel-ta]

▶ two round-trip tickets to Madrid, please dos billetes de ida y vuelta a Madrid, por favor [dos bil-yay-tays day ee-da ee bwel-ta a mad-reed por fa-bor]

▶ I'd like a round-trip ticket to Alicante, leaving on the 3rd and coming back on the 9th quería un billete de ida y vuelta a Alicante, saliendo el día tres y volviendo el día nueve [kair-ee-a oon bil-yay-tay day ee-da ee bwel-ta a a-li-kan-tay sal-yen-doh el dee-a tres ee bolb-yen-doh el dee-a nway-bay]

▶ a round-trip ticket for one car, two adults and two children, please un billete de ida y vuelta para un coche, dos adultos y dos niños, por favor [oon bil-yay-tay day ee-da ee bwel-ta pa-ra oon ko-chay dos a-dool-tohs ee dos noon-yohs por fa-bor]

route la ruta [RRoo-ta]

▶ is there an alternative route we could take? ¿hay alguna ruta alternativa que pudiéramos tomar? [eye al-goo-na RRoo-ta al-tair-na-tee-ba kay pood-yair-a-mos tom-ahr]

row *(of seats)* la fila [fee-la]

▶ can we have seats in the front row? ¿nos puede dar asientos en la primera fila? [nos pway-day dahr as-yen-tohs en la pri-mair-a fee-la]

rowboat el bote de remos [boh-tay day ray-mohs]

▶ can we rent a rowboat? ¿podemos alquilar un bote de remos? [pod-ay-mos al-ki-lahr oon boh-tay day ray-mohs]

rubber ring el flotador [floh-ta-dawr]

▶ where can I buy a rubber ring? ¿dónde puedo comprar un flotador? [don-day pway-doh kom-prahr oon floh-ta-dawr]

run *(on foot, in a car)* la carrera [ka-RRair-a]; *(for skiing)* la pista [pees-ta] ♦ *(on foot)* correr [koRR-air]; *(bus, train)* pasar [pa-sahr]; *(engine)* funcionar [foonth-yoh-nahr] ♦ *(traffic light)* saltarse [sal-tahr-say]

▶ I'm going for a run voy a correr [boy a koRR-air]

▶ the bus runs every half hour el autobús pasa cada media hora [el ow-toh-boos pa-sa kah-da med-ya aw-ra]

running

▶ where can you go running here? ¿dónde se puede ir a correr por aquí? [don-day say pway-day eer a koRR-air por a-kee]

run out of quedarse sin [kay-dahr-say seen]

▶ I've run out of gas me he quedado sin gasolina [may ay kaydah-doh seen ga-so-lee-na]

S

safe seguro(ra) [se-goo-roh] ◆ *(for valuables)* la caja fuerte [ka-CHA fwair-tay]
- is it safe to swim here? ¿se puede nadar sin peligro aquí? [say pway-day na-dahr seen pe-lee-groh a-kee]
- is it safe to camp here? ¿se puede acampar sin peligro aquí? [say pway-day a-kam-pahr seen pe-lee-groh a-kee]
- is there a safe in the room? ¿hay caja fuerte en la habitación? [eye ka-CHa fwair-tay en la a-bi-tath-yohn]

sail *(of a boat)* la vela [bay-la]
- we need to adjust that sail tenemos que ajustar esa vela [ten-ay-mos kay a-CHoos-tahr esa bay-la]

sailboat el velero [bel-air-oh]
- can we rent a sailboat? ¿podemos alquilar un velero? [pod-ay-mos al-ki-lahr oon bel-air-oh]

sailing la vela [bay-la]
- to go sailing ir a navegar [eer a na-beg-ahr]
- I'd like to take beginners' sailing classes me gustaría recibir clases de vela para principiantes [may goos-ta-ree-a RRe-thi-beer kla-says day bay-la pa-ra prin-thip-yan-tays]

salad la ensalada [en-sa-lah-da]
- can I just have a salad? ¿me trae solo una salada, por favor? [may tra-ay soh-loh oon en-sa-lah-da por fa-bor]

sale *(selling)* la venta [ben-ta]; *(at reduced prices)* las rebajas [RRe-ba-CHas]
- is it for sale? ¿está a la venta? [es-ta a la ben-ta]
- can you get your money back on sale items? ¿te devuelven el dinero en los productos de las rebajas? [tay day-bwel-ben el di-nair-oh en los pro-dook-tohs day RRe-ba-CHas]

sales tax el IVA [ee-ba]
- is sales tax included? ¿está incluido el IVA? [es-ta in-kloo-ee-doh el ee-ba]
- can you deduct the sales tax? ¿se puede deducir el IVA? [say pway-day de-doo-theer el ee-ba]

salt la sal [sal] ◆ echar sal a [e-chahr sal a]
- can you pass me the salt? ¿puede pasarme la sal? [pway-day pa-sahr-may la sal]
- it doesn't have enough salt está soso [es-ta soh-soh]

salty salado(da) [sa-lah-doh]
- it's too salty está muy salado [es-ta mwee sa-lah-doh]

same mismo(ma) [mees-moh]
- I'll have the same quiero lo mismo [kyair-oh loh mees-moh]
- the same (as) lo mismo (que) [loh mees-moh (kay)]
- it's the same as yours es lo mismo que tú [es loh mees-moh kay too]

sandwich el bocadillo [bo-ka-deel-yoh]
- a tuna sandwich, please un bocadillo de atún, por favor [oon bo-ka-deel-yoh day a-toon por fa-bor]

Saturday el sábado [sa-ba-doh]
- Saturday, September 13th sábado, trece de septiembre [sa-ba-doh tre-thay day sept-yem-bray]
- it's closed on Saturdays cierra los sábados [thye-RRa los sa-ba-dohs]

sauce la salsa [sal-sa]
- do you have a sauce that isn't too strong? ¿tiene alguna salsa que no sea muy fuerte? [tyen-ay al-goo-na sal-sa kay noh say-a mwee fwair-tay]

sauna la sauna [sow-na]
- is there a sauna? ¿hay sauna? [eye sow-na]

sausage la salchicha [sal-chee-cha]
- I'd like to try some of the hot sausage quería probar un poco de salchicha picante [kair-ee-a pro-bahr oon poh-koh day sal-chee-cha pi-kan-tay]

say decir [deth-eer]
- how do you say 'good luck' in Spanish? ¿cómo se dice 'good luck' en español? [kom-oh say dee-thay good luck en es-pan-yol]

scared
- to be scared estar asustado(da) [estar a-soos-tah-doh]
- I'm scared of spiders me dan miedo las arañas [may dan myay-doh las a-ran-yas]

scheduled flight el vuelo regular [bway-loh RRe-goo-lahr]
- when is the next scheduled flight to Santander? ¿a qué hora es el próximo vuelo regular a Santander? [a kay aw-ra es el prok-si-moh bway-loh RRe-goo-lahr a san-tan-dair]

school (for children) el colegio [ko-leCH-yoh]; (college, university) la universidad [oo-ni-bair-si-dad]
- are you still in school? ¿todavía estás en la universidad? [toh-da-bee-a es-tas en la oo-ni-bair-si-dad]

scoop (of ice cream) la bola [boh-la]
- I'd like a cone with two scoops quería un cucurucho con dos bolas [kair-ee-a oon koo-koo-roo-choh kon dos boh-las]

scooter el escúter [es-koo-tair]
- I'd like to rent a scooter quería alquilar un escúter [kair-ee-a al-ki-lahr oon es-koo-tair]

Scotch *(whiskey)* el whisky escocés [wees-ki es-ko-thays]
▸ a Scotch on the rocks, please un whisky escocés con hielo, por favor [oon wees-ki es-ko-thays kon yay-loh por fa-bor]

Scotch tape® el celo [thay-loh]
▸ do you have any Scotch tape®? ¿tiene celo? [tyen-ay thay-loh]

scrambled eggs los huevos revueltos [way-bohs RRe-bwel-tohs]
▸ I'd like scrambled eggs for breakfast quería huevos revueltos para desayunar [kair-ee-a way-bohs RRe-bwel-tohs pa-ra des-eye-oo-nahr]

screen *(room in a movie theater)* la sala [sa-la]
▸ how many screens does the movie theater have? ¿cuántas salas tiene este cine? [kwan-tas sa-las tyen-ay es-tay thee-nay]

scuba diving el buceo [boo-thay-oh]
▸ can we go scuba diving? ¿podemos ir a bucear? [pod-ay-mos eer a boo-thay-ahr]

sea el mar [mahr]
▸ the sea is rough el mar está bravo [el mahr es-ta brah-boh]
▸ how long does it take to walk to the sea? ¿cuánto se tarda en llegar andando hasta el mar? [kwan-toh say tahr-da en yay-gahr an-dan-doh as-ta el mahr]

seasick mareado(da) [ma-ray-ah-doh]
▸ I feel seasick estoy mareado [es-toy ma-ray-ah-doh]

seasickness el mareo [ma-ray-oh]
▸ can you give me something for seasickness, please? ¿me podría dar algo para el mareo, por favor? [may pod-ree-a dahr al-goh pa-ra el ma-ray-oh por fa-bor]

seaside resort el centro turístico costero [then-troh too-rees-ti-koh kos-tair-oh]
▸ what's the nearest seaside resort? ¿dónde está el centro turístico costero más cercano? [don-day es-ta el then-troh too-rees-ti-koh kos-tair-oh mas thair-kah-noh]

season *(of the year)* la estación [es-tath-yohn]
▸ what is the best season to come here? ¿cuál es la mejor estación para venir aquí? [kwal es la me-CHor es-tath-yohn pa-ra ben-eer a-kee]

season ticket el abono [a-boh-noh]
▸ how much is a season ticket? ¿cuánto cuesta un abono? [kwan-toh kwes-ta oon a-boh-noh]

seat el asiento [as-yen-toh]; *(in a theater, a movie theater)* la butaca [boo-ta-ka]
▸ is this seat taken? ¿está ocupado este asiento? [es-ta o-koo-pah-doh es-tay as-yen-toh]
▸ excuse me, I think you're (sitting) in my seat perdone, me parece que está (sentado) en mi asiento [pair-doh-nay, may pa-re-thay kay es-ta (sen-tah-doh) en mee as-yen-toh]

second *(unit of time)* el segundo [se-goon-doh]; *(gear)* la segunda [se-goon-da] ◆ segundo(da) [se-goon-doh]
▸ wait a second! ¡espera un segundo! [es-pair-a oon se-goon-doh]

▸ is it in second? ¿está en segunda? [es-ta en se-goon-da]

▸ it's the second street on your right es la segunda calle a la derecha [es la se-goon-da kal-yay a la de-re-cha]

second class la segunda clase [se-goon-da kla-say] ◆ en segunda clase [en se-goon-da kla-say]

▸ your seat's in second class su asiento está en la segunda clase [soo as-yen-toh es-ta en la se-goon-da kla-say]

▸ to travel second class viajar en segunda clase [bya-CHahr en se-goon-da kla-say]

see ver [bair]

▸ I'm here to see Dr. Brown estoy aquí para ver al doctor Brown [es-toy a-kee pa-ra bair al dok-tawr brown]

▸ can I see the room? ¿puedo ver la habitación? [pway-doh bair la a-bi-tath-yohn]

▸ I'd like to see the dress in the window me gustaría ver el vestido que hay en el escaparate [may goos-ta-ree-a bair el bes-tee-doh kay eye en el es-ka-pa-ra-tay]

▸ see you soon! ¡hasta pronto! [as-ta pron-toh]

▸ see you later hasta más tarde [as-ta mas tahr-day]

▸ see you (on) Thursday! ¡hasta el jueves! [as-ta el CHway-bays]

self-service *(restaurant, gas station)* autoservicio [ow-toh-sair-beeth-yoh] ◆ *(restaurant, system)* el autoservicio [ow-toh-sair-beeth-yoh]; *(gas station)* la gasolinera autoservicio [ga-so-li-nair-a ow-toh-sair-beeth-yoh]

▸ is it self-service? ¿es autoservicio? [es ow-toh-sair-beeth-yoh]

sell vender [ben-dair]

▸ do you sell stamps? ¿vende sellos? [ben-day sel-yohs]

▸ the radio I was sold is defective la radio que me vendieron es defectuosa [la RRad-yoh kay may bend-yair-on es de-fek-too-oh-sa]

send enviar [emb-yahr]

▸ I'd like to send this package to Toronto by airmail quería enviar este paquete a Toronto por correo aéreo [kair-ee-a emb-yahr es-tay pa-kay-tay a to-ron-toh por ko-RRay-oh a-air-ay-oh]

▸ could you send a tow truck? ¿podría enviar una grúa? [pod-ree-a emb-yahr oo-na groo-a]

separately *(individually)* por separado [por se-pa-rah-doh]

▸ is it sold separately? ¿se vende por separado? [say ben-day por se-pa-rah-doh]

September septiembre [sept-yem-bray]

▸ September 9th nueve de septiembre [nway-bay day sept-yem-bray]

serve *(meal, drink, customer)* servir [sair-beer]; *(town, station)* ir [eer]

▸ when is breakfast served? ¿a qué hora se sirve el desayuno? [a kay aw-ra say seer-bay el des-eye-oo-noh]

▸ are you still serving lunch? ¿todavía están sirviendo la comida? [toh-da-bee-a es-tán seerb-yen-doh la ko-mee-da]

service *(in a restaurant)* el servicio [sair-beeth-yoh] ◆ *(car)* revisar [RRe-bi-sahr]

▸ the service was terrible el servicio era horrible [el sair-beeth-yoh air-a o-RReeb-lay]

▸ we have to have the car serviced tenemos que llevar el coche a revisar [ten-ay-mos kay yay-bahr el ko-chay a RRe-bi-sahr]

service charge el servicio [sair-beeth-yoh]

▸ is the service charge included? ¿está incluido el servicio? [es-ta in-kloo-ee-doh el sair-beeth-yoh]

set *(of cookware)* la batería [ba-tair-ee-a]; *(of keys)* el juego [CHway-goh] ♦ *(sun)* ponerse [pon-air-say]

▸ do you have a spare set of keys? ¿tiene un juego extra de llaves? [tyen-ay oon CHway-goh eks-tra day yah-bays]

▸ what time does the sun set? ¿a qué hora se pone el sol? [a kay aw-ra say poh-nay el sol]

seven siete [syet-ay]

▸ there are seven of us somos siete [som-os syet-ay]

several varios(rias) [bahr-yohs]

▸ I've been before, several years ago ya había estado antes, hace varios años [ya a-bee-a es-tah-doh a-kee a-thay bahr-yohs an-yohs]

shade *(shadow)* la sombra [som-bra]

▸ can we have a table in the shade? ¿nos podría dar una mesa a la sombra? [nos pod-ree-a dahr oo-na may-sa a la som-bra]

shake *(bottle)* agitar [a-CHee-tahr]

▸ to shake hands dar un apretón de manos [dahr oon a-pre-tohn day mah-nohs]

▸ let's shake choca esos cinco [choh-ka e-sohs theen-koh]

shame *(remorse, humiliation)* la vergüenza [bair-gwen-tha]; *(pity)* la pena [pay-na]

▸ (what a) shame! ¡qué pena! [kay pay-na]

shampoo el champú [cham-poo]

▸ do you have any shampoo? ¿tiene champú? [tyen-ay cham-poo]

share compartir [kom-pahr-teer]

▸ we're going to share it: can you bring us two plates? vamos a compartirlo, ¿nos podría traer dos platos? [bah-mos a kom-pahr-teer-loh nos pod-ree-a tra-air dos pla-tohs]

shared *(bathroom, kitchen)* compartido(da) [kom-pahr-tee-doh]

▸ is the bathroom shared? ¿el baño es compartido? [el ban-yoh es kom-pahr-tee-doh]

shaver la maquinilla de afeitar [ma-ki-neel-ya day a-fay-tahr]

▸ where can I buy a new shaver? ¿dónde puedo comprar una maquinilla de afeitar nueva? [don-day pway-doh kom-prahr oo-na ma-ki-neel-ya day a-fay-tahr nway-ba]

sheet *(for a bed)* la sábana [sa-ba-na]; *(of paper)* la hoja [oh-CHa]

▸ could you change the sheets? ¿podría cambiar las sábanas? [pod-ree-a kamb-yahr las sa-ba-nas]

ship el barco [bahr-koh]

▸ when does the ship dock? ¿cuándo atraca el barco? [kwan-doh a-tra-ka el bahr-koh]

shoe el zapato [tha-pa-toh]
- what sort of shoes should you wear? ¿qué tipo de zapatos hay que ponerse? [kay tee-poh day tha-pa-tohs eye kay pon-air-say]

shoe size el número (de zapato) [noo-mair-oh (day tha-pa-toh)]
- what's your shoe size? ¿qué número calza? [kay noo-mair-oh kal-tha]

shop *(store)* la tienda [tyen-da]
- what time do the shops downtown close? ¿a qué hora cierran las tiendas del centro? [a kay aw-ra thee-eRR-an las tyen-das del then-troh]

shopping las compras [kom-pras]
- where can you go shopping around here? ¿dónde se puede ir de compras por aquí? [don-day say pway-day eer day kom-pras por a-kee]

shopping bag la bolsa (de la compra) [bolsa (day la kom-pra)]
- can I have a plastic shopping bag, please? ¿me puede dar una bolsa de plástico, por favor? [may pway-dee-a dahr oo-na bol-sa day plas-ti-koh por fa-bor]

shopping center el centro comercial [then-troh kom-airth-yal]
- I'm looking for a shopping center busco un centro comercial [boos-koh oon then-troh kom-airth-yal]

shop window el escaparate [es-ka-pa-ra-tay]
- we've just been peeking in the shop windows hemos ido de escaparates [ay-mos ee-doh day es-ka-pa-ra-tays]

short *(in time, length)* corto(ta) [kor-toh]; *(in height)* bajo(ja) [ba-CHoh]
- we're only here for a short time nos vamos a quedar aquí muy poco tiempo [nos bah-mos a kay-dahr a-kee mwee poh-koh tyem-poh]
- we'd like to do a shorter trip queríamos hacer una excursión más corta [kair-ee-a-mos a-thair oo-na eks-koors-yohn mas kor-ta]
- I'm two dollars short me faltan dos dólares [may fal-tan dos doh-la-rays]

shortcut el atajo [a-ta-CHoh]
- is there a shortcut? ¿hay un atajo? [eye oon a-ta-CHoh]

short wave la onda corta [on-da kor-ta]
- can you get any English stations on short wave? ¿se puede escuchar alguna emisora inglesa en onda corta? [say pway-day es-koo-chahr al-goo-na e-mi-saw-ra in-glay-sa en on-da kor-ta]

should
- what should I do? ¿que debería hacer? [kay deb-air-ee-a a-thair]

show *(at the theater)* el espectáculo [es-pek-ta-koo-loh]; *(at the movies)* la proyección [pro-yekth-yohn] ♦ *(let see)* enseñar [en-sen-yahr]
- what time does the show begin? ¿a qué hora empieza el espectáculo? [a kay aw-ra em-pyay-tah el es-pek-ta-koo-loh]
- could you show me where that is on the map? ¿me podría enseñar en el mapa dónde está eso? [may pod-ree-a en-sen-yahr en el ma-pa don-day es-ta e-soh]

▶ could you show me the room? ¿me podría enseñar la habitación? [may pod-ree-a en-sen-yahr la a-bi-tath-yohn]

shower *(device, act)* la ducha [doo-cha]; *(of rain)* el chaparrón [cha-pa-RRohn]

▶ I'd like a room with a shower, please quería una habitación con ducha, por favor [kair-ee-a oo-na a-bi-tath-yohn kon doo-cha, por fa-bor]

▶ how does the shower work? ¿cómo funciona la ducha? [kom-oh foonth-yoh-na la doo-cha]

▶ the shower is leaking la ducha no cierra bien [la doo-cha noh thee-e-RRA bien]

shower head la alcachofa de la ducha [al-ka-choh-fa day la doo-cha]

▶ the shower head is broken la alcachofa de la ducha está rota [la al-ka-choh-fa day la doo-cha es-ta RRoh-ta]

shrimp la gamba [gam-ba]

▶ I'm allergic to shrimp soy alérgico a las gambas [soy a-lair-CH-koh a las gam-bas]

shut *(door, window)* cerrar(se) [theRR-ahr-(say)]

▶ the window won't shut la ventana no cierra [la ben-tah-na noh thee-e-RRa]

shutter *(on a window)* la contraventana [kon-tra-ben-tah-na]; *(on a camera)* el obturador [ob-too-ra-dawr]

▶ are there shutters on the windows? ¿las ventanas tienen contraventanas? [las ben-tah-nas tyen-en kon-tra-ben-tah-nas]

shuttle *(vehicle)* el servicio de conexión [sair-beeth-yoh day ko-neks-yohn]

▶ is there a shuttle to the airport? ¿hay un servicio de conexión con el aeropuerto? [eye oon sair-beeth-yoh day ko-neks-yohn kon el eye-roh-pwair-toh]

sick *(unwell)* enfermo(ma) [en-fair-moh]

▶ I feel sick estoy mareado [es-toy ma-ray-ah-doh]

▶ to be sick *(be unwell)* estar enfermo [es-tar en-fair-moh]; *(vomit)* vomitar [bo-mi-tahr]

side *(of the body)* el costado [kos-tah-doh]; *(of an object)* el lado [lah-doh]; *(edge)* el borde [bor-day]; *(opposing part)* el lado [lah-doh]

▶ I have a pain in my right side me duele el costado derecho [may dway-lay el kos-tah-doh de-re-choh]

▶ could we have a table on the other side of the room? ¿nos podría dar una mesa en el otro lado de la sala? [nos pod-ree-a dahr oo-na may-sa en el oh-troh lah-doh day la sa-la]

▶ which side of the road do we drive on here? ¿por qué lado de la carretera tenemos que conducir aquí? [por kay lah-doh day la ka-RRe-tair-a ten-ay-mos kay kon-doo-theer a-kee]

sidewalk la acera [a-thair-a]

▶ the sidewalks are very clean here aquí las aceras están muy limpias [a-kee las a-thair-as est-an mwee leemp-yas]

sight *(seeing)* la vista [bees-ta] • **sights** *(of a place)* los lugares de interés [loo-gah-rays day in-tair-ays]

▶ I'm having problems with my sight tengo problemas con la vista [ten-goh prob-lay-mas kon la bees-ta]

▶ what are the sights that are most worth seeing? ¿cuáles son los lugares de interés que más vale la pena visitar? [kwah-lays son los loo-gah-rays day in-tair-ays kay mas bah-lay la pay-na bi-si-tahr]

sign firmar [feer-mahr]

▶ do I sign here? ¿firmo aquí? [feer-moh a-kee]

signpost la señal [sen-yal]

▶ does the route have good signposts? ¿la ruta está bien señalizada? [la RRoo-ta est-a byen sen-ya-li-thah-da]

silver *(metal)* la plata [pla-ta]

▶ is it made of silver? ¿es de plata? [es day pla-ta]

since desde [des-day] ♦ *(in time)* desde que [des-day kay]; *(because)* ya que [ya kay]

▶ I've been here since Tuesday estoy aquí desde el martes [es-toy a-kee des-day el mahr-tays]

▶ it hasn't rained once since we've been here no ha llovido ni una vez desde que llegamos [noh a yo-bee-doh nee oo-na beth des-day kay yay-gah-mos]

single *(only one)* solo(la) [soh-loh]; *(unmarried)* soltero(ra) [sol-tair-oh] ♦ *(CD)* el single [seen-glay]

▶ not a single one ni uno solo [nee oo-noh soh-loh]

▶ I'm single estoy soltero/soltera [es-toy sol-tair-oh/sol-tair-a]

▶ she's a single woman in her thirties es una mujer soltera de treinta y tantos años [es oo-na mooCH-air sol-tair-a day trayn-ta ee tan-tohs an-yohs]

single bed la cama individual [ka-ma in-di-bid-wal]

▶ we'd prefer two single beds preferiríamos dos camas individuales [pre-fair-ee-ree-a-mos dos ka-mas in-di-bid-wah-lays]

single room la habitación individual [a-bi-tath-yohn in-di-bid-wal]

▶ I'd like to book a single room for 5 nights, please quería reservar una habitación individual para 5 noches, por favor [kair-ee-a re-sair-bahr oo-na a-bi-tath-yohn in-di-bid-wal pa-ra theen-koh no-chays por fa-bor]

sister la hermana [air-mah-na]

▶ I have two sisters tengo dos hermanas [ten-goh dos air-mah-nas]

sit sentarse [sen-tahr-say]

▶ may I sit at your table? ¿me puedo sentar en su mesa? [may pway-doh sen-tahr en soo may-sa]

▶ is anyone sitting here? ¿hay alguien sentado aquí? [eye alg-yen sen-tah-doh a-kee]

site *(of a town, a building)* el emplazamiento [em-pla-tham-yen-toh]; *(archeological)* el yacimiento [ya-thim-yen-toh]

▶ can we visit the site? ¿podemos visitar el yacimiento? [pod-ay-mos bi-si-tahr el ya-thim-yen-toh]

sitting *(for a meal)* el turno [toor-noh]
  ▶ is there more than one sitting for lunch? ¿hay más de un turno para la comida? [eye mas day oon toor-noh pa-ra la ko-mee-da]

six seis [seys]
  ▶ there are six of us somos seis [som-os seys]

sixth sexto(ta) [seks-toh] ◆ el sexto [seks-toh], la sexta [seks-ta]
  ▶ our room is on the sixth floor nuestra habitación está en el sexto piso [nwes-tra a-bi-tath-yohn es-ta en el seks-toh pee-soh]

size *(of a person)* el tamaño [ta-man-yoh]; *(of clothes)* la talla [tal-ya]; *(of shoes)* el número [noo-mair-oh]
  ▶ do you have another size? ¿tiene otra talla? [tyen-ay oh-tra tal-ya]
  ▶ do you have it in a smaller size? ¿lo tiene en una talla más pequeña? [loh tyen-ay en oo-na tal-ya mas pe-kayn-ya]
  ▶ I take or I'm a size 38 *(shoes)* calzo el 38 [kal-thoh el traynt-ta ee o-choh]; *(clothes)* mi talla es el 38 [mee tal-ya es el traynt-ta ee o-choh]

skate *(for skating)* el patín [pa-teen] ◆ patinar [pa-ti-nahr]
  ▶ how much is it to rent skates? ¿cuánto cuesta alquilar patines? [kwan-toh kwes-ta al-ki-lahr pa-tee-nays]
  ▶ can you skate? ¿sabes patinar? [sa-bays pa-ti-nahr]

skating el patinaje [pa-ti-na-CHay]
  ▶ where can we go skating? ¿dónde podemos ir a patinar? [don-day pod-ay-mos eer a pa-ti-nahr]

ski el esquí [es-kee]
  ▶ I'd like to rent a pair of skis for the week, please quería alquilar un par de esquís una semana, por favor [kair-ee-a al-ki-lahr oon pahr day es-kees oo-na se-mah-na por fa-bor]

ski boots las botas de esquí [boh-tas day es-kee]
  ▶ I'd like to rent ski boots quería alquilar botas de esquí [kair-ee-a al-ki-lahr boh-tas day es-kee]

skiing el esquí [es-kee]
  ▶ where can we go skiing near here? ¿dónde podemos esquiar por aquí cerca? [don-day pod-ay-mos es-kee-ahr por a-kee thair-ka]

sleep dormir [dor-meer]
  ▶ I slept well dormí bien [dor-mee byen]
  ▶ I can't sleep no consigo dormir [noh kon-see-goh dor-meer]

sleeping bag el saco de dormir [sa-koh day dor-meer]
  ▶ where can I buy a new sleeping bag? ¿dónde puedo comprar un saco de dormir nuevo? [don-day pway-doh kom-prahr oon sa-koh day dor-meer nway-boh]

sleeping pill el somnífero [som-nee-fair-oh]
  ▶ I'd like some sleeping pills quería somníferos [kair-ee-a som-nee-fair-ohs]

slice *(of bread)* la rebanada [RRe-ba-nah-da]; *(of ham)* la loncha [lon-cha] ♦ cortar [kor-tahr]

▸ a thin slice of ham una loncha fina de jamón [oo-na lon-cha fee-na day CHa-mohn]

slim *(person)* delgado(da) [del-gah-doh]

▸ she's slim está delgada [es-ta del-gah-da]

slow lento(ta) [len-toh]; *(clock, watch)* atrasado(da) [a-tra-sah-doh]

▸ the fog was slow to clear la niebla tardó en levantarse [la nyeb-la tahr-doh en lay-ban-tahr-say]

▸ is that clock slow? ¿ese reloj va atrasado? [se RRe-loCH ba a-tra-sah-da]

slowly despacio [des-path-yoh]

▸ could you speak more slowly, please? ¿puede hablar más despacio, por favor? [pway-day ab-lahr mas des-path-yoh por fa-bor]

small pequeño(ña) [pe-kayn-yoh]

▸ do you have anything smaller? ¿tiene algo más pequeño? [tyen-ay al-goh mas pe-kayn-yoh]

smell *(notice a smell of)* oler [ol-air] ♦ *(have a smell)* oler [ol-air]; *(have a bad smell)* apestar [a-pes-tahr]

▸ can you smell something burning? ¿hueles a quemado? [way-lays a kay-mah-doh]

▸ it smells in here aquí apesta [a-kee a-pes-ta]

smoke el humo [oo-moh] ♦ *(person)* fumar [foo-mahr]

▸ is the smoke bothering you? ¿le molesta el humo? [lay mo-les-ta el oo-moh]

▸ do you mind if I smoke? ¿le importa si fumo? [lay im-por-ta see foo-moh]

▸ no thanks, I don't smoke no, gracias, no fumo [noh grath-yas noh foo-moh]

smoker el fumador [foo-ma-dawr], la fumadora [foo-ma-daw-ra]

▸ are you smokers or nonsmokers? ¿son fumadores o no fumadores? [son foo-ma-daw-rays oh noh foo-ma-daw-rays]

smoking

▸ is smoking allowed here? ¿se puede fumar aquí? [say pway-day foo-mahr a-kee]

▸ I can't stand smoking no aguanto el tabaco [noh ag-wan-toh el ta-ba-koh]

smoking compartment el compartimento de fumadores [kom-par-ti-men-toh day foo-ma-daw-rays]

▸ I'd like a seat in a smoking compartment quiero un asiento en un compartimento de fumadores [kyair-oh oon as-yen-toh en oon kom-par-ti-men-toh day foo-ma-daw-rays]

▸ is there a smoking compartment? ¿hay compartimento de fumadores? [eye kom-par-ti-men-toh day foo-ma-daw-rays]

smoking section la zona de fumadores [thoh-na day foo-ma-daw-rays]

▸ I'd like a table in the smoking section quiero una mesa en la zona de fumadores [kyair-oh oon may-sa en la thoh-na day foo-ma-daw-rays]

sneaker la zapatilla [tha-pa-teel-ya]
  ▸ your sneakers are really trendy! ¡tus zapatillas son súper modernas! [toos tha-pa-teel-yas son soo-pair mod-air-nas]

snorkel el tubo (para buceo) [too-boh (pa-ra boo-thay-oh)]
  ▸ I'd like to rent a snorkel and mask, please quería alquilar un tubo y unas gafas, por favor [kair-ee-a al-ki-lahr oon too-boh ee oo-nas ga-fas por fa-bor]

snow nevar [ne-bahr]
  ▸ it's snowing está nevando [es-ta ne-ban-doh]

snowboard la tabla de snowboard [tab-la day es-nou-boh-ard]
  ▸ I'd like to rent a snowboard quería alquilar una tabla de snowboard [kair-ee-a al-ki-lahr oo-na tab-la day es-nou-boh-ard]

snowboarding el snowboard [es-nou-boh-ard]
  ▸ where can we go snowboarding near here? ¿dónde podemos hacer snowboard por aquí? [don-day pod-ay-mos a-thair es-nou-boh-ard por a-kee]

snow tire el neumático para la nieve [new-ma-ti-koh pa-ra la nyay-bay]
  ▸ do I need snow tires? ¿necesito neumáticos para la nieve? [ne-thes-ee-toh new-ma-ti-kohs pa-ra la nyay-bay]

so *(to such a degree)* tan [tan]; *(also)* también [tam-byen]; *(consequently)* por lo que [por loh kay]
  ▸ it's so big! ¡qué grande es! [kay gran-day es]
  ▸ there's so many choices I don't know what to have hay tanto donde elegir que no sé qué tomar [eye tan-toh don-day e-leCH-eer kay noh say kay tom-ahr]
  ▸ I'm hungry – so am I! tengo hambre – ¡yo también! [ten-goh am-bray – yoh tam-byen]

soap el jabón [CHa-bohn]
  ▸ there's no soap no hay jabón [noh eye CHa-bohn]

socket *(in a wall)* el enchufe [en-choo-fay]
  ▸ is there a socket I can use to recharge my cell? ¿hay algún enchufe que pueda usar para cargar el móvil? [eye al-goon en-choo-fay kay pway-da oo-sahr pa-ra kahr-gahr el mob-eel]

solution la solución [so-looth-yohn]
  ▸ that seems to be the best solution eso parece la mejor solución [e-soh pa-re-thay la me-CHor so-looth-yohn]
  ▸ I'd like some rinsing solution for soft lenses quería solución de enjuague para lentes blandas [kair-ee-a so-looth-yohn day en-CHwa-gay pa-ra len-tays blan-das]

some *(an amount of)* algo [al-goh]; *(a number of)* unos(nas) [oo-nohs] ◆ *(a number)* unos(nas) [oo-nohs]
  ▸ I'd like some coffee quería algo de café [kair-ee-a al-goh day ka-fay]
  ▸ some friends recommended this place unos amigos me recomendaron este sitio [oo-nohs a-mee-gohs may RRe-ko-men-dah-ron es-tay seet-yoh]
  ▸ can I have some? ¿me puede poner un poco? [may pway-day pon-air oon poh-koh]

saying sorry

To apologize, say *perdona* if you are on familiar terms with the person you're talking to, or *perdone* if you don't know them well.

somebody, someone alguien [alg-yen]
- somebody left this for you alguien dejó esto para ti [alg-yen de-CHoh es-toh pa-ra tee]

something algo [al-goh]
- is something wrong? ¿pasa algo? [pa-sa al-goh]

somewhere
- I'm looking for somewhere to stay busco un sitio donde alojarme [boos-koh oon seet-yoh don-day a-lo-CHahr-may]
- somewhere near here en algún lugar cerca de aquí [en al-goon loo-gahr thair-ka day a-kee]
- somewhere else en alguna otra parte [en al-goo-na oh-tra pahr-tay]

son el hijo [ee-CHoh]
- this is my son este es mi hijo [es-tay es mee ee-CHoh]

soon pronto [pron-toh]
- see you soon! ¡hasta pronto! [as-ta pron-toh]
- as soon as possible cuanto antes [kwan-toh an-tays]

sore throat el dolor de garganta [do-lawr day gar-gan-ta]
- I have a sore throat me duele la garganta [may dway-lay la gar-gan-ta]

sorry
- I'm sorry lo siento [loh syen-toh]
- sorry I'm late perdón por llegar tarde [pair-dohn por yay-gahr tahr-day]
- I'm sorry, but this seat is taken perdone, pero este asiento está ocupado [pair-doh-nay pair-oh es-tay as-yen-toh es-ta o-koo-pah-doh]
- sorry to bother you perdone que le moleste [pair-doh-nay kay lay mo-les-tay]
- sorry? *(asking for repetition)* ¿perdón? [pair-dohn]
- no, sorry no, lo siento [noh loh syen-toh]

sound *(of footsteps, conversation, a voice)* el sonido [so-nee-doh]; *(of a TV, radio)* el volumen [bo-loo-men]
- can you turn the sound down? ¿puedes bajar el volumen? [pway-days ba-CHahr el bo-loo-men]

souvenir el recuerdo [RRek-wair-doh]
- where can I buy souvenirs? ¿dónde puedo comprar recuerdos? [don-day pway-doh kom-prahr RRek-wair-dohs]

souvenir shop la tienda de recuerdos [tyen-da day RRek-wair-dohs]

▶ I'm looking for a souvenir shop busco una tienda de recuerdos [boos-koh oo-na tyen-da day RRek-wair-dohs]

spa *(town)* el balneario [bal-nay-ahr-yoh]; *(health club)* el gimnasio [CHim-nas-yoh]; *(bathtub)* la bañera de hidromasaje [ban-yair-a day eed-roh-ma-sa-CHay]

▶ the spa's not working la bañera de hidromasaje no funciona [la ban-yair-a day eed-roh-ma-sa-CHay noh foonth-yoh-na]

space el espacio [es-path-yoh]

▶ is there space for another bed in the room? ¿hay espacio para otra cama en la habitación? [eye es-path-yoh pa-ra oh-tra ka-ma en la a-bi-tath-yohn]

▶ I'd like a space for one tent for two days quería un espacio para una tienda dos días [kair-ee-a oon es-path-yoh pa-ra oo-na tyen-da dos dee-as]

▶ do you have any spaces farther from the road? ¿tiene algún espacio más apartado de la carretera? [tyen-ay al-goon es-path-yoh mas a-par-tah-doh day la ka-RRe-tair-a]

spade *(child's toy)* la pala [pa-la]

▶ my son's left his spade at the beach mi hijo se ha dejado la pala en la playa [mee ee-CHoh say a de-CHah-doh la pa-la en la pleye-a]

spare *(clothes, battery)* de sobra [day soh-bra] ♦ *(tire)* la rueda de repuesto [RRoo-ay-da day RRe-pwes-toh]; *(part)* la pieza de repuesto [pyay-tha day RRe-pwes-toh]

▶ should I take some spare clothes? ¿llevo alguna muda de ropa? [yay-boh al-goo-na moo-da day RRoh-pa]

▶ I don't have any spare cash no me sobra dinero [noh may soh-bra di-nair-oh]

▶ I've got a spare ticket for the game tengo una entrada de sobra para el partido [ten-goh oo-na en-trah-da day soh-bra pa-ra el par-tee-doh]

spare part la pieza de repuesto [pyay-tha day RRe-pwes-toh]

▶ where can I get spare parts? ¿dónde puedo comprar piezas de repuesto? [don-day pway-doh kom-prahr pyay-thas day RRe-pwes-toh]

spare tire la rueda de repuesto [RRoo-ay-da day RRe-pwes-toh]

▶ the spare tire's flat too la rueda de repuesto también está desinflada [la RRoo-ay-da day RRe-pwes-toh tamb-yen es-ta des-in-flah-da]

spare wheel la rueda de repuesto [RRoo-ay-da day RRe-pwes-toh]

▶ there's no spare wheel no hay rueda de repuesto [noh eye RRoo-ay-da day RRe-pwes-toh]

sparkling *(water)* con gas [kon gas]; *(wine)* espumoso(sa) [es-poo-moh-soh]

▶ could I have a bottle of sparkling water, please? ¿me podía traer una botella de agua con gas, por favor? [may pod-ree-a tra-air oo-na bo-tel-ya day ag-wa kon gas por fa-bor]

speak hablar [ab-lahr]

▶ I speak hardly any Spanish casi no hablo español [ka-si noh ab-loh es-pan-yol]

- is there anyone here who speaks English? ¿hay alguien aquí que hable inglés? [eye alg-yen a-kee kay ab-lay in-glays]
- could you speak more slowly? ¿podría hablar más despacio? [pod-ree-a ab-lahr mas des-path-yoh]
- hello, I'd like to speak to Mr...; this is... hola, quería hablar con el señor...; soy... [oh-la kair-ee-a ab-lahr kon el sen-yawr ... soy]
- who's speaking please? ¿de parte de quién? [day pahr-tay day kyen]
- hello, Gary speaking hola, soy Gary [oh-la soy ga-ree]

special el plato del día [pla-toh del dee-a]
- what's today's special? ¿cuál es el plato del día? [kwal es el pla-toh del dee-a]

specialist el especialista [es-peth-ya-lees-ta], la especialista [es-peth-ya-lees-ta]
- could you refer me to a specialist? ¿me podría enviar al especialista? [may pod-ree-a emb-yahr al es-peth-ya-lees-ta]

specialty la especialidad [es-peth-ya-li-dad]
- what are the local specialties? ¿cuáles son las especialidades locales? [kwah-lays son las es-peth-ya-li-dah-days loh-kah-lays]

speed limit el límite de velocidad [lee-mi-tay day bel-o-thi-dad]
- what's the speed limit on this road? ¿cuál es el límite de velocidad en esta carretera? [kwal es el lee-mi-tay day bel-o-thi-dad en es-ta ka-RRe-tair-a]

speedometer el velocímetro [bel-o-thee-met-roh]
- the speedometer's broken el velocímetro está estropeado [el bel-o-thee-met-roh es-ta es-tro-pay-ah-doh]

speed trap el control de velocidad por radar [kon-trohl day bel-o-thi-dad por RRa-dahr]
- are there lots of speed traps in the area? ¿hay muchos controles de velocidad por radar por aquí? [eye moo-chohs kon-troh-lays day bel-o-thi-dad por RRa-dahr por a-kee]

spell escribir [es-kri-beer]
- how do you spell your name? ¿cómo se escribe tu nombre? [kom-oh say es-kree-bay too nom-bray]

spend (money) gastar [gas-tahr]; (time, vacation) pasar [pa-sahr]
- we are prepared to spend up to 200 euros estamos dispuestos a gastar un máximo de 200 euros [es-tah-mos dis-pwes-tohs a gas-tahr oon mak-si-moh day dos-thyen-tohs ew-rohs]
- I spent a month in Spain a few years ago pasé un mes en España hace unos años [pa-say oon mes en es-pan-ya a-thay oo-nohs an-yohs]

spicy picante [pi-kan-tay]
- is this dish spicy? ¿este plato es picante? [es-tay pla-toh es pi-kan-tay]

spoon la cuchara [koo-chah-ra]
- could I have a spoon? ¿me podría traer una cuchara? [may pod-ree-a tra-air oo-na koo-chah-ra]

sport el deporte [de-por-tay]

▶ do you play any sports? ¿practicas algún deporte? [prak-tee-kas al-goon de-por-tay]
▶ I play a lot of sports practico muchos deportes [prak-tee-koh moo-chohs de-por-tays]

sporty *(person)* deportista [de-por-tees-ta]

▶ I'm not very sporty no soy muy deportista [noh soy mwee de-por-tees-ta]

sprain torcerse [tor-thair-say]

▶ I think I've sprained my ankle creo que me he torcido el tobillo [kray-oh kay may ay tor-thee-doh el tob-eel-yoh]
▶ my wrist is sprained me he torcido la muñeca [may ay tor-thee-doh la moon-yay-ka]

square *(in a town)* la plaza [pla-tha]

▶ where is the main square? ¿dónde está la plaza mayor? [don-day es-ta la pla-tha meye-awr]

stain la mancha [man-cha]

▶ can you remove this stain? ¿puede quitar esta marcha? [pway-day ki-tahr es-ta man-cha]

stairs las escaleras [es-ka-lair-as]

▶ where are the stairs? ¿dónde están las escaleras? [don-day es-ta las es-ka-lair-as]

stall *(car, engine)* calarse [ka-lahr-say]

▶ the engine keeps stalling el motor se cala continuamente [el mo-tor say ka-la kon-teen-wa-men-tay]

stamp *(for letter, postcard)* el sello [sel-yoh]

stand *(stall, booth)* el puesto [pwes-toh]; *(in a stadium)* el graderío [gra-dair-ee-oh] ◆ *(tolerate)* aguantar [ag-wan-tahr] ◆ *(be upright)* estar de pie [es-tahr day pyay]; *(get up)* ponerse de pie [pon-air-say day pyay]

▶ where's stand number five? ¿dónde está el graderío número cinco? [don-day es-ta el gra-dair-ee-oh noo-mair-oh theen-koh]

start *(begin)* empezar [em-peth-ahr]; *(function)* arrancar [a-RRan-kahr]

▶ when does the concert start? ¿a qué hora empieza el concierto? [a kay aw-ra em-pyay-tha el konth-yair-toh]
▶ the car won't start el coche no arranca [el ko-chay noh a-RRan-ka]

starving

▶ I'm absolutely starving me muero de hambre [may mwair-oh day am-bray]

States

▶ the States los Estados Unidos [los es-tah-dohs oo-nee-dohs]
▶ I'm from the States soy de los Estados Unidos [soy day los es-tah-dohs oo-nee-dohs]
▶ I live in the States vivo en los Estados Unidos [bee-boh en los es-tah-dohs oo-nee-dohs]
▶ have you ever been to the States? ¿has estado alguna vez en los Estados Unidos? [as es-tah-doh al-goo-na beth en los es-tah-dohs oo-nee-dohs]

station *(railroad, bus, subway)* la estación [es-tath-yohn]; *(TV)* el canal [ka-nal]; *(radio)* la emisora [e-mi-saw-ra]; *(police)* la comisaría [ko-mi-sa-ree-a]

▸ to the train station, please! a la estación de tren, por favor [a la es-tath-yohn day tren por fa-bor]

▸ where is the nearest subway station? ¿dónde está la estación de metro más próxima? [don-day es-ta la es-tath-yohn day met-roh mas prok-si-ma]

stay *(in a place)* quedarse [kay-dahr-say] ◆ *(visit)* la estancia [es-tanth-ya]

▸ we're planning to stay for two nights pensamos quedarnos dos noches [pen-sah-mos kay-dahr-nos dos no-chays]

▸ a two-week stay una estancia de dos semanas [oo-na es-tanth-ya day dos se-mah-nas]

steak un filete [fi-lay-tay]

▸ I'd like a steak and fries quería un filete con patatas fritas [kair-ee-a oon fi-lay-tay kon pa-ta-tas free-tas]

steal robar [RRo-bahr]

▸ my passport was stolen me han robado el pasaporte [may ah RRo-bah-doh el pa-sa-pawr-tay]

▸ our car has been stolen nos han robado el coche [nos an RRo-bah-doh el ko-chay]

steering la dirección [di-rekth-yohn]

▸ there's a problem with the steering hay un problema con la dirección [eye oon prob-lay-ma kon la di-rekth-yohn]

steering wheel el volante [bo-lan-tay]

▸ the steering wheel is very stiff el volante va muy duro [el bo-lan-tay ba mwee doo-roh]

stick shift *(lever)* la palanca de cambio manual [pa-lan-ka day kamb-yoh man-wal]; *(car)* el coche con cambio manual [ko-chay kon kamb-yoh man-wal]

▸ is it a stick shift or an automatic? ¿es un coche con cambio manual o automático? [es oon ko-chay kon kamb-yoh man-wal oh ow-toh-ma-ti-koh]

still todavía [toh-da-bee-a]

▸ how many miles are there still to go? ¿cuántas millas quedan todavía? [kwan-tas meel-yas kay-dan toh-da-bee-a]

▸ we're still waiting to be served todavía estamos esperando a que nos sirvan [toh-da-bee-a es-tah-mos es-pair-an-doh a kay nos seer-ban]

sting *(wasp, nettle)* picar [pi-kahr]

▸ I've been stung by a wasp me ha picado una avispa [may a pi-kah-doh oo-na a-bees-pa]

stomach el estómago [es-toh-ma-goh]

▸ my stomach hurts me duele el estómago [may dway-lay el es-toh-ma-goh]

stomachache el dolor de estómago [do-lor day es-toh-ma-goh]

▸ I have a really bad stomachache tengo un dolor de estómago terrible [ten-goh oon do-lor day es-toh-ma-goh te-RRee-blay]

stop la parada [pa-rah-da] ◆ parar [pa-rahr]

▶ is this the right stop for ...? ¿es ésta la parada de...? [es es-ta la pa-rah-da day]

▶ stop it! ¡para! [pah-ra]

▶ where in town does the shuttle stop? ¿en qué parte de la ciudad para el servicio de conexión? [en kay pahr-tay day la thyoo-dad pah-ra el sair-beeth-yoh day ko-neks-yohn]

▶ please stop here por favor, pare aquí [por fa-bor pah-ray a-kee]

▶ which stations does this train stop at? ¿en qué estaciones para este tren? [en kay es-tath-yoh-nays pah-ra es-tay tren]

▶ do we stop at Salamanca? ¿paramos en Salamanca? [pa-rah-mos en sa-la-man-ka]

store *(place selling goods)* la tienda [tyen-da]

▶ are there any bigger stores in the area? ¿hay tiendas más grandes en la zona? [eye tyen-das mas gran-days en la thoo-na]

store window el escaparate [es-ka-pa-ra-tay]

▶ the store windows are beautifully decorated at Christmas en Navidad los escaparates están con una decoración preciosa [en na-bi-dad los es-ka-pa-ra-tays es-tán kon oo-na de-ko-rath-yohn preth-yoh-sa]

storm la tormenta [tor-men-ta]

▶ is there going to be a storm? ¿va a haber tormenta? [ba a a-bair tor-men-ta]

straight *(line, road)* recto(ta) [RRek-toh]; *(hair)* liso(sa) [lee-soh] ◆ *(in a straight line)* recto [RRek-toh]

▶ you have to keep going straight tienes que continuar recto [tyen-es kay kon-tin-wahr RRek-toh]

street la calle [kal-yay]

▶ will this street take me to the station? ¿esta calle me lleva a la estación? [es-ta kal-yay may yay-ba a la es-tath-yohn]

---

in a store

▶ no, thanks, I'm just looking no, gracias, sólo estoy echando una ojeada [noh grath-yas soh-loh es-toy e-chan-doy oo-na o-CHay-ah-da]

▶ how much is this? ¿cuánto cuesta esto? [kwan-toh kwes-ta es-toh]

▶ I take a size 38/I'm a size 38 mi talla es la treinta y ocho [mee tal-ya es la traynta ee o-choh]

▶ can I try this coat on? ¿puedo probarme este abrigo? [pway-doh pro-bahr-may es-tay a-bree-goh]

▶ can it be exchanged? ¿se puede cambiar? [say pway-day kamb-yahr]

the subway

The subway runs from 6 a.m. to 2 a.m. in Madrid and from 5 a.m. to 12 a.m. in Barcelona (till 2 a.m. Fridays and Saturdays). You can buy individual tickets, but there is also a range of different packages you can use on all types of public transportation which work out cheaper.

streetcar el tranvía [tram-bee-a]
  ▸ can you buy tickets on the streetcar? ¿se pueden comprar los billetes en el tranvía? [day pway-den kom-prahr los bil-yay-tays en el tram-bee-a]

street map el plano de calles [plah-noh day kal-yays]
  ▸ where can I buy a street map? ¿dónde puedo comprar un plano de calles? [don-day pway-doh kom-prahr oon plah-noh day kal-yays]

strong fuerte [fwair-tay]
  ▸ is the current very strong here? ¿la corriente es muy fuerte aquí? [la koRR-yen-tay es mwee fwair-tay a-kee]

stuck
  ▸ someone is stuck in the elevator hay alguien atrapado en el ascensor [eye alg-yen a-tra-pah-doh en el as-then-sawr]

student el estudiante [es-tood-yan-tay], la estudiante [es-tood-yan-tay]
  ▸ I'm a student soy estudiante [soy es-tood-yan-tay]

student discount el descuento para estudiantes [des-kwen-toh pa-ra es-tood-yan-tays]
  ▸ do you have student discounts? ¿hay descuento para estudiantes? [eye des-kwen-toh pa-ra es-tood-yan-tays]

studio (apartment) el estudio [es-tood-yoh]
  ▸ I'm renting a studio apartment alquilo un estudio [al-kee-loh oon es-tood-yoh]

style el estilo [es-tee-loh]
  ▸ she has a lot of style tiene mucho estilo [tyen-ay moo-choh es-tee-loh]

subway el metro [met-roh]
  ▸ can I have a map of the subway? ¿me podría dar un plano del metro? [may pod-ree-a dahr oon plah-noh del met-roh]

subway train el metro [met-roh]
  ▸ when's the last subway train from this station? ¿a qué hora sale el último metro de esta estación? [a kay aw-ra sa-lay el ool-ti-moh met-roh day es-ta es-tath-yohn]

sudden repentino(na) [RRe-pen-tee-noh]
  ▸ all of a sudden de repente [day RRe-pen-tay]

sugar el azúcar [a-thoo-kahr]
  ▸ can you pass me the sugar? ¿me puedes pasar el azúcar? [may pway-days pa-sahr el a-thoo-kahr]

suggest *(propose)* sugerir [sooCH-air-eer]
  ▸ do you have anything else you can suggest? ¿sugieres alguna otra cosa? [sooCH-yair-es al-goo-na oh-tra koh-sa]

suit *(be convenient for)* ir [eer]
  ▸ that suits me perfectly eso me va perfectamente [e-soh may ba pair-fek-ta-men-tay]
  ▸ it doesn't suit me no me va [noh may ba]

suitcase la maleta [ma-lay-ta]
  ▸ one of my suitcases is missing una de mis maletas ha desaparecido [oo-na day mees ma-lay-tas a des-a-pa-re-thee-doh]
  ▸ my suitcase was damaged in transit han dañado una de mis maletas durante el transporte [an dan-yah-doh oo-na day mees ma-lay-tas doo-ran-tay el trans-pawr-tay]

summer el verano [bair-ah-noh]
  ▸ in (the) summer en verano [en bair-ah-noh]

summer vacation las vacaciones de verano [ba-kath-yoh-nays day bair-ah-noh]
  ▸ we've come here for our summer vacation hemos venido aquí de vacaciones de verano [ay-mos be-nee-doh a-kee day ba-kath-yoh-nays day bair-ah-noh]

sun el sol [sol]
  ▸ the sun's very strong at this time of day a esta hora del día el sol es muy fuerte [a es-ta aw-ra del dee-a el sol es mwee fwair-tay]

sunburn las quemaduras (por el sol) [kay-ma-doo-ras (por el sol)]
  ▸ I've got a bad sunburn me he quemado bastante [may ay kay-mah-doh bas-tan-tay]
  ▸ do you have cream for a sunburn? ¿tiene crema para las quemaduras? [tyen-ay kray-ma pa-ra las kay-ma-doo-ras]

Sunday el domingo [dom-in-goh]
  ▸ where can I find a doctor on a Sunday? ¿dónde puedo encontrar un médico el domingo? [don-day pway-doh en-kon-trahr oon may-di-koh el dom-in-goh]
  ▸ are the stores open on Sunday? ¿las tiendas abren los domingos? [las tyen-das a-bren los dom-in-gohs]

sun deck la cubierta superior [koob-yair-ta soo-pair-yawr]
  ▸ how do I get onto the sun deck? ¿cómo subo a la cubierta superior? [kom-oh soo-boh a la koob-yair-ta soo-pair-yawr]

sunglasses las gafas de sol [ga-fas day sol]
  ▸ I've lost my sunglasses he perdido las gafas de sol [ay pair-dee-doh las ga-fas day sol]

sunny *(day, weather)* soleado(da) [sol-ay-ah-doh]
  ▸ it's sunny hace sol [a-thay sol]

sunrise el amanecer [a-ma-neth-air]
  ▸ what time is sunrise? ¿a qué hora es el amanecer? [a kay aw-ra es el a-ma-neth-air]

sunset la puesta de sol [pwes-ta day sol]
  ▸ isn't the sunset beautiful? ¿no es preciosa la puesta de sol? [nog es preth-yoh-sa la pwes-ta day sol]

suntan lotion la loción bronceadora [loth-yohn bron-thay-a-daw-ra]
- I'd like SPF 30 suntan lotion quería loción bronceadora con factor de protección solar treinta [kair-ee-a loth-yohn bron-thay-a-daw-ra kon fak-tawr day pro-tekth-yohn so-lahr trayn-ta]

supermarket el supermercado [soo-pair-mair-kah-doh]
- is there a supermarket nearby? ¿hay un supermercado cerca? [eye oon soo-pair-mair-kah-doh thair-ka]

surcharge el recargo [RRe-kahr-goh]
- do I have to pay a surcharge? ¿tengo que pagar un recargo? [ten-goh kay pa-gahr oon RRe-kahr-goh]

sure seguro(ra) [se-goo-roh]
- are you sure that's how you say it? ¿estás seguro de que se dice así? [es-tas se-goo-roh day kay say dee-thay a-see]

surfboard la tabla de surf [tab-la day soorf]
- is there somewhere we can rent surfboards? ¿hay algún lugar donde podamos alquilar tablas de surf? [eye al-goon loo-gahr don-day pod-ah-mos al-ki-lahr tab-las day soorf]

surfing el surf [soorf]
- can we go surfing around here? ¿podemos hacer surf por aquí? [pod-ay-mos a-thair soorf por a-kee]

surprise la sorpresa [sor-pray-sa]
- what a nice surprise! ¡qué sorpresa tan agradable! [kay sor-pray-sa tan a-gra-dah-blay]

surrounding area los alrededores [al-RRe-de-daw-rays]
- Alicante and the surrounding area Alicante y los alrededores [a-li-kan-tay ee los al-RRe-de-daw-rays]

swallow tragar [tra-gahr]
- the ATM outside has swallowed my credit card el cajero automático ahí fuera se ha tragado mi tarjeta de crédito [el kaCH-air-oh ow-toh-ma-ti-koh a-ee fwair-a say a tra-gah-doh mee tar-CHay-ta day kre-di-toh]
- it hurts when I swallow me duele cuando trago [may dway-lay kwan-doh trah-goh]

swim nadar [na-dahr] ◆ el baño [ban-yoh]
- is it safe to swim here? ¿se puede nadar sin peligro aquí? [say pway-day na-dahr seen pe-lee-groh a-kee]
- to go for a swim ir a darse un baño [eer a dahr-say oon ban-yoh]

swimming pool la piscina [pis-thee-na]
- is there an open-air swimming pool? ¿hay piscina al aire libre? [eye pis-thee-na al eye-ray lee-bray]

switch el interruptor [in-te-RRoop-tawr]
- the switch doesn't work el interruptor no funciona [el in-te-RRoop-tawr noh foonth-yoh-na]

switch off apagar [a-pa-gahr]

▸ where do you switch the light off? ¿cómo se apaga la luz? [kom-oh say a-pah-ga la looth]

▸ my cell was switched off tenía el móvil apagado [ten-ee-a el mob-eel a-pa-gah-doh]

switch on encender [en-then-dair]

▸ where do I switch this light on? ¿cómo se enciende esta luz? [kom-oh say en-thyen-day es-ta looth]

table la mesa [may-sa]

▸ I've reserved a table in the name of... he reservado una mesa a nombre de... [ay RRe-sair-bah-doh oo-na may-sa a nom-bray day]

▸ a table for four, please! una mesa para cuatro, por favor [oo-na may-sa pa-ra kwat-roh por fa-bor]

table tennis el tenis de mesa [ten-ees day may-sa], el ping pong [peen-pon]

▸ are there tables for table tennis? ¿hay mesas para ping pong? [eye mesas pa-ra peen-pon]

table wine el vino de mesa [bee-noh day may-sa]

▸ a bottle of red table wine una botella de vinto tinto de mesa [oo-na bo-tel-ya day bee-noh teen-toh day may-sa]

take coger [koCH-air]; *(carry, lead, accompany)* llevar [yay-bahr]; *(wear)* usar [oo-sahr]

▸ someone's taken my bag alguien me ha cogido el bolso [alg-yen may a koCH-ee-doh el bol-soh]

▸ can you take me to this address? ¿me podría llevar a esta dirección? [may pod-ree-a yay-bahr a es-ta di-rekth-yohn]

▸ are you taking the plane or the train to Madrid? ¿vas a coger el avión o el tren a Madrid? [bas a koCH-air el ab-yohn oh el tren a mad-reed]

▸ which road should I take? ¿qué carretera tengo que coger? [kay ka-RRe-tair-a ten-goh kay koCH-air]

▸ I take a size 40 calzo el 40 [kal-thoh el kwa-ren-ta]

▸ how long does the trip take? ¿cuánto dura el viaje? [kwan-toh doo-ra el bya-CHay]

▸ how long does it take to get to Santander? ¿cuándo se tarda en llegar a Santander? [kwan-toh say tahr-da en yay-gahr a san-tan-dair]

▸ could you take a photo of us? ¿podría hacernos una foto? [pod-ree-a a-thair-nos oo-na foh-toh]

take back *(to a store)* devolver [day-bol-bair]; *(to one's home)* llevar (de vuelta) [yay-bahr (day bwel-ta)]

▸ I'm looking for a present to take back to my son busco un regalo para poder llevárselo a mi hijo [boos-koh oon RRe-gah-loh pa-ra pod-air yay-bahr-say-loh a mee ee-CHoh]

take down *(bags, luggage)* bajar [ba-CHahr]

▸ could you take these bags down, please? ¿podría bajar estas bolsas, por favor? [pod-ree-a ba-CHahr es-tas bol-sas por fa-bor]

take in *(bags, luggage)* entrar [en-trar]

▸ can you have someone take in my bags, please? ¿alguien podría entrar mis bolsas, por favor? [alg-yen pod-ree-a en-trar mees bol-sas por fa-bor]

taken *(seat)* ocupado(da) [o-koo-pah-doh]

▸ sorry, this seat is taken disculpe, este asiento está ocupado [dis-kool-pay es-tay as-yen-toh es-ta o-koo-pah-doh]

take over *(when driving)* tomar el relevo [tom-ahr el RRe-lay-boh]

▸ would you like me to take over from you for a while? ¿quieres que tome el relevo un rato? [kyair-ays kay toh-may el RRe-lay-boh oon RRa-toh]

take up *(bags, luggage)* subir [soo-beer]

▸ can someone take our bags up to our room? ¿podría alguien subir las bolsas a nuestra habitación? [pod-ree-a alg-yen soo-beer las bol-sas a nwes-tra a-bi-tath-yohn]

talk hablar [ab-lahr]

▸ could I talk with you for a moment? ¿puedo hablar contigo un momento? [pway-doh ab-lahr kon-tee-goh oon mo-men-toh]

▸ you have no right to talk to me like that no tienes derecho a hablarme así [noh tyen-es de-re-choh a ab-lahr-may a-see]

tall *(person, tree, building)* alto(ta) [al-toh]

▸ what's that tall building over there? ¿qué es ese edificio alto ahí? [kay es e-say e-di-feeth-yoh al-toh a-ee]

tank *(for gas)* el depósito [de-po-si-toh]

▸ is the tank full? ¿está lleno el depósito? [es-ta yay-noh el de-po-si-toh]

taste el sabor [sa-bawr] ♦ *(sense)* notar sabor a [noh-tahr sa-bawr a]; *(try)* probar [proh-bahr] ♦ saber [sa-bair]

▸ I can't taste anything no noto sabor a nada [noh noh-toh sa-bawr a nah-da]

▸ would you like to taste the wine? ¿quiere probar el vino? [kyair-ay proh-bahr el bee-noh]

▸ it tastes funny sabe raro [sa-bay RRah-roh]

tax el impuesto [im-pwes-toh]

▸ does this price include tax? ¿el precio incluye los impuestos? [el preth-yoh in-kloo-yay los im-pwes-tohs]

taxi el taxi [tak-si]

▸ how much does a taxi cost from here to the station? ¿cuánto cuesta un taxi de aquí hasta la estación? [kwan-toh kwes-ta oon tak-si day a-kee as-ta la es-tath-yohn]

▸ I'd like to reserve a taxi to take me to the airport, please quería reservar un taxi para llevarme al aeropuerto, por favor [kair-ee-a RRe-sair-bahr oon tak-si pa-ra yay-bahr-may al eye-roh-pwair-toh por fa-bor]

taxi driver el taxista [tak-sees-ta], la taxista [tak-sees-ta]
▸ can you ask the taxi driver to wait? ¿podría pedirle al taxista que espere? [pod-ree-a ped-eer-lay al tak-sees-ta kay es-pair-ay]

taxi stand la parada de taxis [pa-rah-da day tak-sis]
▸ where can I find a taxi stand? ¿dónde puedo encontrar una parada de taxis? [don-day pway-doh en-kon-trahr oo-na pa-rah-da day tak-sis]

tea (drink) el té [tay]
▸ tea with milk té con leche [tay kon le-chay]
▸ tea without milk té sin leche [tay seen le-chay]

teach enseñar [en-sen-yahr]
▸ so, you teach Spanish? maybe you could help me! ¿así que enseña español? ¡a lo mejor podía ayudarme! [a-see kay en-sen-ya es-pan-yol a loh me-CHor pod-ee-a a-yoo-dahr-may]

teacher el profesor [pro-fe-sawr], la profesora [pro-fe-saw-ra]
▸ I'm a teacher soy profesor/profesora [soy pro-fe-sawr/pro-fe-saw-ra]

telephone el teléfono [te-lay-fo-noh] ◆ telefonear [te-le-fo-nay-ahr], llamar por teléfono a [ya-mahr por te-lay-fo-noh a]
▸ can I use the telephone? ¿puedo usar el teléfono? [pway-doh oo-sahr el te-lay-fo-noh]

telephone booth la cabina telefónica [ka-bee-na te-le-fo-ni-ka]
▸ is there a telephone booth near here? ¿hay alguna cabina telefónica cerca de aquí? [eye al-goo-na ka-bee-na te-le-fo-ni-ka thair-ka day a-kee]

telephone call la llamada telefónica [ya-mah-da te-le-fo-ni-ka]
▸ I'd like to make a telephone call quería hacer una llamada telefónica [kair-ee-a a-thair oo-na ya-mah-da te-le-fo-ni-ka]

---

taking a taxi

▸ could you call me a taxi, please? ¿podría llamarme un taxi, por favor? [pod-ree-a ya-mahr-may oon tak-si por fa-bor]
▸ to the station/airport, please a la estación/al aeropuerto, por favor [a la es-tath-yohn/eye-roh-pwair-toh por fa-bor]
▸ stop here/at the lights/at the corner, please pare aquí/en el semáforo/en la esquina, por favor [pah-ray a-kee/en el se-ma-fo-roh/en la es-kee-na por fa-bor]
▸ can you wait for me? ¿podría esperarme? [pod-ree-a es-pair-ahr-may]
▸ how much is it? ¿cuánto es? [kwan-toh es]
▸ keep the change quédese con el cambio [kay-day-say kon el kamb-yoh]

television la televisión [te-le-bis-yohn]
 ▸ what's on television tonight? ¿qué hay en televisión esta noche? [kay eye en te-le-bis-yohn es-ta no-chay]

tell decir [de-theer]
 ▸ can you tell me the way to the museum? ¿me podría decir por dónde se va al museo? [may pod-ree-a de-theer por don-day say ba al moo-say-oh]
 ▸ can you tell me what time it is? ¿me podría decir qué hora es? [may pod-ree-a de-theer kay aw-ra es]

temperature *(meteorological)* la temperatura [tem-pe-ra-too-ra]; *(fever)* la fiebre [fyeb-ray]
 ▸ what's the temperature? ¿qué temperatura hace? [kay tem-pe-ra-too-ra a-thay]
 ▸ I've got a temperature tengo fiebre [ten-goh fyeb-ray]

ten diez [dyeth]
 ▸ there are ten of us somos diez [som-os dyeth]

tennis el tenis [ten-ees]
 ▸ where can we play tennis? ¿dónde podemos jugar al tenis? [don-day pod-ay-mos CHoo-gahr al ten-ees]

tennis racket la raqueta de tenis [RRa-kay-ta day ten-ees]
 ▸ can you rent tennis rackets? ¿se pueden alquilar raquetas de tenis? [say pway-den al-ki-lahr RRa-kay-tas day ten-ees]

tent la tienda (de campaña) [tyen-da (day kam-pan-ya)]
 ▸ I'd like to book space for a tent, please quería reservar espacio para una tienda (de campaña) [kair-ee-a RRe-sair-bahr es-path-yoh pa-ra oo-na tyen-da (day kam-pan-ya)]
 ▸ can you put up your tent anywhere? ¿se puede montar la tienda en cualquier lugar? [say pway-day mon-tahr la tyen-da en kwalk-yair loo-gahr]

tent peg la clavija [kla-bee-CHa]
 ▸ we're short of tent pegs nos faltan clavijas [nos fal-tan kla-bee-CHas]

terminal *(in airport)* la terminal [tair-mi-nal]
 ▸ where is terminal 1? ¿dónde está la terminal 1? [don-day es-ta la tair-mi-nal oo-noh]
 ▸ is there a shuttle between terminals? ¿hay un servicio de conexión entre las terminales? [eye oon sair-beeth-yoh day ko-neks-yohn en-tray las tair-mi-nah-lays]

tetanus el tétanos [tay-ta-nohs]
 ▸ I've been vaccinated for tetanus me he vacunado contra el tétanos [may ay ba-koo-nah-doh kon-tra el tay-ta-nohs]

thank agradecer [a-gra-de-thair] ◆ **thanks** gracias [grath-yas]
 ▸ I can't thank you enough no puedo agradecértelo lo suficiente [noh pway-doh a-gra-de-thair-tay-loh loh soo-feeth-yen-tay]
 ▸ thanks for everything (you've done) gracias por todo (lo que has hecho) [grath-yas por toh-doh (loh kay as e-choh)]

thank you! gracias [grath-yas]
- thank you very much! ¡muchas gracias! [moo-chas grath-yas]
- thank you for your help gracias por tu ayuda [grath-yas por too a-yoo-da]

that *(demonstrative use)* ese [e-say]; *(in relative clauses)* que [kay]
- who's that? ¿quién es ese? [kyen es e-say]
- that's right eso es [e-soh es]
- the road that goes to Zaragoza la carretera que va a Zaragoza [la ka-RRe-tair-a ba a tha-ra-goh-tha]
- I'll have that one quiero ese [kyair-oh e-say]

theater *(for plays)* el teatro [tay-at-roh]
- where is there a theater? ¿dónde hay un teatro? [don-day eye oon tay-at-roh]

theft el robo [RRoh-boh]
- I'd like to report a theft quería denunciar un robo [kair-ee-a de-noonth-yahr oon RRoh-boh]

then entonces [en-ton-thays]
- I'll see you then te veré entonces [tay bair-ay en-ton-thays]
- I'll see you at six then te veré entonces a las seis [tay bair-ay en-ton-thays a las seys]

there ahí [a-ee]
- he's over there está ahí [es-ta a-ee]
- there is/are... hay... [eye]
- there's a problem hay un problema [eye oon prob-lay-ma]
- are there any restrooms near here? ¿hay servicios aquí? [eye sair-beeth-yohs a-kee]
- there you are *(handing over something)* aquí tienes [a-kee tyen-es]

thermometer el termómetro [tair-mo-met-roh]
- do you have a thermometer? ¿tiene un termómetro? [tyen-ay oon tair-mo-met-roh]
- the thermometer shows 18 degrees (Celsius) el termómetro marca dieciocho grados Celsius [el tair-mo-met-roh mahr-ka dyeth-ee-o-choh grah-dohs thels-yoos]

---

saying thank you

- thank you gracias [grath-yas]
- thanks, that's very kind of you gracias, es muy amable de tu parte [grath-yas es mwee a-mah-blay day too pahr-tay]
- I can't thank you enough no puedo agradecértelo lo suficiente [noh pway-doh a-gra-de-thair-tay-loh loh soo-feeth-yen-tay]
- thank you for your help gracias por tu ayuda [grath-yas por too a-yoo-da]
- I wanted to thank you for inviting me quería darte las gracias por invitarme [kair-ee-a dahr-tay las grath-yas por in-bi-tahr-may]

thin *(person)* delgado(da) [del-gah-doh]; *(slice, layer, material)* fino(na) [fee-noh]
  ▸ isn't that jacket too thin for a cold evening like this? ¿esa chaqueta no es muy fina para una noche fría como esta? [e-sa cha-kay-ta noh es mwee fee-na pa-ra oo-na no-chay free-a kom-oh es-ta]

thing la cosa [koh-sa]
  ▸ what's that thing for? ¿para qué es esa cosa? [pa-ra kay es e-sa koh-sa]
  ▸ I don't know what the best thing to do is no sé que es lo mejor que puedo hacer [noh say kay es loh me-CHor kay pway-doh a-thair]
  ▸ could you look after my things for a minute? ¿podría cuidar de mis cosas un minuto? [pod-ree-a kwee-dahr day mees koh-sas oon mi-noo-toh]

think pensar [pen-sahr], creer [kray-air]
  ▸ I think (that)... creo que... [kray-oh kay]
  ▸ I thought service charge was included pensaba que el servicio estaba incluido [pen-sah-ba kay el sair-beeth-yoh es-tah-ba in-kloo-ee-doh]
  ▸ I don't think so no creo [noh kray-oh]

third tercero(ra) [tair-thair-oh] ◆ *(fraction)* el tercio [tairth-yoh]; *(gear)* la tercera [tair-thair-a]
  ▸ this is my third time in Spain esta es mi tercera vez en España [es-ta es mee tair-tahir-a beth en es-pan-ya]

thirsty
  ▸ to be thirsty tener sed [ten-air sed]
  ▸ I'm very thirsty tengo mucha sed [ten-goh moo-cha sed]

three tres [tres]
  ▸ there are three of us somos tres [som-os tres]

throat la garganta [gahr-gan-ta]
  ▸ I have a fish bone stuck in my throat tengo una espina clavada en la garganta [ten-goh oo-na es-pee-na kla-bah-da en la gahr-gan-ta]

throat lozenge la pastilla para la garganta [pas-teel-ya pa-ra la gahr-gan-ta]
  ▸ I'd like some throat lozenges quería pastillas para la garganta [kair-ee-a pas-teel-yas pa-ra la gahr-gan-ta]

thunderstorm la tormenta [tor-men-ta]
  ▸ will there be a thunderstorm? ¿habrá tormenta? [ab-ra tor-men-ta]

Thursday el jueves [CHweb-es]
  ▸ we're arriving/leaving on Thursday llegaremos/nos iremos el jueves [yay-ga-ray-mos/nos ee-ray-mos el CHweb-es]

ticket *(for a train, a plane, a bus, the subway)* el billete [bil-yay-tay]; *(for a movie theater, a museum, a sports event)* la entrada [en-trah-da]
  ▸ I'd like a ticket to... quería un billete a... [kair-ee-a oon bil-yay-tay a]
  ▸ how much is a ticket to...? ¿cuánto cuesta un billete a...? [kwan-toh kwes-ta oon bil-yay-tay a]

tickets for public transportation   ⓘ

You can buy tickets for public transportation in *estancos* (tobacco stores) and sometimes in banks. Take a tip: you can buy a single ticket that is valid for 10 trips, which makes good sense. If you're traveling on regional trains, the *Bono 10* card covers 10 journeys, too.

▸ a book of 10 tickets, please un billete de 10 viajes, por favor [oon bil-yay-tay day dyeth bya-CHays por fa-bor]

▸ I'd like to book a ticket quería reservar un billete [kair-ee-a RRe-sair-bahr oon bil-yay-tay]

▸ I'd like three tickets for... quería tres entradas para [kair-ee-a tres en-trah-das pa-ra]

tide la marea [ma-ray-a]

▸ what time does the tide turn? ¿a qué hora cambia la marea? [a kay aw-ra kamb-ya la ma-ray-a]

tight *(piece of clothing)* ajustado(da) [a-CHoos-tah-doh]

▸ these pants are too tight estos pantalones me quedan muy ajustados [es-tohs pan-ta-loh-nays may kay-dan mwee a-CHoos-tah-dohs]

time el tiempo [tyem-poh]; *(by clock)* la hora [aw-ra]; *(occasion)* la vez [beth]

▸ do we have time to visit the town? ¿tenemos tiempo para visitar la ciudad? [ten-ay-mos tyem-poh pa-ra bi-si-tahr la thyoo-dad]

▸ what time is it? ¿qué hora es? [kay aw-ra es]

▸ what time do you close? ¿a qué hora cierra? [a kay aw-ra thee-e-RRa]

▸ could you tell me if the train from Madrid is on time? ¿podría decirme si el tren de Madrid llega a la hora? [pod-ree-a de-theer-may see el tren day mad-reed yay-ga a la aw-ra]

▸ maybe some other time a lo mejor en otra ocasión [a loh me-CHor en oh-tra o-kas-yohn]

▸ three times tres veces [tres beth-ays]

▸ at the same time al mismo tiempo [al mees-moh tyem-poh]

▸ the first time la primera vez [la pri-mair-a beth]

timetable el horario [o-rahr-yoh]

▸ do you have local bus timetables? ¿tiene el horario de los autobuses locales? [tyen-ay el o-rahr-yoh day los ow-toh-boos-es loh-kah-lays]

tip *(gratuity)* la propina [pro-pee-na] ✦ *(give a gratuity to)* dar propina a [dahr pro-pee-na a]

▸ how much should I leave as a tip? ¿cuánto tengo que dar de propina? [kwan-toh ten-goh kay dahr day pro-pee-na] ▸ see box on p. 142

tire *(for a vehicle)* la rueda [RRoo-ay-da], el neumático [new-ma-ti-koh]

▸ the tire's flat la rueda está desinflada [la RRoo-ay-da es-ta des-in-flah-da]

▸ the tire's punctured la rueda está pinchada [la RRoo-ay-da es-ta pin-chah-da]

tipping

A service charge is included on your check (*la cuenta*), but the tip isn't. How much you leave is up to you and depends on the type of establishment. Spaniards differ in the amount they tip, but most people probably round the check up to the nearest suitable whole figure. Around 5–10% would probably be the average.

to *(indicating place, direction)* a [a]; *(in telling time)* menos [may-nos]
▸ when is the next train to Valencia? ¿a qué hora es el próximo tren a Valencia? [a kay aw-ra es el prok-si-moh tren a ba-lenth-ya]
▸ it's twenty to nine son las nueve menos veinte [son las nway-bay may-nos bayn-tay]

tobacco store el estanco [es-tan-koh]
▸ where is the nearest tobacco store? ¿dónde está el estanco más cercano? [don-day es-ta el es-tan-koh mas thair-kah-noh]

today hoy [oy]
▸ what's today's date? ¿a qué fecha estamos hoy? [a kay fe-cha es-tah-mos oy]

toe el dedo del pie [day-doh del pyay]
▸ I think I've broken my toe creo que me he roto un dedo del pie [kray-oh kay may ay RRoh-toh oon day-doh del pyay]

together juntos(tas) [CHoon-tohs]
▸ let's go together vamos juntos [bah-mos CHoon-tohs]

toilet el baño [ban-yoh], el servicio [sair-beeth-yoh]
▸ I need to go to the toilet tengo que ir al baño [ten-goh kay eer al ban-yoh]
▸ do you have to pay to use the toilet? ¿hay que pagar para usar el baño? [eye kay pa-gahr pa-ra oo-sahr el ban-yoh]

toilet paper el papel higiénico [pa-pel eeCH-yay-ni-koh]
▸ there is no toilet paper no hay papel higiénico [noh eye pa-pel eeCH-yay-ni-koh]

toll *(for a road, a bridge)* el peaje [pay-a-CHay]
▸ do you have to pay a toll to use the bridge? ¿hay que pagar peaje para usar el puente? [eye kay pa-gahr pay-a-Chay pa-ra oo-sar el pwen-tay]

toll-free *(number, call)* gratuito(ta) [grat-wee-toh] ◆ *(call)* gratuitamente [grat-wee-ta-men-tay]
▸ there's a toll-free number you can call hay un número gratuito al que puedes llamar [eye oon noo-mair-oh grat-wee-toh al kay pway-days ya-mahr]

tomato el tomate [to-ma-tay]
▸ a kilo of tomatoes un kilo de tomates [oon kee-loh day to-ma-tays]

tomato juice el zumo de tomate [thoo-moh day to-ma-tay]
▸ I'd like a tomato juice quería un zumo de tomate [kair-ee-a oon thoo-moh day to-ma-tay]

tomorrow mañana [man-yah-na]
- can you hold my reservation until tomorrow? ¿puede mantener mi reserva hasta mañana? [pway-day man-ten-air mee RRe-sair-ba as-ta man-yah-na]
- I'm leaving tomorrow morning salgo mañana por la mañana [sal-goh man-yah-na por la man-yah-na]
- see you tomorrow night hasta mañana por la noche [as-ta man-yah-na por la no-chay]

tonight esta noche [es-ta no-chay]
- do you have any beds available for tonight? ¿tiene camas para esta noche? [tyen-ay ka-mas pa-ra es-ta no-chay]

too *(also)* también [tamb-yen]; *(excessively)* demasiado(da) [de-mas-yah-doh]
- enjoy your meal! – you too ¡que aproveche! – tú también [kay a-pro-bech-ay – too tamb-yen]
- she's too tired to... está demasiado cansada para... [es-ta de-mas-yah-doh kan-sah-da pa-ra]
- it's too expensive es demasiado caro [es de-mas-yah-doh kah-roh]
- there are too many people hay demasiada gente [eye de-mas-yah-da-CHen-tay]

tooth el diente [dyen-tay]
- I've broken a tooth me he roto un diente [may ay RRoh-toh oon dyen-tay]

toothache el dolor de muelas [do-lawr day mway-las]
- I have a toothache tengo dolor de muelas [ten-goh do-lawr day mway-las]

toothbrush el cepillo de dientes [thep-eel-yoh day dyen-tays]
- I forgot my toothbrush me he olvidado el cepillo de dientes [may ay ol-bi-dah-doh el thep-eel-yoh day dyen-tays]

toothpaste la pasta de dientes [pas-ta day dyen-tays]
- I'd like to buy some toothpaste quería comprar pasta de dientes [kair-ee-a komprahr pas-ta day dyen-tays]

top *(of a bottle, a tube)* el tapón [ta-pohn]; *(of a pen)* la capucha [ka-poo-cha]; *(of a jar)* la tapa [ta-pa] • *(maximum)* máximo(ma) [mak-si-moh]
- the car drove away at top speed el coche se marchó a toda velocidad [el ko-chay say mahr-choh a toh-da be-lo-thi-dad]

tour el viaje [bya-CHay]
- I'm planning to do a two-week tour of the country estoy planeando un viaje de dos semanas por el país [es-toy pla-nay-an-doh oon bya-CHay day dos se-mah-nas por el pa-ees]

tourist el turista [too-rees-ta], la turista [too-rees-ta] • *(season)* turístico(ta) [too-rees-ti-koh]
- do you get many tourists here? ¿vienen muchos turistas por aquí? [byen-en moo-chohs too-rees-tas por a-kee]

tourist attraction la atracción turística [a-trakth-yohn too-rees-ti-ka]
- what are the main tourist attractions in the area? ¿cuáles son las principales

atracciones turísticas de la zona? [kwah-lays son las prin-thi-pah-lays a-trakth-yoh-nays too-rees-ti-kas day la thoh-na]

tourist class la clase turista [kla-say too-rees-ta]

▸ in tourist class, please en clase turista, por favor [en kla-say too-rees-ta por fa-bor]

tourist guide la guía turística [gee-a too-rees-ti-ka]

▸ we have a good tourist guide with a lot of up-to-date information tenemos una buena guía turística con un montón de información actualizada [ten-ay-mos oo-na bway-na gee-a too-rees-ti-ka kon oon mon-tohn day in-for-math-yohn ak-too-a-li-thah-da]

tourist office la oficina de turismo [o-fi-thee-na day too-rees-moh]

▸ I'm looking for the tourist office estoy buscando la oficina de turismo [es-toy boos-kan-doh la o-fi-thee-na day too-rees-moh]

▸ can I get a street map at the tourist office? ¿en la oficina de turismo puedo conseguir un plano de calles? [en la o-fi-thee-na day too-rees-moh pway-doh kon-se-geer oon pla-noh day kal-yays]

tow remolcar [RRe-mol-kahr]

▸ could you tow me to a garage? ¿me podría remolcar hasta un taller? [may pod-ree-a RRe-mol-kahr as-ta oon tal-yair]

toward *(in the direction of)* hacia [ath-ya]

▸ we're heading toward Segovia vamos hacia Segovia [bah-mos ath-ya se-gohb-ya]

tow away

▸ my car's been towed away se me ha llevado el coche la grúa [say may a yay-bah-doh el ko-chay la groo-a]

towel la toalla [toh-al-ya]

▸ we don't have any towels no tenemos toallas [noh ten-ay-mos toh-al-yas]

▸ could we have more towels? ¿nos podía dar más toallas? [nos pod-ee-a dahr mas toh-al-yas]

---

getting around town

▸ which bus goes to the airport? ¿qué autobús va al aeropuerto? [kay ow-toh-boos ba al eye-roh-pwair-toh]

▸ where does the bus to the station leave from? ¿de dónde sale el autobús a la estación? [day don-day sa-lay el ow-toh-boos a la es-tath-yohn]

▸ I'd like a one-way (ticket) to... quería un billete de ida a... [kair-ee-a oon bil-yay-tay day ee-da a]

▸ can I have a book of tickets, please? ¿me podría dar un talonario de billetes? [may pod-ree-a dahr oon ta-loh-nahr-yoh day bil-yay-tays]

▸ could you tell me where I have to get off to go to...? ¿me podría decir dónde me tengo que bajar para ir a...? [may pod-ree-a de-theer don-day may ten-goh kay ba-CHahr pa-ra eer a]

tower *(of a church, a castle)* la torre [toRR-ay]
▸ can you visit the tower? ¿se puede visitar la torre? [say pway-day bi-si-tar la toRR-ay]

town la ciudad [thyoo-dad]
▸ to go into town ir al centro [eer al then-troh]

town hall el ayuntamiento [a-yoon-tam-yen-toh]
▸ where is the town hall? ¿dónde está el ayuntamiento? [don-day es-ta el a-yoon-tam-yen-toh]

traffic *(vehicles)* el tráfico [tra-fi-koh]
▸ is there a lot of traffic on the freeway? ¿hay mucho tráfico en la autopista? [eye moo-choh tra-fi-koh en la ow-toh-pees-ta]

traffic circle la rotonda [RRo-ton-da]
▸ you turn right at the traffic circle gire a la derecha en la rotonda [CHee-ray a de-re-cha en la RRo-ton-da]

traffic jam el atasco [a-tas-koh]
▸ we got stuck in a traffic jam nos quedamos atrapados en un atasco [nos ke-dah-mos a-tra-pah-dohs en oon a-tas-koh]

traffic lights el semáforo [se-ma-fo-roh]
▸ turn left at the traffic lights gira a la izquierda en el próximo semáforo [CHee-ra a la ith-kyair-da en el prok-si-moh se-ma-fo-roh]

trail *(path)* el camino [ka-mee-noh]
▸ will this trail take us back to the parking lot? ¿este camino nos lleva de vuelta al parking? [es-tay ka-mee-noh nos yay-ba day bwel-ta al pahr-king]

train el tren [tren]
▸ when is the next train to Seville? ¿cuándo es el próximo tren a Sevilla? [kwand-doh es el prok-si-moh tren a se-beel-ya]
▸ I'd like a round-trip ticket for the 9 a.m. train to Madrid tomorrow, please quería un billete de ida y vuelta para el tren de mañana a las nueve de la mañana a Madrid, por favor [kair-ee-a oon bil-yay-tay day ee-da ee bwel-ta pa-ra el tren day man-yah-na a las nway-bay de la man-yah-na a mad-reed por fa-bor]
▸ do you have reduced-price train tickets for seniors? ¿tienen billetes con descuento para jubilados? [tyen-en bil-yay-tays kon des-kwen-toh pa-ra CHoo-bi-lah-dohs]
▸ which platform does the train for Logroño leave from? ¿de qué andén sale el tren de Logroño? [day kay an-dayn sa-lay el tren day loh-gron-yoh]
▸ the train was fifteen minutes late el tren llegó con quince minutos de retraso [el tren yay-goh kon keen-thay mi-noo-tohs day RRe-tra-soh]
▸ where do international trains leave from? ¿dónde salen los trenes internacionales? [day don-day sa-len los tren-ays in-tair-nath-yoh-nah-lays]

tram el tranvía [tram-bee-a]
▸ can you buy tickets on the tram? ¿se pueden comprar los billetes en el tranvía? [say pway-den kom-prahr los bil-yay-tays en el tram-bee-a]

transfer *(of money)* la transferencia [trans-fair-enth-ya] ♦ *(money)* transferir [trans-fair-eer]

▶ I'd like to transfer some money from my savings account quería transferir dinero de mi cuenta de ahorros [kair-ee-a trans-fair-eer di-nair-oh day mee kwen-ta day a-o-RRohs]

travel los viajes [bya-CHays] ♦ *(go on a trip)* viajar [bya-CHahr]

▶ I'd like a window seat facing the direction of travel quería un asiento de ventana mirando hacia el frente [kair-ee-a oon as-yen-toh day ben-tah-na mi-ran-doh ath-ya el fren-tay]

▶ I'm traveling on my own viajo solo [bya-CHoh soh-loh]

travel agency la agencia de viajes [a-CHenth-ya day bya-CHays]

▶ I'm looking for a travel agency estoy buscando una agencia de viajes [es-toy boos-kan-doh oo-na a-CHenth-ya day bya-CHays]

traveler's check el cheque de viaje [che-kay day bya-CHay]

▶ do you take traveler's checks? ¿aceptan cheques de viaje? [a-thep-tan che-kays day bya-CHay]

tree el árbol [ahr-bol]

▶ what type of tree is that? ¿qué tipo de árbol es ese? [kay tee-poh day ahr-bol es es-ay]

trip *(journey)* el viaje [bya-CHay]

▶ have a good trip! ¡buen viaje! [bwen bya-CHay]

trouble el problema [prob-lay-ma]

▶ we didn't have any trouble finding the hotel no tuvimos ningún problema para encontrar el hotel [noh too-bee-mos nin-goon prob-lay-ma pa-ra en-kon-trahr el oh-tel]

▶ I don't want to be any trouble no quiero causar ningún problema [noh kyair-oh kow-sahr nin-goon prob-lay-ma]

▶ it's no trouble no es molestia [noh es mo-lest-ya]

trunk *(of a car)* el maletero [ma-le-tair-oh]; *(piece of luggage)* el baúl [ba-ool]

▶ my things are in the trunk of the car mis cosas están en el maletero del coche [mees koh-sas es-tan en el ma-le-tair-oh del ko-chay]

▶ I've got two small suitcases and a large trunk tengo dos maletas pequeñas y un baúl grande [ten-goh dos ma-lay-tas pe-kayn-yas ee oon ba-ool gran-day]

try *(attempt)* intentar [in-ten-tahr]; *(sample)* probar [pro-bahr]

▶ I'd like to try the local beer me gustaría probar la cerveza local [may goos-ta-ree-a pro-bahr la thair-bay-tha loh-kal]

try on *(dress, shoes)* probarse [pro-bahr-say]

▶ I'd like to try on the one in the window me gustaría probarme el del escaparate [may goos-ta-ree-a pro-bahr-may el del es-ka-pa-ra-tay]

tub *(of ice cream)* la tarrina [ta-ree-na]

▶ do you sell tubs of ice cream to take home? ¿venden tarrinas de helado para llevar a casa? [ben-den ta-ree-nas day e-lah-doh pa-ra yay-bahr a ka-sa]

Tuesday el martes [mar-tes]

▸ we're arriving/leaving on Tuesday llegaremos/nos iremos el martes [yay-ga-ray-mos/nos ee-ray-mos el mar-tes]

tunnel el túnel [too-nel]

▸ is there a toll for using the tunnel? ¿hay peaje para pasar por el túnel? [eye pay-a-CHay pa-ra pa-sahr por el too-nel]

turn *(in a game, order)* el turno [toor-noh]; *(off a road)* el giro [CHee-roh]
◆ *(change direction)* girar [CHi-rahr]

▸ it's your turn es tu turno [es too toor-noh]

▸ is this the turn for the campground? ¿es este el giro del camping? [es es-tay el CHee-roh del kam-peen]

▸ turn left at the lights gira a la izquierda en el semáforo [CHee-ra a la ith-kyair-da en el se-ma-fo-roh]

▸ you have to turn right tienes que girar a la derecha [tyen-es kay CHi-rahr a la de-re-cha]

turn down bajar [ba-CHahr]

▸ can we turn the air-conditioning down? ¿podemos bajar el aire acondicionado? [pod-ay-mos ba-CHahr el eye-ray a-kon-dith-yoh-nah-doh]

▸ how do you turn the volume down? ¿cómo se baja el volumen? [kom-oh say ba-CHa el bo-loo-men]

turn off *(light, appliance, radio)* apagar [a-pa-gahr]; *(electricity)* cortar [kor-tahr]; *(tap)* cerrar [theRR-ahr]

▸ where do you turn the light off? ¿cómo se apaga la luz? [kom-oh say a-pah-ga la looth]

▸ my cell was turned off mi móvil estaba apagado [mee mob-eel es-tah-ba a-pa-gah-doh]

turn on *(light, radio, engine)* encender [en-then-dair]; *(faucet)* abrir [ab-reer]; *(person)* excitar [eks-thi-tahr]

▸ where do I turn this light on? ¿cómo enciendo esta luz? [kom-oh enth-yen-doh es-ta looth]

▸ can you turn on the ignition? ¿puedes dar al contacto? [pway-days dahr al kon-tak-toh]

turn up *(sound, central heating)* subir [soo-beer]

▸ how do you turn up the heating? ¿cómo se sube la calefacción? [kom-oh say soo-bay la ka-lay-fakth-yohn]

TV la televisión [te-le-bis-yohn]

▸ the TV in our room is broken la televisión de nuestro cuarto está estropeada [la te-le-bis-yohn day nwes-troh kwahr-toh es-ta es-tro-pay-ah-da]

TV lounge el salón de televisión [sa-lohn day te-le-bis-yohn]

▸ is there a TV lounge? ¿hay un salón de televisión? [eye oon sa-lohn day te-le-bis-yohn]

twelve doce [doh-thay] ◆ *(noon, midnight)* las doce [doh-thay]
- there are twelve of us somos doce [so-mos doh-thay]
- it's twelve o'clock son las doce [son las doh-thay]

twice dos veces [dos beth-ays]
- the ferry runs twice a day el ferry funciona dos veces por día [el fe-RRi foonth-yoh-na dos beth-ays por dee-a]

twin el gemelo [CHe-may-loh], la gemela [CHe-may-la] ◆ gemelo(la) [CHe-may-loh]
- twin brother hermano gemelo [air-mah-noh CHe-may-loh]
- twin sister hermana gemela [air-mah-na CHe-may-la]

twin beds las camas gemelas [ka-mas CHe-may-las]
- a room with twin beds una habitación con camas gemelas [oo-na a-bi-tath-yohn kon ka-mas CHe-may-las]

two dos [dos]
- there are two of us som-os dos [somos dos]

U

umbrella el paraguas [pa-rag-was]
- could you lend me an umbrella? ¿me podría prestar un paraguas? [may pod-ree-a pres-tahr oon pa-rag-was]

unacceptable inaceptable [een-a-thep-tah-blay]
- it's completely unacceptable! ¡es completamente inaceptable! [es kom-play-ta-men-tay een-a-thep-tah-blay]

saying that you have understood/not understood

- oh, I see...! ah, ya veo...! [ah ya bay-oh]
- sorry, but I didn't understand perdón, no le he entendido [pair-dohn noh lay ay en-ten-dee-doh]
- I'm a little confused estoy un poco confundido [es-toy oon poh-koh kon-foon-dee-doh]
- I don't understand your question no entiendo su pregunta [noh ent-yen-doh soo pre-goon-ta]
- sorry, but I still don't understand perdón, pero sigo sin entender [pair-dohn pair-oh see-goh seen en-ten-dair]

underpass el paso subterráneo [pa-soh soob-teRR-ah-nay-oh]
 ▸ is the underpass safe at night? ¿el paso subterráneo es seguro por la noche? [el pa-soh soob-teRR-ah-nay-oh es se-goo-roh por la no-chay]

understand entender [en-ten-dair]
 ▸ I can understand Spanish, but I can't really speak it entiendo el español, pero no lo hablo [ent-yen-doh el es-pan-yol pair-oh noh loh ab-loh]
 ▸ I understand a little entiendo un poco [ent-yen-doh oon poh-koh]
 ▸ I don't understand a word no entiendo nada [noh ent-yen-doh nah-da]
 ▸ do you understand? ¿entiende? [ent-yen-day]

unit (of condominium complex) la unidad [oo-ni-dad]
 ▸ we'd prefer a unit with air-conditioning preferíamos una unidad con aire acondicionado [pre-fe-ree-a-mos oo-na oo-ni-dad kon eye-ray a-kon-dith-yoh-nah-doh]

United States (of America)
 ▸ the United States los Estados Unidos (de América) [es-tah-dohs oo-nee-dohs(day a-mair-i-ka)]
 ▸ I'm from the United States soy de los Estados Unidos (de América) [soy day los es-tah-dohs oo-nee-dohs (day a-mair-i-ka)]
 ▸ I live in the United States vivo en los Estados Unidos (de América) [bee-boh en los es-tah-dohs oo-nee-dohs (day a-mair-i-ka)]
 ▸ have you ever been to the United States? ¿has estado en los Estados Unidos (de América)? [as es-tah-doh en los es-tah-dohs oo-nee-dohs (day a-mair-i-ka)]

unleaded (gas) sin plomo [seen ploh-moh] ◆ la gasolina sin plomo [ga-so-lee-na seen ploh-moh]
 ▸ do you have premium or just regular unleaded? ¿tiene súper o sólo normal sin plomo? [tyen-ay soo-pair oh soh-loh nor-mal seen ploh-moh]

until hasta [as-ta]
 ▸ I'm staying until Sunday me quedo hasta el domingo [may kay-doh as-ta el do-meen-goh]
 ▸ until noon hasta el mediodía [as-ta el med-yoh-dee-a]

up (to a higher position) hacia arriba [ath-ya a-RRee-ba]; (in a higher position) arriba [a-RRee-ba] ◆
 ▸ what's up? (what's wrong) ¿qué pasa? [kay pa-sa]; (as greeting) ¿qué te cuentas? [kay tay kwen-tas]
 ▸ what are you up to tonight? ¿qué piensas hacer esta noche? [kay pyen-sas a-thair es-ta no-chay]

urgent urgente [oor-CHen-tay]
 ▸ it's not urgent no es urgente [noh es oor-CHen-tay]

urgently urgentemente [oor-CHen-tay-men-tay]
 ▸ I have to see a dentist urgently tengo que ver a un dentista urgentemente [ten-goh kay bair a oon den-tees-ta oor-CHen-tay-men-tay]

US(A)

- the US los Estados Unidos [los es-tah-dohs oo-nee-dohs]
- I'm from the US soy de los Estados Unidos [soy day los es-tah-dohs oo-nee-dohs]
- I live in the US vivo en los Estados Unidos [bee-boh en los es-tah-dohs oo-nee-dohs]
- have you ever been to the US? ¿has estado en los Estados Unidos? [as es-tah-doh los es-tah-dohs oo-nee-dohs]

use usar [oo-sahr]

- could I use your cellphone? ¿podría usar su móvil? [pod-ree-a oo-sahr soo mob-eel]

vacancy la habitación libre [a-bi-tath-yohn lee-bray]

- do you have any vacancies for tonight? ¿tiene alguna habitación libre para esta noche? [tyen-ay al-goo-na a-bi-tath-yohn lee-bray pa-ra es-ta no-chay]

vacation las vacaciones [ba-kath-yoh-nays]

- are you here on vacation? ¿estás aquí de vacaciones? [es-tas a-kee day ba-kath-yoh-nays]
- I'm on vacation estoy de vacaciones [es-toy day ba-kath-yoh-nays]

valid válido(da) [ba-li-doh]

- is this ticket valid for the exhibit too? ¿esta entrada es válida también para la exhibición? [es-ta en-trah-da es ba-li-da tamb-yen pa-ra la ek-si-beeth-yohn]
- how long is this ticket valid for? ¿cuál es la validez de este billete? [kwal es la ba-li-deth day es-tay bil-yay-tay]
- my passport is still valid mi pasaporte todavía es válido [mee pa-sa-pawr-tay toh-da-bee-a es ba-li-doh]

vegetable la verdura [bair-doo-ra]

- does it come with vegetables? ¿viene con verdura? [byen-ay kon bair-doo-ra]

vegetarian vegetariano(na) [be-CHe-tahr-yah-noh] ◆ el vegetariano [be-CHe-tahr-yah-noh], la vegetariana [be-CHe-tahr-yah-na]

- I'm a vegetarian soy vegetariano/vegetariana [soy be-CHe-tahr-yah-noh/be-CHe-tahr-yah-na]
- do you have vegetarian dishes? ¿tienen platos vegetarianos? [tyen-en pla-tohs be-CHe-tahr-yah-nohs]

vending machine la máquina expendedora [ma-ki-na eks-pen-de-daw-ra]

- the vending machine isn't working la máquina expendedora no funciona [la ma-ki-na eks-pen-de-daw-ra noh foonth-yoh-na]

vertigo el vértigo [bair-ti-goh]

- I suffer from vertigo tengo vértigo [ten-goh bair-ti-goh]

very muy [mwee]
- I'm very hungry tengo mucha hambre [ten-goh moo-cha am-bray]
- very much mucho [moo-choh]
- very near muy cerca [mwee thair-ka]

view *(panorama)* la vista [bees-ta]
- I'd prefer a room with an ocean view preferiría una habitación con vista al mar [pre-fair-i-ree-a oon a-bi-tath-yohn kon bees-ta al mahr]

villa el chalé [cha-lay]
- we'd like to rent a villa for one week queríamos alquilar un chalet una semana [kair-ee-a-mos al-ki-lahr oon cha-lay oo-na se-mah-na]

virus el virus [bee-roos]
- I must have picked up a virus he debido de contraer un virus [ay de-bee-doh day kon-tra-air oon bee-roos]

visa el visado [bi-sah-doh]
- do you need a visa? ¿hace falta visado? [a-thay fal-ta bi-sah-doh]

visit la visita [bi-see-ta] ♦ visitar [bi-si-tahr]
- is this your first visit to Madrid? ¿es su primera visita a Madrid? [es soo pri-mair-a bi-see-ta a mad-reed]
- I'd like to visit the castle me gustaría visitar el castillo [may goos-ta-ree-a bi-si-tahr el kas-teel-yoh]

voicemail el correo de voz [ko-RRay-oh day both]
- I need to check my voicemail quería consultar mi correo de voz [kair-ee-a kon-sool-tahr mee ko-RRay-oh day both]

voucher el vale [bah-lay]
- I haven't received the voucher no he recibido el vale [noh ay re-thi-bee-doh el bah-lay]

waist la cintura [thin-too-ra]
- ▸ it's a little bit tight at the waist me aprieta un poco la cintura [may ap-ree-ay-ta oon poh-koh la thin-too-ra]

wait esperar [es-pair-ahr]
- ▸ have you been waiting long? ¿hace mucho que esperas? [a-thay moo-choh kay es-pair-as]

waiter el camarero [ka-ma-rair-oh]
- ▸ waiter, could we have the check, please? camarero, la cuenta, por favor [ka-ma-rair-oh la kwen-ta por fa-bor]

wait for esperar [es-pair-ahr]
- ▸ are you waiting for the bus? ¿estás esperando el autobús? [es-tas es-pair-an-doh el ow-toh-boos]
- ▸ I'm waiting for them to call back estoy esperando a que me llamen [es-toy es-pair-an-doh a kay may yah-men]
- ▸ don't wait for me no me esperes [noh may es-pair-ays]

waiting room la sala de espera [sa-la day es-pair-a]
- ▸ is there a waiting room near the platform? ¿hay una sala de espera cerca del andén? [eye oo-na sa-la day es-pair-a thair-ka del an-dayn]

waitress la camarera [ka-ma-rair-a]
- ▸ the waitress has already taken our order la camarera ya ha anotado nuestro pedido [la ka-ma-rair-a ya a a-noh-tah-doh nwes-troh pe-dee-doh]

wake despertar [des-pair-tahr] ◆ despertarse [des-pair-tahr-say]
- ▸ could you wake me at 6:45? ¿me podría despertar a las siete menos cuarto? [may pod-ree-a des-pair-tahr a las sye-tay may-nos kwahr-toh]
- ▸ I always wake early siempre me despierto temprano [syem-pray may des-pyair-toh tem-prah-noh]

wake up despertar [des-pair-tahr] ◆ despertarse [des-pair-tahr-say]
- ▸ a noise woke me up in the middle of the night un ruido me despertó en mitad de la noche [oon roo-ee-doh may des-pair-toh en mi-tad day la no-chay]
- ▸ I have to wake up very early tomorrow to catch the plane tengo que despertarme muy temprano mañana para coger el avión [ten-goh kay des-pair-tahr-may mwee tem-prah-noh man-yah-na pa-ra koCH-air el ab-yohn]

walk el paseo [pa-say-oh] ◆ *(go on foot)* pasear [pa-say-ahr] ◆ *(person)* acompañar [a-kom-pan-yahr]; *(distance)* caminar [ka-mi-nahr]

water

It isn't the custom for a jug of water to be brought to your table in Spain. You have to order bottled water: either noncarbonated (*agua sin gas*), sparkling (*agua con gas*), or *fría* or *del tiempo* (cold or room temperature).

- are there any interesting walks in the area? ¿hay paseos interesantes en la zona? [eye pa-say-ohs in-tair-e-san-tays en la thoh-na]
- let's go for a walk vamos a dar un paseo [bah-mos a dahr oon pa-say-oh]
- how long would it take me to walk it? ¿cuánto me llevaría caminando? [kwan-toh may yay-ba-ree-a ka-mi-nan-doh]

walking boots las botas de senderismo [boh-tas day sen-dair-ees-moh]
- do you need walking boots? ¿hacen falta botas de senderismo? [a-then fal-ta boh-tas day sen-dair-ees-moh]

wallet la cartera [kahr-tair-a]
- I've lost my wallet he perdido la cartera [ay pair-dee-doh la kahr-tair-a]

want *(wish, desire)* querer [ke-rair]
- I don't want to go there no quiero ir ahí [noh kyair-oh eer a-ee]

warm caliente [kal-yen-tay]
- it's warm hace calor [a-thay ka-lawr]
- where can I buy some warm clothing for the trip? ¿dónde puedo comprar ropa de abrigo para la excursión? [don-day pway-doh kom-prahr RRoh-pa day a-bree-goh pa-ra la eks-koors-yohn]

warn avisar [a-bi-sahr]
- no one warned me about that! ¡nadie me avisó de eso! [nad-yay may a-bi-soh day e-soh]

wash lavar [la-bahr] • lavarse [la-bahr-say]
- where can I wash my hands? ¿dónde puedo lavarme las manos? [don-day pway-doh la-bahr-may las mah-nohs]

watch el reloj [RRe-loCH] • *(look at)* mirar [mi-rahr]; *(guard)* vigilar [bi-CHi-lahr]
- my watch has been stolen me han robado el reloj [may an RRo-bah-doh el RRe-loCH]
- can you watch my bags for a minute? ¿podría vigilarme las bolsas un minuto? [pod-ree-a bi-CHi-lahr-may las bol-sas oon mi-noo-toh]

water el agua [ag-wa]
- could I have some hot water, please? ¿me podía traer agua caliente, por favor? [may pod-ree-a tra-air ag-wa kal-yen-tay por fa-bor]
- there's no hot water no hay agua caliente [noh eye ag-wa kal-yen-tay]

water ski el esquí acuático [es-kee a-kwa-ti-koh]
▶ can I rent water skis here? ¿puedo alquilar esquís acuáticos aquí? [pway-doh al-ki-lahr es-kees a-kwa-ti-kohs a-kee]

water skiing el esquí acuático [es-kee a-kwa-ti-koh]
▶ can I go water skiing anywhere around here? ¿puedo hacer esquí acuático por aquí? [pway-doh a-thair es-kee a-kwa-ti-koh por a-kee]

wave *(of water)* la ola [oh-la]
▶ the waves are very big today hoy las olas son muy grandes [oy las oh-las son mwee gran-days]

way *(means)* la forma [for-ma]; *(direction)* la dirección [di-rekth-yohn]; *(route, path)* el camino [ka-mee-noh]
▶ what's the best way of getting there? ¿cuál es la mejor forma de llegar ahí? [kwal es la me-CHor for-ma day yay-gahr a-ee]
▶ which way is it to the station? ¿por dónde se va a la estación? [por don-day say ba a la es-tath-yohn]
▶ I went the wrong way fui por el camino equivocado [fwee por el ka-mee-noh e-ki-bo-kah-doh]
▶ is this the right way to the cathedral? ¿por aquí se va a la catedral? [por a-kee say ba a la ka-te-dral]
▶ on the way en el camino [en el ka-mee-noh]
▶ all the way *(push)* hasta el fondo [as-ta el fon-doh]
▶ no way! ¡ni hablar! [nee ab-lahr]

way out la salida [sa-lee-da]
▶ where's the way out? ¿dónde está la salida? [don-day es-ta la sa-lee-da]

weak *(person)* débil [deb-eel]; *(drink)* muy poco cargado(da) [mwee poh-koh kahr-gah-doh]
▶ I feel very weak me siento muy débil [may syen-toh mwee deb-eel]
▶ could I have a very weak coffee? ¿me podría poner un café muy poco cargado? [may pod-ree-a pon-air oon ka-fay mwee poh-koh kahr-gah-doh]

asking the way

▶ can you show me where we are on the map? ¿me podría mostrar en el mapa dónde estamos? [may pod-ree-a mos-trahr en el ma-pa don-day es-tah-mos]
▶ where is the station/the post office? ¿dónde está la estación/la oficina de correos? [don-day es-ta la es-tath-yohn/la o-fi-thee-na day ko-RRay-ohs]
▶ excuse me, how do you get to the Prado Museum? perdón, ¿cómo se va al Museo del Prado? [pair-dohn kom-oh say ba al moo-say-oh del prah-doh]
▶ is it far? ¿está lejos? [es-ta lay-CHohs]
▶ is it within walking distance? ¿se puede ir andando? [say pway-day eer an-dan-doh]

wear *(piece of clothing, glasses)* llevar [yay-bahr]
  ▸ is what I'm wearing all right? ¿lo que llevo está bien? [loh kay yay-boh es-ta byen]

weather el tiempo [tyem-poh]
  ▸ what is the weather like today? ¿qué tiempo hace hoy? [kay tyem-poh a-thay oy]
  ▸ is the weather going to change? ¿va a cambiar el tiempo? [ba a kamb-yahr el tyem-poh]

weather forecast el pronóstico del tiempo [pro-nos-ti-koh del tyem-poh]
  ▸ what's the weather forecast for tomorrow? ¿cuál es el pronóstico del tiempo para mañana? [kwal es el pro-nos-ti-koh del tyem-poh pa-ra man-yah-na]

website address la dirección del sitio web [di-rekth-yohn del seet-yoh web]
  ▸ can you give me your website address? ¿me podrías dar la dirección de tu sitio web? [may pod-ree-as dahr la di-rekth-yohn day too seet-yoh web]

Wednesday el miércoles [myair-ko-les]
  ▸ we're arriving/leaving on Wednesday llegaremos/nos iremos el miércoles [yay-ga-ray-mos/nos ee-ray-mos el myair-ko-les]

week la semana [se-mah-na]
  ▸ how much is it for a week? ¿cuánto es por semana? [kwan-toh es por se-mah-na]
  ▸ I'm leaving in a week me voy dentro de una semana [may boy den-troh day oo-na se-mah-na]
  ▸ two weeks dos semanas [dos se-mah-nas]

weekly semanal [se-ma-nal]
  ▸ is there a weekly rate? ¿hay una tarifa semanal? [eye oo-na ta-ree-fa se-ma-mal]

welcome bienvenido(da) [byen-ben-ee-doh] ◆ la bienvenida [byen-ben-ee-da]
◆ *(person)* dar la bienvenida a [dahr la byen-ben-ee-da a]
  ▸ welcome! ¡bienvenido! [byen-ben-ee-doh]
  ▸ you're welcome *(in reply to thanks)* de nada [day nah-da]
  ▸ you're welcome to join us únete a nosotros cuando quieras [oo-nay-tay a no-soh-trohs kwan-doh kyair-as]

well *(in health)* bien [byen] ◆ bien [byen]
  ▸ I'm very well, thank you estoy muy bien, gracias [es-toy mwee byen grath-yas]
  ▸ get well soon! ¡que te mejores pronto! [kay tay me-CHor-ays pron-toh]
  ▸ well played bien jugado [byen CHoo-gah-doh]

well done *(steak)* pasado(da) [pa-sah-doh]
  ▸ well done, please pasado, por favor [pa-sah-doh por fa-bor]

what qué [kay]
  ▸ what? *(asking for repetition)* ¿qué? [kay]
  ▸ what is it? *(what's this thing?)* ¿qué es eso? [kay es e-soh]; *(what's the matter?)* ¿qué pasa? [kay pa-sa]
  ▸ what's up? *(what's wrong?)* ¿qué pasa? [kay pa-sa]; *(as greeting)* ¿qué te cuentas? [kay tay kwen-tas]

- what's your name? ¿cómo te llamas? [kom-oh tay yah-mas]
- what's it called? ¿cómo se llama? [kom-oh say yah-ma]
- what time is it? ¿qué hora es? [kay aw-ra es]
- what day is it? ¿qué día es? [kay dee-a es]
- what desserts do you have? ¿qué postres tienen? [kay pos-trays tyen-en]

wheel la rueda [RRoo-ay-da]

- could you help me change the wheel? ¿podría ayudarme a cambiar la rueda? [pod-ree-a a-yoo-dahr-may a kamb-yahr la RRoo-ay-da]

when cuándo [kwan-doh] ◆ cuando [kwan-doh]

- when was it built? ¿cuándo fue construido? [kwan-doh fway kons-troo-ee-doh]
- when is the next train to Madrid? ¿cuándo es el próximo tren a Madrid? [kwan-doh es el prok-si-moh tren a mad-reed]

where dónde [don-day]

- where do you live? ¿dónde vives? [don-day bee-bes]
- where are you from? ¿de dónde eres? [day don-day air-ays]
- excuse me, where is the nearest bus stop, please? perdón, ¿dónde está la parada de autobús más próxima? [pair-dohn don-day es-ta la pa-rah-da day ow-toh-boos mas prok-si-ma]

which qué [kay] ◆ *(in questions)* cuál [kwal]; *(in relative clauses)* qué [kay]

- which hotel would you recommend for us? ¿qué hotel nos recomendaría? [kay oh-tel nos RRe-ko-men-da-ree-a]
- which way should we go? ¿qué camino deberíamos coger? [kay ka-mee-noh deb-air-ee-a-mos koCH-air]
- which do you prefer? ¿cuál prefieres? [kwal pref-yair-es]

while

- I'm only planning to stay for a while sólo planeo quedarme poco tiempo [soh-loh pla-nay-oh ke-dahr-may poh-koh tyem-poh]

white *(in color)* blanco(ca) [blan-koh]

- I need a white T-shirt necesito una camiseta blanca [ne-thes-ee-toh oo-na ka-mi-say-ta blan-ka]

white wine el vino blanco [bee-noh blan-koh]

- a glass of white wine, please un vaso de vino blanco, por favor [oon ba-soh day bee-noh blan-koh por fa-bor]

who quién [kyen]

- who are you? ¿quién eres? [kyen air-es]
- who should I speak to about the heating? ¿con quién tengo que hablar sobre la calefacción? [kon kyen ten-goh kay ab-lahr soh-bray la ka-lay-fakth-yohn]
- who's calling? ¿de parte de quién? [day pahr-tay day kyen]

whole entero(ra) [en-tair-oh]

- we spent the whole day walking pasamos el día entero paseando [pa-sah-mos el dee-a en-tair-oh pa-say-an-doh]

▶ on the whole we had a good time en general lo pasamos bien [en CHen-e-ral loh pa-sah-mos byen]

whole-wheat integral [in-te-gral]

▶ I'd like some whole-wheat bread quería pan integral [kair-ee-a pan in-te-gral]

why ¿por qué? [por kay]

▶ why not? ¿por qué no? [por kay noh]

wide *(river, road)* ancho(cha) [an-choh]

▶ 2 meters wide dos metros de ancho [dos met-rohs day an-choh]

will

▶ I'll be arriving at six llegaré a las seis [yay-ga-ray a las seys]

win ganar [gan-ahr]

▶ who's winning? ¿quién gana? [kyen ga-na]

wind el viento [byen-toh]

▶ there's a strong west wind hay un fuerte viento oeste [eye oon fwair-tay byen-toh oh-es-tay]

window *(of a building, plane)* la ventana [ben-tah-na]; *(of a car, at a station, in a post office)* la ventanilla [ben-ta-neel-ya]; *(of a store)* el escaparate [es-ka-pa-ra-tay]

▶ I can't open the window no consigo abrir la ventana [noh kon-see-goh ab-reer la ben-tah-na]

▶ I'm cold: could you close your window? tengo frío, ¿podría cerrar la ventana? [ten-goh free-oh pod-ree-a theRR-ahr la ben-tah-na]

▶ I'd like to see the dress in the window quería ver el vestido del escaparate [kair-ee-a bair el bes-tee-doh del es-ka-pa-ra-tay]

▶ where's the window for buying tickets? ¿dónde está la ventanilla para comprar entradas? [don-day es-ta la ben-ta-neel-ya pa-ra kom-prahr en-trah-das]

window seat el asiento de ventana [as-yen-toh day ben-tah-na]

▶ I'd like a window seat if possible quería un asiento de ventana si fuera posible [kair-ee-a oon as-yen-toh day ben-tah-na see fwair-a po-see-blay]

windshield el parabrisas [pa-ra-bree-sas]

▶ could you clean the windshield? ¿podría limpiar el parabrisas? [pod-ree-a limp-yahr el pa-ra-bree-sas]

windsurfing el windsurf [win-soorf]

▶ is there anywhere around here I can go windsurfing? ¿dónde puedo hacer windsurf por aquí? [don-day pway-doh a-thair win-soorf por a-kee]

windy *(day, weather)* ventoso(sa) [ben-toh-soh]

▶ it's windy hace viento [a-thay byen-toh]

wine el vino [bee-noh]

▶ this wine is not chilled enough el vino no está lo suficientemente frío [el bee-noh noh es-ta loh soo-feeth-yen-te-men-te free-oh]

wishes and regrets

▶ I hope it won't be too busy espero que no estés demasiado ocupado [es-pair-oh kay noh es-tays de-mas-yah-doh o-koo-pah-doh]

▶ it'd be great if you stayed sería genial si te pudieras quedar [sair-ee-a CHen-yal see tay pood-yair-as ke-dahr]

▶ if only we had a car! ¡ojalá tuviéramos un coche! [o-CHa-la toob-yair-a-mos oon ko-chay]

▶ unfortunately, we couldn't get there in time desgraciadamente, no conseguimos llegar a tiempo [des-grath-yah-da-men-te noh kon-se-gee-mos yay-gahr a tyem-poh]

▶ I'm really sorry you couldn't make it siento mucho que no pudieras asistir [syen-toh moo-choh kay noh pood-yair-as a-sis-teer]

wine list la lista de vinos [lees-ta day bee-nohs]

▶ can we see the wine list, please? ¿podemos ver la lista de vinos, por favor? [pod-ay-mos bair la lees-ta day bee-nohs por fa-bor]

wish el deseo [de-say-oh] ◆ desear [de-say-ahr]

▶ best wishes! ¡mis mejores deseos! [mees me-CHor-ays de-say-ohs]

▶ we wish you good luck te deseamos buena suerte [tay des-ay-ah-mos bway-na swair-tay]

with con [kon]

▶ thanks, but I'm here with my boyfriend gracias, pero estoy aquí con mi novio [grath-yas pair-oh es-toy a-kee kon mee nob-yoh]

withdraw *(money)* sacar [sa-kahr]

▶ I'd like to withdraw 100 euros quería sacar 100 euros [kair-ee-a sa-kahr thyen ew-rohs]

wishing someone something

▶ Happy Birthday! ¡feliz cumpleaños! [fe-leeth koom-play-an-yohs]

▶ Merry Christmas! ¡feliz Navidad! [fe-leeth na-bi-dad]

▶ Happy New Year! ¡feliz Año Nuevo! [fe-leeth an-yoh nway-boh]

▶ enjoy your vacation! ¡que disfrutes de las vacaciones! [kay dis-froo-tays day las ba-kath-yoh-nays]

▶ enjoy your meal! ¡que aproveche! [kay a-pro-bech-ay]

▶ good night! ¡buenas noches! [bway-nas no-chays]

▶ congratulations! ¡felicidades! [fe-li-thi-dah-days]

without sin [seen]
 ▸ a tuna sandwich without mayonnaise un bocadillo de atún sin mayonesa [oon bo-ka-deel-yoh day a-toon seen meye-oh-nay-sa]

woman la mujer [mooCH-air]
 ▸ where's the women's changing room? ¿dónde está el probador de señoras? [don-day es-ta el pro-ba-dawr day sen-yaw-ras]

wonderful maravilloso(sa) [ma-ra-beel-yoh-soh]
 ▸ that's wonderful! ¡qué maravilloso! [kay ma-ra-beel-yoh-soh]
 ▸ the weather was wonderful el tiempo fue maravilloso [el tyem-poh fway ma-ra-beel-yoh-soh]

word la palabra [pa-lab-ra]
 ▸ I don't know what the word is in English no sé cómo se dice eso en inglés [noh say kom-oh say dee-thay e-soh en in-glays]
 ▸ I don't understand a word no entiendo nada [noh ent-yen-doh nah-da]

work *(employment)* el trabajo [tra-ba-CHoh] ◆ *(do a job)* trabajar [tra-ba-CHahr]; *(function)* funcionar [foonth-yoh-nahr]
 ▸ to be out of work no tener trabajo [noh ten-air tra-ba-CHoh]
 ▸ I work in marketing trabajo en márketing [tra-ba-CHoh en mahr-ke-teen]
 ▸ the heating's not working la calefacción no funciona [la ka-le-fakth-yohn noh foonth-yoh-na]
 ▸ how does the shower work? ¿cómo funciona la ducha? [kom-oh foonth-yoh-na la doo-cha]

workday el día laborable [dee-a la-boh-rah-blay]
 ▸ is tomorrow a workday? ¿mañana es día laborable? [man-yah-na es dee-a la-boh-rah-blay]

world el mundo [moon-doh]
 ▸ what part of the world are you from? ¿de qué parte del mundo eres? [day kay pahr-tay del moon-doh air-es]

worried preocupado(da) [pray-o-koo-pah-doh]
 ▸ I'm worried about his health estoy preocupado por su salud [es-toy pray-o-koo-pah-doh por soo sa-lood]

worry preocuparse [pray-o-koo-pahr-say]
 ▸ don't worry! ¡no te preocupes! [noh tay pray-o-koo-pes]

worth el valor [ba-lawr]
 ▸ how much is it worth? ¿cuánto vale? [kwan-toh bah-lay]
 ▸ it's well worth a visit vale la pena una visita [bah-lay la pay-na oo-na bi-see-ta]
 ▸ what's worth seeing in this town? ¿qué vale la pena ver en esta ciudad? [kay bah-lay la pay-na bair en es-ta thyoo-dad]

wound la herida [air-ee-da]
 ▸ I need something for disinfecting a wound necesito algo para desinfectar una herida [ne-thes-ee-toh al-goh pa-ra des-in-fek-tahr oo-na air-ee-da]

wrap (up) envolver [em-bol-bair]
> • can you wrap it (up) for me? ¿me lo puede envolver? [may loh pway-day em-bol-bair]

wrist la muñeca [moon-yay-ka]
> • I've sprained my wrist me he torcido la muñeca [may ay tor-thee-doh la moon-yay-ka]

write *(gen)* escribir [es-kri-beer]; *(check)* extender [eks-ten-dair] ◆ escribir [es-kri-beer]
> • I have some letters to write tengo que escribir unas cartas [ten-goh kay es-kri-beer oo-nas kahr-tas]

wrong *(incorrect)* incorrecto(ta) [in-ko-RRek-toh]
> • to be wrong *(person)* estar equivocado [es-tahr e-ki-bo-kah-doh]
> • I'm sorry, but I think you're wrong perdona, pero creo que estás equivocado [pair-doh-na pair-oh kray-oh kay es-tas e-ki-bo-kah-doh]
> • sorry, I dialed the wrong number perdón, me he equivocado (de número) [pair-dohn may ay e-ki-bo-kah-doh (day noo-mair-oh)]
> • you've got the wrong number se ha equivocado (de número) [say a e-ki-bo-kah-doh (day noo-mair-oh)]
> • this is the wrong train este es el tren equivocado [es-tay es el tren e-ki-bo-kah-doh]
> • what's wrong? ¿qué pasa? [kay pa-sa]
> • there's something wrong with the switch le pasa algo al interruptor [lay pa-sa al-goh al in-tair-oop-tawr]

X, Y, Z

X-ray la radiografía [RRad-yoh-gra-fee-a]
> • do you think I should have an X-ray? ¿le parece que debería hacerme una radiografía? [lay pa-re-thay kay de-bair-ee-a a-thair-may oo-na RRad-yoh-gra-fee-a]

year el año [an-yoh]
> • we came here last year vinimos aquí el año pasado [bi-nee-mos a-kee el an-yoh pa-sah-doh]
> • I'm 21 years old tengo 21 años [ten-goh beyn-ti-oon an-yohs]

yellow amarillo(lla) [a-ma-reel-yoh]
> • the yellow one el amarillo [el a-ma-reel-yoh]

Yellow Pages®
> • do you have a copy of the Yellow Pages? ¿tiene una copia de las páginas amarillas? [tyen-ay qa kohp-ya day las pa-CHee-nas a-ma-reel-yas]
> • why don't you look in the Yellow Pages? ¿por qué no lo miras en las páginas amarillas? [por kay noh loh mee-ras en las pa-CHee-nas a-ma-reel-yas]

yes sí [see]
  ▸ yes, please sí, por favor [see por fa-bor]
  ▸ it doesn't matter – yes it does! no importa – ¡sí que importa! [noh im-por-ta –see kay im-por-ta]

yet todavía [toh-da-bee-a]
  ▸ I've not been there yet todavía no he estado ahí [toh-da-bee-a noh ay es-tah-doh a-ee]

yogurt el yogur [yo-goor]
  ▸ do you have any organic yogurt? ¿tiene yogures orgánicos? [tyen-ay yo-goo-rays or-ga-ni-kohs]

young man el joven [CHoh-ben]
  ▸ who is that young man? ¿quién es ese joven? [kyen es e-say CHoh-ben]

young person el joven [CHoh-ben], la joven [CHoh-ben]
  ▸ are there any discounts for young people? ¿hay descuentos para los jóvenes? [eye des-kwen-tohs pa-ra los CHoh-ben-es]

young woman la joven [CHoh-ben]
  ▸ who is the young woman he's with? ¿quién es la joven con la que está? [kyen es la CHoh-ben kon la kay es-ta]

youth hostel el albergue juvenil [al-bair-gay CHoo-ben-eel]
  ▸ I'd like to book two beds for three nights in a youth hostel quería reservar dos camas tres noches en un albergue juvenil [kair-ee-a re-sair-bahr dos ka-mas tres no-chays en oon al-bair-gay CHoo-ben-eel]

zone *(on public transportation)* la zona [thoh-na]
  ▸ I'd like a ticket for zones one to four quería un billete para las zonas uno a cuatro [kair-ee-a oon bil-yay-tay pa-ra las thoh-nas oo-noh a kwat-roh]

Spanish language and Hispanic culture

Spanish around the world: who speaks it and where?

Spanish is the native language of over 350 million people in the world, making it the world's second-most spoken language, next to Chinese with around 1.3 billion speakers (English has around 340 million). In addition to Spain, Spanish is the official language of Argentina, Bolivia, Chile, Colombia, Costa Rica, Cuba, the Dominican Republic, Ecuador, El Salvador, Equatorial Guinea, Guatemala, Honduras, Mexico, Nicaragua, Panama, Paraguay, Peru, Uruguay, and Venezuela. It is also widely spoken in several other countries, including Canada, Morocco, the Philippines, and the United States.

Spanish in the US

Spanish is the second-most common language in the US after English. It is spoken by around 30 million native citizens over the age of five. This represents 12% of the population and is the fifth largest Spanish-speaking community in the world, after Mexico, Colombia, Spain and Argentina. Spanish is the joint official language of New Mexico, alongside English. Spanish has been spoken around northern New Mexico, southern Colorado and the US-Mexico border since the 17th century.

Where did the Spanish language come from?

The Spanish language has a long and colorful history. Modern Spain and Portugal make up the Iberian Peninsula, which occupies a critical strategic position between East and West, between the Mediterranean and the Atlantic, between Europe, Africa and the Middle East. This has meant that from the very earliest times, different peoples invaded, stayed for a while and went, leaving their influences. The earliest people living there that we have any trace of were the Celtiberians. Their Celtic language probably died out in the first century AD.

Phoenicians, Carthaginians, Romans…

During the thousand years before the birth of Christ, the Phoenicians, then the Carthaginians, then the Romans regarded Spain as a prize worth possessing. But, as happened elsewhere in Europe, it was to be the Romans who would most influence the language that would be spoken in Spain in the future. After the defeat of the Carthaginian general Hannibal, they ruled the Iberian peninsula for almost 800 years.

Vulgar Latin

The Latin that the Roman armies brought with them was not the Classical Latin of Rome but what came to be called Vulgar Latin, the language of the *vulgus*, the ordinary people. This mingled with the languages of the Celtiberians and the remaining Carthaginians to form the strain of Vulgar Latin that was spoken for centuries in the peninsula. Modern Spanish has a great many words derived from Latin. Some examples are the Spanish words for *father, mother, bread*, and *wine*, in Latin **pater, mater, panis, vinum** and in Spanish **padre, madre, pan, vino**. Vulgar Latin in all the forms it took around Roman Europe is what unites what are called the **Romance** languages, meaning languages that have Latin as the most significant part of their background.

After the Romans

In 409 the Empire was crumbling and the Germanic tribes that the Romans called Barbarians swept across Europe and grabbed, among other prizes, the Iberian peninsula. It was the Visigoths who established themselves in Spain and effectively created the kingdom of Hispania. But the Visigoths were very Romanized and successful though they were in uniting the kingdom, they never really succeeded in imposing their Gothic language and in the 8th century another contest for the domination of Spain took place...

The Moors

In the year 711 a Muslim army crossed the Strait of Gibraltar from North Africa and invaded the Iberian peninsula. These were the people who would soon be called the Moors (from the French *Maure*, as they came from the region of Mauretania in North Africa). They pushed swiftly up through Spain and across the Pyrenees into France and were only finally stopped in 733 at Tours.

They brought with them an extraordinarily rich culture that was to leave its imprint on the whole of Europe. But it was in Spain and Portugal, where they stayed for 800 years, that the impact was greatest. The language of the Moors quickly gained in influence and Arabic and a related dialect called Mozarabic were soon widely spoken, except in a few small kingdoms in the north, such as Asturias, where Vulgar Latin lived on.

The emergence of Spanish

As time went on, the Christian kingdoms began to take back the territories they had lost to the Moors and the Romance dialects again gained ground. The dominant of these was Castilian, which originated in the north central plains. The language that emerged was a rich mix, as Castilian borrowed many words from Mozarabic. In the 13th century a standardized Spanish language began to emerge, based on the Castilian dialect.

The *reconquista*

It was the Catholic monarchs Ferdinand of Aragon and Isabella of Castile who made Castilian the official language of the kingdom and it was also they who, in 1492, finally pushed out the Moors from their last stronghold in Granada. This event was baptized the **reconquista**.

Arabic words in Spanish

Given the length of time that Spain remained under Moorish rule, as well as its proximity to North Africa, it was no doubt inevitable that Spanish should assimilate a great many Arabic words. The extent to which this is the case sets Spanish (and Portuguese) apart from other Romance languages – modern Spanish is estimated to have at least 4,000 words of Arabic origin. Over the centuries, it took in vocabulary from every area of life. From **aceite** (*oil*), **arroz** (*rice*), **atún** (*tuna*), **azúcar** (*sugar*), **limón** (*lemon*), **naranja** (*orange*), **espinaca** (*spinach*), **café** (*coffee*), not forgetting **alcohol**, to **alcázar** (*palace*), **alfombra** (carpet), **algodón** (*cotton*), **baño** (*bathroom*), and **guitarra** (*guitar*). It is easy to see too that many of these Arabic words have come into English via Spanish.

Castilian and Adalusian

Castilian became the main language of Spain and Spanish people refer to Spanish as **castellano** rather than **español.** The main dialect, Andalusian (**andaluz**) is spoken in Andalusia in the extreme south of the country. The main differences are in pronunciation but Andalusian also has a good many words that are particular to it. Other regions such as Estramadura, Murcia, La Mancha, and Madrid have very similar dialects. Perhaps the most striking thing is the tendency not to pronounce the final consonant of a word. Andalusian is of course the language of **flamenco** and is spoken by all classes in Andalusia. However, in the rest of Spain, it is quite looked down upon and in theater and film is often associated with comic characters. People with ambitions in the media generally learn to speak Castilian.

The other languages of modern Spain

Cultural and historical diversity remain, unsurprisingly, a strong feature of modern-day Spain. Outside Spanish, three main languages are spoken in Spain today. All were severely repressed during the Franco era but are once more very much alive – and officially recognized – today.

Basque

Basque (in Basque **euskara**) is an ancient language spoken by the Basque people in the Basque Country of southwest France and northwest Spain. The Basques are held to be one of the most culturally distinct groups in Europe. Fascinatingly, it has not to date been possible to establish any link between their language, which has around a million speakers, and any other anywhere in the world.

Catalan

Catalan (**catalán**) is a Romance language which developed out of Vulgar Latin around 900. It has about 12 million speakers spread over Catalonia and Valencia, the Balearic Islands, Andorra (where it is the sole official language), the Roussillon region of France and parts of Aragon and Sardinia. It has taken in influences from Castilian over the centuries. However, it is not at all a dialect of Castilian but is in fact a relative of Occitan.

Galician

Galician (**gallego**) is also a Romance language. It developed as Galician-Portuguese out of Vulgar Latin at the beginning of the Middle Ages and still remains close to modern Portuguese. Along with Castilian it is the official language of Galicia in north eastern Spain and is also spoken in areas of the neighboring provinces of Asturia and Castile and Leon, as well as in many Latin American countries. There are thought to be around 2 million speakers.

The conquest of the Americas

The *reconquista* of Spain, finally accomplished in 1492 was seen as a crusade on the part of the Christian armies of northern Spain. In the same spirit, Spain set out to conquer the Americas and, by analogy to what had happened in Spain, called themselves the **conquistadores** (*the conquerors*). Christopher Columbus discovered the Americas in 1492 and this set off the colonization of the immense area that is now Latin America. It was a sorry era of Spanish history, accomplished with appalling cruelty towards the native peoples of these lands. Most of them attained independence in the 19th century. Spanish remains the official language of most of the colonized countries.

Spanish words in English

Spanish words have come into English over the centuries by a variety of routes. Many have come through general world trade. However, it is unsurprising that it has been through the contact between the US and Latin America that a great many words have been adopted. A particularly rich source was the vocabulary of the cowboys who moved north from Latin America to work in what is now the southwest of the US. Then of course there is much that has come in more recently, particularly in the realm of food.

Cowboys

Many familiar words come from Spanish. Some examples are: **corral**, **ranch** (from *rancho*), **savannah** (from Spanish *zavana* from the Indian language Taino *zabana*), **barbecue** (via Spanish from Taino *barbacoa*), **bronco** (meaning *rough*), **rodeo**, **lasso**, **buckaroo** (from *vaquero* meaning *cowboy*), **mustang** and **canoe** (Spanish *canoa* from Haitian *canoua*).

The natural world

The conquest of the Americas led to the discovery of a great deal of flora and fauna previously unknown to the **conquistadores**. So, via Spanish, we have **pampa**, **papaya**, **banana**, **avocado**, **iguana**, **jaguar**, **llama**, **alligator** (from *el lagarto* meaning *lizard*) and **mosquito**, to name only a very few.

Eating, drinking, dancing – and other amusements

Recent times have seen an explosion in the popularity of Latin American cooking, coming especially via Mexico and giving us **jalapeño**, **taco**, **burrito**, **guacamole**, **nacho**, **salsa** to name but a few. More directly from Spanish we have **paella**, **tortilla**, **sangría**, **margarita**, **tequila** and also **chocolate**, originally from Nahuatl *xocolatl*. Rather more risky pleasures give us tobacco, cigar, alcohol, marijuana, cocaine (via Spanish from Quechua *kúka*), whilst in music and dance we have inherited **flamenco**, **tango**, **rumba**, **bolero** and **guitar**. And of course we can always don a **poncho** or a **sombrero**.

And here are just a few more everyday words we have inherited from Spanish: **pim(i)ento**, **hacienda**, **fiesta**, **incommunicado**, **patio**, **cargo**, **cafeteria**, **pronto**, **plaza**, **junta**, **macho** and **aficionado**.

True friends and false friends

Despite the fact that Spanish and English have quite different origins, there are a good many words which are similar in both languages. These are usually derived from Greek or Latin. **Romántico**, for instance, does mean *romantic*, **conferencia** means *conference* and **contexto**, **sarcástico**, **patriótico**, **democrático**, **cliente**, **equivalente**, **indiferente**, **patente**, **suficiente**, **atención**, **circulación**, **edición**, **indicación**, **proposición** are just a few more of the Spanish words which have the same meaning as their English equivalent.

It is wise to be cautious, however, because you never know when an apparently 'true friend' may turn out to be a 'false friend' and cause embarrassment, if not worse! In fact, speaking of embarrassment, if you tell a Spanish-speaker that you are **embarazada,** they may be more surprised than you expected, as this means *pregnant*! Similarly, don't be shocked if someone you have just met tells you they are **constipado,** as this just means they have a cold. Here is a list of some of the most common deceptively similar words:

actual	current, at the present time
asistir	to attend, to be present
atender	to look after, attend to
biblioteca	library (bookstore is **librería**)
campo	country(side), field
carpeta	folder, briefcase

compromiso	commitment (an engaged couple are said to be **comprometidos**)
desgracia	misfortune, bad luck
disgusto	displeasure
discusión	argument (**argumento** means plot, storyline)
decepción	disappointment
excitado	sexually aroused
en absoluto	not at all
fábrica	factory
largo	long
molestar	to bother, to annoy (with no sexual connotation)
quieto	still
rape	monkfish/anglerfish
recordar	to remember
sano	healthy
sensible	sensitive
suceso	event (success is **éxito**)
simpático	friendly

English loanwords in Spanish

Spanglish

The English language has a varying degree of influence on everyday Spanish, depending largely on the country's geographical proximity and socio-economic relationship with the US. In some countries, such as Mexico, the use of Spanglish is widespread. This is when English words are integrated into Spanish speech patterns. So you might hear somebody say **'voy a vacunear la carpeta'** *(I'm going to vacuum the carpet)* or **'voy a parquear el carro'** *(I'm going to park the car)*, or someone might point up in the street and say **'¡mira! ¡un gato en el rufo del bildin!'** *(look! there's a cat on the roof of the building!)*.

At work

Generally, direct loanwords from English are more frequent in Latin American Spanish, particularly technical and business terms. These words often have a Spanish equivalent in Spain. Latin Americans, for example, will refer to their computer as their **computadora**, whereas in Spain the word **ordenador** is used. Having said this, there are many English words which are commonly used in Spain and Latin America alike, such as **manager, holding, budget, planning, marketing, telemarketing, sponsor, eslogan, overtime, overbooking,** and **training**. And people might discuss this morning's **meeting** during their **coffee break** or over **lonche**.

Internet

The Internet (**internet**, with no article) is one area where the trend of English borrowing is most apparent. **Surfear** on the **web**, **chatear on line** through your **módem** are common fare, as is the universal **e-mail** (often shortened to **mail** and also known as **emilio**) which you might send to the people on your **mailing** (mailing list).

Again, in Spain many computer terms have their Spanish equivalent, often a literal translation of the English. So **e-mail** is also referred to as **correo electrónico**, **navegar** is just as common as **surfear**, and you can design your own **página web** or **sitio de internet** and give it a **punto com** domain name. The mouse is **el ratón** and you use it to **hacer click**.

Sports and leisure

Sports is another important area for English borrowings. The sacred **fútbol** (referring to soccer, American football is specified as **fútbol americano**) is full of anglicisms, such as **penalti, chutar, gol, fan, ranking**, and most other sports have kept their English name, such as **basket** (without *ball*), **hockey, voleibol, béisbol, golf,** and **tenis**.

In the world of show business and publicity, actors go to **castings**, to do an **acting** for a **spot** (a TV commercial) and directors often work from **storyboards**. An actress might be described as having **mucho feeling**. The word **design** is much used, in the world of fashion (**una falda design** -- a designer skirt) and also to describe décor (**un restaurante muy design**).

Many words ending in **-ing** have become common usage. You might **hacer un footing** (go jogging) in the morning and then go and do a little **shopping**, buy a **sofa** for your **living** (living room) and maybe drop into a salon and get a **peeling**, then go and get your car from the **parking**. If you are looking for somewhere to live you might consider a **loft de alto standing** (top quality, luxury), or you may just be looking for a vacation **leasing**.

Spanish language and culture

Fast food

Fast food culture has brought words such as **sandwich** (always made with sliced bread, as opposed to the traditional **bocadillo**), **hamburguesa, ketchup, coca cola,** all of which you can find in a **fast food** (meaning a fast food *restaurant*) or a **self** (self-service restaurant). A curious borrowing is the **bikini**, which in some parts of Spain not only refers to swimwear but to a ham and cheese toasted sandwich.

English words in youth talk

The use of English words definitely gives a certain cool to youth talk, and expressions have developed around this. **Montar un show** is to kick up a fuss, **flipar** is to be amazed by something, **chute** is a hit off drugs but is used figuratively to describe a strong sensation, **un freaky** is a weirdo, **chequear** is to check something out. Young people often have **piercings**, generally work on their **look,** and talk about their favorite **dj** (or **deejay**) and the music they're into using words like: **new-wave, pop, funky, gothic, rock, roots, drum and bass, techno, hard-core, electro, trance, grunge,...** Popular activities are **hacer zapping** (flipping through TV channels), and more exciting pursuits such as, **rafting** (white-water rafting), **esquí, hacer snowboard,** and **puenting** (bungee jumping).

Youth slang

The vocabulary young people use and the way they alter the language is a way for them to define themselves socially and culturally, therefore slang tends to be very specific to a particular country or area. The way young people talk in Mexico is different from the way young people talk in Argentina or Paraguay, and Spanish slang from the Iberian Peninsula is different again. For example, in Spain the hip way to say *man* and *woman* is **tío** and **tía** (literally meaning *uncle* and *aunt*) or **pavo** and **pava**, whereas in Argentina they say **tipo** and **mina** and in Chile they say **mino** and **mina** or **gallo** and **galla**. Mexicans use **chavo** and **chava**.

There are innumerable friendly forms of address in Spanish slang. A favorite in Argentina is **boludo** (literally *big balls*), and in Mexico they have **huevón**, which means the same thing. **Guapa** (beautiful) is often used to address women in Spain. Also in Spain, **¿que pasa?** means *what's up?* whereas in Latin America generally it's more common to say **¿que onda?**. The Italian **ciao** is used more and more for 'goodbye,' along with **hasta luego** (see you later).

If something is cool, for Spanish people it's **chulo** or **guay**, for Mexicans it's **perro**, and in Chile they say **de miedo** or **bacán**. The opposite in Spain is **chungo**.

A walk on the wild side

The vocabulary of going out, of alcohol and drugs, is full of slang. A beer in Mexico is a **chela** and marijuana is **mota**. In Spain, a glass of beer is a **caña**, **maria** is marijuana and a joint is **un porro** or **un canuto.** If someone offers you **chocolate** you might not get what you expect as it also means hashish, and if you hear the words **camello** and **caballo** they may not be talking about animals but refering to a *drug dealer* and *heroin*.

Everyday forms of speech

All over the Spanish speaking world the use of diminutives is very popular. The suffix **-ito** or **-ita** is often added to names (**Paquito, Lolita...**) and to forms of address like **chiquita** (*little girl*), **muchachito** (*young boy*), but is frequently used with all kinds of words, giving them a more friendly sound. For example, **¿vamos a tomar un cafecito?** (*should we go for a coffee?*) or **¿estás cansadita?** (*are you tired?*).

Young people often abbreviate words, like **profe** (**profesor** *teacher*), **cole** (**colegio** *junior high school*), **mani** (**manifestación** *demonstration*), **finde** (**fin de semana** *weekend*), **peli** (**película** *movie*) and **sinpa** (**sin pagar** *leaving without paying*). Cellphone text messages are full of cryptic abbreviations like **k** (**qué?** *what?*), **qndo** (**¿cuándo?** *when?*), **hno** (**hermano** *brother*) and **kero** (**quiero** *I love*).

Hispanic culture

In Latin American countries, the predominantly Catholic traditions of the Spanish conquerors combined with indigenous folklore, and later with the rituals of the African slaves (often referred to as **criollo**), to create a rich and complex fusion of cultures. Unsurprisingly then, there are many contrasts between the customs and cultural characteristics of these countries and those of Spain, but also many similarities.

In Latin America and Spain alike, people take time to enjoy the good things in life, like eating and socializing, and value their leisure time, which can be scarce due to long working days, particularly in Latin America, where the economic situation tends to be more difficult. This determination to enjoy life is reflected particularly in the numerous festivals that take place.

Spanish language and culture

Religious celebrations

Religious festivals are often occasions for celebration and ritual. In Latin America the Catholic tradition has usually been laid on top of indigenous and Creole customs. In Mexico, el **Día de los Muertos** (the Day of the Dead or All Souls' Day, on November 2nd) is a very important festival which reflects Aztec rituals surrounding death. It is a colorful celebration where people leave flowers and gifts for their dead relatives and friends, who are believed to leave the afterworld and revisit their earthly homes on this day. It demonstrates an attitude towards death which is quite different from the solemnity of the Judeo-Christian tradition.

Having said this, even in Spain religious celebrations often have elements of ancient popular ritual which have survived from pagan times. An interesting festival in this respect is **Semana Santa** (Holy Week), which is observed all over the country but is particularly impressive in **Seville**. Throughout the week there are processions bearing statues of Jesus and the Virgin Mary from all the churches of the city. These statues often take on a very personal character. **La Macarena** from the area of **La Triana** is particularly popular and people shout **¡guapa!** (*beautiful one!*) and throw flowers as she passes, almost as if she were made of flesh and blood. Each area of the city has its own statue and bearing it is a great honor which the men usually pay for – how much depends on how close they get to the statue.

In Latin American countries, people also participate in processions at Easter-time. In Guatemala, for example, they carry platforms on which plays are performed that re-enact the entry into Jerusalem, the death and the resurrection of Christ. Antigua is particularly famous for this celebration and people there decorate the path of the procession with carpets of flowers or sawdust combined with pine needles and dye.

Knights and Kings

A good example of the fusion of Spanish and Creole customs is the festival of **Santiago** in Puerto Rico. **Santiago** was a Spanish knight who is said to have won a great battle against the Moors, and who was adopted by the Yoruba slaves when they were forbidden to worship their own god. There is a big procession with dancing and music based on **bomba** and **plenta** rhythms, which combine African and Spanish elements. The most exciting part of the festival is *The Devils against the Christians* where people mime the battle between the Christians and the Moors, many of them wearing either bright clothes, bells, flowers and white masks to represent the 'good' Spanish Caballeros, or devil masks with horns to represent the 'evil' Moors.

Another important festival in all Latin American countries is the **Fiesta Patria** or Independence Day, which commemorates independence from the Spanish crown, and often involves processions through the cities, sometimes, as in the case of Guatemala, with flaming torches.

When December comes, in Spain and Latin America all the boys and girls start to write their letter to the Three Kings, or to their favorite King: **Melchor, Gaspar** or **Baltasar**, to tell them what gifts they would like to receive. On the 24th they receive small presents and the grown-ups celebrate Christmas with a big meal, but for their main presents they have to wait for Epiphany, January 6th which is when the Three Kings arrive. There are also processions on this day.

Colors of Spain

Spain is a very varied country and the culture and traditions can be quite different from one area to another. In the south the Moorish occupation (8th – 15th century) left a rich heritage which is particularly apparent in the architecture, for example the spectacular **Alhambra** palace, in Granada and the great Mosque of Cordoba.

The south of Spain is also famous, of course, for flamenco and bullfights, and these traditions are very much alive. Going to bullfights is still a popular activity and the **toreros** (*bullfighters*) are stars. People even follow the fights on television. In other parts of the country bullfighting is not so popular, in fact in Catalonia it is banned altogether, but there are other variants such as the festival of **St Fermin** in Pamplona, when the young men run with the bulls through the streets of the city, daring each other to get as close as possible to the animals.

Flamenco became famous worldwide thanks to a few great stars like **Camaron de La Isla, Paco de Lucía** and **Joaquín Cortés**, but it comes from the very close-knit gypsy community and is a fascinating fusion of elements from places as far apart as India and Africa. The guitar itself, perhaps the most representative instrument of flamenco, is probably of Indian origin. Flamenco singing and dancing is an art form which draws on the deepest passions of the performers and its spirit is described by the word **duende**.

Popular dances have sprung from the flamenco tradition, such as the **Sevillanas**. This dance is obligatory during the **Feria de Abril** in **Sevilla,** when everyone gets dressed up (polka-dot dresses for the women and bolero jackets and breeches for the men) and parties for two weeks. The **feria** is also the name for the site where this takes place, which is set up with lots of tents in which people meet to drink **manzanilla** (a light, dry sherry), eat and dance.

There are different songs and dances in different areas of Spain. In Aragón, for example, they have the **jota**, Madrid is famous for its **coplas,** and Catalonia for the **sardana.** There are also strong elements of Celtic culture in Spain. These are clearly reflected in the music, for example, of Galicia, which has much in common with traditional Irish music.

Music today

The music of Spain nowadays tends to combine different influences. Ska is particularly popular and more and more modern bands are making what they call **mestizo** music, which combines different musical cultures such as flamenco, hip hop, reggae and Latin American rhythms.

Latin American music, due to its close association with dance, is based on an incredible variety of rhythmic patterns. The **tango** from Argentina, the **cumbia** from Columbia, the **son** from Cuba, the **bachata** from the Dominican Republic, the **salsa** and the **merengue** are just a few examples. **Rancheras** are the popular songs performed by **mariachi** bands in Mexico. Other musical traditions date back to the pre-Columbian Indians, such as the **guaíno** from Peru and Bolivia. Indigenous music has also combined with creole music in some places such as in Peru where it has given birth to the **chicha**.

Lifestyle

Common to all Hispanic countries is a predominantly Latin or Mediterranean attitude to the family, where ties are very strong and leaving home is not necessarily considered a desirable thing. Many single men over thirty continue to live at home. Children are adored but not spoiled, and firmly taught to respect their elders. They usually participate in adult activities, such as mealtimes, but are expected to behave themselves.

As in all Latin and Mediterranean cultures, the street is the venue for all kinds of activity, like taking a **paseo** (stroll), meeting your friends, window-shopping, watching other people and being watched, and having a cool drink on one of the many **terrazas**.

Food and drink

Food is very important and the necessary time is taken to enjoy and digest it, hence the famous **siesta**. It is also one of the best opportunities for conversation, another greatly valued pastime. The main meal of the day is eaten around 2 or 3 p.m., and often people won't go back to work until 4 or 5. In the hotter climates this is partly to avoid the unbearable heat of the middle of the day.

Going out to eat almost every day is common in Spain, especially at lunchtime, and the tapas tradition is widespread. This is when customers are given a little something to eat for free with their glass of wine. Apparently the plate this food was served on was originally placed on top of the glass, hence the word **tapa**, which means *lid*. You can eat very well in many parts of Spain by just wandering from one **tasca** (tapas bar) to the next having a few glasses of wine. Tapas can include all kinds of things from olives to grilled sardines to canapés or **montaditos** (slices of bread with any number and variety of ingredients on them). In the north of Spain, the tapas aren't usually free but it is nonetheless common to see a variety of mouth-watering morsels lined up on the bar.

Spanish cooking is typically Mediterranean and includes olive oil, a wide variety of fresh vegetables, seafood, fish and meat. People eat all imaginable forms of pig meat, the best-known and most highly valued being **jamón serrano** (*cured ham*), whole legs of which can be seen everywhere, in shops, in bars and in people's homes. Blood sausage, known as **morcilla** is also very popular and is sometimes made with rice. Another typical dish is **tortilla española**, a potato omelette. There are many varieties of cheese, the most widespread being **manchego**, which ranges from **tierno** (soft) to **curado** (well aged). Surprisingly, people say that the best seafood can be found in Madrid because it is traditionally rushed, fresh, every day for the pleasure of the royal family, but wonderful fish and seafood can of course be found all around the coast. Spain also boasts some very good wines, like Rioja and Ribera del Duero.

Traditional food in Latin America

Latin American food is very varied and includes indigenous, Asian, African, Creole and European influences. The single most important crop is corn, which has been cultivated since Mayan times and provides the staple food source, along with beans and rice. It is used to make **tortillas**, which can be found with a variety of fillings all over Latin America, and other dishes including **pozole** (*corn stew*).

Mexican cuisine is famous internationally and combines a wide variety of fresh fruit, vegetables and spices, particularly the different varieties of chili peppers. One famous item is **mole poblano**, which is a sauce made with chocolate, an ingredient that was much used by the Aztecs and came to Europe via Spain around 1500.

Argentina and Uruguay are famous for their high-quality beef, which is usually eaten grilled (**asado**). **Empanadas** (pastry stuffed with different things, including spicy meat and sweetcorn) can be found everywhere and a popular dessert is **dulce de leche**, made with condensed milk. And of course no Argentinian can be without his **mate**, a herb which is mixed with boiling water, poured from a handy thermos, to make a refreshing infusion.

Good wines can also be found in Latin America, the best-known perhaps being Chilean.

Leisure

In Latin America and Spain alike, soccer is **el Deporte Rey** (the king of sports). Several Latin American nations are renowned for their level of professional excellence and many of their players are bought by European teams. Some Latin American countries have achieved international renown in other sports too, such as Cuba in track and field, Puerto Rico in basketball and Columbia in cycling. Baseball is popular in Cuba and the Dominican Republic.

In Spain, it is difficult to avoid hearing people talk about soccer, particularly if Barcelona are playing against Madrid, as there is a lot of conflict between these two cities and their teams are among the best in Europe.

Cycling is also a popular sport in Spain and **La Vuelta** is among the top three cycling events in Europe, along with *Le Tour de France* and *Il Giro* in Italy. Many people follow the race on television and turn out in their hundreds, sometimes even thousands, at the different stages of the tour.

In the last couple of decades, skiing has become a much more affordable and popular pursuit. Many people go up to the Pyrenees, often to France and Andorra which have better slopes, to practice their slaloming. Snowboarding is popular too.

Spain has some beautiful beaches, not all of which have been taken over by tourism, and the Spanish know where to find the most unspoiled of them. People are very proud of their country and love to enjoy the varied countryside and the good food and wine. The Balearic Islands (Menorca, Mallorca, Ibiza, and Formentera) are also a popular destination for the summer months.

Spanish–English dictionary

a [a] *prep* to; at ▸ a las siete at seven o'clock

abajo [a-ba-CHoh] *adv* down

abandonar [a-ban-do-nahr] *v* to abandon, to leave

abierto, ta [ab-yair-toh] *adj* open

abrigo [ab-ree-goh] *m* coat

abril [ab-reel] *m* April

abrir [ab-reer] *v* to open

absoluto, ta [ab-so-loo-toh] *adj* absolute ▸ en absoluto (not) at all

absorbente [ab-sawr-ben-tay] *adj* absorbent

aburrido, da [a-boo-RRee-doh] *adj* bored; boring ▸ estar aburrido to be bored ▸ ser aburrido to be boring

acá [a-ka] *adv* here

acabar [a-ka-bahr] *v* to finish, to end ▸ acabar de hacer algo to have just done something

academia [a-ka-daym-ya] *f* school; academy

acampar [a-kam-pahr] *v* to camp (out)

acantilado [a-kan-ti-lah-doh] *m* cliff

acaso [a-ka-soh] *adv* ▸ por si acaso just in case

acceder [ak-thay-dair] *v* to access

acceso [ak-thay-soh] *m* access; entrance ▸ 'acceso pasajeros' 'passenger entrance'

accesorio [ak-thay-sawr-yo] *m* accessory

accidente [ak-thi-den-tay] *m* accident

aceite [a-thay-tay] *m* oil ▸ aceite de girasol/de oliva sunflower/olive oil

aceituna [a-thay-too-na] *f* olive

aceptar [a-thep-tahr] *v* to accept

acera [a-thair-a] *f* sidewalk

acerca [a-thair-ka] *prep* ▸ acerca de about

acercarse [a-thair-kahr-say] *v* to approach; to get close; *(to someone)* to come up to

acoger [a-koCH-air] *v* to take in

acomodarse [a-kom-oh-dahr-say] *v* to make yourself comfortable

acompañar [a-kom-pan-yahr] *v* to accompany; to go with

aconsejar [a-kon-say-CHahr] *v* to advise

acontecimiento [a-kon-teth-im-yen-toh] *m* event

acordar [a-kor-dahr] *v* to agree

acordarse [a-kor-dahr-say] *v* to remember ▸ acordarse de hacer algo to remember to do something

acostarse [a-kos-tahr-say] *v* to go to bed

acostumbrar [a-kos-toom-brahr] *v* to be in the habit of ▸ acostumbrarse a to get used to

actividad [ak-ti-bi-dad] *f* activity

acto [ak-toh] *m* act

actualidad [ak-too-a-li-dad] *f* ▸ de actualidad topical ▸ en la actualidad currently, nowadays

actuar [akt-wahr] *v* to act; to behave

acuerdo [a-kwair-doh] *m* agreement ▸ de acuerdo OK, all right ▸ estar de acuerdo to agree

adaptarse [a-dap-tahr-say] *v* to adapt

adelantado, da [a-day-lan-tah-doh] *adj* ahead, in front; advanced; *(clock)* fast

‣ por adelantado in advance

adelante [a-day-lan-tay] *adv* forward ✦ *excl* come in!; go ahead! ‣ más adelante *(in time)* later; *(in space)* further on

adelgazar [a-del-ga-thahr] *v* to lose weight

además [a-day-mas] *adv* besides; also, too ‣ además de as well as

adentro [a-den-troh] *adv* inside

adiós [ad-yohs] *excl* goodbye!

adjuntar [ad-CHoon-tahr] *v* to attach, to enclose

administrativo, va [ad-mi-nis-tra-tee-boh] *adj* administrative

admitir [ad-mi-teer] *v* to admit

adónde [a-don-day] *adv* where (to)?

aduana [ad-wah-na] *f* customs

advertir [ad-bair-teer] *v* to warn

aéreo, a [a-air-ay-oh] *adj* air; *(view, photo)* aerial

aeropuerto [eye-roh-pwair-toh] *m* airport

afeitarse [a-fay-tahr-say] *v* to shave

aficionado, da [a-feeth-yon-ah-do] *adj* amateur ‣ ser aficionado a algo to like something a lot

aficionarse a [a-feeth-yon-ahr-say a] *v* to become keen on, to become fond of

afortunadamente [a-for-too-nah-da-men-tay] *adv* luckily

afuera [af-wair-a] *adv* outside

afueras [af-wair-as] *fpl* outskirts

agencia [a-CHenth-ya] *f* agency ‣ agencia de viajes travel agency

agente [a-CHen-tay] *m, f* agent; representative ‣ agente de policía police officer

agosto [a-gos-toh] *m* August

agotado, da [a-goh-tah-doh] *adj* exhausted, tired out; sold out

agotarse [a-goh-tahr-say] *v* to get tired out; to sell out

agradecer [a-gra-day-thair] *v* to be grateful ‣ agradecer algo a alguien to thank somebody for something

agridulce [a-gri-dool-thay] *adj* sweet-and-sour

agrio, gria [ag-ryo] *adj* sour

agrupación [a-groo-path-yohn] *f* group

agua [ag-wa] *f* water

aguacate [ag-wa-kat-ay] *m* avocado

agujero [a-gooCH-air-oh] *m* hole

ahí [a-ee] *adv* there

ahogarse [a-o-gahr-say] *v* to drown; to suffocate

ahora [a-aw-ra] *adv* now

ahorrar [a-o-RRahr] *v* to save

ahorro [a-o-RRoh] *m* saving

ahumado, da [a-oo-mah-doh] *adj* smoked

aire [eye-ray] *m* air ‣ aire acondicionado air conditioning ‣ al aire libre in the open air

ajillo [a-CHeel-yoh] *m* minced garlic ‣ al ajillo with garlic

ajo [a-CHoh] *m* garlic

ala [a-la] *f* wing

alarma [a-lahr-ma] *f* alarm

albaricoque [al-ba-ri-koh-kay] *m* apricot

albergar [al-bair-gahr] *v* to put up, to accommodate

albergue [al-bair-gay] *m* hostel; refuge ‣ albergue juvenil youth hostel

albóndiga [al-bon-dig-a] *f* meatball

albufera [al-boo-fair-a] *f* lagoon

alcachofa [al-ka-choh-fa] *f* artichoke

alcalde, sa [al-kal-day] *m, f* mayor

alcanzar [al-kan-thahr] *v* to reach; *(bus, train)* to catch

alcaparra [al-ka-pa-RRa] *f* caper

alcohol [al-koh-ol] *m* alcohol

alcohólico, ca [al-ko-o-li-koh] *adj* alcoholic

aldea [al-day-a] *f* village, hamlet

alegrarse [a-leg-rahr-say] *v* to be pleased ▸ alegrarse de to be glad that

alegre [a-leg-ray] *adj* happy, cheerful; bright; lively

alegría [a-leg-ree-a] *f* happiness, joy

alergia [a-lairCH-ya] *f* allergy

alerta [a-lair-ta] *f* alert; warning ◆ *excl* look out! ▸ dar la alerta to raise the alarm ▸ 'alerta roja' 'red alert'

aletas [a-lay-tas] *fpl (for diving)* flippers

algo [al-goh] *pron* something ◆ *adv* rather, slightly

algodón [al-go-dohn] *m* cotton

alguien [alg-yen] *pron* someone, somebody

alguno, na [al-goo-noh] *adj* some; any ◆ *pron* one ▸ algún día some day

alimento [a-li-men-toh] *m* food

alioli [a-li-oh-li] *m* aioli, garlic mayonnaise

aliviar [a-lib-yahr] *v* to relieve

allá [al-ya] *adv (space)* over there; *(time)* back in ▸ allá tú that's your problem

allí [al-yee] *adv* there

almacén [al-ma-thayn] *m* store ▸ grandes almacenes department store

almejas [al-may-CHas] *fpl* clams

almendra [al-men-dra] *f* almond

almendrado [al-men-drah-doh] *m* almond cookie

almíbar [al-mee-bahr] *m* syrup ▸ melocotón en almíbar canned peaches

almohada [al-moh-ah-da] *f* pillow

almuerzo [alm-wair-thoh] *m* lunch; breakfast

alojamiento [a-loh-CHam-yen-toh] *m* accommodations

alojarse [a-loh-CHahr-say] *v* to stay

alquilar [al-ki-lahr] *v* to rent, to rent out ▸ 'se alquila' 'for rent'

alquiler [al-ki-lair] *m* rent; rental ▸ de alquiler for rent

alrededor [al-RRe-de-dor] *adv* around ▸ alrededor (de) around; about

alrededores [al-RRe-de-dor-ays] *mpl* surrounding area

alterar [al-tair-ahr] *v* to alter, to change

altitud [al-ti-tood] *f* altitude

alto, ta [al-toh] *adj* high; tall; loud ◆ *adv* loudly; high ◆ *excl* halt!, stop!

altura [al-too-ra] *f* height; altitude ▸ dos metros de altura two meters in height, two meters tall

alubias [a-loob-yas] *fpl* beans

alud [a-lood] *m* avalanche; landslide

alumno, na [a-loom-noh] *m, f* pupil, student

amanecer [a-man-e-thair] *m* dawn ▸ al amanecer at dawn

amar [a-mahr] *v* to love

amarillo, lla [a-ma-reel-yoh] *adj & m* yellow

ambientador [amb-yen-ta-dawr] *m* air freshener

ambiente [amb-yen-tay] *m* atmosphere; life, things going on ▸ medio ambiente environment

ambos, bas [am-bohs(bas)] *adj* both ◆ *pron* both of them

ambulancia [am-boo-lanth-ya] *f* ambulance

ambulatorio [am-boo-la-tawr-yoh] *m* health center, clinic

amistad [a-mis-tad] *f* friendship

Al Andalus

Arab influence can be seen all over Andalusia, which is hardly surprising as the region was occupied by the Arabs from the 8th to the 15th century. It was a very rich period when Muslims, Christians and Jews lived side by side. Among the great buildings remaining from the period are the famous *Alhambra* palace in Granada; Córdoba's *mezquita* (mosque), begun in 785 but later partially destroyed so that a cathedral could be built within it; and Seville's *Alcázar* palace with its *mudéjar* style.

ampliar [amp-lee-ahr] *v* to enlarge; to extend; to widen

amueblado, da [am-way-blah-doh] *adj* furnished

ancho, cha [an-choh] *adj* wide ♦ *m* width ▸ dos metros de ancho two meters wide

anchoa [an-choh-a] *f* anchovy

anciano, na [anth-yah-noh] *adj* old, elderly

andar [an-dahr] *v* to walk

Andalucía [an-da-loo-thee-a] *f* Andalusia

andén [an-dayn] *m* platform

anguila [ang-gee-la] *f* eel

angula [ang-goo-la] *f* young eel, elver

animado, da [a-ni-mah-doh] *adj* lively

animar [a-ni-mahr] *v* to cheer up; to liven up

ánimo [a-ni-moh] *excl* ▸ ¡ánimo! come on!, cheer up!

aniversario [a-ni-bair-sahr-yoh] *m* anniversary

anoche [a-no-chay] *adv* last night

anochecer [a-no-che-thair] *m* nightfall, dusk ▸ al anochecer at dusk

anotar [a-noh-tahr] *v* to note down

ansiedad [ans-yay-dad] *f* anxiety

ante [an-tay] *prep* before ▸ ante todo above all

anteanoche [an-tay-a-no-chay] *adv* the night before last

anteayer [an-tay-a-yair] *adv* the day before yesterday

anterior [an-tair-yawr] *adj* previous; before

antes [an-tes] *adv* before ▸ antes de before ▸ lo antes posible as soon as possible

anticipar [an-ti-thi-pahr] *v (date)* to bring forward; *(payment)* to pay in advance

antigüedad [an-tig-way-dad] *f* age; ancient times; antique

antiguo, gua [an-teeg-woh] *adj* old, former; antique; ancient

anual [an-wal] *adj* annual

anular [a-noo-lahr] *v* to cancel, to annul

añadir [an-ya-deer] *v* to add

año [an-yoh] *m* year ▸ tengo treinta años I'm thirty years old

apagar [a-pa-gahr] *v* to put out; to turn off

aparato [a-pa-rat-oh] *m* machine, appliance, device; piece of equipment

aparcamiento [a-pahr-kam-yen-toh] *m* parking lot; parking

aparcar [a-pah-kahr] *v* to park

apartamento [a-pahr-ta-men-toh] *m* apartment

apellido

Who said macho? In Spain you take the family names of both of your parents, with your father's name coming before your mother's. Both of them must appear on official documents, even if it's more common to use only your father's name in everyday life. As for married women, in the past they might have taken their husband's last name, but nowadays they virtually always use their own parental names.

apartar [a-pahr-tahr] *v* to put to one side, to set aside

aparte [a-pahr-tay] *adv* & *adj* apart
▶ aparte de as well as, apart from

apellido [a-pel-yee-doh] *m* last name

apenas [a-pay-nas] *adv* hardly, scarcely

aperitivo [a-per-i-tee-boh] *m* aperitif; appetizer

apetecer [a-pe-te-thair] *v* to feel like, to want

apetito [a-pe-tee-toh] *m* appetite

apio [ap-yoh] *m* celery

aplazar [ap-la-thahr] *v* to postpone

aplicar [ap-li-kahr] *v* to apply

apoyar [a-poh-yahr] *v* to lean, to rest; to support

apreciar [a-preth-yahr] *v* to think highly of, to be fond of; to appreciate, to value; to notice

aprender [a-pren-dair] *v* to learn

apresurarse [a-pres-oo-rahr-say] *v* to hurry

apretar [a-pre-tahr] *v* to squeeze; to tighten

aprisa [a-pree-sa] *adv* quickly

aprobar [a-proh-bahr] *v* to approve; *(exam)* to pass

aprovechar [a-pro-be-chahr] *v* to take advantage of, to make the most of

aproximarse [a-prok-si-mahr-say] *v* to approach, to come closer

apto, ta [ap-toh] *adj* suitable ▶ 'no apto para menores' 'not suitable for minors'

apuntar [a-poon-tahr] *v* to write down; to point

apuntarse [a-poon-tahr-say] *v* to enroll, to put one's name down

aquel [a-kel] *adj* that ▶ aquella casa that house

aquél [a-kel] *pron* that one

aquello [a-kel-yoh] *pron* that

aquí [a-kee] *adv* here

árbol [ar-bol] *m* tree

arbusto [ar-boos-toh] *m* bush

aperitivo

In Spain, drinking an aperitif is a perfect opportunity to meet up with friends or family, especially at lunchtime on Sundays. With a glass of wine, vermouth or beer, you can nibble on *pinchos* (snacks) stuck on toothpicks (*palillos*). The waiter tallies up the bill by counting the *palillos*, so don't swallow them!

archipiélago [ar-chip-yay-la-goh] *m* archipelago, group of islands

área [ahr-ay-a] *f* area, zone ▸ 'área de descanso' 'rest area' ▸ 'área de recreo' 'recreation area'

arena [a-ray-na] *f* sand

arenque [a-ren-kay] *m* herring

armario [ar-mahr-yoh] *m* closet

arrancar [a-RRan-kahr] *v* to pull up/out, to tear out; *(engine)* to start

arrastrar [a-RRas-trahr] *v* to drag

arreglar [a-RReg-lahr] *v* to repair, to mend

arriba [a-RRee-ba] *adv (position)* above; *(direction)* up ▸ más arriba further up

arrojar [a-RRo-CHahr] *v* to throw; to be sick, to vomit

arroyo [a-RRo-yoh] *m* stream

arroz [a-RRoth] *m* rice ▸ arroz con leche rice pudding

arte [ar-tay] *m* art

artesanía [ar-te-sa-nee-a] *f* craftwork ▸ de artesanía handcrafted

artículo [ar-tee-koo-loh] *m* article ▸ artículos de lujo luxury goods

asado, da [a-sah-doh] *adj* roast, baked ♦ *m* roast

asador [a-sa-dawr] *m* roaster; *(restaurant)* grill, grillroom

asearse [a-say-ahr-say] *v* to get washed and dressed

asegurarse [a-seg-oo-rahr-say] *v* ▸ asegurarse de (que) to make sure (that)

aseo [a-say-oh] *m* toilet; cleanliness, personal hygiene

así [a-see] *adj & adv* like this, like that ▸ así es that's right

asiento [as-yen-toh] *m* seat

asma [as-ma] *f* asthma

asociación [a-sohth-yath-yohn] *f* association

aspecto [as-pek-toh] *m* appearance, look; aspect

astuto, ta [as-too-toh] *adj* shrewd, cunning

asunto [a-soon-toh] *m* subject, matter; affair ▸ no es asunto tuyo it's none of your business

asustar [a-soos-tahr] *v* to frighten

asustarse [a-soos-tahr-say] *v* to be scared

atajo [a-ta-CHoh] *m* short cut

atar [a-tahr] *v* to tie

atardecer [a-tahr-de-thair] *m* dusk ▸ al atardecer at dusk

atención [a-tenth-yohn] *f & excl* attention

atender [a-ten-dair] *v* to look after, to take care of; to deal with; *(customer)* to serve; *(patient)* to treat

aterrizar [a-te-RRi-thahr] *v* to land

ático [a-ti-koh] *m* top-floor apartment

atractivo, va [a-trak-tee-boh] *adj* attractive ♦ *m* appeal; attraction

atrás [a-tras] *adv* back, backwards; in the back, at the back; earlier, ago ▸ años atrás years ago

atrasado, da [a-tra-sah-do] *adj* behind, delayed; backward; *(clock)* slow

atrasar [a-tra-sahr] *v* to put back

atraso [a-tra-soh] *m* delay

atravesar [a-tra-bes-ahr] *v* to go through, to cross

atropellar [a-tro-pel-yahr] *v* to run over, to knock down

atún [a-toon] *m* tuna

aun [own] *adv* even ♦ *conj* even

aún [a-oon] *adv* still

aunque [own-kay] *conj* although

ausencia [ow-senth-ya] *f* absence

auténtico, ca [ow-ten-ti-koh] *adj* genuine, authentic

autonomía [ow-ton-om-ee-ya] *f* autonomy, independence; autonomous region

autopista [ow-toh-pees-ta] *f* expressway, freeway ▸ autopista de peaje turnpike, tollway

autorizar [ow-to-ri-thahr] *v* to authorize

autovía [ow-toh-bee-a] *f* divided highway

auxiliar [owk-seel-yahr] *m, f* assistant ◆ *v* to help

auxilio [owk-seel-yoh] *m* help ◆ *excl* help!, assistance ▸ ¡auxilio! help! ▸ 'primeros auxilios' 'first aid'

avanzar [a-ban-thahr] *v* to advance, to move forward; to make progress

avda. *abbr of* **avenida** ave

ave [ah-bay] *f* bird

AVE [ah-bay] *m abbr of* **Alta Velocidad Española** Spanish high-speed train

avellana [a-bel-yah-na] *f* hazelnut

avenida [a-ben-ee-da] *f* avenue

aventura [a-ben-too-ra] *f* adventure

avería [a-bair-ee-a] *f* fault, breakdown

averiarse [a-bair-yahr-say] *v* to break down ▸ 'averiado' 'broken down''out of order'

avión [ab-yohn] *m* plane, airplane

avioneta [ab-yoh-nay-ta] *f* light aircraft

avisar [a-bi-sahr] *v* to warn; to inform

ayer [a-yair] *adv* yesterday

ayuda [a-yoo-da] *f* help

ayudar [a-yoo-dahr] *v* to help

ayuntamiento [a-yoon-tam-yen-toh] *m* town hall, city hall; town council, city council

azafata [a-tha-fa-ta] *f* hostess

azafrán [a-tha-fran] *m* saffron

azotea [a-thoh-tay-a] *f* flat roof

azúcar [a-thoo-kahr] *m* sugar

azul [a-thool] *adj & m* blue

b

bacalao [ba-ka-low] *m* cod

bahía [ba-ee-a] *f* bay

bailar [beye-lahr] *v* to dance

bajar [ba-CHahr] *v* to go down, to come down; to lower; to turn down

bajo, ja [ba-CHoh] *adj* low; short ◆ *adv* softly, in a low voice ◆ *prep* under

balneario [bal-nay-ahr-yoh] *m* spa

balsa [bal-sa] *f* raft; pond, pool

banco [ban-ko] *m* bank; bench

bandeja [ban-day-CHa] *f* tray

bandera [ban-dair-a] *f* flag

banderilla [ban-de-reel-ya] *f (bullfighting)* barbed dart stuck in the bull's back

bañador [ban-ya-dawr] *m* swimsuit; swimming trunks

bañarse [ban-yahr-say] *v* to have a bath; to go for a swim

baño [ban-yoh] *m* bathroom ▸ darse un baño to have a bath; to go for a swim

bar [bahr] *m* bar ▸ bar musical bar with music (where one can dance)

barato, ta [ba-ra-toh] *adj & adv* cheap

barca [bahr-ka] *f* boat

barco [bahr-koh] *m* ship, boat ▸ barco de vela sailboat

barra [ba-RRa] *f* bar; slash ▸ 'barra libre' 'free bar' ▸ barra de pan baguette, thin loaf of French bread

barranco [ba-RRan-koh] *m* gully

barrera [ba-RRair-ra] *f* barrier; *(bull-fighting)* front row of seats

barrio [baRR-yoh] *m* neighborhood, area

base [ba-say] *f* base

basta [bas-ta] *excl* ▸ ¡basta! enough!

bastante [bas-tan-tay] *prep & adv* enough

bastar [bas-tahr] *v* to be enough

basura [ba-soo-ra] *f* garbage

batido [ba-tee-doh] *m* milk shake

bazar [ba-thahr] *m* hardware store

beber [beb-air] *v* to drink

bebida [beb-ee-da] *f* drink

belleza [bel-yay-tha] *f* beauty

bello, lla [bel-yoh] *adj* beautiful

bellota [bel-yoh-ta] *f* acorn

beneficiar [be-ne-fith-yahr] *v* to benefit

berberechoss [bair-be-re-chohs] *mpl* cockles

berenjena [be-ren-CHay-na] *f* eggplant

beso [bay-soh] *m* kiss

besugo [bes-oo-goh] *m* sea bream

bien [byen] *adv* well, properly ◆ *adj* good ◆ *m* good ▸ ¡bien! great!; fine!

bienvenida [byem-ben-ee-da] *f* welcome

billete [bil-yay-tay] *m* ticket; bill, bank-note ▸ billete de ida y vuelta round-trip ticket

biscuit [bis-kweet] *m* ▸ biscuit glacé ice cream

bistec [bis-tek] *m* steak ▸ bistec de ternera veal steak, beefsteak ▸ bistec a

la plancha grilled steak

bisutería [bi-soo-tair-ee-ya] *f* costume jewelry

bizcocho [bith-ko-choh] *m* sponge cake

blanco, ca [blan-koh] *adj & m* white

boca [boh-ka] *f* mouth

bocadillo [bok-a-deel-yo] *m* sandwich

bodega [bod-ay-ga] *f* wine cellar; winery; bar

bogavante [bog-a-ban-tay] *m* lobster

bolígrafo [bol-ee-graf-oh] *m* ballpoint pen

bollo [bol-yoh] *m* roll, bun

bolsa [bol-sa] *f* bag

bolsillo [bol-seel-yoh] *m* pocket

bolso [bol-soh] *m* purse

bombero [bom-bair-oh] *m* fireman

bombón [bom-bohn] *m* chocolate

bonito, ta [bon-ee-toh] *adj* pretty, nice ◆ *m* tuna, bonito

bono [boh-noh] *m* voucher

bonobús [boh-noh-boos] *m* bus pass

boquerones [bok-e-roh-nes] *mpl* (fresh or pickled) anchovies

borde [bor-day] *m* edge ▸ al borde de on the edge of

borracho, cha [bo-RRa-choh] *adj* drunk ◆ *m, f* drunk, drunkard

borrar [bo-RRahr] *v* to erase

bosque [bos-kay] *m* wood, forest

bote [boh-tay] *m* jar, can; boat

botella [bot-el-ya] *f* bottle

botellón [bo-tel-yohn] *m* gathering of young people in a park or square etc. to drink alcohol and enjoy themselves

botón [bot-ohn] *m* button

botones [bot-oh-nes] *m* bellhop

brasa [bras-a] *f* ▸ a la brasa barbecued

bravo, va [brah-boh] *adj* wild, fierce;

botellón

Botellones began in the 1990s, but still continue, despite having been banned in many places. What's the idea? A group of young people get together, anything between five and five hundred of them (or even more), and meet up in a square or a park on the weekend. They spend the whole night talking, singing, yelling and, of course, getting drunk, maybe having a smoke... That's young people!

rough ◆ *excl* ▸ ¡bravo! bravo!

brazo [bra-thoh] *m* arm

brécol [bray-kol] *m* broccoli

breve [bray-bay] *adj* brief, short

broncearse [bron-thay-ahr-say] *v* to get a tan

bucear [boo-thay-ahr] *v* to dive

bueno, na, [bway-noh] *adj* good ◆ *adv* all right ▸ ¡buenas! hi, hello

buey [bwey] *m* ox ▸ buey de mar crab

bulto [bool-toh] *m* lump, bump; item of

luggage ▸ 'un (solo) bulto de mano' (just) one piece of hand luggage

buñuelo [boon-yoo-ay-loh] *m* fritter ▸ buñuelo de viento cream-filled dough-nut

buque [boo-kay] *m* ship

burro, rra [boo-RRoh] *m, f* donkey

buscar [boos-kahr] *v* to look for

butaca [boo-ta-ka] *f* seat; armchair

buzón [boo-thohn] *m* mail box

C

c/ *abbr of* **calle** st

caballa [ka-bal-ya] *f* mackerel

caballero [ka-bal-yair-oh] *m* man, gentleman ▸ 'caballeros' *(toilets)* 'gentlemen, men'

caballo [ka-bal-yoh] *m* horse

cabello [ka-bel-yoh] *m* hair ▸ cabello de ángel pumpkin preserve

caber [ka-bair] *v* to fit ▸ sólo caben cuatro personas there's room for only four people

cabeza [ka-bay-tha] *f* head

cabina [ka-bee-na] *f* cabin ▸ cabina telefónica phone booth

cabo [kah-boh] *m (geography)* cape

cabra [kab-ra] *f* (nanny) goat

cada [kah-da] *adj* each; every ▸ cada dos días every two days ▸ cada uno each

cadena [ka-day-na] *f* chain

caducar [ka-doo-kahr] *v* to expire; to go past its sell-by date

caducidad [ka-doo-thi-thad] *f* ▸ fecha de caducidad sell-by date

caer [ka-air] *v* to fall ▸ cae en domingo it falls on a Sunday

café [ka-fay] *m* coffee; café ▸ café con leche coffee with milk ▸ café solo black coffee

caja [ka-CHa] *f* box; cash register; checkout ▸ caja de ahorros savings

Camino de Santiago

This is the famous route that links the Pyrenees with Santiago de Compostela in Galicia, where the remains of the apostle St. James are said to be buried. Pilgrimages began in the Middle Ages and died out during the 17th century, but since the 1960s they have gradually come back into favor. Nowadays, thousands follow the old pilgrim's route to Santiago every year, on foot, on horseback or even by bicycle.

bank ▸ 'caja rápida' 'express checkout' ▸ caja fuerte safe

cajero, ra [kaCH-air-oh] *m, f* cashier

cajón [ka-CHohn] *m* drawer

cala [kah-la] *f* cove

calabacín [ka-la-ba-theen] *m* zucchini

caldo [kal-doh] *m* broth

calefacción [ka-lay-fakth-yohn] *f* heating

calendario [ka-len-dahr-yoh] *m* calendar

calentar [ka-len-tahr] *v* to heat up, to warm up

calidad [ka-li-dad] *f* quality

caliente [kal-yen-tay] *adj* hot

callar [kal-yahr] *v* to shut up

calle [kal-yay] *f* street

callejero [kal-yeCH-air-oh] *m* street map

callejón [kal-ye-CHohn] *m* alley ▸ callejón sin salida cul-de-sac, dead end

callos [kal-yohs] *mpl* tripe ▸ callos a la madrileña tripe with ham, pork sausage, peppers and onion

calor [ka-lawr] *m* heat

calzada [kal-thah-da] *f* roadway; pavement

calzado [kal-thah-doh] *m* footwear

cama [ka-ma] *f* bed ▸ cama individual single bed ▸ cama de matrimonio double bed

cámara [ka-ma-ra] *f* camera; chamber; inner tube ▸ cámara fotográfica camera

camarero, ra [ka-ma-rair-oh] *m, f* waiter, waitress

camarón [ka-ma-rohn] *m* shrimp

camarote [ka-ma-roh-tay] *m* cabin

cambiar [kam-byahr] *v* to change; to move

cambio [kam-byoh] *m* change; exchange, exchange rate

caminar [ka-mi-nahr] *v* to walk

camino [ka-mee-noh] *m* path, track; way ▸ 'camino particular' 'private road'

camisa [ka-mee-sa] *f* shirt

camiseta [ka-mi-say-ta] *f* T-shirt; undershirt

campamento [kam-pa-men-toh] *m* camp ▸ ir de campamento to go camping

camping [kam-ping] *m* campground ▸ camping gas portable gas stove ▸ 'camping naturista' 'nudist campground' ▸ hacer camping to go camping

campo [kam-poh] *m* field; country ▸ campo de golf golf course

cancelar [kan-thel-ahr] *v* to cancel

canción [kanth-yohn] *f* song

cangrejo [kan-gray-CHoh] *m* crab

cansado, da [kan-sah-doh] *adj* tired ▸ estar cansado to be tired

cansarse [kan-sahr-say] *v* to get tired

Cantábrico [kan-tab-ri-koh] *m* ▸ el mar Cantábrico the Cantabrian Sea

cantar [kan-tahr] *v* to sing

cante [kan-tay] *m* Andalusian folk song ▸ cante flamenco flamenco singing ▸ cante jondo traditional-style flamenco singing

cantidad [kan-ti-dad] *f* quantity, amount; sum (of money)

cantina [kan-tee-na] *f* canteen, dining hall; buffet, cafeteria

caña [kan-ya] *f* glass of beer

capaz [ka-path] *adj* able, capable ▸ ser capaz de to be capable of

capítulo [ka-pee-too-loh] *m* chapter

cara [kah-ra] *f* face; (of record) side; (of coin) heads ▸ tener buena cara to look good, to look well

caracol [ka-ra-kol] *m* snail

carajillo [ka-ra-CHeel-yoh] *m black coffee with a dash of brandy, whisky, etc.*

caramelo [ka-ra-may-loh] *m* piece of candy; caramel

cárcel [kahr-thel] *f* prison

carga [kahr-ga] *f* loading; cargo; burden; charge; refill ▸ 'carga y descarga' 'loading and unloading'

cargar [kahr-gahr] *v* to load; to charge; to carry

carne [kahr-nay] *f* meat; flesh

carné [kahr-nay] *m* card ▸ carné de identidad identity card ▸ carné de conducir driver's license

caro, ra [kah-roh] *adj & adv* expensive

carpa [kahr-pa] *f* marquee; carp

carrera [ka-RRair-a] *f* race; (university) degree

carrete [ka-RRay-tay] *m* roll of film

carretera [ka-RRay-tair-a] *f* road

carril [ka-RReel] *m* (of freeway) lane

carta [kahr-ta] *f* (à la carte) menu; letter

cartera [kahr-tair-a] *f* wallet; briefcase

casa [ka-sa] *f* house ▸ casa de campo country house

casarse [ka-sahr-say] *v* to get married

cascada [kas-kah-da] *f* waterfall

casco [kas-koh] *m* helmet ▸ casco antiguo old town

caserío [ka-se-ree-oh] *m* farmhouse

casi [ka-si] *adv* almost

casilla [ka-seel-ya] *f* box

castaña [kas-tan-ya] *f* chestnut

castigar [kas-ti-gahr] *v* to punish

castillo [kas-teel-yoh] *m* castle

casualidad [kas-wa-li-dad] *f* coincidence ▸ por casualidad by any chance

catálogo [ka-ta-loh-goh] *m* catalog

Cataluña [ka-ta-loon-ya] *f* Catalonia

catar [ka-tahr] *v* to taste

cataratas [ka-ta-ra-tas] *fpl* waterfall

catarro [ka-ta-RRoh] *m* cold, chill

cava [kah-ba] *m* cava, Spanish sparkling wine

caza [ka-tha] *f* hunting, shooting; game

cazuela [kath-way-la] *f* earthenware dish ▸ pollo a la cazuela chicken casserole

cebolla [theb-ol-ya] *f* onion

cebolleta [theb-ol-yay-ta] *f* scallion

ceder [thed-air] *v* to give way, to yield ▸ 'ceda el paso' 'yield'

celebrar [thel-eb-rahr] *v* to celebrate

cementerio [them-en-tair-yoh] *m* cemetery

cena [thay-na] *f* evening meal, dinner

centeno [then-tay-noh] *m* rye

céntimo [then-ti-moh] *m* cent

centollo [then-tol-yoh] *m* spider crab

centralita [then-tra-lee-ta] *f* switchboard

centro [then-troh] *m* center ▸ centro turístico tourist resort ▸ centro ciudad downtown

cepillo [thep-eel-yoh] *m* brush ▸ cepillo de dientes toothbrush

cepo [thay-poh] *m* (*of vehicle*) Denver boot

cerca [thair-ka] *adv* near, nearby

cercanías [thair-ka-nee-as] *m* local train ◆ *fpl* surrounding area, environs

cerdo, da [thair-doh] *m*, *f* hog

cereza [thair-ay-tha] *f* cherry

cero [thair-oh] *num* zero

cerrado, da [thair-RRah-doh] *adj* closed ▸ 'cerrado por vacaciones' 'closed for vacation'

cerrar [thair-RRahr] *v* to close, to shut; (*faucet*) to turn off; (*zipper*) to zip up

cerro [theRR-oh] *m* hill

certificado, da [thair-ti-fi-kah-doh] *adj* (*mail*) registered

cerveza [thair-bay-tha] *f* beer ▸ cerveza negra dark beer

césped [thes-ped] *m* lawn, grass ▸ 'prohibido pisar el césped' 'keep off the grass'

chalé [cha-lay] *m* detached house, single dwelling (with garden); cottage; (mountain) chalet

champú [cham-poo] *m* shampoo

chaqueta [cha-kay-ta] *f* jacket

charla [chahr-la] *f* chat

charlar [chahr-lahr] *v* to chat

cheque [chek-ay] *m* check

chicle [cheek-lay] *m* chewing gum

chico, ca [cheek-oh] *m*, *f* boy, girl

chipirón [chip-i-rohn] *m* baby squid

▸ chipirones en su tinta baby squid in their ink

chistorra [chis-to-RRa] *f* long thin spicy pork sausage

chocar [chok-ahr] *v* to crash; to surprise, to shock

chopito [chop-ee-toh] *m* baby cuttlefish ▸ chopitos fritos fried baby cuttlefish

choque [chok-ay] *m* crash, collision

chuleta [choo-lay-ta] *f* (*meat*) chop

chuletón [choo-lay-tohn] *m* (*meat*) large chop

chupito [choo-pee-toh] *m* (*of liquor*) shot, nip

churrasco [choo-RRas-koh] *m* barbecued steak

churro [choo-RRoh] *m* stick of dough, deep-fried and sprinkled with sugar

Cía *abbr of* compañía Co.

ciego, ga [thyay-goh] *m*, *f* blind person

ciento [thyen-toh] *num* hundred ▸ por ciento percent

cierre [thye-RRay] *m* closure, closing; fastener, zipper

cierto, ta [thyair-toh] *adj* true, correct; certain

cigala [thi-gah-la] *f* Norway lobster, langoustine

cigarrillo [thi-ga-RReel-yoh] *m* cigarette

cigarro [thi-ga-RRoh] *m* cigarette; cigar

cinco [theen-koh] *num* five

circuito [theer-kwee-toh] *m* circuit

circulación [theer-koo-lath-yohn] *f* traffic; circulation

ciruela [theer-way-la] *f* plum

cita [thee-ta] *f* date; appointment

ciudad [thyoo-dad] *f* city, town

civilización [thi-bi-li-thath-yohn] *f* civilization

claro, ra [klah-roh] *adj* clear; obvious,

churros

It would be a crime to leave Spain without having tasted *chocolate con churros*. *Churros* are little fritters shaped into fluted sticks and sprinkled with sugar that you dip into really thick hot chocolate. They are delicious! Eat them for breakfast, at tea-time, or really early in the morning after a night on the town!

evident; light ◆ *excl* ▸ ¡claro! of course!

clase [kla-say] *f* class; type, sort ▸ viajar en primera clase to travel first class ▸ clase preferente business class

cláusula [klow-soo-la] *f* clause

cliente [klee-en-tay] *m, f* customer, client

clima [klee-ma] *m* climate

cobrador, ra [kob-ra-dawr] *m, f* bus conductor

cobrar [kob-rahr] *v* to charge ▸ ¿me cobra, por favor? could I pay, please?

cobro [kob-roh] *m* ▸ a cobro revertido *(phone call)* collect

cocer [ko-thair] *v* to cook; to boil

coche [ko-chay] *m* car, automobile ▸ coche cama sleeping car ▸ coche restaurante dining car

cochinillo [ko-chi-neel-yoh] *m* suckling pig

cocido [ko-thee-doh] *m* stew

cocina [ko-thee-na] *f* kitchen; stove; cooking

código [ko-di-goh] *m* code

coger [koCH-air] *v* to take; to catch

col [kol] *f* cabbage

cola [koh-la] *f* line ▸ hacer cola to wait in line

colaborar [ko-la-bo-rahr] *v* to collaborate ▸ colaborar en to contribute to

colchón [kol-chohn] *m* mattress

colchoneta [kol-choh-nay-ta] *f* airbed

colegio [ko-leCH-yoh] *m* school

colgar [kol-gahr] *v* to hang up

coliflor [ko-li-flor] *f* cauliflower

colina [ko-lee-na] *f* hill

colocar [ko-lo-kahr] *v* to place, to put

comarca [ko-mahr-ka] *f* area

combatir [kom-ba-teer] *v* to fight

combinación [kom-bi-nath-yohn] *f* combination

combinado [kom-bi-nah-doh] *m* cocktail ▸ plato combinado single course meal, served on one plate

comedor [ko-me-dawr] *m* dining room

comentario [ko-men-tahr-yoh] *m* commentary

comenzar [ko-men-thahr] *v* to start

comer [ko-mair] *v* to eat

comercio [ko-mairth-yoh] *m* trade, business; store, shop

comida [ko-mee-da] *f* food; meal; lunch ▸ 'comida rápida' 'fast food' ▸ 'comidas caseras' 'home cooking' ▸ 'comidas para llevar' 'take out meals'

comisaría [ko-mi-sa-ree-a] *f* police station

como [kom-oh] *adv & conj* like; as; such as

cómo [kom-oh] *adv* how?

compañero, ra [kom-pan-yair-oh] *m, f* colleague; classmate, workmate

compañía [kom-pan-yee-a] *f* company

comunidad autónoma

17 in number, the *comunidades autónomas* are autonomous regions that were set up after the adoption of the Constitution in 1978. They each have their own legislative body which is elected by direct universal suffrage. Their powers vary, but they administer such aspects of government as the health service, education, public transportation and so on; some even have their own police forces. There are also two *ciudades autónomas* (autonomous cities), the Spanish enclaves of Ceuta and Melilla on the North African coast.

compartimiento [kom-pahr-tim-yen-toh] *m* compartment

compartir [kom-pahr-teer] *v* to share

complejo, ja [kom-play-CHoh] *adj* complex

completo, ta [kom-play-to] *adj* complete

complicado, da [kom-pli-kah-doh] *adj* complicated

comportarse [kom-por-tahr-say] *v* to behave

compra [kom-pra] *f* purchase ▸ hacer la compra to do the shopping ▸ ir de compras to go shopping

comprar [kom-prahr] *v* to buy

comprobar [kom-pro-bahr] *v* to check

común [ko-moon] *adj* common; ordinary

comunicar [ko-moo-ni-kahr] *v* to communicate ▸ comunica *(on 'phone)* the line's busy

comunidad [ko-moo-ni-dad] *f* community ▸ comunidad autónoma *name given to each of the 17 regions of Spain which have their own government and autonomy in certain matters*

con [kon] *prep* with

conceder [kon-thed-air] *v* to give

concentrarse [kon-then-trahr-say] *v* to concentrate; to gather together

concierto [konth-yair-toh] *m* concert

concluir [kon-kloo-eer] *v* to conclude

concreto, ta [kon-kray-toh] *adj* specific, definite; concrete

condimento [kon-di-men-toh] *m* seasoning

condón [kon-dohn] *m* condom

conducir [kon-doo-theer] *v* to drive

conejo [ko-nay-CHoh] *m* rabbit

confecciones [kon-fekth-yoh-nays] *fpl* fashions

conferencia [kon-fair-enth-ya] *f* (long-distance) call ▸ poner una conferencia to make a long-distance call

confiar [kon-fi-ahr] *v* to confide; to entrust ▸ confiar en to trust in ▸ confiar en que to hope that

confirmar [kon-feer-mahr] *v* to confirm

confluencia [kon-floo-enth-ya] *f* confluence; junction

confundir [kon-foon-deer] *v* to confuse ▸ confundir algo/a alguien con to mistake something/someone for

confundirse [kon-foon-deer-say] *v* to get confused; to make a mistake

congelados [kon-CHe-lah-dohs] *mpl* frozen food

conjunto [kon-CHoon-toh] *m* outfit; group, band

conmigo [kon-mee-goh] *pron* with me

conocer [ko-no-thair] *v* to know; to meet

conocido, da [ko-no-thee-doh] *adj* well-known; familiar

consciente [kons-thyen-tay] *adj* conscious ▸ ser consciente de to be aware of

consecuencia [kon-sek-wenth-ya] *f* consequence

conseguir [kon-se-geer] *v* to achieve; to get, to manage to obtain

consejo [kon-say-CHoh] *m* piece of advice

consentir [kon-sen-teer] *v* to allow

conserje [kon-sair-CHay] *m* concierge; porter

consigna [kon-seeg-na] *f* checkroom

consistorio [kon-sis-tawr-yoh] *m* city council

constar [kon-stahr] *v* to appear, to figure ▸ constar de to be made up of ▸ me consta que I know that

constipado [kon-sti-pah-doh] *m* cold, chill

consulta [kon-sool-ta] *f* query, inquiry; consultation ▸ 'consulta (médica)' 'doctor's office'

consultorio [kon-sool-tawr-yoh] *m* (doctor's, dentist's) office

consumición [kon-soo-mith-yohn] *f* drink ▸ 'consumición obligatoria' 'customers must purchase a drink'

consumir [kon-soo-meer] *v* to consume; to use (up); to eat, to drink

consumo [kon-soo-moh] *m* consumption

contar [kon-tahr] *v* to count; to tell, to relate

contener [kon-te-nair] *v* to contain

contento, ta [kon-ten-toh] *adj* happy, content

contestación [kon-tes-tath-yohn] *f* answer

contestador [kon-tes-ta-dawr] *m* ▸ contestador automático answering machine

contestar [kon-tes-tahr] *v* to answer

contigo [kon-tee-goh] *pron* with you

continente [kon-ti-nen-tay] *m* continent

contra [kon-tra] *prep* against

contrabando [kon-tra-ban-doh] *m* smuggling; contraband

contraindicado, da [kon-tra-in-di-kah-doh] *adj* contraindicated ▸ 'contraindicado durante el embarazo' 'not to be taken during pregnancy'

contrario, ria [kon-trahr-yoh] *adj* opposing; opposite ▸ al contrario on the contrary

contraseña [kon-tra-sayn-ya] *f* password

contratiempo [kon-tra-tyem-poh] *m* setback, mishap

control [kon-trol] *m* control ▸ 'control de pasaportes' 'passport check'

convencer [kom-ben-thair] *v* to convince, to persuade

conveniente [kom-ben-yen-tay] *adj* convenient; advisable, a good idea

convertirse [kom-bair-teer-say] *v* to convert ▸ convertirse en to become

cónyuge [kon-yoo-CHay] *m, f* spouse

coñac [kon-yak] *m* brandy

copa [koh-pa] *f* glass; cup; (alcoholic) drink ▸ ir de copas to go out drinking ▸ tomar una copa to have a drink

corazón [ko-ra-thohn] *m* heart

cordero, ra [kor-dair-oh] *m, f* lamb

cordillera [kor-dil-yair-a] *f* mountain range ▸ la cordillera Cantábrica the Cantabrian Mountains

cornete [kor-nay-tay] *m* cornet, cone

corredor, ra [ko-RRay-dawr] *m* runner; racecar driver

correo [ko-RRay-oh] *m* mail ▸ correo aéreo airmail ▸ correo certificado certified mail ▸ correo electrónico e-mail ▸ enviar algo por correo to mail something

Correos *m* post office ▸ 'Correos (y Telégrafos)' 'post office'

correr [ko-RRair] *v* to run; to go fast; to rush; to flow

correspondencia [ko-RRes-pon-denth-ya] *f* correspondence

corresponder [ko-RRes-pon-dair] *v* to correspond

corriente [koRR-yen-tay] *adj* normal, regular; common

cortado [kor-tah-doh] *m* coffee with a dash of milk

cortante [kor-tan-tay] *adj* sharp, cutting

cortar [kor-tahr] *v* to cut; to close ▸ 'cortado por obras' 'closed for road-work'

corte [kor-tay] *m* cut; haircut

cortesía [kor-te-see-a] *f* politeness, courtesy

cortijo [kor-tee-CHoh] *m* farm, farmhouse

corto, ta [kor-toh] *adj* short

cosa [koh-sa] *f* thing

cosecha [ko-se-cha] *f* harvest; vintage

costa [kos-ta] *f* coast

costar [kos-tahr] *v* to cost

costilla [kos-teel-ya] *f* rib; chop

costumbre [kos-toom-bray] *f* custom; habit ▸ tener la costumbre de to be in the habit of

coto [koh-toh] *m* reserve ▸ 'coto (priva-do) de caza' '(private) game reserve'

crecer [kre-thair] *v* to grow

creer [kray-air] *v* to believe; to think ▸ creer en to believe in

cremallera [kray-mal-yair-a] *f* zipper

criatura [kree-a-too-ra] *f* child, baby; creature

cristal [kris-tal] *m* glass; crystal; piece of glass; window pane

croqueta [kro-kay-ta] *f* croquette

cruce [kroo-thay] *m* crossroads

crucero [kroo-thair-oh] *m* cruise

crudo, da [kroo-doh] *adj* raw; under-done, undercooked

crujiente [krooCH-yen-tay] *adj* crisp, crunchy

crustáceo [kroos-tath-ay-oh] *m* crusta-cean

cruz [krooth] *f* cross

cruzar [kroo-thahr] *v* to cross

cuaderno [kwa-dair-noh] *m* exercise book, workbook

cuadrado, da [kwad-rah-doh] *adj* square

cuadro [kwad-roh] *m* picture, painting; table, diagram

cuajada [kwa-CHah-da] *f* cottage cheese ▸ cuajada con miel cottage cheese with honey

cual [kwal] *pron* which ▸ el/la cual whom ▸ lo cual which

cuál [kwal] *pron* which?, which one?; what?

cualidad [kwa-li-dad] *f* quality

cualquier, a [kwal-kyair] *adj* any ▸ en cualquier lugar anywhere ▸ cualquier cosa anything

cualquiera [kwal-kyair-a] *pron* anyone

cuando [kwan-doh] *conj* when

cuándo [kwan-doh] *adv* when?

cuanto, ta [kwan-toh] *pron* ▸ unos cuantos, unas cuantas quite a few ▸ cuantos/cuantas quieras as many as you like ▸ cuanto antes as soon as possible ▸ en cuanto as soon as

cuánto, ta [kwan-toh] *adj* how much?, how many; what a lot of ...! ◆ *pron* how much?, how many?

cuarto, ta [kwahr-toh] *num* fourth ◆ *m* room; quarter ▸ cuarto de baño bathroom ▸ cuarto de hora quarter of an hour

cuatro [kwat-roh] *num* four

cubierta [koob-yair-ta] *f (of boat)* deck; *(of book)* cover

cubierto, ta [koob-yair-toh] *adj* covered ▸ a cubierto under cover

cubito [koo-bee-toh] *m* cube ▸ cubito de hielo ice cube

cuchara [koo-cha-ra] *f* spoon

cuchillo [koo-cheel-yoh] *m* knife

cucurucho [koo-koo-roo-choh] *m* cornet, cone

cuenta [kwen-ta] *f (bar, restaurant)* bill, check; account

cuento [kwen-toh] *m* story

cuero [kwair-oh] *m* leather

cuerpo [kwair-poh] *m* body

cueva [kway-ba] *f* cave

cuidado [kwee-dah-doh] *m* care ◆ *excl* look out!, be careful! ▸ cuidado con... watch... ▸ estar al cuidado de in charge

of ▸ tener cuidado to be careful, to take care

cuidar [kwee-dahr] *v* to take care of ▸ cuidar de to take care of

cuidarse [kwee-dahr-say] *v* to take care of oneself ▸ cuidarse de to be careful about

culpa [kool-pa] *f* guilt ▸ tienes la culpa you're to blame, it's your fault

cumbre [koom-bray] *f* summit

cumpleaños [koom-play-an-yohs] *m* birthday ▸ ¡feliz cumpleaños! happy birthday!

cumplir [koom-pleer] *v (law)* to obey; *(order, threat)* to carry out; *(promise)* to keep; *(years)* to be; *(deadline)* to expire ▸ cumplir con su deber to do one's duty

cuneta [koo-nay-ta] *f* gutter; ditch

cura [koo-ra] *f* cure ▸ cura de reposo rest cure

curado, da [koo-ra-doh] *adj* cured; matured

curar [koo-rahr] *v* to cure; *(wound)* to dress

curarse [koo-rahr-say] *v* to get better, to recover

curioso, sa [koor-yoh-soh] *adj* curious, inquisitive, nosy; strange, odd

curva [koor-ba] *f* curve; bend ▸ 'curva peligrosa' 'dangerous bend'

cuyo, ya [koo-yoh] *adj* whose

d

D. *abbr of* **don** Mr.

dañar [dan-yahr] *v* to damage, to harm

daño [dan-yoh] *m* damage, harm ▸ daños y perjuicios damages ▸ hacer daño to hurt; to harm

dar [dahr] *v* to give; to hit; *(button, key)* to press ▸ ¡qué más da! what does it matter? ▸ dar a to look onto

dátil [da-teel] *m* date

dato [da-toh] *m* piece of information ▸ datos personales personal details

dcha. *abbr of* **derecha** r

d. de J.-C. *abbr of* **después de Jesucristo** A.D.

de [de] *prep* of; from ▸ el coche de mi padre my father's car ▸ la piscina del hotel the hotel pool ▸ un reloj de oro a gold watch ▸ trabaja de camarero he works as a waiter

debajo [de-ba-CHoh] *adv* underneath ▸ debajo de under

deber [de-bair] *v* to owe; to have to, must ▸ debido a due to, because of ▸ deben de ser las diez it must be ten o'clock ▸ ¿qué le debo? how much do I owe you?, how much is it?

deberse [de-bair-say] *v* ▸ deberse a to be due to

débil [deb-eel] *adj* weak

década [de-ka-da] *f* decade

décimo, ma [de-thi-moh] *num* tenth

decir [de-theer] *v* to say, to tell ▸ ¿diga?, ¿dígame? *(on 'phone)* hello?

dedicar [de-di-kahr] *v* to dedicate

dedo [day-doh] *m* finger; toe ▸ dedo

pulgar thumb

deducir [de-doo-theer] *v* to deduce

defecto [day-fek-toh] *m* defect, fault

defender [de-fen-dair] *v* to defend

dejar [de-CHahr] *v* to leave; to allow, to let; to lend ▸ dejar de to stop

dejarse [de-CHahr-say] *v* to leave (behind) ▸ dejar algo en algún sitio to leave something somewhere ▸ me he dejado el paraguas I forgot my umbrella

delante [de-lan-tay] *adv* in front, at the front; opposite ▸ delante de in front of; opposite

delgado, da [del-gah-doh] *adj* thin

demás [de-mas] *adj* other ▸ lo demás the rest ▸ los demás the others ▸ todo lo demás everything else

demasiado, da [de-mas-yah-doh] *adj & pron* too much, too many ◆ *adv* too

demora [de-maw-ra] *f* delay

demostrar [de-mos-trahr] *v* to show, to demonstrate

denominación [de-no-mi-nath-yohn] *f* ▸ 'denominación de origen' *guarantee that a product comes from a particular region and meets certain standards of quality*

dentro [den-troh] *adv* inside ▸ dentro de *(place)* inside, in; *(time)* within

denunciar [de-noonth-yahr] *v* to report (to the police)

dependiente, ta [de-pend-yen-tay] *m, f* sales clerk

deporte [de-por-tay] *m* sport ▸ deportes

de invierno winter sports

deportivo, va [de-por-tee-boh] *adj (of sneakers, clothes etc.)* sports

depósito [de-po-si-toh] *m* deposit; warehouse ▸ depósito de gasolina gas tank

deprisa [de-pree-sa] *adv* quickly

derecha [de-re-cha] *f* right

derecho, cha [de-re-choh] *adj* right ▸ todo derecho straight ahead

derrota [de-RRoh-ta] *f* defeat

derrumbar [de-RRoom-bahr] *v* to demolish

derrumbarse [day-RRoom-bahr-say] *v* to collapse

desarrollar [de-sa-RRol-yahr] *vt* to develop

desarrollo [de-sa-RRol-yoh] *m* development

desayuno [de-sa-yoo-noh] *m* breakfast

descafeinado, da [des-ka-fay-nah-doh] *adj* decaffeinated

descansar [des-kan-sahr] *v* to rest

descanso [des-kan-soh] *m* rest

descender [des-then-dair] *v* to go down, to drop, to fall

descolgar [des-kol-gahr] *v* to pick up

desconocer [des-ko-no-thair] *v* not to know

descubierto, ta [des-koob-yair-toh] *adj* bare, uncovered; clear, cloudless

descubrir [des-koob-reer] *v* to discover, to find out; to uncover

descuento [des-kwen-toh] *m* discount, reduction

descuidar [des-kwee-dahr] *v* to neglect

descuidarse [des-kwee-dahr-say] *v* to let oneself go

desde [dez-day] *prep* since; from

desear [de-say-ahr] *v* to want, to desire;

to wish ▸ te deseo suerte I wish you luck

desechable [de-se-chab-lay] *adj* disposable

desechos [de-se-chohs] *mpl* waste

desembarcar [de-sem-bahr-kahr] *v* to disembark

desembocadura [de-sem-bok-a-doo-ra] *f* mouth, estuary

desenchufar [de-sen-choo-fahr] *v* to unplug

desfiladero [des-fee-la-dair-oh] *m* ravine, gorge

desgracia [des-grath-ya] *f* misfortune, disaster ▸ por desgracia unfortunately

deshacer [de-sa-thair] *v* to undo ▸ deshacer la maleta to unpack

desierto [des-yair-toh] *n* desert

desierto, ta [des-yair-toh] *adj* deserted

desistir [de-sis-teer] *v* to give up ▸ desistir de (hacer) algo to stop (doing) something

desnatado, da [des-na-tah-doh] *adj (milk)* skim

desnudarse [des-noo-dahr-say] *v* to undress

desodorante [de-soh-doh-ran-tay] *m* deodorant

desorientarse [de-sawr-yen-tahr-say] *v* to get disoriented

despacho [des-pa-choh] *m* office ▸ despacho de billetes ticket office, box office

despacio [des-path-yoh] *adv* slowly

despedida [des-pe-dee-da] *f* goodbye; farewell party

despedir [des-pe-deer] *v* to say goodbye to, to see off; to dismiss, to fire

despegar [des-pe-gahr] *v* to take off

despejado, da [des-pe-CHah-doh] *adj* clear

Día de los Inocentes

The Day of the Innocents, December 28th, is the equivalent of our April Fools' Day. It commemorates the massacre of all baby boys in Bethlehem under the age of two by Herod, alarmed by the prospect of a new Messiah, Jesus, as a rival king of the Jews. Newspapers print spoof news stories and people play practical jokes on each other. In Spain the traditional joke (*inocentada*) is to have a *monigote* (a paper cut-out of a person) stuck on your back.

despeñadero [des-pen-ya-dair-oh] *m* precipice

desperdicios [des-pair-deeth-yohs] *mpl* waste; scraps

desperfecto [des-pair-fek-toh] *m* flaw

despertador [des-pair-ta-dawr] *m* alarm clock

despertarse [des-pair-tahr-say] *v* to wake up

despierto, ta [des-pyair-toh] *adj* awake

desplazarse [des-pla-thahr-say] *v* to travel; to move around

desprenderse [des-pren-dair-say] *v* to come off, to become detached

después [des-pwes] *adv* afterwards, later; then ▸ después de after

destacar [des-ta-kahr] *v* to highlight, to emphasize; to stand out

destruir [des-troo-eer] *v* to destroy

desventaja [des-ben-ta-CHa] *f* disadvantage

desviar [des-bi-ahr] *v* to divert

desviarse [des-bi-ahr-say] *v* to turn off; to go off course ▸ desviarse del tema to go off the subject

detalle [day-tal-yay] *m* detail

detener [de-te-nair] *v* to stop; to arrest

determinar [de-tair-mi-nahr] *v* to establish

detrás [day-tras] *adv* behind, at the back ▸ detrás de behind; (*in sequence*) after

deuda [de-oo-da] *f* debt

devolución [day-bo-looth-yohn] *f* return; refund ▸ 'no se admiten devoluciones' 'no goods may be exchanged or returned'

devolver [day-bol-bair] *v* to return

día [dee-a] *m* day ▸ del día today's ▸ día del espectador (*cinema*) day when discounts are offered on tickets ▸ día festivo holiday ▸ día laborable working day

diario, ria [dee-ahr-yoh] *adj* daily ◆ *m* newspaper

dibujo [di-boo-joh] *m* drawing

diciembre [deeth-yem-bray] *m* December

diente [dyen-tay] *m* tooth

diestro, tra [dyes-troh] *adj* right-handed; skillful ◆ *m* bullfighter

dieta [dyay-ta] *f* diet

diez [dyeth] *num* ten

diferencia [di-fe-renth-ya] *f* difference ▸ a diferencia de unlike

digital [di-CHi-tal] *adj* digital

dinero [din-air-oh] *m* money ▸ dinero suelto (loose) change

dirección [di-rekth-yohn] *f* direction; management

directo, ta [di-rek-toh] *adj* direct ▸ en directo live

dirigirse [di-ri-CHeer-say] *v* ▸ dirigirse a (*place*) to head for; (*person*) to speak to

discapacitado, da [dis-ka-pa-thi-tah-doh] *m, f* disabled

disculparse [dis-kool-pahr-say] *v* to excuse oneself

discutir [dis-koo-teer] *v* to argue; to question; to discuss

diseño [di-sayn-yoh] *m* design

disfrutar [dis-froo-tahr] *v* to enjoy oneself ▸ disfrutar de to enjoy

disminuir [dis-min-weer] *v* to drop, to fall

disponerse [dis-po-nair-say] *v* ▸ disponerse a to be about to

distancia [dis-tanth-ya] *f* distance

distintivo [dis-tin-tee-boh] *m* emblem, badge

distinto, ta [dis-teen-toh] *adj* different

distraer [dis-tra-air] *v* to keep amused; to distract

distraerse [dis-tra-air-say] *v* to keep oneself amused; to get distracted

distrito [dis-tree-toh] *m* district ▸ distrito postal postal district

diversión [di-bairs-yohn] *f* fun, entertainment

divertido, da [di-bair-tee-do] *adj* fun, enjoyable

divertirse [di-bair-teer-say] *v* to enjoy oneself

dividir [di-bi-deer] *v* to divide (up)

divisas [di-bee-sas] *fpl* foreign currency

doblar [dob-lahr] *v* to double; to fold

▸ doblar la esquina to go around the corner

doble [dob-lay] *adj & m* double

documentación [do-koo-men-tath-yohn] *f* papers, documents

doler [do-lair] *v* to hurt, to be painful

dolor [do-lawr] *m* pain

doméstico, ca [do-mes-ti-koh] *adj* domestic ▸ animal doméstico pet

domicilio [do-mi-theel-yoh] *m* address

domingo [do-min-goh] *m* Sunday

don [don] *m* gift

donde [don-day] *adv & conj* where ▸ de/desde donde from where ▸ ésta es la casa donde nací this is the house I was born in

dónde [don-day] *adv* where? ▸ ¿de/desde dónde? where … from?

dormir [dor-meer] *v* to sleep

dormirse [dor-meer-say] *v* to go to sleep; to oversleep

dormitorio [dor-mi-tawr-yoh] *m* bedroom

dorso [dor-soh] *m* back ▸ 'instrucciones al dorso' 'see back for instructions'

dos [dos] *num* two

dosis [do-sees] *f* dose

Dr. *abbr of* **doctor** Dr.

Dra. *abbr of* **doctora** Dr.

ducha [doo-cha] *f* shower

dudar [doo-dahr] *v* to doubt

dueño, ña [dwayn-yoh] *m, f* owner

dulce [dool-thay] *adj* sweet ◆ *m* piece of candy ▸ dulces sweet things

durante [doo-ran-tay] *adv* for; during ▸ durante tres días for three days

duro, ra [doo-roh] *adj & adv* hard

echar [e-chahr] *v* to put into add; to pour; to throw; to throw out, to expel; to fire ▸ echa sal a la sopa put some salt in the soup ▸ la han echado she's been fired

edad [ay-dad] *f* age ▸ la Edad Media the Middle Ages ▸ tercera edad senior citizens

edificio [e-di-feeth--yoh] *m* building

educado, da [e-doo-kah-doh] *adj* polite

efectivo [e-fek-tee-boh] *m* cash ▸ en efectivo in cash

efecto [e-fek-toh] *m* effect ▸ efectos personales personal effects ▸ efectos secundarios side effects

ej. *abbr of* **ejemplo** e.g.

ejemplar [e-CHem-plahr] *adj* exemplary ♦ *m* copy; specimen

ejemplo [e-CHem-ploh] *m* example

ejercicio [eCH-air-theeth-yoh] *m* exercise

el [el] *art* the ▸ el libro the book ▸ el coche the car ▸ el agua water ▸ el de la esquina the one on the corner

él [el] *pron* he; him; it ▸ mi hermano es él he's my brother

elección [e-lekth-yohn] *f* election

electricidad [e-lek-tri-thi-dad] *f* electricity

electrodoméstico [e-lek-troh-doh-mes-ti-koh] *m* electrical appliance

elegir [e-le-CHeer] *v* to choose; to elect

ello [el-yoh] *pron* it, that

ellos [el-yohs, el-yas] *pron* they; them

embajada [em-ba-CHah-da] *f* embassy

embarazada [em-ba-ra-thah-da] *adj* pregnant

embarazo [em-ba-ra-thoh] *m* pregnancy

embarcadero [em-bar-ka-dair-oh] *m* jetty

embarcarse [em-bar-kahr-say] *v* to board

embargo [em-bahr-goh] ▸ sin embargo however

embarque [em-bahr-kay] *m* boarding

embotellado, da [em-bo-tel-yah-doh] *adj* bottled; blocked with traffic

embutidos [em-boo-tee-dohs] *mpl* cold cured meats

emergencia [e-mair-CHenth-ya] *f* emergency

emocionante [e-mohth-yo-nan-tay] *adj* exciting

empanada [em-pa-nah-da] *f* turnover

empanadilla [em-pa-na-deel-ya] *f* small turnover

empeorar [em-pay-aw-rahr] *v* to worsen

empezar [em-pe-thahr] *v* to begin ▸ empezar a to begin to

emplear [em-play-ahr] *v* to employ; to use

emprender [em-pren-dair] *v* to embark on, to undertake

empresa [em-pray-sa] *f* company, firm

empujar [em-poo-CHahr] *v* to push ▸ 'empujar' 'push'

en [en] *prep* in; on ▸ en diez minutos in ten minutes ▸ en diciembre/en verano in December/in summer ▸ en la mesa on the table ▸ en casa/en el trabajo/en el colegio at home/at work/at school ▸ en avión/en tren by plane/by train

enamorarse [e-na-mo-rahr-say] *v* to fall in love

encantado, da [en-kan-tah-doh] *excl* delighted ▸ ¡encantado! pleased to meet you!

encantar [en-kan-tahr] *v* to delight ▸ ¡me encanta! I love it!

encargado, da [en-kahr-gah-doh] *m, f* manager

encargar [en-kahr-gahr] *v* to order

encender [en-then-dair] *v* to light

encerrar [en-thay-RRahr] *v* to lock in, to shut in

enchufar [en-choo-fahr] *v* to plug in

encierro [enth-yeRR-oh] *m* running of the bulls

encima [en-thee-ma] *adv* on top; on top of that ▸ encima de on top of

encoger [en-koCH-air] *v* to shrink

encontrar [en-kon-trahr] *v* to find ▸ encontrarse con alguien to bump into somebody

encrucijada [en-kroo-thi-CHah-da] *f* crossroads

encuentro [en-kwen-troh] *m* meeting; game, match

enero [e-nair-oh] *m* January

enfadarse [en-fa-dahr-say] *v* to get angry

enfermar [en-fair-mahr] *v* to fall ill, to get sick

enfermería [en-fair-me-ree-a] *f* infirmary

enfermo, ma [en-fair-moh] *adj* ill, sick ♦ *m, f* sick person, patient ▸ ponerse enfermo to fall ill, to get sick

enfrente [en-fren-tay] *adv* opposite

enhorabuena [e-naw-ra-bway-na] *excl* ▸ ¡enhorabuena! congratulations! ▸ dar

la enhorabuena a alguien to congratulate somebody

enlace [en-la-thay] *m* connection; link

ensaimada [en-seye-mah-da] *f* light spiral-shaped sweet bun

ensalada [en-sa-lah-da] *f* salad ▸ ensalada catalana salad with cold cured meats ▸ ensalada verde green salad ▸ ensalada mixta mixed salad ▸ ensalada del tiempo *salad made with whatever's freshly available* ▸ ensalada variada mixed salad

ensaladilla [en-sa-la-deel-ya] *f* salad ▸ ensaladilla rusa Russian salad

enseguida [en-se-gee-da] *adv* right away

enseñar [en-sen-yahr] *v* to teach; to show

entender [en-ten-dair] *v* to understand

entero, ra [en-tair-oh] *adj* whole, entire

entonces [en-ton-thes] *adv* then

entrada [en-trah-da] *f* entry; entrance; ticket ▸ 'entrada libre' 'free admission'

entrantes [en-tran-tays] *mpl (on menu)* appetizers

entrar [en-trahr] *v* to enter, to go in, to come in

entre [en-tray] *prep* between; among

entrega [en-tray-ga] *f* handing over; delivery

entregar [en-tre-gahr] *v* to hand over, to give; to deliver

entremeses [en-tray-may-says] *mpl* hors d'oeuvres

entrenarse [en-tray-nahr-say] *v* to train

entresuelo [en-tray-sway-loh] *m* mezzanine

entretanto [en-tray-tan-toh] *adv* meanwhile

envase [em-ba-say] *m* container, bottle

‣ **envase sin retorno** non-returnable container

enviar [emb-yahr] *v* to send

envío [em-bee-oh] *m* dispatch; delivery; remittance

envolver [em-bol-bair] *v* to wrap up

equipaje [e-kee-pa-CHay] *m* baggage ‣ **equipaje de mano** carry-on luggage

equipo [e-kee-poh] *m* team; equipment

equivocarse [e-kee-boh-kahr-say] *v* to make a mistake

ermita [air-mee-ta] *f* country chapel

error [e-RRawr] *m* mistake

escabeche [es-ka-be-chay] *m* pickle

escala [es-kah-la] *f* scale; layover

escalar [es-ka-lahr] *v* to climb

escalera [es-ka-lair-a] *f* stairs, staircase ‣ **escalera mecánica** escalator

escalope [es-ka-loh-pay] *m* (*meat*) scallop

escalopín [es-ka-loh-peen] *m* fillet ‣ **escalopines de ternera** fillets of veal

escaparse [es-ka-pahr-say] *v* to escape; to run away

escaparate [es-ka-pa-ra-tay] *m* store window

escarola [es-ka-roh-la] *f* curly endive, escarole

escaso, sa [es-ka-soh] *adj* scant; scarce ‣ **andar escaso de** to be short of

escena [es-thay-na] *f* scene

escoger [es-koCH-air] *v* to choose

esconder [es-kon-dair] *v* to hide

escribir [es-kri-beer] *v* to write

escrito [es-kree-toh] *m* document

escuchar [es-koo-chahr] *v* to listen

escuela [es-kway-la] *f* school

escultura [es-kool-too-ra] *f* sculpture

ese, sa [ay-say] *adj* that

ése, sa [ay-say] *pron* that one

esfuerzo [es-fwair-thoh] *m* effort

eso [ay-soh] *pron* that

espacio [es-path-yoh] *m* space ‣ **por un espacio de dos horas** for two hours

España [es-pan-ya] *n* Spain

español, la [es-pan-yol] *adj* Spanish ‣ *n* Spaniard

espárrago [es-pa-RRa-goh] *m* asparagus tip

especia [es-peth-ya] *f* spice

especial [es-peth-yal] *adj* special

especie [es-peth-yay] *f* species; sort, kind ‣ **en especie** in kind

espectáculo [es-pek-ta-koo-loh] *m* show; sight, spectacle

espectador, ra [es-pek-ta-dawr] *m*, *f* member of the audience, viewer, spectator

espejo [es-pay-CHoh] *m* mirror

esperar [es-pe-rahr] *v* to hope; to expect; to wait

espinacas [es-pi-na-kas] *fpl* spinach

espléndido, da [es-plen-di-doh] *adj* splendid, magnificent

esposo, sa [es-poh-soh] *m*, *f* husband, wife

espuma [es-poo-ma] *f* froth, foam, lather; surf

esquí [es-kee] *m* skiing; ski ‣ **esquí acuático** water skiing

esquina [es-kee-na] *f* corner

establecimiento [es-tab-le-thim-yen-toh] *m* establishment; premises, store, business

estación [es-tath-yohn] *f* station; season ‣ **'estación de servicio'** 'gas station'

estacionamiento [es-tath-yoh-nam-yen-toh] *m* parking ‣ **'estacionamiento**

limitado' 'restricted parking zone'
▸ 'estacionamiento prohibido' 'no parking'

estacionar [es-tath-yoh-nahr] *v* to park
▸ 'no estacionar' 'no parking'

estadio [es-tad-yoh] *m* stadium

estado [es-tah-doh] *m* state ▸ estado civil marital status

estanco [es-tan-koh] *m* tobacco store (also selling stamps)

estanque [es-tan-kay] *m* pool, pond

estar [es-tahr] *v* to be ▸ esta calle está sucia this street is dirty ▸ la comida estará para las tres lunch will be ready for three o'clock

estarse [es-tahr-say] *v* ▸ ¡estate quieto! keep still!

estatua [es-tat-wa] *f* statue

este, ta [es-tay] *adj* this

este [es-tay] *m* east

éste, ta [es-tay] *pron* this one

estilo [es-tee-loh] *m* style

esto [es-toh] *pron* this

estofado, da [es-to-fah-doh] *adj* stewed ◆ *m* stew

estrecho, cha [es-tre-choh] *adj* narrow ◆ *m* strait

estrella [es-trel-ya] *f* star

estreñimiento [es-tren-yeem-yen-toh] *m* constipation

estropear [es-tro-pay-ahr] *v* to damage, to ruin

estropearse [es-tro-pay-ahr-say] *v* to break down; to go bad

estudio [es-tood-yoh] *m* studio apartment; study

estupendo, da [es-too-pen-doh] *adj* wonderful, fantastic ◆ *excl* ▸ ¡estupendo! fantastic!

Euskadi [ews-ka-di]the Basque Country

euskera [ews-kair-a] *n* Basque (language)

exceder [eks-the-dair] *v* to exceed

excepto [eks-thep-toh] *adv* except
▸ 'excepto festivos' 'except holidays'

exceso [eks-thay-soh] *m* excess ▸ exceso de equipaje excess baggage

excursión [eks-koors-yohn] *f* excursion, trip ▸ ir de excursión to go on a trip

éxito [ek-si-toh] *m* success

expedir [eks-pe-deer] *v* to issue; to dispatch

expendedor, ra [eks-pen-de-dawr] *m, f* vendor ▸ expendedor automático automatic vending machine

expendedora [eks-pen-de-daw-ra] *f* machine ▸ expendedora de billetes ticket machine

exponer [eks-po-nair] *v* to exhibit, to display

exposición [eks-po-seeth-yohn] *f* exhibition

expreso [eks-pray-soh] *m* express

extender [eks-ten-dair] *v* to extend, to stretch; to spread; to issue

extensión [eks-tens-yohn] *f* extension; area

exterior [eks-tair-yawr] *adj* external

extra [eks-tra] *adj* & *m* extra

extraer [eks-tra-air] *v* to extract

extranjero, ra [eks-tran-CHair-oh] *adj* foreign ◆ *m, f* foreigner

extraño, ña [eks-tran-yoh] *adj* strange ◆ *m, f* stranger

extraviar [eks-trab-yahr] *v* to lose

extremo, ma [eks-tray-moh] *adj* extreme ◆ *m* end; extreme

fabada [fa-bah-da] *f* ▸ fabada (asturiana) *bean stew with pork sausage and bacon*

fábrica [fab-ri-ka] *f* factory

facilidad [fa-thi-li-dad] *f* ease

fallar [fal-yahr] *v* to fail, to go wrong; to get it wrong

Fallas [fal-yas] *celebrations in Valencia during which figures are burnt*

fallo [fal-yoh] *m* mistake; fault

falso, sa [fal-soh] *adj* false

falta [fal-ta] *f* lack, shortage; absence ▸ echar en falta to miss ▸ hace falta pan we need bread

faltar [fal-tahr] *v* to be missing, to be absent; to be needed, to be lacking ▸ ¡no faltaba más! of course!

fama [fa-ma] *f* fame

familia [fa-meel-ya] *f* family ▸ familia numerosa large family

famoso, sa [fa-moh-soh] *adj* famous

farmacia [far-math-ya] *f* pharmacy ▸ 'farmacia de guardia' 'duty pharmacy'

faro [fah-roh] *m* lighthouse

fatal [fa-tal] *adj* awful, terrible; fatal

favor [fa-bor] *m* favor ▸ estar a favor de to be in favor of ▸ hacer un favor to do a favor ▸ pedir un favor to ask a favor ▸ por favor please

favorecer [fa-bo-re-thair] *v* to suit; to favor

febrero [fe-brair-oh] *m* February

fecha [fe-cha] *f* date ▸ fecha de caducidad sell-by date; expiration date ▸ fecha de nacimiento date of birth

felicidad [fe-li-thi-dad] *f* happiness

felicidades [fe-li-thi-da-des] *excl* ▸ ¡felicidades! happy birthday!; congratulations!

feliz [fe-leeth] *adj* happy

feo, a [fay-oh] *adj* ugly

feria [fair-ya] *f* fair; festival

ferrocarril [fe-RRoh-ka-RReel] *m* railroad

festividad [fes-ti-bi-dad] *f* festivity

festivo, va [fes-tee-bo] *adj* festive; cheerful ♦ *n* public holiday

fiambres [fi-am-brays] *mpl* cold cuts

Fallas de Valencia

The origins of *las fallas* are obscure, but they probably have their roots in ancient pagan festivals celebrating the end of winter which were later assimilated by the Christian church. Nowadays, huge papier-mâché and wooden structures called *ninots* with their satirical depictions of people and topical events are put on display in the streets of the city, around March 15th, in a ceremony called the *plantà*. There they stay until the night of March 19th, the feast of St Joseph, patron saint of carpenters, when they are all set alight – except one – in the *cremà* (burning).

Feria de Abril

Two weeks after Easter, the *feria* of Seville is held in a large park where more than 1,000 *casetas* are put up. These canvas stands are rented by the well-off, and by some institutions and associations, as places where they can welcome friends, families and business associates to have a drink and dance *sevillanas* day and night. The *feria* is an occasion for the *sevillanos* to display not only their fine clothes, but also their magnificent horses.

fiar [fee-ahr] *v* to give credit ▸ 'aquí no se fía' 'no credit given'

ficha [fee-cha] *f* index card; checker, counter, domino; *(in casino)* chip

fideos [fi-day-ohs] *mpl* noodles

fideua [fi-day-wa] *f* *dish similar to a seafood paella, but made with noodles instead of rice*

fiebre [fi-eb-ray] *f* fever

fiesta [fi-es-ta] *f* party; fiesta; holiday ▸ fiesta patronal *celebrations for the feast day of the local patron saint*

figurar [fi-goo-rahr] *v* to appear, to figure in

figurarse [fi-goo-rahr-say] *v* to imagine

fijar [fi-CHahr] *v* to fix ◆ **fijarse** [fi-CHahr-say] *v* ▸ fijarse en algo to notice something; to watch something

fila [fee-la] *f* row; line

filtro [feel-troh] *m* filter ▸ filtro solar sun cream

fin [fin] *m* end ▸ fin de semana weekend ▸ 'fin de zona de estacionamiento' 'end of parking zone'

final [fee-nal] *adj* final ◆ *m* end, ending ◆ *f* final

finca [feen-ka] *f* property; estate

fino, na [fee-noh] *adj* thin; fine; polite, refined ◆ *m* dry sherry

firmar [feer-mahr] *v* to sign

físico, ca [fee-si-koh] *adj* physical ◆ *n* physique

flamenco [fla-men-koh] *m* flamenco ▸ see box on p. 28

flan [flan] *m* crème caramel ▸ flan con nata crème caramel with whipped cream

fiestas

Some are religious and others pagan in origin, but there is hardly a day of the year when there isn't a fiesta of some sort happening in some corner of Spain, though most of them take place in the summer months. Every town, village and even neighborhood has a patron saint whose feast day will be celebrated with dancing, music, processions, mock battles recalling the expulsion of the Moors, *romerías* (pilgrimages), bull-running, firework displays, sports competitions or what have you. You name it, they do it! And you can bet that eating and drinking will always play a prominent part in the festivities.

flamenco

Created by the Gypsies of Andalusia, the *cante jondo* expresses the despair of being rejected. It became *flamenco* in the 19th century when, accompanied by the classical guitar, it was sung in taverns. It came back into fashion in the 1920s, thanks to Lorca, and is still very popular today. There are four basic styles (*palos*): *soleare*, *siguiriya*, *tango* and *fandango*.

flecha [fle-cha] *f* arrow ▸ 'siga la flecha' 'follow the arrow'

flor [flor] *f* flower

flora [flaw-ra] *f* flora

flotador [flo-ta-dawr] *m (for swimming)* inflatable ring

folleto [fol-yay-toh] *m* leaflet

fonda [fon-da] *f* boarding house; cheap restaurant

forastero, ra [fo-ras-tair-oh] *m, f* stranger

forestal [fo-res-tal] *adj* forest

forma [for-ma] *f* shape, form; way ▸ estar en forma to be fit

formalidad [for-ma-li-dad] *f* formality; reliability

formulario [for-moo-lahr-yoh] *m* form

fortaleza [for-ta-lay-tha] *f* strength

fotografía [foh-toh-gra-fee-a] *f* photograph

fracaso [fra-ka-soh] *m* failure

frambuesa [fram-bway-sa] *f* raspberry

francés, esa [fran-thays] *adj* French

franqueo [frang-kay-oh] *m* postage

frasco [fras-koh] *m* bottle; jar

frecuente [fre-kwen-tay] *adj* frequent

freír [fre-eer] *v* to fry

frente [fren-tay] *f* forehead

fresa [fray-sa] *f* strawberry

fresco, ca [fres-koh] *adj* fresh; cool

fricandó [fri-kan-doh] *m* fricassee

frigorífico [free-go-ree-fi-koh] *m* refrigerator

frío, a [free-oh] *adj & m* cold

fritada [fri-tah-da] *f* dish or meal of fried food

frito, ta [free-toh] *adj* fried

frontera [fron-tair-a] *f* border

fruta [froo-ta] *f* fruit

fruto [froo-toh] *m* fruit ▸ frutos secos nuts

fuego [fway-goh] *m* fire ◆ *excl* ▸ ¡fuego! fire!

fuente [fwen-tay] *f* fountain; source; serving dish

fuera [fwair-a] *adv* outside, out

fuerte [fwair-tay] *adj* strong; loud; intense ◆ *adv* hard; loud

fuerza [fwair-tha] *f* strength

fumador, ra [foo-ma-dawr] *m, f* smoker ▸ 'no fumador' 'non-smoking' ▸ 'fumador' 'smokers'

fumar [foo-mahr] *v* to smoke ▸ 'prohibido fumar' 'no smoking'

función [foonth-yohn] *f* job, function; showing; performance

funcionar [foonth-yoh-nahr] *v* to work ▸ el ascensor no funciona the elevator is out of order

fundirse [foon-deer-say] *v* to melt

furgoneta [foor-goh-nay-ta] *f* van

futuro, ra [foo-too-roh] *adj & n* future

g

gafas [ga-fas] *fpl* glasses, spectacles

galería [ga-le-ree-a] *f* gallery

gallego, ga [gal-yay-goh] *adj* Galician

galleta [gal-yay-ta] *f* cookie

gallina [gal-yee-na] *f* hen

gamba [gam-ba] *f* prawn ▸ gambas al ajillo prawns with garlic ▸ gambas a la plancha grilled prawns

gana [ga-na] *f* wish, desire ▸ tener ganas de to feel like ▸ no me da la gana I can't be bothered, I don't feel like it ▸ de buena/mala gana willingly/reluctantly

ganador, ra [ga-na-dawr] *m, f* winner

ganar [ga-nahr] *v* to win; to earn

ganga [gan-ga] *f* bargain

garbanzo [gahr-ban-thoh] *m* chickpea

garganta [gahr-gan-ta] *f* throat

gaseosa [ga-say-oh-sa] *f* soda

gasóleo [ga-so-lah-yoh] *m* diesel, gas oil

gasolina [ga-soh-lee-na] *f* gasoline ▸ (gasolina) súper premium gasoline

gasolinera [ga-so-li-nair-a] *f* gas station

gastar [gas-tahr] *v* to spend; to use up

gastarse [gas-tahr-say] *v* to spend; to wear out

gasto [gas-toh] *m* expense

gastronomía [gas-tro-no-mee-a] *f* gastronomy

gato, ta [ga-toh] *m, f* cat

gelatina [CHe-la-tee-na] *f* gelatin; Jell-O®

género [CHe-ne-roh] *m* kind, type, genre; goods; material; gender

generoso, sa [CHaynayroso] *adj* generous

genio [CHen-yoh] *m* genius ▸ mal genio bad temper

gente [CHen-tay] *f* people

genuino, na [CHen-wee-noh] *adj* genuine, real

gerente [CHe-ren-tay] *m, f* manager

gimnasia [CHim-nas-ya] *f* exercise, gymnastics

ginebra [CHi-neb-ra] *f* gin

girar [CHi-rahr] *v* to turn

girasol [CHi-ra-sol] *m* sunflower

giro [CHee-roh] *m* turn, rotation; money order

glorieta [glawr-yay-ta] *f* traffic circle; arbor

gobierno [gob-yair-noh] *m* government

golfo [gol-foh] *m* gulf

golosina [go-lo-see-na] *f* piece of candy

golpe [gol-pay] *m* blow; bump, knock ▸ de golpe suddenly

golpear [gol-pe-ahr] *v* to hit

gordo, da [gor-doh] *adj* fat ◆ *m, f* fat person

gorra [go-RRa] *f* cap

gorro [go-RRo] *m* hat, cap, bonnet

gota [goh-ta] *f* drop

grabar [gra-bahr] *v* to record; to engrave

gracia [grath-ya] *f* funny thing; grace, elegance ▸ no me hace gracia I don't think it's funny

gracias [grath-yas] *fpl* thanks ▸ muchas gracias thank you very much

Guardia Civil

This police force, some of whom still wear black three-cornered hats, nowadays has a less negative image than when it was an instrument of Francoist repression (notably in the assassination of Lorca). Dressed in their olive green uniforms (the *policía nacional* is in navy blue), they are in charge of rural areas, the road network and customs.

gradas [grah-das] *fpl* stands (of stadium), grandstand

grado [grah-doh] *m* degree

granada [gra-nah-da] *f* pomegranate

grande [gran-day] *adj* big, large

granel [gra-nel] *adv* ▸ a granel *(dry goods)* loose; *(wine, oil)* from the barrel; in bulk

granizado [gra-ni-thah-doh] *m* granita, slush

granja [gran-CHa] *f* farm; café, tea shop

grano [grah-noh] *m* grain; spot, pimple

grasa [gra-sa] *f* fat, grease

gratinado [gra-ti-nah-doh] *adj* au gratin

gritar [gri-tahr] *v* to shout

grúa [groo-a] *f* tow truck; crane

grueso, sa [groo-ay-soh] *adj* thick

grupo [groo-poh] *m* group ▸ grupo sanguíneo blood type

gruta [groo-ta] *f* cave, grotto

guante [gwan-tay] *m* glove

guapo, pa [gwa-poh] *adj* good-looking; nice

guardar [gwar-dahr] *v* to keep, to save; to guard; to put away

guardarropa [gwar-da-RRoh-pa] *m* cloakroom

guardia [gwahrd-ya] *m, f* police officer ▸ un guardia civil a civil guard ▸ la Guardia Civil the Civil Guard ▸ guardia de seguridad security guard ▸ guardia municipal/urbano local police officer ▸ de guardia on duty

guía [gee-a] *m, f* guide ◆ *f* guidebook ▸ guía telefónica phone book ▸ guía turística tourist guide

guiar [gee-ahr] *v* to guide

guindilla [gin-deel-ya] *f* chili

guisado [gi-sah-doh] *m* stew

guisante [gi-san-tay] *m* pea

guitarra [gi-ta-RRa] *f* guitar

gustar [goos-tahr] *v* to like ▸ me gusta I like it ▸ no le gusta la carne he doesn't like meat

gusto [goos-toh] *m* taste; pleasure ▸ mucho gusto pleased to meet you

h

haba [ah-ba] *f* broad bean

haber [a-bair] *v* to have ▸ hay muchos problemas there are a lot of problems ▸ haber de to have to ▸ hay que reservar you have to make a reservation ▸ ¿qué hay? what's new?

habichuela [a-bi-chway-la] *f* bean

habitación [a-bi-tath-yohn] *f* room; bedroom ▸ habitación doble/individual double/single room

hablar [ab-lahr] *v* to speak

hacer [a-thair] *v* to make; to do; to build ▸ hace buen/mal tiempo the weather's good/bad ▸ hace dos días two days ago

hacerse [a-thair-say] *v* to become

hacia [ath-ya] *prep* towards ▸ hacia aquí/ allí here/there ▸ hacia atrás/adelante backwards/forwards ▸ hacia las tres at about three o'clock

hacienda [ath-yen-da] *f* country estate; property

hallarse [al-yahr-say] *v* to be

hambre [am-bray] *f* hunger ▸ tener hambre to be hungry

hamburguesa [am-boor-gay-sa] *f* hamburger

harina [a-ree-na] *f* flour

hasta [as-ta] *prep* until ◆ *adv* even

hecho, cha [e-choh] *adj* done ◆ *m* fact

helado, da [e-lah-doh] *adj* frozen ◆ *m* ice cream

hembra [em-bra] *f* female

herida [e-ree-da] *f* wound

herirse [e-reer-say] *v* to injure oneself

hermano, na [air-mah-noh] *m, f* brother, sister

herramienta [e-RRam-yen-ta] *f* tool

hervir [air-beer] *v* to boil

hielo [yay-loh] *m* ice

hierro [ye-RRoh] *m* iron

hígado [ee-ga-doh] *m* liver

higo [ee-goh] *m* fig

hijo, ja [ee-CHoh] *m, f* son, daughter

hijos [ee-CHohs] *mpl* children

hilera [i-lair-a] *f* row

hilo [ee-loh] *m* thread

hispánico, ca [ees-pa-ni-koh] *adj* Hispanic

hispano, na [ees-pah-noh] *adj* Hispanic

Hispanoamérica [ees-pah-no-a-mair-i-ka] *n* Spanish America

historia [ees-tawr-ya] *f* history; story

hogar [oh-gahr] *m* home

hoja [oh-CHa] *f* leaf; sheet (of paper)

hojaldre [o-CHal-dray] *m* puff pastry

hola [oh-la] *excl* ▸ ¡hola! hi!

hombre [om-bray] *m* man ▸ ¡hombre! hey! ▸ hombre de negocios businessman

hora [aw-ra] *f* time; hour; appointment ▸ 'horas convenidas' 'by appointment only'

horario [o-rahr-yoh] *m* schedule; working hours, business hours

horchata [or-cha-ta] *f* *cold drink made from tiger nuts, sugar and water*

horizonte [o-ri-thon-tay] *m* horizon

horno [or-noh] *m* oven ▸ **al horno** baked, roasted

hortaliza [or-ta-lee-tha] *f* vegetable

hospedarse [os-pe-dahr-say] *v* to stay

hospital [os-pi-tal] *m* hospital

hostal [os-tal] *m* cheap hotel

hostelería [os-te-le-ree-a] *f* the hotel and catering trade

hotel [o-tel] *m* hotel

hoy [oy] *adv* today

huelga [wel-ga] *f* strike

hueso [way-soh] *m* bone; pit, stone

huésped, da [wes-ped] *m, f* guest

▸ **habitación de huéspedes** guest room

huevo [way-boh] *m* egg ▸ **huevo duro** hardboiled egg ▸ **huevo estrellado/frito** fried egg ▸ **huevos a la flamenca** *eggs baked with tomato sauce, chorizo and peas* ▸ **huevos al plato** baked eggs ▸ **huevo pasado por agua** soft-boiled egg

humano, na [oo-mah-noh] *adj & m* human

humedad [oo-me-dad] *f* humidity, dampness

humo [oo-moh] *m* smoke

humor [oo-mawr] *m* humor; mood

ibérico, ca [i-bair-i-koh] *adj* Iberian

ida [ee-da] *f* outward journey ▸ **billete de ida y vuelta** round-trip ticket

idea [i-day-a] *f* idea

identidad [i-den-ti-dad] *f* identity

identificarse [i-den-ti-fi-kahr-say] *v* to identify oneself

idioma [id-yoh-ma] *m* language

iglesia [i-glays-ya] *f* church

igual [i-gwal] *adj* equal, the same ▸ **me da igual** I don't mind either way ▸ **da igual** it doesn't matter ▸ **igual que** the same as

igualmente [i-gwal-men-tay] *adv* equally ▸ **¡que te diviertas mucho! – igualmente** enjoy yourself! – the same to you!

impedir [im-pe-deer] *v* to prevent

imponer [im-po-nair] *v* to impose

importante [im-por-tan-tay] *adj* important

importar [im-por-tahr] *v* to matter; to import ▸ **no importa** it doesn't matter

▸ **¿te importa que venga con nosotros?** do you mind if she comes with us?

importe [im-por-tay] *m* price, cost

imprescindible [im-pres-thin-dee-blay] *adj* essential

impreso [im-pray-soh] *m* printed document, form

imprevisto [im-pre-bees-toh] *m* unforeseen circumstance

impuesto [im-pwes-toh] *m* tax

incendio [in-thend-yoh] *m* fire ▸ **'peligro de incendio'** 'fire hazard'

incluido, da [in-kloo-ee-doh] *adj* included

inclusive [in-kloo-see-bay] *adv* inclusive ▸ **'vacaciones del 1 al 15, ambos inclusive'** 'vacation from the 1st to the 15th inclusive'

incluso [in-kloo-soh] *adv* even

indemnizar [in-dem-ni-thahr] *v* to compensate

indicaciones [in-di-kath-yoh-nes] *fpl* instructions

industria [in-doos-tri-a] *f* industry; factory

infancia [in-fanth-ya] *f* childhood

infantil [in-fan-teel] *adj* children's

inferior [in-fair-yawr] *adj* lower; inferior ▸ inferior a below

información [in-for-math-yohn] *f* information ▸ 'información' 'information desk'

informativo [in-for-ma-tee-boh] *m* the news

informe [in-for-may] *m* report

infracción [in-frakth-yohn] *f* offense

ingrediente [in-gred-yen-tay] *m* ingredient

ingreso [in-gray-soh] *m* entry; admission; deposit; income

inicio [i-neeth-yoh] *m* start, beginning

inmediato, ta [in-med-ya-toh] *adj* immediate ▸ de inmediato right away

inmóvil [in-mo-beel] *adj* still, immobile

inolvidable [in-ol-bi-dah-blay] *adj* unforgettable

inquietarse [in-kyet-ahr-say] *v* to worry

inquilino, na [in-ki-lee-noh] *m, f* tenant

insatisfecho, cha [in-sa-tis-fe-choh] *adj* dissatisfied

inscribirse [in-skri-beer-say] *v* to enroll; to register

insecticida [in-sek-ti-thee-da] *m* insecticide

insecto [in-sek-toh] *m* insect

instalación [in-sta-lath-yohn] *f* installation

instalaciones [in-sta-lath-yoh-nays] *fpl* facilities

instante [in-stan-tay] *m* moment ▸ al instante immediately

instituto [in-sti-too-toh] *m* high school; institute

instrucción [in-strookth-yohn] *f* education

instrucciones [in-strookth-yohn-ays] *fpl* instructions

intenso, sa [in-ten-soh] *adj* intense

intentar [in-ten-tahr] *v* to try

intento [in-ten-toh] *m* attempt

intercambio [in-tair-kamb-yoh] *m* exchange

interés [in-tair-ays] *m* interest

interesante [in-tair-e-san-tay] *adj* interesting

interesar [in-tair-e-sahr] *v* to interest ▸ interesarse en/por to be interested in

interior [in-tair-yawr] *adj* inside, inner, interior ◆ *m* inside

interrumpir [in-te-RRoom-peer] *v* to interrupt

interurbano, na [in-ter-oor-bah-noh] *adj* inter-city; long-distance

intervenir [in-tair-be-neer] *v* to intervene; to take part; to operate on

intoxicación [in-tok-si-kath-yohn] *f* poisoning ▸ intoxicación alimentaria food poisoning

introducir [in-tro-doo-theer] *v* to introduce; to enter ▸ 'introducir monedas' 'insert coins'

inundación [in-oon-dath-yohn] *f* flood

inválido, da [im-ba-li-doh] *m, f* disabled

investigar [im-bes-ti-gahr] *v* to investigate; to research

invierno [imb-yair-noh] *m* winter

invitar [in-bi-tahr] *v* to invite ▸ invitar a

alguien a to invite somebody to

ir [eer] v to go; to work ▸ ¿cómo te va? how are things? ▸ voy a reservar una habitación I'm going to book a room ▸ ir bien to be convenient ▸ ¿le va bien el lunes? is Monday all right for you? ▸ ¡qué va! not at all!, you must be joking! ▸ vamos, no te enfades come on, don't get upset

irse [eer-say] v to leave

isla [ees-la] f island

islote [ees-loh-tay] m islet

itinerario [i-ti-ne-rahr-yoh] m route

IVA [ee-ba] m abbr of **impuesto sobre el valor añadido** sales tax ▸ 'IVA (no) incluido' 'sales tax (not) included'

izda abbr of **izquierda** l

izquierda [ith-kyair-da] f left ▸ a la izquierda on the left

izquierdo, da [ith-kyair-doh] adj left; left-hand

j

jabón [CHa-bohn] m soap

jamón [CHa-mohn] m ham

jarabe [CHa-ra-bay] m syrup

jardín [CHar-deen] m garden

jarra [CHa-RRa] f large glass; pitcher

jarro [CHa-RRoh] m pitcher

jefe, fa [CHe-fay] m, f boss; chief

jerez [CHe-reth] m sherry

joven [CHoh-ben] adj young ◆ m, f young person

joya [CHoy-a] f piece of jewelry

judía [CHoo-deey-a] f bean ▸ judía tierna/verde green bean ▸ judía seca/blanca navy bean

juego [CHway-goh] m game ▸ Juegos Olímpicos Olympic Games

jueves [CHwe-bays] m Thursday

juez [CHweth] m, f judge

jugar [CHoo-gahr] v to play

jugo [CHoo-goh] m juice

jamón

This is a specialty of Andalusia, though excellent *jamón* is produced in Extremadura and in Teruel and Salamanca too. The least expensive is *jamón del país*, locally produced in various regions of Spain. Next up on the scale comes *jamón serrano*, mainly from the mountain areas of the south and southwest. A superior type of *serrano* is *jamón ibérico*, produced from free-range pigs which feed mainly on acorns; this is salted and then cured for two years in the pure dry air of the high sierra. But the Rolls Royce of hams is *jamón de Jabugo*, from the village of that name, 2,200 feet up in the *Sierra Morena*, traditionally the home of the very finest hams.

Jerez

This world-famous wine is truly astonishing. The secret of its unique flavor lies in the technique known as *solera* with its pyramids of barrels. Smaller quantities of younger wines in the top barrels are mixed with larger quantities of older ones in the lower barrels to ensure consistent aroma, flavor and quality. The wine to be bottled is drawn from the bottom barrels. The English love the *fino*, *amontillado* and *oloroso* varieties so much that they brought the word 'sherry' into the English language.

juicio [CHweeth-yoh] *m* trial; judgement ▸ a mi juicio in my opinion

julio [CHool-yoh] *m* July

junio [CHoon-yoh] *m* June

junto, ta [CHoon-toh] *adv* together ▸ junto a next to ▸ todo junto all together

juventud [CHoo-ben-tood] *f* youth

juzgado [CHooth-gah-doh] *m* court

laborable [la-bo-rah-blay] *adj* working, work ◆ *m* working day, weekday ▸ 'sólo laborables' 'weekdays only'

laboral [la-bo-ral] *adj* working, labor

lado [lah-doh] *m* side ▸ al otro lado de on the other side of ▸ al lado de next to

ladrón, ona [lad-rohn] *m, f* thief

lago [lah-goh] *m* lake

laguna [la-goo-na] *f* lagoon

lamentar [la-men-tahr] *v* to regret

lámpara [lam-pa-ra] *f* lamp

lana [lah-na] *f* wool

lancha [lan-cha] *f* launch ▸ lancha motora motorboat

langosta [lan-gos-ta] *f* crawfish

langostino [lan-gos-tee-noh] *m* prawn ▸ langostinos a la plancha grilled prawns ▸ langostinos al ajillo prawns with garlic

lanzar [lan-thahr] *v* to throw; to launch

lanzarse [lan-thahr-say] *v* to throw oneself ▸ se lanzó a la piscina he threw himself into the pool

lápiz [la-peeth] *m* pencil ▸ lápiz de labios lipstick ▸ lápiz de ojos eyeliner

largo, ga [lahr-goh] *adj* long ◆ *m* length ▸ a lo largo de along ▸ de largo recorrido *(train)* long-distance ▸ cinco metros de largo five meters long

lata [la-ta] *f* can ▸ en lata canned

laurel [low-rel] *m* bay ▸ hoja de laurel bay leaf

lavabo [la-bah-boh] *m* washbowl, washbasin; bathroom

lavado [la-bah-doh] *m* wash ▸ 'lavado automático' 'automatic car wash'

lenguas oficiales

¿Hablas español? - ¡Sí! But it's not always that simple. Although *castellano*, the language of Castile, is the main language of the country, *catalán* (from Catalonia), *vasco* (from the Basque country), *gallego* (from Galicia) and *valenciano* (from Valencia) are also official languages.

▸ 'lavado en seco' 'dry-cleaning'

lavadora [la-ba-daw-ra] *f* washing machine

lavandería [la-ban-de-ree-a] *f* laundry

lavar [la-bahr] *v* to wash

laxante [lak-san-tay] *m* laxative

leche [le-chay] *f* milk ▸ leche condensada condensed milk ▸ leche entera whole milk ▸ leche frita *dessert made from milk, flour and sugar dipped in beaten egg and fried*

lechuga [le-choo-ga] *f* lettuce

leer [lay-air] *v* to read

legumbre [le-goom-bray] *f* pulse, legume

lejos [lay-CHohs] *adv* far away ▸ lejos de a long way from ▸ a lo lejos in the distance

lengua [len-gwa] *f* tongue; language

lenguado [len-gwah-doh] *m (fish)* sole

lenguaje [len-gwa-CHay] *m* language

lentes [len-tays] *mpl* glasses ▸ lentes de contacto contact lenses

lenteja [len-tay-CHa] *f* lentil

lento, ta [len-toh] *adj* slow

letra [let-ra] *f* letter; lyrics, words

letrero [let-rair-oh] *m* sign

levantar [lay-ban-tahr] *v* to lift

levante [lay-ban-tay] *m* the east ▸ el Levante the eastern provinces of Spain: Castellón, Valencia, Alicante and Murcia

ley [ley] *f* law

libertad [li-bair-tad] *f* freedom

libre [lee-bray] *adj* free

libreta [li-bray-ta] *f* notebook; bankbook, passbook

libro [lee-broh] *m* book

licor [li-kawr] *m* liquor, liqueur

lidia [leed-ya] *f* bullfighting, bullfight

lienzo [li-en-thoh] *m* canvas

ligar [li-gahr] *v* to tie, to bind; to chat up ▸ ligar con alguien *(fam)* to score with somebody

ligero, ra [li-CHair-oh] *adj* light

límite [lee-mi-tay] *m* limit

limón [li-mohn] *m* lemon

limonada [li-mo-nah-da] *f* lemonade

limpiar [limp-yahr] *v* to clean

limpieza [limp-yay-tha] *f* clean, cleaning; cleanliness

limpio, pia [limp-yoh] *adj* clean

lindo, da [leen-doh] *adj* pretty, nice

línea [lee-nay-a] *f* line

líquido [lee-ki-doh] *m* liquid

liso, sa [lee-soh] *adj* smooth; plain, not patterned

lista [lees-ta] *f* list ▸ lista de correos *(at post office)* general delivery ▸ lista de precios price list

listo, ta [lees-toh] *adj* clever, bright ▸ estar listo to be ready

litro [lee-troh] *m* liter

llama [yah-ma] *f* flame

llamada [ya-mah-da] *f* call ▸ llamada telefónica telephone call

llamar [ya-mahr] *v* to call; to knock ▸ **llamar por teléfono** to telephone

llamarse [ya-mahr-say] *v* to be called

llano, na [yah-noh] *adj* flat ✦ *m* plain

llanura [ya-noo-ra] *f* plain

llave [yah-bay] *f* key

llegada [yay-gah-da] *f* arrival ▸ **'llegadas internacionales'** 'international arrivals'

llegar [yay-gahr] *v* to arrive ▸ **llegar a** to reach, to arrive in, to arrive at ▸ **llegar de** to arrive from, to get back from

llenar [yay-nahr] *v* to fill

lleno, na [yay-noh] *adj* full

llevar [yay-bahr] *v* to take; to wear; to carry ▸ **lleva gafas** she wears glasses ▸ **no llevamos dinero** we have no money on us

llover [yo-bair] *v* to rain ▸ **llueve** it's raining

llovizna [yo-beeth-na] *f* drizzle

lluvia [yoob-ya] *f* rain

lo [loh] *pron* it; him; you; thing, things ▸ **lo mejor** the best thing ▸ **lo peor** the worst thing ▸ **lo que dices no es verdad** what you say is true ▸ **me gusta lo nuevo** I like new things

local [loh-kal] *adj* local

localidad [loh-ka-li-dad] *f* place, town; seat; ticket

loción [lohth-yohn] *f* lotion ▸ **loción bronceadora** suntan lotion

loco, ca [loh-koh] *adj* & *m, f* crazy, mad

lógico, ca [lo-CHi-koh] *adj* logical; understandable

lograr [log-rahr] *v* to achieve; to manage to

lomo [loh-moh] *m* back; loin ▸ **lomo de cerdo** loin of pork ▸ **lomo embuchado** *cured pork loin, shaped like a sausage* ▸ **lomos de merluza** loin of hake

loncha [lon-cha] *f* slice

longaniza [lon-ga-nee-tha] *f* *type of pork sausage, eaten cold*

longitud [lon-CHi-tood] *f* length ▸ **dos metros de longitud** two meters long

luego [loo-ay-goh] *adv* later, then ✦ *conj* therefore ▸ **desde luego** of course

lugar [loo-gahr] *m* place ▸ **tener lugar** to take place ▸ **en cualquier lugar** anywhere ▸ **en primer lugar** firstly, in the first place

lujo [loo-CHoh] *m* luxury

luna [loo-na] *f* moon

lunes [loo-nays] *m* Monday

luz [looth] *f* light; lamp

macedonia [ma-the-dohn-ya] *f* mixed vegetables ▸ **macedonia de frutas** fruit salad

macho [ma-choh] *adj* male

madera [ma-dair-a] *f* wood

madre [mad-ray] *f* mother

madrileño, ña [mad-ri-layn-yoh] *adj* from Madrid, of Madrid

madrugada [mad-roo-gah-da] *f* early morning

maduro, ra [ma-doo-roh] *adj* mature, ripe, aged

mal [mal] *adj* bad; wrong; sick ✦ *adv* badly; wrong ✦ *m* evil, bad thing;

damage, harm ▸ sentar mal *(food)* to disagree with one; *(clothes)* to not suit one; *(attitude)* to put one out ▸ no está nada mal it's not bad at all

malecón [ma-lay-kohn] *m* jetty; waterfront

malestar [ma-les-tahr] *m* unease; discomfort

maleta [ma-lay-ta] *f* suitcase ▸ hacer las maletas to pack

maletero [ma-le-tair-oh] *m (of car)* trunk

maletín [ma-le-teen] *m* briefcase

Mallorca [mal-yor-ka] *n* Majorca

malo, la [ma-lo] *adj* bad; wrong; sick

manantial [ma-nant-yal] *m* spring

mandar [man-dahr] *v* to send; to order, to tell ▸ mandar hacer algo a alguien to tell somebody to do something

mando [man-doh] *m* ▸ mando a distancia remote control

manera [ma-nair-a] *f* way, manner

mango [man-goh] *m* handle

mano [mah-noh] *f* hand ▸ 'hecho a mano' 'handmade' ▸ de segunda mano second-hand ▸ echar una mano a alguien to give somebody a hand ▸ a mano derecha/izquierda on the right/left

manta [man-ta] *f* blanket

manteca [man-tay-ka] *f* fat ▸ manteca de cacao cocoa butter ▸ manteca de cerdo lard

mantecado [man-tay-kah-doh] *m* crumbly shortcake cookie

mantener [man-te-nair] *v* to keep, to maintain

mantequilla [man-te-keel-ya] *f* butter

manzana [man-thah-na] *f* apple; *(of street)* block

manzanilla [man-tha-neel-ya] *f* chamomile tea; type of dry sherry

mañana [man-yah-na] *f* morning ◆ *adv* tomorrow ▸ por la mañana in the morning ▸ mañana por la mañana tomorrow morning ▸ pasado mañana the day after tomorrow

mapa [ma-pa] *m* map

máquina [ma-ki-na] *f* machine

maquinilla [ma-ki-neel-ya] *f* razor

mar [mahr] *m* sea

maravilla [ma-ra-beel-ya] *f* wonder

marca [mahr-ka] *f* make, brand

marcha [mahr-cha] *f* march ▸ poner en marcha to start ▸ salir de marcha to go out on the town

marco [mahr-koh] *m* frame

marea [ma-ray-a] *f* tide

mareado, da [ma-ray-ah-doh] *adj* dizzy ▸ estar mareado to feel nauseous

mareo [ma-ray-oh] *m* dizziness; sickness (nausea), airsickness, seasickness, travel sickness

marfil [mahr-feel] *m* ivory

margen [mahr-CHen] *m* margin; bank, riverbank

marido [ma-ree-doh] *m* husband

marina [mah-ree-na] *f* navy

mariscada [ma-ris-kah-da] *f* seafood meal

marisco [ma-rees-koh] *m* seafood

marisma [ma-rees-ma] *f* marsh

mármol [mahr-mol] *m* marble

martes [mahr-teys] *m* Tuesday

marzo [mahr-thoh] *m* March

más [mas] *adj & adv & pron* more ▸ más peras/aire more pears/air ▸ más o menos more or less ▸ ¿quién/qué más? who/what else? ▸ más barato cheaper

masa [ma-sa] *f* mixture, dough, pastry; mass

masaje [ma-sa-CHay] *m* massage

materia [ma-tair-ya] *f* subject; matter; material

material [ma-tair-yal] *adj* & *n* material

matrícula [ma-tree-koo-la] *f* enrollment, enrollment fees; license plate

máxima [mak-si-ma] *f* maximum temperature

máximo, ma [mak-si-moh] *adj* & *m* maximum

mayo [meye-oh] *m* May

mayor [meye-or] *adj* older, oldest; bigger, biggest ◆ *m, f* adult, grown-up ▸ **soy mayor que tú** I'm older than you ▸ **él es el mayor** he's the oldest ▸ **la mayor parte** the greater part ▸ **el mayor barco del mundo** the biggest ship in the world

mayoría [meye-o-ree-a] *f* majority

mazapán [ma-tha-pan] *m* marzipan

me [may] *pron* me; myself

mediados [med-yah-dohs] *mpl* ▸ **a mediados de agosto** around the middle of August

mediano, na [med-yah-noh] *adj* medium-sized

medianoche [med-ya-no-chay] *f* midnight

mediante [med-yan-tay] *prep* by means of, through

medicamento [me-di-ka-men-toh] *m* medicine

médico, ca [me-di-koh] *m, f* doctor ▸ **médico de guardia** doctor on duty

medida [me-dee-da] *f* measure

medio, dia [med-yoh] *adj* half; average ◆ *m* middle; environment; way ▸ **media hora** half an hour ▸ **medios de transporte** means of transport

mediodía [med-yoh-dee-a] *m* midday

medir [me-deer] *v* to measure

mejillón [me-CHil-yohn] *m* mussel

mejor [me-CHor] *adj* & *adv* better, best ▸ **el mejor** the best ▸ **lo mejor** the best thing ▸ **mejor que mejor** so much the better

mejorar [me-CHo-rahr] *v* to improve; to get better

melocotón [me-lo-ko-tohn] *m* peach

melón [me-lohn] *m* melon ▸ **melón con jamón** melon with cured ham

membrillo [mem-breel-yoh] *m* quince

memoria [me-mor-ya] *f* memory ▸ **de memoria** from memory

mencionar [menth-yoh-nahr] *v* to mention

menestra [me-nes-tra] *f* mixed vegetables ▸ **menestra de verduras** vegetable stew

menor [men-or] *adj* younger, youngest; smaller, smallest ◆ *m, f* minor ▸ **ser menor de edad** to be under age ▸ **un problema menor** a minor problem

Menorca [men-or-ka] *n* Minorca

menos [may-nos] *adv* less, fewer; except ▸ **menos manzanas/aire** fewer apples/less air ▸ **el/la/lo menos...** the least ▸ **acudieron todos menos él** they all came except him ▸ **a menos que** unless ▸ **al/por lo menos** at least ▸ **3 euros de menos** 3 euros too little ▸ **las dos menos diez** ten to two ▸ **un poco menos** a little less

mensaje [men-sa-CHay] *m* message

mentira [men-tee-ra] *f* lie

menudo, da [men-oo-doh] *adj* small ▸ **a menudo** often

mercadillo [mair-ka-deel-yoh] *m* street market, outdoor market, open-air market

mercado [mair-kah-doh] *m* market

mercancía [mair-kan-thee-a] *f* goods

merienda [me-ryen-da] *f* tea; snack

merluza [mair-loo-tha] *f* hake ▸ merluza a la plancha grilled hake ▸ merluza a la romana hake in batter

mero [mair-oh] *m* grouper ▸ mero a la plancha grilled grouper

mes [mes] *m* month ▸ el mes que viene next month

mesa [may-sa] *f* table

meseta [me-say-ta] *f* plateau

mesón [me-sohn] *m* inn; traditional bar or restaurant

metálico, ca [me-ta-li-koh] *adj* metallic ▸ en metálico in cash

meter [me-tair] *v* to put

mezclar [meth-klahr] *v* to mix

mezquita [meth-kee-ta] *f* mosque

mi [mi] *adj* my ▸ mis libros my books

mí [mi] *pron* me

miedo [myay-doh] *m* fear ▸ tener miedo de to be afraid of

mientras [myen-tras] *conj* while; as long as ▸ mientras que whereas ▸ mientras esté aquí while I'm here

miércoles [myair-ko-les] *m* Wednesday

mínimo, ma [mee—ni-moh] *adj* & *n* minimum

minoría [mi-no-ree-a] *f* minority

minusválido, da [mi-noos-ba-li-doh] *m, f* handicapped person

mío [mee-oh] *adj* & *pron* mine ▸ un amigo mío a friend of mine

mirador [mi-ra-dawr] *m* viewing point

mirar [mi-rahr] *v* to look

mismo, ma [mees-mo] *adj* same ▸ el mismo the same ▸ ahora mismo right now ▸ lo mismo (que) the same (as) ▸ me da lo mismo it's all the same to me

mitad [mi-tad] *f* half; middle

mixto, ta [meeks-toh] *adj* mixed ◆ *m* ham and cheese sandwich

mochila [mo-chee-la] *f* backpack

modo [moh-doh] *m* way ▸ no podía aguantarlo, de modo que me fui I couldn't stand it, so I left ▸ de ningún modo no way ▸ de todos modos anyway

molestar [mo-les-tahr] *v* to bother, to disturb ▸ 'no molestar' 'do not disturb'

molestia [mo-lest-ya] *f* nuisance, bother; discomfort

moneda [mo-nay-da] *f* coin; currency

monitor, ra [mo-ni-tawr] *m, f* instructor, monitor

montado [mon-tah-doh] *m* small slice of bread with a savory topping

montaña [mon-tan-ya] *f* mountain

montar [mon-tahr] *v* to ride ▸ montar a caballo to ride horseback

monte [mon-tay] *m* mountain

montón [mon-tohn] *m* heap, pile ▸ un montón de loads of

morcilla [mor-theel-ya] *f* blood sausage

moreno, na [mo-ray-noh] *adj* dark-haired; dark-skinned; tanned, sunburnt

mosquito [mos-kee-toh] *m* mosquito

mostaza [mos-ta-tha] *f* mustard

mostrador [mos-tra-dawr] *m* counter ▸ 'mostrador de facturación' 'check-in desk'

mostrar [mos-trahr] *v* to show

motivo [mo-tee-bo] *m* reason, motive ▸ con motivo de because of; on the occasion of

motora [mo-taw-ra] *f* motorboat

mover [mo-bair] *v* to move

moverse [mo-bair-say] *v* to move (about)

movida

In the 1980s the *movida* (the scene) was like a champagne cork popping after the drab decades of the Francoist era. The film director Pedro Almodóvar is the enfant terrible of this artistic revival that set out to shock. But now, in *Malasaña*, the part of Madrid where it was born, the *movida* has given way to new types of creativity.

movida [mo-bee-da] *f* things going on, life; bother, problems

móvil [mo-beel] *m* mobile phone

muchacha [moo-cha-cha] girl

muchacho [moo-cha-choh] *m* boy

mucho, cha [moo-choh] *adj* a lot of ◆ *adv* a lot ◆ *pron* a lot ▸ muchos piensan que... many think that ... ▸ como mucho at the most ▸ ¡con mucho gusto! I'd be delighted! ▸ mucho antes long before ▸ mucho después much later

muerte [mwair-tay] *f* death

muestra [mwes-tra] *f* sample; exhibition; *(of affection, etc.)* sign

mujer [mooCH-air] *f* woman

multa [mool-ta] *f* fine

municipio [moo-ni-theep-yoh] *m* municipality, town

museo [moo-say-oh] *m* museum

música [moo-si-ka] *f* music

muslo [moos-loh] *m* thigh; *(of chicken)* leg ▸ ¿muslo o pechuga? leg or breast?

muy [mwee] *adv* very

n

nabo [nah-boh] *m* turnip

nacer [na-thair] *v* to be born

nacionalidad [nath-yo-na-li-dad] *f* nationality

nada [nah-da] *pron* nothing ◆ *adv* at all ▸ de nada not at all, you're welcome ▸ no me gusta nada I don't like it at all

nadar [na-dahr] *v* to swim

nadie [nah-yay] *pron* nobody

naranja [na-ran-CHa] *f* & *adj* & *m* orange ▸ naranja exprimida fresh orange juice

nata [na-ta] *f* cream ▸ nata montada whipped cream

natillas [na-teel-yas] *fpl* custard

natural [na-too-ral] *adj* natural ▸ ser natural de to come from

naturaleza [na-too-ra-lay-tha] *f* nature

náutico, ca [now-ti-koh] *adj* nautical ▸ club náutico yacht club

Navidad [na-bi-dad] *n* Christmas ▸ ¡Feliz Navidad! Merry Christmas!

neblina [neb-lee-na] *f* mist

necesidad [ne-thes-i-dad] *f* need, necessity

necesitar [ne-thes-i-tahr] *v* to need

negar [ne-gahr] *v* to deny; to refuse

‣ **negarse a** to refuse to

negro, gra [nay-groh] *adj* black

nervios [nair-byohs] *mpl* nerves

nervioso, sa [nair-byoh-soh] *adj* nervous ‣ **estar nervioso** on edge ‣ **ser nervioso** to be high-strung

nevada [ne-bah-da] *f* snowfall

nevar [ne-bahr] *v* to snow ‣ **nieva** it's snowing

nevera [ne-bair-a] *f* refrigerator

ni [ni] *conj* neither ◆ *adv* even ‣ **no es alto ni bajo** he's neither tall nor short ‣ **no he comido ni una manzana** I haven't even eaten an apple ‣ **no me quedaré ni un minuto más** I'm not staying a minute more ‣ **no quiero ni pensarlo** I don't even want to think about it

niebla [nyeb-la] *f* fog

nieve [nyay-bay] *f* snow

ningún [nin-goon] *adj* no ◆ *pron* none ‣ **en ninguna parte** nowhere ‣ **ninguno de ellos lo vio** none of them saw it

niña [neen-ya] little girl

niño [neen-ya] *m* little boy

nivel [ni-bel] *m (of building)* level

no [noh] *adv* no ‣ **no quiero ir** I don't want to go ‣ **¡cómo no!** of course!

noche [no-chay] *f* evening; night ‣ **¡buenas noches!** *(greeting)* good evening!; *(when leaving)* good night! ‣ **por la noche** at night ‣ **a las 8 de la noche** eight o'clock in the evening ‣ **esta noche voy al cine** I'm going to the movies tonight ‣ **de noche** at night ‣ **es de noche** it's dark ‣ **ayer por la noche** last night

Nochebuena [no-chay-bway-na] *f* Christmas Eve

Nochevieja [no-chay-byay-CHa] *f* New Year's Eve

nombre [nom-bray] *m* name ‣ **nombre de pila** first name, given name ‣ **¿nombre y apellidos?** name and last name?

norma [nor-ma] *f* rule

norte [nor-tay] *m* north

nos [nos] *pron* we ‣ **nos queremos** we love each other

nosotros, tras [no-soh-trohs] *pron* we, us, ourselves ‣ **entre nosotros** between ourselves

nota [noh-ta] *f* note

notar [noh-tahr] *v* to notice; to feel ‣ **se nota que...** you can tell that ...

noticia [no-teeth-ya] *f* piece of news

noticias [no-teeth-yas] *fpl* news

novedad [no-be-dad] *f* new thing, novelty, newness

novela [no-bay-la] *f* novel

noveno, na [no-bay-noh] *num* ninth

noviembre [nob-yem-bray] *m* November

novillada [no-beel-yah-da] *f* bullfight with young bulls

nube [noo-bay] *f* cloud

nuestro, tra [nwes-troh] *adj* our ◆ *pron* ours ‣ **el nuestro es azul** ours is blue

nueve [nway-bay] *num* nine

nuevo, va [nway-boh] *adj* new ‣ **de nuevo** again

nuez [nweth] *f* walnut

núm. *abbr of* **numero** No., no.

numerado, da [noo-me-rah-doh] *adj* numbered

número [noo-me-roh] *m* number; *(shoe)* size ‣ **número de teléfono** telephone number

numeroso, sa [noo-me-roh-soh] *adj* numerous, many

nunca [noon-ka] *adv* never

o [oh] *conj* or ▸ rojo o verde red or green

obedecer [o-be-de-thair] *v* to obey

objetivo, va [ob-CHe-tee-boh] *adj* objective ◆ *n* aim, objective; target; lens

objeto [ob-CHay-toh] *m* object ▸ con objeto de with the aim of ▸ 'objetos perdidos' 'lost and found'

obra [oh-bra] *f* work; construction site ▸ obra maestra masterpiece ▸ obra de teatro play ▸ 'en obras' 'work in progress'

obsequio [ob-sek-yoh] *m* gift

oca [oh-ka] *f* goose

ocho [o-choh] *num* eight

ocio [ohth-yoh] *m* leisure, free time

octavo, va [ok-tah-boh] *num* eighth

octubre [ok-too-bray] *m* October

ocupado, da [o-koo-pah-doh] *adj* busy ▸ 'ocupado' *(sign on toilet)* 'occupied'

ocurrir [o-koo-RReer] *v* to happen ▸ ¡ni se te ocurra! don't even think of it!

odiar [ohd-yahr] *v* to hate

oeste [oh-es-tay] *m* west

oferta [o-fair-ta] *f* offer ▸ oferta y demanda supply and demand

oficina [o-fi-thee-na] *f* office ▸ oficina de correos post office ▸ oficina de objetos perdidos lost and found ▸ oficina de turismo tourist office

oficio [o-feeth-yo] *m* trade, job

ofrecer [o-fre-thair] *v* to offer

oído [o-ee-doh] *m* hearing; (inner) ear

oír [o-eer] *v* to hear ▸ ¡oiga! excuse me!

ojo [o-CHoh] *m* eye ▸ ¡ojo! look out!

ola [oh-la] *f* wave ▸ ola de calor heat wave ▸ ola de frío cold spell

ole [o-lay] *excl* ▸ ¡ole! bravo!

oler [o-lair] *v* to smell ▸ oler bien/mal to smell good/terrible

olor [o-lawr] *m* smell ▸ un olor a a smell of

olvidar [ol-bi-dahr] *v* to forget ▸ olvidarse de hacer algo to forget to do something

once [on-thay] *adj* eleven

opción [opth-yohn] *f* option

ONCE

This organization, created in 1938, works towards reintegrating people with physical disabilities, particularly the visually handicapped, into society. The lottery is one of its sources of financing. Its members sell *cupones*, and there's a draw every day except Saturday. Friday's winning ticket is called the *cuponazo* and the prize is bigger. So take a chance, at least you'll be doing your part!

operación [o-pe-rath-yohn] *f* operation ▸ operación salida mass exodus of cars from big cities at the start of a public holiday ▸ operación retorno mass return home after a public holiday

opinar [o-pi-nahr] *v* to think

oponerse [o-po-nair-say] *v* to object; to oppose, to be against

oportunidad [o-por-too-ni-dad] *f* opportunity; bargain

óptica [op-ti-ka] *f* optician

opuesto, ta [o-pwes-toh] *adj* opposing ▸ opuesto a opposed to

orden [or-den] *m* order

ordenador [or-de-na-dawr] *m* computer

ordenar [or-de-nahr] *v* to order; to tidy

ordinario, ria [or-di-nahr-yoh] *adj* coarse, vulgar; poor-quality; ordinary

oreja [o-ray-CHa] *f* ear

organización [or-ga-ni-thath-yohn] *f* organization

origen [o-ree-CHen] *m* origin

original [o-ree-CHi-nal] *adj* original; unusual

orilla [o-reel-ya] *f* shore; bank, riverbank

os [os] *pron* you, yourselves ▸ os vi ayer I saw you yesterday

oscuro, ra [os-koo-roh] *adj* dark ▸ a oscuras in the dark

ostra [os-tra] *f* oyster

otoño [o-ton-yoh] *m* autumn

otro, tra [oh-tro] *adj* other ◆ *pron* another one; other ▸ el otro día the other day ▸ dame otro give me another one ▸ otros prefieren la playa others prefer the beach

oveja [o-bay-CHa] *f* sheep

p

paciente [path-yen-tay] *adj & m, f* patient

padecer [pa-de-thair] *v* to suffer ▸ padecer de to suffer from

padre [pa-dray] *m* father

padres [pa-drays] *mpl* parents

paella [pa-el-ya] *f* paella

pagado, da [pa-gah-doh] *adj* paid

pagar [pa-gahr] *v* to pay ▸ 'pague en caja' 'please pay at the desk'

---

paella

In the 19th century it was a poor man's dish made up of leftovers, but now it's a popular lunchtime dish with both rich and poor and there are many different types. Just take some rice, cook it in a saffron-flavored broth with your choice of fish, seafood, chicken, rabbit, pork, chorizo, green beans, etc. and there you are; there are even vegetarian paellas! It's Spain's nearest thing to a national dish and you can get good ones all over Spain, but the best ones are from Valencia, of course!

parador nacional

The first *parador nacional de turismo* was opened in 1928 by King Alfonso XIII. Offering from 3- to 5-star accommodation, there are now over 90 of them, mainly castles, manor houses, former palaces, monasteries, all steeped in history, which have been turned into hotels, although there are a few purpose-built ones. There is even one in the *Alhambra* in Granada. If you don't stay in one, at least have a drink there or enjoy typical local food in the restaurant.

página [paCH-i-na] *f* page

país [pa-ees] *m* country

paisaje [peye-sa-CHay] *m* countryside, landscape

País Vasco [peyes-bas-koh] *n* Basque Country

pájaro [paCH-a-roh] *m* bird

pala [pa-la] *f* spade

palabra [pa-lab-ra] *f* word

palacio [pa-lath–yoh] *m* palace

palco [pal-koh] *m* (*in theater*) box

pálido, da [pa-li-doh] *adj* pale

palomitas [pa-loh-mee-tas] *fpl* popcorn

pan [pan] *m* bread ▸ pan integral wholewheat bread ▸ pan de molde packaged sliced bread ▸ pan con tomate bread rubbed with tomato flesh ▸ pan tostado Melba toast

pantalla [pan-tal-ya] *f* screen

pantano [pan-tah-noh] *m* reservoir; marsh

papel [pa-pel] *m* paper; role

papelera [pa-pe-lair-a] *f* wastepaper basket, trashcan

paquete [pa-kay-tay] *m* package, parcel

par [par] *adj* even ◆ *m* pair ▸ un par de... a pair of ...

para [pa-ra] *prep* for ▸ esta agua no es buena para beber this water is not good to drink ▸ salir para Sevilla to leave for Seville ▸ ¿estará listo para el lunes? will it be ready for Monday? ▸ la comida está lista para servir lunch is ready to serve

parada [pa-rah-da] *f* stop ▸ parada de autobús bus stop ▸ parada de taxis taxi stand

parador [pa-ra-dawr] *m* ▸ parador (nacional) state-owned quality hotel

paraguas [pa-rag-was] *m* umbrella

paraíso [pa-ra-ee-soh] *m* paradise

paralelo, la [pa-ra-lay-loh] *adj* parallel

parar [pa-rahr] *v* to stop ▸ 'para en todas las estaciones' 'stops at all stations'

parecer [pa-re-thair] *v* to seem; to look, to sound ▸ parecía contento he seemed happy ▸ parecía cansado you look tired ▸ parece que se está nublando el cielo it looks as if it's clouding over

parecerse [pa-re-thair-say] *v* ▸ parecerse a to look like

pared [pa-red] *f* wall

pareja [pa-ray-CHa] *f* couple; partner

paro [pah-roh] *m* unemployment ▸ estar en el paro to be unemployed

parque [pahr-kay] *m* park ▸ parque acuático water park ▸ parque infantil playground ▸ parque zoológico zoo

parquímetro [par-kee-met-roh] *m* parking meter

paseo

At weekends or at holiday time, at around 7 or 8 o'clock in the evening, it might seem as if the whole of Spain goes out for a stroll with their friends or family before they eat dinner: it's *paseo* time. They take a leisurely walk through the neighborhood streets or along the seafront, enjoying the opportunity to say hello to their neighbors or acquaintances. It's a nice custom that shouldn't be missed.

parrilla [pa-RReel-ya] *f* grill ▸ a la parrilla grilled

parte [pahr-tay] *f* part; place; share ▸ ¿de parte de quién? who's calling, please? ▸ en alguna parte somewhere ▸ en otra parte somewhere else ▸ en parte to a certain extent ▸ en/por todas partes all over, everywhere

particular [par-ti-koo-lahr] *adj* private; particular

partida [par-tee-da] *f* departure; game ▸ partida de nacimiento birth certificate

partido [par-tee-doh] *m* game, match; *(political)* party

partir [par-teer] *v* to leave, to depart; to split ▸ a partir de from

pasa [pa-sa] *f* raisin

pasado, da [pa-sah-doh] *adj & n* past

pasaje [pa-saCH-ay] *m* passengers; ticket; alley, passage

pasajero, ra [pa-saCH-air-oh] *adj & m, f* passenger

pasaporte [pa-sa-por-tay] *m* passport

pasar [pa-sahr] *v* to go past, to pass; to come in, to go in; to happen; to spend ▸ el autobús pasa por mi casa the bus goes past my house ▸ el Manzanares pasa por Madrid the Manzanares flows through Madrid ▸ 'no pasar' 'no entry' ▸ pasar de largo to go past ▸ pasarlo bien to have a good time ▸ ¡pase! come in! ▸ ¿qué pasa? what's going on?

▸ pasé una semana en Vigo I spent a week in Vigo

Pascua [pas-kwa] *f* Easter; Passover

Pascuas *fpl* ▸ ¡Felices Pascuas! Merry Christmas!

pasear [pa-say-ahr] *v* to stroll, to walk; to drive, to ride

paseo [pa-say-oh] *m* stroll, walk; drive, ride

pasillo [pa-seel-yo] *m* corridor, aisle

paso [pa-soh] *m* step ▸ de paso on one's way, while one's at it ▸ a dos pasos just round the corner ▸ paso de cebra crosswalk ▸ paso a nivel grade crossing ▸ paso de peatones crosswalk ▸ 'paso subterráneo' 'underpass' ▸ 'prohibido el paso' 'no entry' ▸ 'ceda el paso' 'yield'

pasta [pas-ta] *f* pasta; cookie; dough, money ▸ pasta de dientes toothpaste

pastel [pas-tel] *m* cake

pastilla [pas-teel-ya] *f* tablet, pill

pata [pa-ta] *f* leg ▸ pata negra type of top-quality cured ham

patata [pa-ta-ta] *f* potato ▸ patatas bravas *sautéed potatoes with mayonnaise and spicy tomato sauce* ▸ patatas fritas French fries; potato chips

patio [pat-yoh] *m* patio

pato, ta [pa-toh] *m, f* duck

pavo, va [pah-boh] *m, f* turkey

paz [path] *f* peace ▸ dejar en paz to leave alone

peaje [pay-a-CHay] *m* toll

peatón [pay-a-tohn] *m* pedestrian ▸ 'prohibido peatones' 'no pedestrians'

pechuga [pe-choo-ga] *f (of chicken)* breast ▸ ¿muslo o pechuga? leg or breast?

pedazo [pe-da-thoh] *m* bit, piece

pedir [pe-deer] *v* to ask for; to order

pegar [pe-gahr] *v* to hit; to stick

película [pe-lee-koo-la] *f* film, movie

peligro [pe-lee-groh] *m* danger

pelo [pay-loh] *m* hair; fur

pelota [pe-loh-ta] *f* ball

pena [pay-na] *f* shame, pity ▸ valer la pena to be worthwhile

pendiente [pend-yen-tay] *adj* outstanding, pending ◆ *m* earring ◆ *f* slope

pensar [pen-sahr] *v* to think ▸ pensar en to think of, to think about

pensión [pens-yohn] *f* pension; guesthouse ▸ media pensión hotel room with breakfast and a main meal included ▸ pensión completa hotel room with all meals included

peor [pay-awr] *adj & adv* worse, worst ▸ es peor alumno que su hermano he's a worse student than his brother ▸ es cada vez peor it's getting worse ▸ el/la peor the worst ▸ lo peor the worst thing

pepino [pe-pee-noh] *m* cucumber

pequeño, ña [pe-kayn-yoh] *adj* small

pera [pair-a] *f* pear

perder [pair-dair] *v* to lose; to miss

perejil [pe-re-CHeel] *m* parsley

perfecto, ta [pair-fek-toh] *adj* perfect

periodo [pair-yoh-doh] *m* period

perjudicar [pair-CHoo-di-kahr] *v* to damage, to harm, to affect adversely

perjuicio [pair-CHweeth-yoh] *m* damage, harm

permanecer [pair-ma-ne-thair] *v* to stay

permiso [pair-mee-soh] *m* permission; permit ▸ permiso de conducir driver's license

pero [pay-roh] *conj* but

perrito [pe-RRee-toh] *m* puppy ▸ perrito caliente hotdog

perro, rra [pe-RRo] *m, f* dog ▸ 'cuidado con el perro' 'beware of dog' ▸ 'no se admiten perros' 'no dogs allowed'

perseguir [pair-say-geer] *v* to chase, to pursue; to persecute

persona [pair-soh-na] *f* person

personal [pair-soh-nal] *adj* personal ◆ *m* personnel, staff ▸ 'sólo personal autorizado' 'authorized personnel only'

pertenecer [pair-te-ne-thair] *v* to belong

pertenencias [pair-te-nenth-yas] *fpl* belongings

pesado, da [pe-sah-doh] *adj* heavy

pesca [pes-ka] *f* fishing

pescadilla [pes-ka-deel-ya] *f* whiting

pescadito [pes-ka-dee-to] *m* whitebait ▸ pescadito frito fried whitebait

pescado [pes-kah-doh] *m* fish

pescar [pes-kahr] *v* to fish

pésimo, ma [pe-si-moh] *adj* terrible

peso [pay-soh] *m* weight

pez [peth] *m* fish ▸ pez espada swordfish

picar [pi-kahr] *v* to chop, to mince, to grind; to nibble, to have a bite; to bite; to itch, to tickle; to sting; *(ticket)* to punch; *(sun)* to be strong

pico [pee-koh] *m* peak, summit; beak ▸ las tres y pico just after three ▸ tiene cuarenta y pico he's forty something ▸ ciento y pico 100-odd

pie [pyay] *m* foot ▸ a pie on foot ▸ en pie

standing ‣ **pies de cerdo** pig's trotters

piedra [pyed-ra] *f* stone, rock

pieza [pyay-tha] *f* piece

píldora [peel-do-ra] *f* pill

pimienta [pim-yen-ta] *f* pepper ‣ **pimienta negra** black pepper

pimiento [pim-yen-toh] *m* pepper ‣ **pimientos del piquillo** small slightly hot red peppers

pinchazo [peen-cha-thoh] *m* flat tire; prick

pincho [peen-choh] *m* bar snack, tapa ‣ **pincho moruno** pork kebab

pintado, da [pin-tah-doh] *adj* painted ‣ **'recién pintado'** 'wet paint'

pintar [pin-tahr] *v* to paint

pintoresco, ca [pin-to-res-koh] *adj* picturesque

pintura [pin-too-ra] *f* paint

piña [peen-ya] *f* pineapple ‣ **piña en almíbar** canned pineapple

Pirineos [pi-ri-nay-ohs] *mpl* Pyrenees

pisar [pi-sahr] *v* to step on, to tread on; *(brake, accelerator)* to put one's foot on ‣ **'prohibido pisar el césped'** 'keep off the grass'

piso [pee-soh] *m* apartment; floor, story

pista [pees-ta] *f* clue; trail; track, racetrack; runway; ski slope; (tennis) court; (dance) floor

pisto [pees-toh] *m* ratatouille

placa [pla-ka] *f* plate; plaque; badge

placer [pla-thair] *m* pleasure

plancha [plan-cha] *f* sheet; iron; griddle ‣ **a la plancha** grilled

planchar [plan-chahr] *v* to iron

plano, na [plah-noh] *adj* flat ✦ *m* plan

planta [plan-ta] *f* plant; floor, story

plástico, ca [plas-ti-koh] *adj & m* plastic

plata [pla-ta] *f* silver

plátano [pla-ta-noh] *m* banana; *(tree)* London plane

platea [pla-tay-a] *f (in theater)* orchestra

plato [pla-toh] *m* plate, platter; dish; course ‣ **plato combinado** single course meal, served on one plate ‣ **plato principal** main course ‣ **plato del día** today's special ‣ **platos caseros** home cooking

playa [pla-ya] *f* beach; seaside ‣ **'playa naturista'** 'nudist beach'

playeras [pla-yair-as] *fpl* beach shoes

plaza [pla-tha] *f* square ‣ **plaza de toros** bullring

plazo [pla-thoh] *m (of time)* period; installment ‣ **a corto/largo plazo** in the short/long term ‣ **a plazos** in installments

plegable [ple-gah-blay] *adj* folding

población [pob-lath-yohn] *f* population; village, town, city

poblado, da [pob-lah-doh] *adj* inhabited ✦ *m* settlement

pobre [poh-bray] *adj* poor ✦ *m, f* poor person

poco, ca [poh-koh] *adj & pron* little ‣ **dentro de poco** soon ‣ **hace poco** not long ago ‣ **poco a poco** little by little ‣ **por poco me caigo** I almost fell ‣ **tengo poco dinero** I don't have much money ‣ **un poco (de)** a little

poder [po-dair] *v* to be able to ✦ *m* power

policía [po-li-thee-a] *f* police (force) ✦ *m, f* police officer ‣ **policía municipal/urbana** local police

polideportivo [po-li-de-por-tee-boh] *m* sports center

póliza [po-li-tha] *f* policy

pollo [pol-yoh] *m* chicken ‣ **pollo a la**

plancha grilled chicken ▸ pollo al ajillo chicken with garlic ▸ pollo al curry curried chicken ▸ pollo asado roast chicken

polo [poh-loh] *m* pole; polo shirt; Popsicle®

polvo [pol-boh] *m* powder, dust

polvorón [pol-bo-rohn] *m* very crumbly shortcake

pomada [poh-mah-da] *f* ointment

pomelo [poh-may-loh] *m* grapefruit

poner [po-nair] *v* to put; to turn on, to switch on; *(fax)* to send; *(movie)* to show ▸ pon la radio turn the radio on ▸ ¿qué ponen en la tele? what's on TV? ▸ póngame una cerveza a beer, please

ponerse [po-nair-say] *v* to go, to get, to become; *(clothes)* to put on ▸ ponerse malo/ enfermo to get sick

por [por] *prep* for; because of; by; through; to; per; down, up, along; in, at ▸ cerrado por reformas closed for renovations ▸ lo hizo por ella he did it because of her ▸ por mensajero/fax by courier/fax ▸ entramos por la puerta principal we went in through the main door ▸ lo hice por complacerte I did it to please you ▸ cien euros por persona a hundred euros per person ▸ iba por la calle I was walking down the street ▸ por la mañana/tarde in the morning/ afternoon ▸ por la noche at night ▸ ¿por dónde vive? where does she live? ▸ por todas partes all over, everywhere

porque [por-kay] *conj* because ▸ ¿por qué? why?

portaequipajes [por-ta-e-ki-pa-CHays] *m* roof rack; luggage rack; trunk

portátil [por-ta-teel] *adj* portable

portero, ra [por-tair-oh] *m, f* porter; superintendent; goalkeeper

posada [poh-sah-da] *f* inn

poseer [po-say-air] *v* to own, to have

posibilidad [po-si-bi-li-dad] *f* possibility

posición [po-sith-yohn] *f* position

positivo, va [po-si-tee-bo] *adj* positive

postal [pos-tal] *f* postcard

posterior [pos-tair-yawr] *adj* rear, back; subsequent

postre [pos-tray] *m* dessert ▸ de postre for dessert ▸ postre de la casa house dessert

potencia [po-tenth-ya] *f* power

practicar [prak-ti-kahr] *v (sport)* to do ▸ practicar la natación to swim

práctico, ca [prak-ti-koh] *adj* practical

prado [prah-doh] *m* meadow

precio [preth-yoh] *m* price ▸ precio fijo fixed price ▸ precio de coste cost price

precioso, sa [preth-yoh-soh] *adj* gorgeous; precious

precipicio [pre-thi-peeth-yoh] *m* precipice

preciso, sa [pre-thee-soh] *adj* exact, precise ▸ es preciso que vengas. you must come

preferencia [pre-fe-renth-ya] *f* preference

prefijo [pre-fee-CHo] *m* area code, country code

pregunta [pre-goon-ta] *f* question ▸ hacer una pregunta to ask a question

preguntar [pre-goon-tahr] *v* to ask ▸ preguntar por alguien to ask after somebody

premio [prem-yoh] *m* prize

prenda [pren-da] *f* article of clothing

prensa [pren-sa] *f* press

preocupado, da [pray-o-koo-pah-doh] *adj* worried

preocuparse [pray-o-koo-pahr-say] *v* to

worry ▸ **preocuparse de** to take care of, to see to ▸ **preocuparse por** to worry about

presa [pray-sa] *f* reservoir, dam; prey

presenciar [pre-senth-yahr] *v* to witness

presente [pre-sen-tay] *adj* present

presidente, ta [pre-si-den-tay] *m, f* president

presión [prays-yohn] *f* pressure ▸ **presión sanguínea** blood pressure

prestar [pres-tahr] *v* to lend

prever [pray-bair] *v* to foresee; to forecast

previo, via [pray-byoh] *adj* previous

primavera [pree-ma-bair-a] *f* spring

primer [pree-mair] *num* first

primero, ra [pree-mair-oh] *num & m, f & adv* first ▸ **lo primero** the first thing ▸ **primera clase** first class ▸ **a primeros de** at the beginning of

principal [preen-thi-pal] *adj* main ◆ *m* second floor

príncipe [preen-thi-pay] *m* prince

principio [prin-theep-yoh] *m* start, beginning; principle ▸ **a principios de** at the beginning of ▸ **al principio** at first

prioridad [pree-o-ri-dad] *f* priority

prisa [pree-sa] *f* hurry ▸ **darse prisa** to hurry ▸ **tener prisa** to be in a hurry

privado, da [pri-bah-doh] *adj* private

probador [pro-ba-dawr] *m* fitting room

probar [pro-bahr] *v* to prove, to show; to try on; to taste, to try; to test

problema [pro-blay-ma] *m* problem

procedencia [pro-the-denth-ya] *f* origin; point of departure

proceder [pro-the-dair] *v* to proceed ▸ **proceder de** to come from, to arrive from

producir [pro-doo-theer] *v* to produce

producto [pro-dook-toh] *m* product

programación [pro-gra-math-yohn] *f* programs; programming

prohibido, da [proh-i-bee-doh] *adj* forbidden ▸ 'prohibido aparcar' 'no parking' ▸ 'prohibido el paso' 'no entry' ▸ 'prohibido el paso a personas ajenas a la obra' 'authorized personnel only' ▸ 'prohibido fijar carteles' 'post no bills' ▸ 'prohibido fumar' 'no smoking' ▸ 'prohibida la entrada a menores' 'adults only'

prohibir [pro-i-beer] *v* to ban

pronto [pron-toh] *adv* soon; early ▸ **de pronto** suddenly ▸ **tan pronto como** as soon as

propiedad [prop-yay-dad] *f* property ▸ 'propiedad privada' 'private property'

propina [pro-pee-na] *f* tips ▸ 'no se aceptan propinas' 'no tipping'

proponer [pro-po-nair] *v* to propose

proporcionar [pro-porth-yo-nahr] *v* to supply, to provide

propósito [pro-po-si-toh] *m* purpose, intention ▸ **a propósito** by the way; on purpose ▸ **a propósito de** speaking of

propuesta [prop-wes-ta] *f* proposal

provecho [pro-be-choh] *m* benefit ▸ ¡**buen provecho!** enjoy your meal!

provenir [pro-be-neer] *v* ▸ **provenir de** to come from

provincia [pro-beenth-ya] *f* province

provisional [pro-bis-yo-nal] *adj* temporary

provocar [pro-bo-kahr] *v* to cause; to provoke

próximo, ma [prok-si-moh] *adj* next; nearby ▸ **el próximo lunes** next Monday

proyecto [pro-yek-toh] *m* project

público, ca [poo-bli-koh] *adj* public ▸ **en público** in public

pueblo [pway-bloh] *m* people; village

puente [pwen-tay] *m* bridge ▸ **hacer puente** to have a long weekend ▸ **puente aéreo** air shuttle

puerro [pwe-RRoh] *m* leek

puerta [pwair-ta] *f* door; gate ▸ **puerta de embarque** boarding gate ▸ **puerta principal** main door

puerto [pwair-toh] *m* port, harbor; mountain pass

pues [pways] *conj* then; because ▸ **pues no sé** well, I don't know ▸ **¡pues claro!** but of course!

puesto, ta [pwes-toh] *m* on ▸ **con las botas puestas** with one's boots on

pulpa [pool-pa] *f* pulp; flesh

pulpo [pool-poh] *m* octopus

pulsar [pool-sahr] *v* to press

punta [poon-ta] *f* point; tip, end

punto [poon-toh] *m* point; place; dot, period ▸ **en su punto** *(in general)* just right; *(steak)* medium ▸ **a punto de** about to, on the point of ▸ **en punto** on the dot, sharp ▸ **punto de encuentro** meeting point

puntual [poon-twal] *adj* punctual

puro, ra [poo-roh] *adj* pure ◆ *m* cigar

PVP *m abbr of* **precio de venta al público** *recommended retail price*

pza. *abbr of* **plaza** sq.

q

que [kay] *conj* that; than ▸ **ése es el chico con el que hablé** that's the boy (whom) I spoke to ▸ **la persona de la que te hablo es médico** the person (who) I'm talking about is a doctor ▸ **la playa a la que fui es preciosa** the beach (that) I went to is beautiful ▸ **espero que te diviertas** I hope (that) you enjoy yourself ▸ **¡que te diviertas!** enjoy yourself! ▸ **¡que sí/no!** yes/no! ▸ **hace más calor que ayer** it's warmer than yesterday ▸ **gana más que su marido** she earns more than her husband

qué [kay] *pron & adj* what?, which? ▸ **¿qué?** what? ▸ **¿qué talla necesita?** what size do you need? ▸ **¿qué color prefiere?** which color do you prefer?

quedar [kay-dahr] *v* to be left; to be; to

fit ▸ **no queda pescado** there's no fish left ▸ **le queda perfecto** it fits you perfectly ▸ **quedar con alguien** to arrange to meet somebody ▸ **quedar en hacer algo** to arrange to do something

quedarse [kay-dahrsay] *v* to stay; to take ▸ **me quedo con la verde** I'll take the green one

quejarse [kay-CHahr-say] *v* to complain

quemarse [kay-mahr-say] *v* to get burnt; to get sunburnt

querer [kay-rair] *v* to want; to love ▸ **ven cuando quieras** come whenever you want ▸ **te quiero** I love you ▸ **sin querer** accidentally

queso [kay-soh] *m* cheese

quien [kyen] *pron* who, whom

Quijote

To avoid the punishment of having his right hand cut off after a duel, Cervantes fled to Rome and entered service with a cardinal. He lost his left hand fighting, languished in Turkish jails, was eventually ransomed, returned to Spain, married a woman 22 years his junior, and, in 1605, wrote *Quijote*, one of the major literary works of all time. Quite a full life, wasn't it?

---

quién [kyen] *pron* who?, whom?
▸ ¿quién te lo dijo? who told you?
quieto, ta [kyay-toh] *adj* still
Quijote [ki-CHoh-tay] *n* Don Quixote
quinto, ta [keen–toh] *num* fifth

quiosco [kyos-koh] *m* newsstand
quirófano [ki-ro-fa-noh] *m* operating room
quitar [ki-tahr] *v* to take off, to remove; to take away; to steal

r

ración [RRath-yohn] *f* helping, portion
rallar [RRal-yahr] *v* to grate
ramo [RRah-moh] *m* branch
ranura [RRa-noo-ra] *f* slot
rape [RRa-pay] *m* angler fish, monkfish
rápido, da [RRa-pi-doh] *adj* fast ♦ *adv* quickly
raptar [RRap-tahr] *v* to kidnap
raqueta [RRa-kay-ta] *f* racket
raro, ra [RRah-roh] *adj* strange, odd; rare
rastro [RRas-troh] *m* trace; trail, sign
▸ el rastro flea market
rato [RRa-toh] *m* while ▸ dentro de un rato in a while ▸ hace un rato a while ago
raya [RRa-ya] *f* stripe ▸ a/de rayas striped
rayo [RRa-yoh] *m* ray; flash of lightning
▸ rayos X X-rays
razón [RRa-thohn] *f* reason ▸ 'se vende

piso: razón aquí' 'apartment for sale: inquire within' ▸ tener razón to be right
reaccionar [RRay-akth-yoh-nahr] *v* to react
real [RRay-al] *adj* real; royal
realidad [RRay-al-i-dad] *f* reality
realizar [RRay-al-i-thahr] *v* to make, to do, to perform, to carry out
rebaja [RRe-ba-CHa] *f* reduction in price, discount ▸ rebajas sales
rebajar [RRe-ba-CHahr] *v* to reduce
rebanada [RRe-ba-nah-da] *f* slice (of bread)
rebozado, da [RRe-bo-thah-doh] *adj* in batter
recado [RRe-kah-doh] *m* errand, message
recambio [RRe-kamb-yoh] *m* spare part
recepción [RRe-thepth-yohn] *f* reception
receta [RRe-thay-ta] *f* recipe; prescription

recetar [RRe-thet-ahr] *v* to prescribe

recibir [RRe-thi-beer] *v* to receive

recibo [RRe-thee-boh] *m* receipt

recién [RReth-yen] *adv* newly ▸ recién hecho freshly made ▸ recién nacido newborn ▸ 'recién pintado' 'wet paint'

reciente [RReth-yen-tay] *adj* recent

recinto [RRe-theen-toh] *m* enclosure, area

recipiente [RRe-thip-yen-tay] *m* container

reclamación [RRe-kla-math-yohn] *f* claim; complaint ▸ 'reclamaciones y quejas' 'complaints'

recoger [RRe-koCH-air] *v* to gather, to pick up; to tidy ▸ recoger a alguien to pick somebody up

reconocer [RRe-ko-no-thair] *v* to recognize; to examine

recordar [RRe-kor-dahr] *v* to remember

recorrido [RRe-ko-RRee-doh] *m* route ▸ tren de largo recorrido long-distance train •

recta [RRek-ta] *f* straight line; straight stretch of road

recto, ta [RRek-toh] *adj & adv* straight ▸ todo recto straight ahead ▸ siga recto go straight ahead

recuerdo [RRe-kwair-doh] *m* memory; souvenir ▸ dale recuerdos a tu madre give my best wishes to your mother

recuperación [RRe-koo-pair-ath-yohn] *f* recovery

recursos [RRe-koor-sohs] *mpl* resources

red [RRed] *f* net; network

redondo, da [RRe-don-doh] *adj* round

reducir [RRe-doo-theer] *v* to reduce

reembolso [RRay-em-bol-soh] *m* refund ▸ contra reembolso cash on delivery, COD

reemplazar [RRay-em-pla-thahr] *v* to replace

referirse [RRe-fe-reer-say] *v* ▸ referirse a algo to refer to something

reflexionar [RRe-fleks-yoh-nahr] *v* to reflect, to think

refresco [RRe-fres-koh] *m* soft drink

refrigerado, da [RRe-friCH-air-ah-doh] *adj* air-conditioned

refugio [RRe-fooCH-yoh] *m* shelter, refuge

regalar [RRe-ga-lahr] *v* to give (as a present), to give away

regalo [RRe-gah-loh] *m* gift, present

registrar [RRe-CHis-trahr] *v* to register, to record; to search

registro [RRe-CHees-troh] *m* register; registry office; search

regresar [RRe-gray-sahr] *v* to return

reino [RRey-noh] *m* kingdom

reír [RRe-eer] *v* to laugh ▸ reírse de to laugh at

relación [RRe-lath-yohn] *f* connection, link; relationship ▸ en relación a with regard to

relacionar [RRe-lath-yoh-nahr] *v* to relate ▸ relacionarse con alguien to hang out with somebody ▸ relacionarse con algo to be related to something

relativo, va [RRe-la-tee-boh] *adj* relative ▸ relativo a relating to

relieve [RRel-yay-bay] *m* relief

relleno, na [RRel-yay-noh] *adj* filled; stuffed ◆ *m* filling; stuffing

reloj [RRe-loCH] *m* clock; watch

remar [RRe-mahr] *v* to row

remedio [RRe-mayd-yoh] *m* solution; remedy

remite [RRay-mee-tay] *m* return address

Reyes Magos

If you're spending Christmas in Spain and believe in Santa Claus, think again! In Spain it isn't Santa who brings presents, but the Three Wise Men, Melchior, Gaspar and Balthazar. They come on January 6th, and so does the *roscón de reyes*, a traditional cake in which a figurine of a king is hidden.

remitente [RRay-mi-ten-tay] *m, f* sender

remo [RRay-moh] *m* oar

remolacha [RRay-mo-la-cha] *f* beetroot

remoto, ta [RRay-mo-toh] *adj* remote

RENFE [RRen-fay] *f Spanish national railroad company*

renovar [RRay-noh-bahRR] *v* to renew

renta [RRen-ta] *f* income; rent

renunciar [RRe-noonth-yahr] *v* to give up, to relinquish ▸ **renunciar a algo** to renounce something; to turn something down

repartir [RRe-par-teer] *v* to divide, to share out; to hand out, to give out; to deliver

repetición [RRe-pe-teeth-yohn] *f* repetition

repetir [RRe-pe-teer] *v* to repeat

repostería [RRe-pos-tair-ee-a] *f* cakes, pastries, sweets

requesón [RRe-kay-sohn] *m* cheese similar to ricotta

resbalar [RRes-ba-lahr] *v* to slip, to slide; to be slippery

reserva [RRe-sair-ba] *f* reservation, booking ✦ *m* vintage wine ▸ **un reserva del 99** a '99 vintage wine ▸ **'reserva anticipada'** 'advance booking' ▸ **reserva natural** nature reserve

reservado, da [RRe-sair-bah-doh] *adj* reserved

resfriarse [RRes-fri-ahr-say] *v* to catch a cold

resguardo [RRes-gwahr-doh] *m* receipt, ticket

residencia [RRe-si-denth-ya] *f* residence; home; boarding house

resolver [RRe-sol-bair] *v* to solve

respecto [RRes-pek-toh] *m* ▸ **con respecto a** regarding, with regard to

responder [RRes-pon-dair] *v* to answer; to respond

respuesta [RRes-pwes-ta] *f* reply

resto [RRes-toh] *m (remainder)* rest

resuelto, ta [RRes-wel-toh] *adj* solved

resultado [RRe-sool-tah-doh] *m* result

retirado, da [RRe-ti-rah-doh] *adj* retired; remote

retorno [RRe-tor-noh] *m* return

retrasar [RRe-tra-sahr] *v* to put off, to postpone; to delay, to hold up ✦ **retrasarse** *v* to be late

retraso [RRe-tra-soh] *m* delay ▸ **con retraso** delayed ▸ **llevar retraso** to be late

retrato [RRe-tra-toh] *m* portrait

retrete [RRe-tre-tay] *m* toilet

revelado [RRe-bel-ah-doh] *m* developing

revelar [RRe-bel-ahr] *v* to develop; to reveal

revés [RRe-bays] *m* ▸ **al revés** the wrong way around; back to front; upside down

revisar [RRe-bi-sahr] *v* to check (over)

revisor, ra [RRe-bi-sawr] *m, f* ticket collector

revista [RRe-bees-ta] *f* magazine

revuelto, ta [RRe-bwel-toh] *m* untidy, messy, messed up

rey [RRey] *m* king

riada [RRi-ah-da] *f* flood

ribera [RRi-bair-a] *f* riverbank

rico, ca [RRee-koh] *adj* rich; nice, delicious

riesgo [RRi-es-goh] *m* risk ▸ a todo riesgo fully comprehensive

rincón [RRin-kohn] *m* corner

riñón [RRin-yohn] *m* kidney ▸ riñones al jerez kidneys in sherry

río [RRee-oh] *m* river

rioja [RRi-oh-CHa] *m* Rioja wine

robar [RRo-bahr] *v* to steal, to rob

roca [RRo-ka] *f* rock

rodar [RRo-dahr] *v* to roll; *(film)* to shoot

rodear [RRo-day-ahr] *v* to go around; to surround

rogar [RRo-gahr] *v* to ask ▸ les rogamos que confirmen su asistencia please confirm whether you will be able to attend

rojo, ja [RRo-CHoh] *adj & m* red

rollito [RRol-yee-toh] *m* roll

rollo [RRol-yoh] *m* roll; reel

romería [RRo-mair-ee-a] *f* pilgrimage; religious procession

romper [RRom-pair] *v* to break, to tear

ron [RRon] *m* rum

ronda [RRon-da] *f* round

ropa [RRoh-pa] *f* clothes ▸ ropa blanca linen ▸ ropa interior underwear

roto, ta [RRoh-toh] *adj* broken

rotonda [RRo-ton-da] *f* traffic circle

rótulo [RRo-too-loh] *m* sign

rueda [RRoo-ay-da] *f* wheel

ruido [RRoo-ee-doh] *m* noise

rumbo [RRoom-boh] *m* course ▸ rumbo a heading for

ruta [RRoo-ta] *f* route

S *abbr of* **San** St.

sábado [sa-ba-doh] *m* Saturday ▸ cada sábado, todos los sábados every Saturday ▸ el sábado pasado last Saturday ▸ el sábado por la mañana/tarde/ noche on Saturday morning/afternoon/evening ▸ este sábado this Saturday

sábana [sa-ba-na] *f* sheet

saber [sa-bair] *v* to know ▸ saber a to taste of ▸ saber bien/mal to taste good/ bad ▸ saber algo de to know something about

sabor [sa-bawr] *m* taste; flavor ▸ tener sabor a to taste like

sacar [sa-kahr] *v* to take out; to get ▸ sacar billetes/entradas to buy tickets ▸ sacar dinero to withdraw money ▸ sacar una copia de to make a copy of

saco [sa-koh] *m* sack ▸ saco de dormir sleeping bag

Sagrada Familia

Begun in 1883, the most original church in Europe is still under construction! After giving Barcelona a fantastic series of buildings which mix Art Nouveau, Gothic and Islamic influences, Gaudí dropped everything in 1914 to concentrate on what became his life's work. He ended up living as a recluse on the site for 16 years and died in complete penury. Run over by a tram, his body lies in the crypt.

sagrado [sa-grah-doh] *adj* sacred, holy

sal [sal] *f* salt ▶ sales de baño bath salts

sala [sah-la] *f* room ▶ 'sala climatizada' 'air-conditioning' ▶ 'sala de espera' 'waiting room' ▶ sala de estar living room ▶ sala de fiestas night club

salchicha [sal-chee-cha] *f* sausage

salchichón [sal-chi-chohn] *m* salami-like sausage

saldo [sal-doh] *m* balance ▶ saldos remnants

salida [sa-lee-da] *f* exit, way out; departure ▶ 'salida sin compra' *sign in store showing the special exit for customers who have made no purchases* ▶ 'salida de socorro/emergencia' 'emergency exit' ▶ 'salidas internacionales' 'international departures'

salir [sa-leer] *v* to go out; to leave; to come out; *(sun)* to rise

salmón [sal-mohn] *m* salmon ▶ salmón ahumado/fresco smoked/fresh salmon

salmonete [sal-moh-nay-tay] *m* red mullet

salpicón [sal-pi-kohn] *m* ▶ salpicón de marisco cold seafood with chopped tomato, onion and peppers in oil and vinegar

salsa [sal-sa] *f* sauce; salsa ▶ salsa bechamel white sauce ▶ salsa rosa cocktail sauce

saltar [sal-tahr] *v* to jump (over)

saltarse [sal-tahr-say] *v (red traffic light)* to go through

salteado, da [sal-tay-ah-doh] *adj* sautéed

salto [sal-toh] *m* jump ▶ salto de agua waterfall

salud [sa-lood] *f* health ▶ estar bien/mal de salud to be in good/poor health ▶ ¡(a tu) salud! to your health!

saludar [sa-loo-dahr] *v* to greet

salvaje [sal-ba-CHay] *adj* wild

salvar [sal-bahr] *v* to save

salvavidas [sal-ba-bee-das] *m* lifebelt; lifeguard

sandía [san-dee-a] *f* water melon

sanfaina [san-feye-na] *f* ratatouille

sanfermines [san-fair-mee-nays] *mpl* Pamplona bullfighting festival

sangre [san-gray] *f* blood

sanidad [sa-ni-dad] *f* health; (public) health service

sanitarios [sa-ni-tahr-yohs] *mpl* bathroom furniture

sano, na [sah-noh] *adj* healthy ▶ sano y salvo safe and sound

santo, ta [san-toh] *adj* holy, saintly ✦ *m, f* saint

sardina [sar-dee-na] *f* sardine ▶ sardinas a la plancha grilled sardines

sanfermines

For most people, *sanfermines* means just one thing: brave (or foolish, some would say) young men dressed in the traditional white costume and red sash running with the bulls which are being driven through the narrow streets of the old town from their pens to the bullring. This is the *encierro* and it takes place each morning of the *sanfermines* (July 7th through the 14th) when Pamplona celebrates the Feast of San Fermín, patron saint of the city. Of course, there's much much more going on, but since Hemingway it's the bulls that capture most people's imagination.

---

satisfacer [sa-tis-fa-thair] *v* to satisfy

satisfecho, cha [sa-tis-fe-choh] *adj* satisfied

se [say] *pron* one, oneself; himself, herself, itself; to him, to her; themselves; to them; yourself, yourselves; to you; each other, one another ▸ el niño se lesionó the child injured himself ▸ siéntese sit yourself down ▸ yo se lo daré I'll give it to him ▸ si usted quiere, yo se las mandaré if you wish, I'll send them to you ▸ se quieren they love each other ▸ 'se habla inglés' 'English spoken' ▸ se ha suspendido la excursión the trip has been canceled

secador [se-ka-dawr] *m* dryer ▸ secador de cabello hair dryer

secar [se-kahr] *v* to dry

sección [sekth-yohn] *f* section

secretaría [se-kre-ta-ree-a] *f* secretariat, secretary's office

sed [sed] *f* thirst ▸ dar sed to make one thirsty ▸ tener sed to be thirsty

seda [say-da] *f* silk

sedante [say-dan-tay] *m* sedative

sede [say-day] *f* headquarters

seguir [se-geer] *v* to follow; to continue, to carry on, to go on ▸ mi abuelo sigue trabajando my grandfather still works

según [se-goon] *prep* according to ◆ *adv* it depends, depending; as

segundo, da [se-goon-doh] *num* & *n* second

seguramente [se-goo-ra-men-tay] *adv* most probably

seguridad [se-goo-ri-dad] *f* security; safety; certainty ▸ Seguridad Social Medicaid

seguro, ra [se-goo-roh] *adj* safe; sure; definite ◆ *m* insurance (policy); safety catch ◆ *adv* definitely ▸ estar seguro to be sure ▸ ¡seguro que sí! of course!

seis [say-ees] *num* six ◆ *fpl* six o'clock ▸ a las seis at six o'clock ▸ doscientos seis two hundred six ▸ treinta y seis thirty-six ▸ de seis en seis in sixes ▸ los seis all six of them

selecto, ta [se-lek-toh] *adj* select

sello [sayl-yoh] *m* stamp

selva [sel-ba] *f* jungle

semáforo [se-ma-fo-roh] *m* traffic light

semana [say-mah-na] *f* week ▸ Semana Santa Holy Week ▸ see box on p. 58

semejante [say-may-CHan-tay] *adj* similar; such ..., such a ...

semidesnatado, da [se-mi-des-na-tah-doh] *adj* 2% (milk)

semilla [se-meel-ya] *f* seed

Semana Santa

During Holy Week the faithful carry religious statues or sculpted scenes of Christ's passion, the *pasos*, in procession. They are escorted by the penitents from various *cofradías* (brotherhoods), dressed in long tunics and wearing pointed hoods with two holes cut for their eyes. In Seville, you sometimes hear *saetas*, poems that are sung from up on the balconies.

sencillo, lla [sen-theel-yoh] *adj* simple

sendero [sen-dair-oh] *m* path

sentar [sen-tahr] *v* ▸ sentar bien/mal a alguien *(food)* to agree/not to agree with somebody; *(clothes, etc.)* to suit/not to suit somebody; *(comments)* to please/upset somebody

sentarse [sen-tahr-say] *v* to sit down

sentido [sen-tee-doh] *m* sense ▸ 'sentido único' 'one-way'

sentir [sen-teer] *v* to feel ▸ lo siento I'm sorry ▸ sentirse bien/mal to feel well/ill

señas [sayn-yas] *fpl* address; signs; details

señal [sen-yal] *f* signal, sign; mark; *(on phone)* tone

señalar [sen-ya-lahr] *v* to indicate, to point out; to mark

señor, ra [sen-yawr] *m* man, gentleman ▸ ¡señor! sir! ▸ 'señores' *(toilets)* 'gentlemen'

señora [sen-yawr-a] *f* woman, lady; wife ▸ ¡señora! madam! ▸ 'señoras' *(toilets)* 'ladies'

señorita [sen-yo-ree-ta] *f* young lady

sepia [sayp-ya] *f* cuttlefish ▸ sepia a la plancha grilled cuttlefish

septiembre [septyem--bray] *m* September ▸ a principios/mediados/finales de septiembre at the beginning/in the middle/at the end of September ▸ el pasado/próximo (mes de) septiembre last/next September ▸ en septiembre in September ▸ este (mes de) septiembre this September ▸ uno de los septiembres más lluviosos one of the wettest Septembers ▸ el nueve de septiembre the ninth of September

séptimo, ma [sep-ti-moh] *num* seventh

ser [sair] *v* to be ▸ mi abrigo es rojo my coat is red ▸ son turistas they are tourists ▸ son las tres de la tarde it's three o'clock in the afternoon ▸ hoy es San José today is Saint Joseph's Day ▸ fue construido por los romanos it was built by the Romans ▸ ¿cuánto es? how much is it? ▸ o sea in other words ▸ ser de to be from; to be made of ▸ ser para to be for ▸ este trapo es para limpiar los cristales this cloth is for cleaning the windows

serio, ria [sair-yoh] *adj* serious

servicio [sair-beeth-yoh] *m* service; toilet, bathroom ▸ 'servicio (no) incluido' 'service (not) included' ▸ servicios mínimos skeleton service ▸ servicio público public service ▸ servicio de revelado rápido fast film developing service ▸ servicios toilets

servilleta [sair-bil-yay-ta] *f* napkin

servir [sair-beer] *v* to serve ▸ servir de algo to be useful for something
• servirse [sair-beer-say] *v* to help oneself ▸ 'sírvase usted mismo' 'help yourself'

Siglo de Oro

The 'Golden Age,' a time of great literary and artistic achievement, began with the discovery of America in 1492. Charles V became head of the Holy Roman Empire, the largest-ever European empire, and Spain annexed the other colonial power, Portugal, in 1580. But decline set in, beginning with the spread of the ideas of Luther and the defeat of the previously invincible Spanish Armada in 1588.

seta [say-ta] *f* (wild) mushroom ▸ setas al ajillo/con gambas mushrooms with garlic/prawns

sevillanas [se-bil-yah-nas] *fpl popular dance and song from Seville*

sexto, ta [seks-toh] *num* sixth ▸ el sexto the sixth ▸ la sexta the sixth ▸ el sexto día the sixth day ▸ en sexto lugar, en sexta posición in sixth place

si [see] *conj* if

sí [see] *adv* yes ◆ *pron* ▸ sí mismo himself, yourself ▸ sí misma herself, yourself ▸ sí mismos themselves, yourselves ▸ sí mismas themselves, yourselves

sidra [see-dra] *f* cider

siempre [syem-pray] *adv* always ▸ desde siempre always ▸ como siempre as usual

sierra [sye-RRa] *f* mountain range

siete [sye-tay] *num* seven

siglo [see-gloh] *m* century

signo [seeg-noh] *m* sign

siguiente [sig-yen-tay] *adj & m, f* next ▸ ¡siguiente! next!

silencio [si-lenth-yoh] *m* silence

similar [si-mi-lahr] *adj* similar

simpático, ca [sim-pa-ti-koh] *adj* nice, friendly

sin [seen] *prep* without

sino [see-noh] *conj* but; except ▸ no el lunes, sino el martes not Monday, but Tuesday

sintético, ca [sin-tay-ti-koh] *adj* synthetic

síntoma [seen-toh-ma] *m* symptom

siquiera [seek-yair-a] *adv* even ▸ dime siquiera su nombre at least give me his name ▸ no tengo ni siquiera diez euros I don't even have ten euros

sitio [seet-yoh] *m* place; room, space ▸ en otro sitio someplace else

situar [sit-wahr] *v* to place, to put; to locate

s/n *abbr* of **sin número** no number

sobrar [soh-brahr] *v* to be left over; to be more than enough

sobrasada [soh-bra-sah-da] *f type of spreadable spicy pork sausage from Majorca*

sobre [soh-bray] *m* envelope ◆ *prep* about; over, above; about, around ▸ una artículo sobre Valencia an article about Valencia

sobreático [soh-bray-a-ti-koh] *m* floor built on top of the attic floor

sobrecarga [soh-bray-kahr-ga] *f* overload, excess load

sobrepasar [soh-bray-pa-sahr] *v* to exceed

sociedad [sohth-yay-dad] *f* society; club, association

socio, cia [sohth-yoh] *m, f* member; partner

socorrer [so-ko-RRair] *v* to aid, to help

socorro [so-ko-RRoh] *m* aid, help ◆ *excl* ▸ ¡socorro! help!

sofocante [so-fo-kan-tay] *adj* stifling

sofrito [so-free-toh] *m* type of sauce made from fried onions, garlic and tomato

sol [sol] *m* sun; (at bullring) seats in the sun ▸ hace sol it's sunny

solamente [sol-la-men-tay] *adv* only

solar [soh-lahr] *adj* solar ◆ *m* lot, piece of land

soleado, da [so-lay-ah-doh] *adj* sunny

soler [so-lair] *v* ▸ no suelo levantarme tarde I don't usually get up late ▸ solía venir los domingos he used to come on Sundays

solicitud [so-li-thi-tood] *f* application (form)

sólido, da [so-li-doh] *adj & m* solid

solo, la [soh-loh] *adj* alone

sólo [soh-loh] *adv* only

solomillo [so-lo-meel-yoh] *m* fillet steak

soltar [sol-tahr] *v* to release, to let out, to let go of

soltero, ra [sol-tair-oh] *adj* single, unmarried ◆ *m, f* single person

solucionar [soh-looth-yoh-nahr] *v* to solve

sombra [som-bra] *f* shadow, shade; (at bullring) seats in the shade

sombrero [som-brair-oh] *m* hat

sombrilla [som-breel-ya] *f* sunshade, beach umbrella

somnífero [som-nee-fay-roh] *m* sleeping pill

sonar [so-nahr] *v* to ring, to go off; to sound

sonido [so-nee-doh] *m* sound

sonreír [son-ray-eer] *v* to smile

soñar [son-yahr] *v* to dream ▸ soñar con to dream about

sopa [soh-pa] *f* soup ▸ sopa de ajo garlic soup with bread and beaten egg ▸ sopa de cebolla onion soup ▸ sopa de marisco/de pescado shellfish/fish soup

soplar [soh-plahr] *v* to blow

sorbete [sor-bay-tay] *m* sorbet ▸ sorbete de frambuesa/de limón raspberry/lemon sorbet

sordo, da [sor-doh] *adj* deaf ◆ *m, f* deaf person

sorpresa [sor-pray-sa] *f* surprise

sótano [so-ta-noh] *m* basement; cellar

Sr. *abbr of* señor Mr.

Sra. *abbr of* señora Mrs.

Sres. *abbr of* señores Messrs.

Srta. *abbr of* señorita Miss

Sta. *abbr of* santa St.

Sto. *abbr of* santo St.

su [soo] *adj* his, her, its; their; your ▸ Juan y su madre Juan and his mother ▸ María y su hermano María and her brother ▸ ¡usted y sus chistes! you and your jokes!

suave [swah-bay] *adj* soft; gentle; mild

subir [soo-beer] *v* to go up; to rise; to put up, to raise; to climb, to walk up

submarinismo [soob-ma-ri-nees-moh] *m* scuba diving

subrayar [soob-RRa-yahr] *v* to underline

subterráneo, a [soob-tay-RRah-nay-oh] *adj* underground

subtítulo [soob-tee-too-loh] *m* subtitle

suburbio [soo-boorb-yoh] *m* suburb

suceder [soo-thed-air] *v* to happen ▸ ¿qué le sucede? what's the matter (with you)?

suceso [soo-thay-soh] *m* event

sucio, cia [sooth–yoh] *adj* dirty

sudar [soo-dahr] *v* to sweat

sueldo [swel-doh] *m* wages

suelo [sway-loh] *m* floor

suelto [swel-toh] *m* loose change ▸ ¿tiene suelto? do you have any change?

sueño [swayn-yoh] *m* dream; sleep ▸ tener sueño to feel sleepy

suerte [swair-tay] *f* luck ◆ *excl* ▸ ¡suerte! good luck!

suficiente [soo-fith-yen-tay] *adj* enough

sugerencia [soo-CHe-renth-ya] *f* suggestion

sujetar [soo-CHe-tahr] *v* to hold

sumergirse [soo-mair-CHeer-say] *v* to submerge

suministro [soo-mi-nees-troh] *m* supply

superar [soo-pe-rahr] *v* to overcome; to beat; to exceed

superior [soo-pair-yawr] *adj* superior, better; upper ▸ superior a better than; higher than

suplemento [soo-ple-men-toh] *m* supplement

suponer [soo-po-nair] *v* to suppose; to involve

supuesto [soo-pwes-toh] *adj* alleged, supposed ▸ por supuesto of course

sur [soor] *m* south

surtido, da [soor-tee-doh] *m* selection

sustituir [soos-tit-weer] *v* to replace ▸ sustituir algo/a alguien por to replace something/somebody with

susto [soos-toh] *m* fright ▸ dar un susto a alguien to frighten somebody ▸ ¡qué susto! what a fright!

suyo, ya [soo-yoh] *adj* his, hers; yours; theirs

tabaco [ta-ba-koh] *m* tobacco, cigarettes

taberna [ta-bair-na] *f* bar

tabla [tab-la] *f* board; plank; table, list
▸ tabla de planchar ironing board

tablao [tab-low] *m* ▸ tablao flamenco *club where flamenco shows are performed*

tablero [tab-lair-oh] *m* board

tableta [tab-lay-ta] *f (chocolate)* bar; tablet

taco [ta-koh] *m (of ham, cheese)* cube, piece

tajada [ta-CHah-da] *f* slice

Talgo [tal-goh] *m Spanish high-speed inter-city train*

taller [tal-yair] *m* workshop; studio; garage, repair shop

talón [ta-lohn] *m* heel; check

tamaño [ta-man-yoh] *m* size

también [tam-byen] *adv* also

tampoco [tam-poh-koh] *adv* neither

tanto, ta [tan-toh] *adj* so much, so many ◆ *pron* so much, so many ◆ *adv* so ▸ tanto por ciento so much percent

tapas

The most common explanation for the origin of *tapas* is that they were pieces of bread put on glasses to keep flies from swimming in them. But none of that should stop you tasting these delicious snacks. There's a huge variety (olives, cheese, cold meat, octopus, fried fish, squid, prawns, stuffed peppers, tortilla, etc.). Don't be afraid to make a meal of them.

tapa [ta-pa] *f* lid, cover; tapa, bar snack
▸ 'tapas variadas' selection of tapas

tapar [ta-pahr] *v* to cover; to put the lid on, to put the top on, to put the stopper in, to cork

tapón [ta-pohn] *m* stopper, cork, bottle top

taquilla [ta-keel-ya] *f* box office, ticket office; locket

tardar [tahr-dahr] *v* to take ▸ tardamos dos horas para ir it took us two hours to get there

tarde [tahr-day] *f* afternoon, evening ◆ *adv* late; too late ▸ ¡buenas tardes! good afternoon; good evening ▸ es muy tarde it's very late ▸ llegar tarde to arrive late ▸ el museo abre por la tarde the museum opens in the afternoon

tarifa [ta-ree-fa] *f* price, charge, fare ▸ tarifa plana flat rate

tarjeta [tar-CHay-ta] *f* card ▸ 'se aceptan tarjetas' 'credit cards accepted' ▸ tarjeta de crédito credit card ▸ tarjeta de embarque boarding pass ▸ tarjeta postal postcard

tarta [tahr-ta] *f* cake, tart ▸ tarta de chocolate chocolate cake ▸ tarta helada ice-cream cake

tasa [ta-sa] *f* rate

tasca [tas-ka] *f* traditional (cheap) bar

tauromaquia [tow-roh-mak-ya] *f* bullfighting

taxímetro [tak-see-met-roh] *m* taximeter

taza [ta-tha] *f* cup

te [tay] *pron* you, to you

té [tay] *m* tea

teatro [tay-a-tro] *m* theater

tecla [tek-la] *f (on keyboard)* key

tejanos [te-CHah-nohs] *mpl* jeans

tejido [te-CHee-doh] *m* cloth, fabric, material

tel. *abbr of* **teléfono** tel.

tela [tay-la] *f* cloth, fabric, material; canvas

telearrastre [tay-lay-a-RRas-tray] *m* ski lift, ski tow

telediario [tay-lay-dyahr-yoh] *m* television news

teléfono [tay-lay-fo-noh] *m* telephone ▸ (teléfono) móvil cell phone, mobile phone

telesilla [tay-lay-seel-ya] *f* chairlift

tema [tay-ma] *m* topic, subject

temblor [tem-blawr] *m* tremor; shaking, trembling

tempestad [tem-pes-tad] *f* storm

templado, da [tem-plah-doh] *adj* mild, temperate; warm, lukewarm

temporada [tem-po-rah-da] *f* season ▸ de temporada seasonal ▸ temporada alta/baja high/low season

temporal [tem-po-ral] *m* storm

temprano, na [tem-prah-noh] *adv* early

tenedor [te-ne-dawr] *m* fork

tener [ten-air] *v* to have; to be ▸ tengo dos hijos I have two children ▸ ¿cuántos años tienes? how old are you? ▸ tiene cuarenta años he is forty years old ▸ tener frío/calor to be hot/cold ▸ ten el libro que me pediste here's the book you asked me for

tenso, sa [ten-soh] *adj* tense

tentempié [ten-tem-pyay] *m* snack

tercero, ra [tair-thair-oh] *num* third

tercio [tairth-yoh] *m* third

terminal [tair-mi-nal] *f* terminal; terminus

término [tair-mi-noh] *m* term; end ▸ término municipal *area under the jurisdiction of a city council*

ternera [tair-nair-a] *f* veal

terremoto [te-RRe-moh-toh] *m* earthquake

terreno [te-RRay-noh] *m* land, terrain, ground; plot of land

terrón [te-RRohn] *m* ▸ terrón de azúcar sugar cube

ti [tee] *pron* you ▸ me acordaré de ti I will remember you

tibio, bia [teeb-yoh] *adj* lukewarm

tiempo [tyem-poh] *m* time; weather ▸ a tiempo in time; on time ▸ al mismo tiempo que at the same time as ▸ del tiempo *(fruit)* in season; *(drink)* at room temperature ▸ hace tiempo some time ago

tienda [tyen-da] *f* shop, store; tent ▸ tienda de campaña tent ▸ tienda de comestibles grocery store ▸ tienda de ultramarinos grocery store

tierno, na [tyair-noh] *adj* tender

tierra [tye-RRa] *f* earth, soil, land; dirt ▸ tierra adentro inland

tijeras [tiCH-air-as] *fpl* scissors

tila [tee-la] *f* linden blossom tea

timbre [teem-bray] *m* bell

tinta [teen-ta] *f* ink

tinto [teen-toh] *m* red wine

típico, ca [tee-pi-koh] *adj* typical

tirar [ti-rahr] *v* to pull; to throw, to throw away ▸ 'tirar' 'pull'

toalla [twal-ya] *f* towel ▸ toalla de baño bath towel ▸ toalla de playa beach towel

tocar [toh-kahr] *v* to touch ▸ 'no tocar' 'please do not touch'

tocino [to-thee-noh] *m* bacon; pork fat

todavía [toh-da-bee-a] *adv* still

todo, da [toh-doh] *adj* all ◆ *pron* everything ▸ todo está listo everything is ready ▸ han venido todos everyone has come ▸ todo el día all day ▸ ante todo above all ▸ sobre todo especially

tomar [toh-mahr] *v* to take; to have, to eat, to drink ▸ tomar el fresco to get some fresh air ▸ tomar el sol to sunbathe ▸ tomar una copa to have a drink

tónica [to-ni-ka] *f* tonic water

tópico, ca [to-pi-koh] *adj* to be applied locally

torcer [tor-thair] *v* to turn; to twist

tormenta [tor-men-ta] *f* storm

toro [toh-roh] *m* bull ▸ see box on p. 64

toros [toh-ros] *mpl* bulls, bullfighting

torre [to-RRay] *f* tower

torta [tor-ta] *f* cake

tortilla [tor-teel-ya] *f* omelet ▸ tortilla (a la) francesa plain omelet ▸ tortilla de atún/de champiñones tuna/mushroom omelet ▸ tortilla de gambas/de jamón prawn/ham omelet ▸ tortilla de patatas potato omelet

tos [tos] *f* cough

toros

It's a controversial subject, even in Spain itself, but one that can't be avoided. Arising from the ritual sacrifices in the Mediterranean area in pagan times, the *corrida* unfolds in three *tercios*: the *picadores* (horsemen with lances) weaken the bulls; then the *banderilleros* stick *banderillas* (barbed darts) into the bull's back. Then the *matador* in his *traje de luces* (literally, suit of lights) tires the bull with his cape and finally kills the animal with an *estocada* (sword thrust).

toser [tos-air] *v* to cough

tostada [tos-tah-da] *f* slice of toast

tóxico, ca [tok-si-koh] *adj* poisonous, toxic

trabajar [tra-ba-CHahr] *v* to work

trabajo [tra-ba-CHoh] *m* job; work; piece of work

traer [tra-air] *v* to bring ▸ me trajo un regalo de Cuba she brought me a present from Cuba ▸ nos trajo a casa he brought us home

tráfico [tra-fi-koh] *m* traffic

traje [tra-CHay] *m* suit ▸ traje de chaqueta woman's two-piece suit ▸ traje de baño swim suit ▸ traje de luces bullfighter's outfit

trampolín [tram-po-leen] *m* diving board; ski jump

tranquilo, la [tran-kee-lo] *adj* quiet, calm, peaceful

transbordador [trans-bor-da-dawr] *m* ferry

transbordo [trans-bor-doh] *m (train, plane)* change ▸ hacer transbordo to change

transferencia [trans-fair-enth-ya] *f* transfer

tránsito [tran-si-toh] *m* traffic

transporte [trans-por-tay] *m* transportation ▸ transporte privado private

transportation ▸ transporte público public transportation

tranvía [tram-bee-a] *m* streetcar

tras [tras] *prep* after; behind

trasero, ra [tra-sair-oh] *adj* rear, back

trasladarse [tras-la-dahr-say] *v* to move; to be transferred

tratar [tra-tahr] *v* to treat; to deal with ▸ tratar de to try to

través [tra-bays] *prep* ▸ a través de vía, through

travesía [tra-be-see-a] *f* crossing, journey; side street

trayecto [tra-yek-toh] *m* journey

tren [tren] *m* train ▸ tren de cercanías local train ▸ tren de lavado car wash

tres [trays] *num* three

trigo [tree-goh] *m* wheat

triple [tree-play] *adj & m* triple ▸ el triple (de) three times

tripulación [tri-poo-lath-yohn] *f* crew

triunfar [tri-oon-fahr] *v* to win; to be successful

tropezar [tro-pay-thahr] *v* to trip (up)

trozo [tro-thoh] *m* bit, piece

trucha [troo-cha] *f* trout ▸ trucha a la navarra trout fried with ham

tu [too] *adj* your ▸ tus libros your books

tú [too] *pron* you ▸ el responsable eres tú you are responsible

tumbarse [toom-bahr-say] *v* to lie down

tumbona [toom-boh-na] *f* beach recliner

turismo [too-rees-moh] *m* tourism; private car ▸ turismo ecológico eco-tourism ▸ turismo rural rural tourism

turista [too-rees-ta] *m, f* tourist

turno [toor-noh] *m* turn ▸ 'espere su turno' 'wait your turn'

turrón [too-RRohn] *m* nougat-like sweet made with almonds, sugar and honey, traditionally eaten at Christmas

tuyo, ya [too-yoh] *adj* your ◆ *pron* yours ▸ este es el tuyo this is yours ▸ una amiga tuya a friend of yours

último, ma [ool-ti-moh] *adj* last ▸ a últimos de at the end of ▸ por último finally

ultramarinos [ool-tra-ma-ree-nohs] *m* grocery store

un [oon]one

único, ca [oo-ni-koh] *adj* only; unique

uno, na [oo-noh] *adj & pron* one ▸ había cincuenta y un turistas there were fifty-one tourists ▸ uno/una de one of ▸ cuesta unos veinte euros it costs about twenty euros ▸ había unas doce personas there were about twelve people

urbanización [oor-ba-ni-thathyohn] *f* housing development

urgencia [oor-CHenth-ya] *f* urgency ▸ tuvieron que ir a urgencias they had to go to the emergency room

usar [oo-sahr] *v* to use

uso [oo-soh] *m* use

usted [oos-ted] *pron* you (formal) ▸ me gustaría hablar con usted I would like to speak to you ▸ ¿cómo están ustedes? how are you?

usual [oos-wal] *adj* usual

usuario, ria [oos-wahr-yoh] *m, f* user

uva [oo-ba] *f* grape

vaca [ba-ka] *f* cow; beef

vacaciones [ba-kath-yoh-nays] *fpl* vacation ▸ estar/ir de vacaciones to be on vacation ▸ 'cerrado por vacaciones' 'closed for vacation'

vacío, a [ba-thee-oh] *adj* empty ▸ al vacío vacuum-packed

vacuna [ba-koo-na] *f* vaccine

vado [bah-doh] *m* (of river or stream) ford ▸ 'vado permanente' 'keep clear'

vajilla [ba-CHeel-ya] *f* earthenware; set of matching dishes

vale [ba-lay] *m* voucher, coupon

valer [ba-lair] *v* to be worth; to cost; to

venta

These are Andalusian country inns. From the 15th to 18th century, all of Spain's smugglers did their deals there. Flat broke, Don Quixote left a slate behind him in some of them! Today, they offer a unique atmosphere, the chance to taste game in season or to smoke a *faria*, the poor man's cigar born from the old smuggling trade.

be good, to be useful ▸ ¿vale? OK?, all right? ▸ ¡vale ya! that's enough! ▸ ¿te vale así? is that all right for you? ▸ eso no vale that's not fair ▸ más vale que no le digas nada you'd better not tell him anything

válido, da [ba-li-doh] *adj* valid

valle [bal-yay] *m* valley

valor [ba-lawr] *m* value; price

vapor [ba-pawr] *m* steam ▸ al vapor steamed

vaqueros [ba-kair-ohs] *mpl* jeans

variar [bar-yahr] *v* to vary; to alter, to change ▸ para variar for a change

variedad [bar-yay-dad] *f* variety

varios, rias [bahr-yohs] *adj* several; various ▸ 'varios' 'miscellaneous'

varón [ba-rohn] *m* boy, man, male

vasco, ca [bas-koh] *adj & m, f* Basque ▸ a la vasca Basque-style

vaso [ba-soh] *m* glass

vecino, na [beth-ee-noh] *adj* nearby, neighboring ◆ *m, f* neighbor

vegetariano, na [be-CHe-tar-yah-noh] *m, f* vegetarian

vehículo [be-ee-koo-loh] *m* vehicle

vela [bay-la] *f* candle; sail

velocidad [bel-o-thi-dad] *f* speed ▸ 'velocidad controlada por radar' 'speed cameras used'

vencer [ben-thair] *v* to beat, to defeat; to win, to be victorious; to expire, to be due

venda [ben-da] *f* bandage

vender [ben-dair] *v* to sell

veneno [ben-ay-noh] *m* poison

venir [ben-eer] *v* to come ▸ ven conmigo come with me ▸ el texto viene en inglés the text is in English ▸ el año que viene next year

venta [ben-ta] *f* sale ▸ 'en venta' 'for sale'

ventaja [ben-ta-CHa] *f* advantage

ventana [ben-tah-na] *f* window

ventanilla [ben-ta-neel-ya] *f* window

ver [bair] *v* to see ▸ desde aquí no veo nada I can't see a thing from here ▸ verse con alguien to see somebody ▸ nos vemos mañana see you tomorrow

veranear [be-ra-nay-ahr] *v* to spend the summer

verano [be-rah-noh] *m* summer ▸ en verano in summer

verbena [bair-bay-na] *f* open-air party or festival

verdad [bair-dad] *f* truth ▸ de verdad really; honestly ▸ ¿verdad? isn't it?, don't they, didn't he, aren't you, etc. ▸ era bueno, ¿verdad? it was good, wasn't it?

verde [bair-day] *adj & m* green

verdura [bair-doo-ra] *f* greens, vegetables ▸ verdura con patatas greens and boiled potatoes

vergüenza [bair-gwen-tha] *f* shame ▸ how embarrassing!

vestido [bes-tee-doh] *m* dress

vestirse [bes-teer-say] *v* to get dressed, to dress

vez [beth] *f* time ▸ a veces sometimes ▸ ¿has estado en Madrid alguna vez? have you ever been to Madrid? ▸ de vez en cuando from time to time ▸ muchas veces many times ▸ pocas veces rarely, not often ▸ rara vez rarely ▸ tres veces al día three times a day ▸ una vez once ▸ pedir la vez to ask who's the last person waiting to be served

vía [bee-a] *f* route, road; railroad track, platform ▸ por vía aérea by air

viajar [bya-CHahr] *v* to travel

viaje [bya-CHay] *m* travel ▸ estar de viaje to be away on a trip ▸ ir de viaje to go away on a trip ▸ viaje de novios honeymoon ▸ ¡buen viaje! bon voyage!

vida [bee-da] *f* life

vidrio [bee-dri-oh] *m* glass

vieira [byay-ra] *f* scallop

viejo, ja [byay-CHoh] *adj* old ◆ *m, f* old person

viento [byen-toh] *m* wind

viernes [byair-nays] *m* Friday ▸ Viernes Santo Good Friday

vigente [bi-CHen-tay] *adj* current, in force, in use

vigilar [bi-CHi-lahr] *v* to watch (over), to guard

vinagre [bi-na-gray] *m* vinegar

vino [bee-noh] *m* wine ▸ vino de la casa house wine ▸ vino blanco/rosado/tinto white/rosé/red wine

visado [bi-sah-doh] *m* visa

visita [bi-see-ta] *f* visit ▸ 'visitas guiadas' 'guided tours'

visitar [bi-si-tahr] *v* to visit

vista [bees-ta] *f* sight; view ▸ ¡hasta la vista! see you!

viva [bee-ba] *excl* long live!, up! ▸ ¡viva España! God save Spain!

vivienda [bib-yen-da] *f* home; housing

vivir [bib-eer] *v* to live

vivo, va [bee-boh] *adj* alive, living; bright, lively; sharp-witted, astute ▸ estar vivo to be alive

volar [bol-ahr] *v* to fly

volver [bol-bair] *v* to return, to go back ▸ no pienso volver a ese hotel I'm not going back to that hotel

volverse *v* to turn round; to return; to become, to go ▸ se volvió loco he went crazy

vomitar [bo-mi-tahr] *v* to vomit

VOSE *f abbr of* **versión original subtitulada en español** original version with Spanish subtitles

vosotros, tras [boh-soh-trohs] *pron* you

voz [both] *f* voice

vuelo [bway-loh] *m* flight ▸ vuelo charter/regular charter/scheduled flight ▸ 'vuelos nacionales' 'domestic flights'

vuelta [bwel-ta] *f* return; change ▸ dar una vuelta to go for a walk ▸ dar vueltas to go round, to spin ▸ darse la vuelta to turn around ▸ estar de vuelta to be back ▸ a la vuelta when we get back

vuestro, tra [bwes-troh] *adj* your ◆ *pron* yours ▸ este es el vuestro this one is yours ▸ una amiga vuestra a friend of yours

y

y [ee] *conj* and
ya [ya] *adv* already; right now

yate [ya-tay] *m* yacht
yo [yoh] *pron* I ▸ soy yo it's me

z

zanahoria [tha-na-awr-ya] *f* carrot
zapato [tha-pa-toh] *m* shoe
zarzuela [thar-thway-la] *f* seafood stew;
Spanish light opera
zona [thoh-na] *f* area, zone ▸ 'zona de
estacionamiento limitado y vigilado'
'patrolled restricted parking zone'
▸ zona verde green area, park
zumo [thoo-moh] *m* juice ▸ zumo de
fruta/de naranja fruit/orange juice